STANTON

Lincoln's Secretary of War

EDWIN McMASTERS STANTON

STANTON

Lincoln's Secretary of War

BY

FLETCHER PRATT

GREENWOOD PRESS, PUBLISHERS
WESTPORT, CONNECTICUT

CONTENTS

Between many chapters is a brief BACKDROP of excerpts from contemporary newspaper accounts, public notices, advertisements, letters, and other documents of Stanton's time.

v

BOOK III.   *The Third Career*

APPENDIX.   *The Controversies*

MAPS

PREFACE

THE object in this biography is not so much to make Stanton an attractive person as a credible one. He was certainly attractive to some people; one need only cite the letters written by him to his second wife, Ellen, while he was in California. There need only be mentioned the fact that after Stanton became Secretary of War, Lincoln spent more time with him than with any other person. This was not due to a thirst for news from the fronts alone. News, often very important news, came through the Navy Department also, but there is no record of the President's spending a night on the sofa in the presence of Mr. Welles.

Also, even Andrew Johnson, at a time when the two men were opposed to each other on the most important issue before the government, still preferred Stanton's advice on points not connected with the controversy—on the testimony of Gideon Welles, who disliked Stanton from the first time he heard of him, and whose dislike never grew dim. That is, there were people who liked Stanton for his efficiency, for his work, without caring much about him personally; and there were also people who liked him personally, without relation to his work.

Not much time will be devoted to this aspect of the case. This is primarily a work of correction. The portrait of a kind of monster, a malignant Radical who betrayed Lincoln's and Johnson's confidence in order to carry out purposes of his own, not only fails to accord with the record—and the record is set down very elaborately in more than 300 volumes—it also fails to accord with any psychological possibility. And it is also a judgment which does little honor to the memory of Lincoln. What! was the President, so seldom mistaken in his estimates of people, consistently mistaken about the man with whom he associated most intimately for three years?

How has this misstatement, this peculiar picture of Stanton come about? Partly it arose because the Secretary of War has had no defenders during the period when modern biography was being written. The most recent biography previous to this one is Frank Abial Flower's, written in 1900 for the most part, published in 1905 in a small edition by a small house, and a partisan, if carefully documented volume. Since that time the technique of biography has undergone a complete change. In fact, new techniques have been added, including the "debunking" method, which consists in discovering what was wrong in any figure thought well of by the previous generation.

There is also the always-present tendency to use in biography, because it is the easiest way, a not very excusable method —that of making your subject taller by diminishing the stature of everyone around him. Stanton has been peculiarly the victim of this process of denigration, because almost everyone in his circle has been the subject of biographies in recent years —Lincoln, Welles, Seward, Judge Black, Andrew Johnson, Grant, Sherman, and Thomas among others. This is most especially true of McClellan; for reasons that need investigation, McClellan-olatry has approached the sectarian level, and it is a requirement of the faith to regard Stanton as the Antichrist.

In the second place, blaming a great deal on Stanton has proved useful in party politics. The line goes like this: The Congressional reconstruction program was a failure. Stanton preferred it to Johnson's reconstruction plan. Therefore, Stanton was one of the members of a villainous conspiracy which put through the evil Congressional program instead of John-son's good one.

There is some wobbly logic here and much ignoring of facts, but the line of argument has been particularly used by those "liberals" who, on the one hand say they wish to wipe out all discrimination against the Negro, and yet who are required by their political position to assure Southerners of their essential sympathy for Dixie. Claude Bowers is a good example; he does the trick by saying that everything done to make the Negro more than a second-class citizen today is a noble advancement of civilization, while everything done for the same purpose in the 1860s was done out of the most contemptible motives.

It is not hard for this school to present Thaddeus Stevens as merely a fierce and revengeful old man, and they have no particular difficulty with the erratic Sumner—though on this front the defense has not yet been heard from. Neither of them did anything before or during the war that merited special consideration. But with Stanton the case is otherwise. He has to be explained somehow, and the explanation most frequently adopted is that from the beginning he was a master of intrigue and treachery, who somehow pulled the wool over Lincoln's eyes. That this explanation coincides nicely with the one adopted by the McClellan claque only helped to establish it as the true one. But it results in the portrait of a man who never lived; and the effort here, without attempting to justify everything Stanton ever did, is to annotate that incredible portrait in correction and explanation.

In the course of that explanation, very free use of official letters and telegrams has been made, especially during the Civil War period. In many cases they have not been quoted completely, because they are often long-winded and contained a good deal of extraneous matter, but it has not seemed advisable to insert ellipses for each omission, because it makes for hard reading and the original texts are readily available to anyone who wishes to assure himself that no essential injustice has been done.

The reason for the use of these telegrams instead of summarizing their content is that they formed an essential part of the medium in which Stanton moved. It is impossible to form any true picture of his actions and the compulsions upon him unless one is aware of the material he had to work with. He was constantly required to make snap decisions that would have far-reaching effects on the basis of what those sheets of telegraphic flimsy told him; and what they told him was sometimes not true and nearly always incomplete. There was no time, for example, to send a trained investigator to Nashville to find out whether General Wilson really needed horses or not; his request either had to be refused, or he would have to be given what he wanted by instant and arbitrary action.

For the same reason—to present the picture of events as they actually impinged on Stanton's consciousness—the usual method of carrying one campaign or series of events through to its conclusion before taking up another has not been adopted here. That usual method is neater, but it does not tell what was really happening. It was an essential feature of the life Stanton lived as Secretary of War that he was constantly called upon to be the ringmaster of a three-ring circus. The Gettysburg campaign was carried on in the midst of a bitter controversy over prisoner-of-war exchange, and at the same time supplies had to be expedited to Grant for the siege of Vicksburg, means had to be found to improve Rosecrans' cavalry, the Missouri situation called for daily correspondence, and machinery for the administration of the Draft Act was being worked out. No true view of the man and what he faced can be achieved unless it is realized that he was constantly faced with the necessity for decisive action in several different areas at once, on top of dealing with the requests of several dozen minor visitors a day—the people who wanted passes, contracts and so on.

Nor is it possible to obtain any true picture of the man and what he did without the realization that these thousands of official letters, telegrams and papers constitute the only life he had during the war period. Before Stanton's appointment as Secretary there were (for instance) the letters to Buchanan, and a very revealing picture they give. After he moved into the War Office, there were private letters to nobody; he hardly wrote a dozen during the war, and some of those he wrote remained unmailed. He had no private life, in fact; went nowhere but on business and even spent a good part of his nights at the department. It is because the war occupied so much of his time that it has been necessary to see him only

under official circumstances during it; there were no other
circumstances.

A word about bibliography. The main sources for the Civil
War period are so well known as hardly to need repeating
here. Sources not usually consulted are the biographies of
Stanton by Flower (the 1905 book) and George C. Gorham
(Houghton, Mifflin, 1899); Schlesinger's "Age of Jackson"
(Little, Brown, 1945), Brigance's biography of Judge Black
(University of Pennsylvania Press, 1934), and a large num-
ber of letters and clippings kindly loaned by Mr. Gideon T.
Stanton, to whom thanks are hereby unreservedly rendered.
Mr. John Goodrum Miller also is officially thanked for help
in locating old court reports. Lest anyone should accuse me of
not having read the works of Otto Eisenschiml, I will say that
I have read them, and it seems unnecessary to say anything
more about them.

in the Steubenville saddlery while the type for the next issue of his paper was being set, and was much beholden to the doctor for giving literary form to his forceful ideas.

By the time he became aware of Lundy, the sickly infant Edwin had become a healthy boy, though an undersized one compared with the other Stantons—whether because of the difficulties at his birth or the diet that was the usual reason for stunting in pioneer communities, it is not clear. He was just coming out of a kindergarten school kept by a Miss Randle, where he seems to have spent much of his time sleeping with his head in the good lady's lap, and just entering the seminary of Henry Orr, around the block from his father's place. Two years later, Ed Stanton, aetat ten, was transferred to the Reverend George Buchanan's Latin school. A notable activity of mind, housed in a body that could not keep abreast of those around it in outdoor sports, found expression in studies—both those assigned to him and those he undertook for himself.

He is described at this date as imperious, self-reliant, never once getting into a fight with another boy, but loving to deliver lectures to his companions, to which they listened not unwillingly, for the boy Stanton possessed something of the gift of wonder. Part of the material for these lectures was furnished by the natural history museum of insects, birds, and small animals which his father helped him to collect, the doctor being a great hand at trotting around the countryside in search of herbs, which he unsuccessfully tried to persuade his neighbors to grow commercially. Part of the lecturing was done by demonstration; young Edwin Stanton early learned to make pets of snakes, and used to wander into the house with a pair of them coiling around his arms and neck to the horror of his mother and the three other children who had now been added to the family.

But most frequently of all, the lecture, delivered in the family stable, would be on God, Moses, the flood of Noah, or the Bible, and it would end with a prayer meeting at which Ed Stanton offered the invocation. He had turned twelve by a little more than a month when he was given preliminary tests and admitted a probationary member of the Methodist church

—his mother's denomination, which had become his father's also. His thirteenth birthday was five days gone when he passed a final examination and became a full member. Six days later, on December 30, 1827, Dr. David Stanton tumbled across his threshold, struck dead by apoplexy; and it was discovered that his extensive practice had produced no estate but the house he lived in.

II

THUS far the public records. They give nothing of the flavor of the society in which Edwin M. Stanton grew up, the medium through which he moved toward maturity. It was first of all a society on the make, growing richer and easier. The old log cabins, where the only light came through a door left open and four squares of greased paper, were vanishing so fast that one of the favorite sports of boyhood was making huge bonfires of shavings from the new houses and tossing in horse chestnuts to hear them pop. Everyone expected to live a better life than his father's, and counted on his son's being still better. If the advance were not rapid enough to satisfy, it must be because there was something wrong with the ground or the neighborhood; the family packed its goods into a Conestoga wagon and set off for richer lands toward the sunset, while another family moved in from the east to replace them. William Dean Howells' grandfather changed farms four times in the space of ten years, always moving a little farther west; and Mr. William Faux, the intelligent British traveler, noted four empty houses on his way through in one direction, all of which were filled by new-come immigrants from over the mountains when he went back. As a by-product, these movements and changes produced an endless crop of lawsuits, of a kind not known in more settled jurisdictions.

It was a postpioneering society, in which household skills were adequate to supply household needs for all but the most recondite articles. Two years before Dr. Stanton's death, the opening of the Erie Canal had begun to shift the region's reliance on home industry toward dependence on the products of associative labor, but throughout Stanton's boyhood the incoming products had not yet swamped local ability to produce most things, nor had it elaborated taste beyond the possibilities of local production.

The only vehicles were still the mountain-crossing Conestoga and farm-built two-wheeled chaises, considered very elegant. If a man wanted a chair, he built one; or arranged a swap with a neighbor who was a little better at chair carpentry. People raised their own wool, as they had always, and considered a sheep too valuable an animal to eat. But now, before spinning the wool into cloth, they took it to a mill for mechanical carding, and so eliminated the heaviest part of the labor. The mill itself was another example of the decline but not elimination of home skills; iron for its spindles now came down the river from Pittsburgh, which had not yet acquired the "h" but which had already developed the largest metal industry in America. The metal came in crude form; the spindles had to be forged by a blacksmith, who then rounded them with a hand file, since there were no lathes beyond the mountains. Another English traveler noted that there was one of these blacksmiths every two or three miles along the road and that all of them were furiously busy. When the first steamboat came up the river, the entire town of Steubenville declared a holiday and rushed to the bank—where all hands had to latch onto lines and pull her in, since her engine had broken down.

Yet the dominant factor in that eastern Ohio society of the 1820s was the abundance and cheapness of the food that poured from the ground, almost at the touch of a hand. The farms were not large—the land had been taken up in plots of 40, 80, more rarely 160 acres, and there was as yet no process of concentration—but every one produced far more than the family that lived on it could use. Labor could be had for fifty cents a day and found; it was not worth hiring for the purpose of gathering additional produce into barns.

Partly this was due to the movement of Midwestern trade, which was down the river system to New Orleans, then around the coast to Baltimore, Philadelphia, New York, and so across the mountains to Pittsburgh, with an exchange of goods at each transfer point. At the time Ed Stanton was born, Ohio was sending her wheat along this route, but by the date of his father's death, it cost a whole dollar to ship a barrel of produce to the Crescent City, and the new lands in Illinois and Missouri could do it cheaper. So the wheat stayed home and became part of the general surplus.

The intelligent Mr. Faux found bedbugs in his blankets, but his night's lodging, with a breakfast of beef, pork, steaks, eggs, and coffee, with plenty for the horses, cost him fifty cents, or about one-third the price of an inferior meal in a London tavern. A farmer offered him land for $10 an acre; cherries grew along every roadside fence and were free for the taking; apples cost nothing except in large quantities, and peaches were six cents a peck.

Especially peaches. The early settlers who moved tentatively across the great river after Mad Anthony Wayne broke the tribes at Fallen Timbers, looked to their orchards for the graces of the table. The normal diet was a rather monotonous procession of meat and grain products. Sweets were restricted to wild honey, poultry was too hard to handle in uncleared country, potatoes were used as a cereal substitute, and the other vegetables had not yet found their way to the table. It was only a few years since a sprig of the British nobility got himself nicknamed "Turnip" Townshend for suggesting that the pesky things were good for humans to eat. The settlers planted orchards, then; long rows of apple trees. Since it takes some years for apples to come into fullest bearing, the rows were interlined with peaches, which would grow more rapidly and die out about the time the apples became important.

Soil and climate deceived the settlers badly. The peaches not only grew and produced beyond all expectation; they refused to make room for the apples when the latter came in, growing taller, wider, and producing more fruit than any peaches in the history of the world. When Mr. Alard Welby came from England to investigate the products of American democracy in the 1820s, those Ohio peaches were almost the only objects to win his favor; he found them with branches intertwined, "literally breaking down with fruit." Dried to "peach leather" (home canning had not been invented), they formed the orderly of the winter diet. Fermented and distilled to peach brandy, they provided the farmer with his only reliable cash crop, as well as with the bottle of spirits that sat on every dinner table except in Quaker homes. European doctors valued it highly as a specific against gout.

The men who raised the fruit and made the brandy were mining the soil and lowering the water table, but they did not know it; they were restlessly looking for greater plenty in the midst of one of the world's most abundant regions, but they did not realize it; they were in an age of rapid transitions, but they were unaware of that; they only knew that they were members of a successful, expanding, libertarian society, in an age of hope and glory. There had been Indians, but they were far away. There had been England, but she existed now only as a memory of the intoxicating hour when the news from New Orleans sent every citizen into the streets to shout all night past illuminated windows. What did they have to worry about?

They had their souls to worry about. The old Calvinistic predestination and original sin obviously did not accord with the facts of life in a land where a man could so easily change his own destiny by hitching his horses to a Conestoga wagon and setting out for the blacklands of Illinois or the forests of Michigan. There was no theatre; no sports but on the most childish level; no music or pictures or art forms of any type; the society was too new for Society. There were not even schools, except as private enterprises. The lack of all forms of intellectual-emotional life had not been felt during the frontier period, while the struggle for existence absorbed all one's waking hours, but the frontier had now moved some distance westward and Ohio was a land whose easy abundance begat a certain amount of leisure not yet filled by the civilized amenities. Cincinnati, said a French visitor, was a "sad little town," where there was absolutely nothing to do with one's time. The only available activities were drinking, politics, and introspection.

Under the circumstances it is not surprising that a pair of young brothers (whose names are now lost) had been moved to address groups of their contemporaries in words that roused them to "a pungent sense of sin." That was in Kentucky, which the frontier had earlier left behind, and in 1800. The fire lit by those two young men spread into the Great Revival, which saw people coming from many miles to camp meetings, where praying, preaching, and exhorting went on from dawn to dusk for seven days on end, and the spiritually wounded screamed as they jerked across the ground in "exercises" designed to drive the devil from their bodies.

But the flame had by no means died down; it rekindled across the whole of the Northwest Territory as soon as the frontier was pushed far enough back to allow it to burn. When Mr. Welby was going to Steubenville, he found all the roads covered with dust, because of the enormous number of horses and wagons that had passed in the direction of a great religious camp meeting, attended by more than four thousand people. There was nothing in the least unusual in little Ed Stanton's holding prayer meetings in the stable. The Reverend George, his teacher, was an exhorter of great power, and the boy himself was only following at a distance in the footsteps of the Evangelist of Indian Creek, a lad of twelve, who stood on a stump urging people to come to Jesus until two men had to uphold his arms.

III

LUCY Norman Stanton's father was wealthy enough to have cared for her and her brood as well when she became a widow, but he was far away in Culpeper, Virginia, and she never let him know there was any financial stringency. Instead, she added a few books and some groceries to the stock of medicines her husband had left her, and opened a general store on the ground floor of the Market Street house. It was not a success, in spite of the fact that young Edwin turned the slow-moving stock of books into a rental library at a charge of ten cents per volume per term. A few months after his father's death, the boy had to leave school and take a clerkship in the bookstore of James Turnbull, at a salary of $50 for the first year, $75 for the second, and $100 for the third. The salary beyond that point was not fixed, but it seems to have been understood that he would stay four years more, filling out a normal apprenticeship.

Additional comments on life in early Ohio are furnished by the facts that a town of two thousand people could support a bookstore, and that a thirteen-year-old clerk was so little out of the ordinary that Mr. Turnbull frequently employed young Stanton on such business as buying paper for the publishing business which he ran on the side. As for the boy himself, he had secured the keys of fairyland; he read every book in the place, so much busying himself with the pursuit that prospective customers found it difficult to attract his attention. He was never hesitant in expressing opinions of what he read; he showed a conventional appreciation of the works of Shakespeare, but his true favorite among poets was James Montgomery. He was fond of declaiming passages from that author's "The World Before the Flood," which was so mercilessly cut up by Jeffrey in the *Edinburgh Review*. Critical taste in literature is always somewhat slow in developing, and in some individuals it never appears at all.

At the close of the hundred-dollar year, the boy expressed a desire to complete his education at college, and his legal guardian, a shadowy lawyer named Daniel Collier, secured a release from the apprenticeship and let him go. The place chosen was Kenyon College at Gambier, then only recently founded by Episcopal Bishop Philander Chase, but already famous everywhere beyond the Alleghanies as "The Star of the West." Where the money for this expedition came from is not altogether clear. Collier advanced some of the funds from his own pocket. Possibly there was something left of the hundred dollars, for cash needs were not great, and it is probable that the young brother, Darwin Stanton, was earning something by this date.

In any event, Edwin Stanton reached Kenyon by stage in

time for the summer term of 1831, after a two-day halt at Wooster to recover from a violent attack of asthma, which had bothered him earlier and now became a serious and permanent feature of his life. It was the first time he had ever been on his own, and he at once gave evidence that he intended to remain independent. Guardian Collier reminded Edwin when he left that his father had wished him to become a doctor, and urged him to bend his studies in that direction; but young Stanton chose an "irregular course" in classics, mathematics, political economy, and history that bore no relation to a medical career. His mother was so ardent a Methodist that itinerant ministers of that sect usually made the Stanton home a port of call; but the young man had not been at Kenyon six months before he switched over to the Episcopal faith, and in it he remained.

It is possible to view the change of religion as a phase of the same passion for intellectual activity that led him to read all the books in Turnbull's store. The antics and noisy repetitions of the "Shouting Methodists" were not well calculated to appeal to a mind that wished faith and reason to go hand in hand. Episcopal insistence on logic, Episcopal latitudinarianism on minor points of conduct doubtless had an appeal as well. Everyone agrees that young Stanton was peculiarly observant; he could hardly have missed the fact that the agonies of the camp-meeting followers were largely fireworks. They could shuck off their sins in a glorious paroxysm on Tuesday, then get drunk and beat up the wife on Wednesday; or declaim against the sin of public dancing at a prayer meeting, but experience no particular qualms about leading Louisa into the bushes on the way home.

But the appeal of the religion itself is hardly the whole explanation, for there are two incidents of independence, not one. In fact, it is impossible to escape the impression that Stanton wished to demonstrate that he would not have the dogmas, the arrangements of others, thrust upon him. It was not so much that at sixteen he knew what he wanted as that he was sure he did not want to be forced to do anything.

So he became in religion an Episcopalian, and in learning a free-lance, and slipped easily into the life of the Star of the

West, where the morning bell rang at five, recitations began twenty minutes later and lasted all day, except for the hours spent in sweeping one's own room, making one's bed, or working one's share in the college fields or on the college roads. It was a close-hauled regime, not the type that would strike one offhand as attractive, but it was not notably harder than life at home, and he loved every minute of it, cherishing for all his life the fondest recollections of his college.

Well he might; for it was at Kenyon that Stanton first encountered politics and the forces that were to furnish his reason for existence.

BACKDROP

Columbus Gazette

INFORMATION WANTED. Miss Margaret and Miss Ann Glass, daughters of the late William Glass, of the town of Cormon in the county of Tyrone, Ireland, having lost their parents, and understanding that their uncles, Robert & James Glass resided some where in the state of Ohio, have arrived at Columbus, in said state, but have not been able to hear anything respecting their uncles. Any information respecting them would be thankfully acknowledged.

Printers in this state, generally, will have the goodness to give this two or three insertions.

Ohio State Journal

The Jew Bill, as it is called, has at length passed the legislature of Maryland, and the Jews of that state now possess the same political privileges as other citizens.

Granville Wanderer

To Wise Men, Matrons and Maids, the subscriber has by purchase and deed obtained of Wm. Bushness and Co. of the state of Virginia, the right of constructing, using and vending their new and useful machine for spinning WOOL and COTTON. It is called THE PLEASANT SPINNER or FAMILY FACTORY.

SALT FOR WHEAT. The subscriber will give one bushel of SALT, in exchange for two bushels of WHEAT.—C. Humphrey & Sons.

Columbus Gazette

ATKINSON & MARTIN, HATTERS, Return their thanks to their friends for the liberal encouragement they have received and inform them that they have removed their Hat Manufactory, to the house recently occupied by Mr. Thomas Johnson book-binder, two doors north of Robinson's Tavern, high street, where they are prepared to accommodate the public on as reasonable terms as can be had in this country; they now have in addition to their former assortment Elastic Water Proof Hats, ALSO WOOL HATS of a superior quality. Lambs wool taken for hats at fifty cents a pound. CASH FOR MUSKRAT SKINS.

2

MR. ATTORNEY STANTON

EDWIN STANTON, of course, had not escaped politics earlier. No active mind could do so in a milieu where nine-tenths of the text of newspapers was devoted to the subject, and where it ranked second only to the neighbors' private affairs as a topic of conversation. Not everyone in Steubenville went to camp meetings, but down to children so small they had to be carried, there were no absentees from the great social event of the year—the erection of the party pole, made of hickory and decorated with streamers, if one were a Jackson Democrat; made of ash, with a live coon tied to the top, if one were for Henry Clay of Ashland, Kentucky.

But in the days before Kenyon, young Stanton's politics were of the emotional and family variety. He followed the lead of his father, Mr. Turnbull, Daniel Collier, and other members of the business community; and they were all for Henry Clay and the American System. The orderliness of that system, its stability, the ease with which it found solutions for the problems most pressing in the West—internal improvements and the supply of manufactured goods—were exactly calculated to appeal to a community where the profits of business were considerable, although the means of doing business were not keeping pace with the growth of the population. If, as his opponents alleged, Clay's system had a slight squint toward aristocracy, this was hardly a drawback in Steubenville. There was a strong

16

admixture of Quaker ideology in that town, and though many Quakers, like Dr. Stanton, had dropped away from formal connections with the sect, they retained a certain tendency to regard themselves as still a peculiar people, a little better than the river roustabouts and backwoods migrant laborers who swore by the name of Andrew Jackson. Not an aristocracy of birth, as it might have been in England; but of sound principles and good works.

For that matter, the Ohioans who voted for Clay in 1824 found little difficulty in transferring their allegiance to Jackson in 1828, when Clay was not a candidate. Old Hickory was the hero of New Orleans, the voice of the growing West, a kind of kitchen Clay, whose backers beyond the Alleghanies were careful to present him as an advocate of a protective tariff and internal improvements. Among the splinter groups that claimed to have inherited the old Jeffersonian Democracy, there were as yet no principles save those of discontent over the failure of Mr. President Adams to solve an economic crisis. There were no parties except those that grouped themselves around individual leaders who offered specific annotations of practice in interpreting the great Jeffersonian dream. That these annotations in the cases of Clay, Adams, and Daniel Webster had transformed the dream itself into a kind of Hamiltonism was as yet suspected by no one except a few impossible mugwumps like John Randolph of Roanoke, and a few passé doctrinaires like John Taylor of Caroline. Their pure Jeffersonian agrarianism was so obviously impractical in a country already feeling beyond the Mississippi that they were reduced to the role of ineffective and complaining criticism.

Jackson, then, offered a change of men rather than of measures when he succeeded John Quincy Adams in the Presidency. It was only in 1830, with his veto of a bill authorizing the United States to subscribe to the stock of a private turnpike company in Kentucky, that the cloven hoof began to appear. By 1831, when Edwin Stanton went off to college, there were horns and a tail. Andrew Jackson had publicly expressed his belief that the Bank of the United States was an unconstitutional and oppressive institution. Thomes Hart Benton, Jackson's wheel horse in the Senate, made it clear that the President would oppose renewal of the bank's expiring charter—and Henry Clay was on the other side.

Thus was launched the titanic struggle that was to dominate American politics for the next fourteen years and to end by altering both the political and economic character of the nation. But it was not the only struggle, and the bank was not the only issue; for John C. Calhoun chose the precise moment of Jackson's deepest preoccupation with the economic question to bring from the theoretical to the active level his famous doctrine of the absolute sovereignty of the states. In 1832 a South Carolina state convention declared the tariffs of 1828 and 1832 null and void within the state limits and, with something like apprehension, people wondered what Jackson would do.

On December 10 he told them, in a proclamation to the people of South Carolina which has ever since been regarded as the ablest state paper he ever put out. The hand that did the actual writing was that of Edward Livingston, but there is no possible doubt about whose ideas are being expressed:

The [South Carolina] ordinance is founded, not on the indefeasible right of resisting acts which are plainly unconstitutional and too oppressive to be endured, but on the strange position that any one State may not only declare an act of Congress void, but prohibit its execution; that they may do this consistently with the Constitution; that the true construction of that instrument permits a State to retain its place in the Union and yet be bound by no other of the laws than it may choose to consider constitutional.

I consider the power to annul a law of the United States, assumed by one State, incompatible with the existence of the Union, contradicted expressly by the Constitution, unauthorized by its spirit, inconsistent with every principle on which it was founded, and destructive of the great object for which it was formed.

A small majority of the citizens of one State of the Union have elected delegates to a State convention; that convention has ordained that the revenue laws of the United States must be repealed, or they are no longer a member of the Union. To say that any State may at pleasure secede from the Union is to say that the United States is not a nation, because it would be a solecism to contend that any part of a nation might dissolve its connection with the other parts, to their injury or ruin, without committing an offense. Secession, like any other revolutionary act, may be morally justified by the extremity of oppression; but to call it a constitutional right is confounding the meaning of terms.

It is the intent of this instrument to *proclaim* not only that the duty imposed on me by the Constitution "to take care that the laws be faithfully executed" shall be performed to the extent of the powers already vested in me by law, but to warn the citizens of South Carolina of the danger they will incur by obedience to the illegal and disorganizing ordinance of the convention.

The document produced something like an explosion of sentiment for the Union. Ten thousand people gathered before the New York City Hall to express their approval of Jackson's course and their disapproval of South Carolina's; Philadelphia, Boston, Baltimore held monster mass meetings for the same purposes; ten states denounced nullification through their legislatures, and Virginia sent a special commissioner to beg that South Carolina reconsider. John Quincy Adams in the House defended the man who had replaced him, and in the Senate, Daniel Webster, the old man of the mountains, stoked his boilers with apple brandy and stood up to boom like a battery of fifty cannon in favor of the President he detested. Even in South Carolina itself there were meetings of protest and the ominous formation of committees of correspondence as in the old days before the Revolution. Calhoun would have to find a sharper quirt to drive his mare to take the fence.

In the halls of Kenyon College the noise of these shoutings was by no means muted. The place had a literary and debating society, the Philomathesian, to which young Stanton had gravitated as naturally as a sunflower toward light. By the spring of 1832, being in his Junior course, the young man who had lectured in his father's barn was a leader in the group. The Calhoun view of the Constitution as a compact among sovereign states came up naturally as a topic of discussion, for it had been floating around, just below the level of action, ever since the "Tariff of Abominations" roused Carolina sensibilities and Calhoun brought out his famous "Exposition" to prove that the states were guardians of the Constitution. If one of them found a federal law in conflict with the fundamental instrument (said he), that law stood suspended until an amendment to the Constitution corrected the error. The doctrine was carefully worked out, for Calhoun's logical powers were great.

At Kenyon defenders of the Calhoun doctrine were by no means wanting, since the reputation of the Star of the West had spread rapidly and far. It was already the leading Episcopal college beyond the Alleghanies, and as much of the planter aristocracy belonged to that communion, its sons came there naturally. But it is easy to see how the language of nullification that they spoke sounded like Chinese to the young men from the Northwest Territory who formed the remainder of the student body. The state sovereign? They hardly thought of themselves as citizens of a state at all. Indeed, many of them were not, being from areas still under territorial government. In all the Northwest Territory very few persons had been born in the states where they lived, and those few were mostly very young. The states themselves were new and experimental entities, convenient for handling local affairs, but little more. The national government, which sold people their lands, protected them from Indians, and built post roads, was the solid and permanent reality, from which favors and powers flowed down to the states rather than in the other direction.

When Southerners from Kentucky, Tennessee, Alabama, and Louisiana pronounced for nullification, they produced a feeling against themselves which was exacerbated by an additional sense of betrayal. The major line of political fission in the nation had seldom been sharply geographical, but insofar as it was, that line followed the crest of the Alleghanies. The West gave the casting vote for war in 1812, had fought as a unit for easy money and debtor-relief laws under John Quincy Adams, and in 1828 it was Western votes that put Andrew Jackson into the White House. It was utterly shocking that these Southern Westerners should be so lost to a sense of community interest as to turn on their own man, in the name of a metaphysic that promised to reduce the status of the Republic to that of a federation of Indian tribes.

Nor was it surprising that the Northern members of the Philomathesian Society, under the leadership of Edwin Stanton, conducted the debates in a tone which led the Southerners to resign in a body and form a new literary club, in which they would not have to listen to such language. In the tempestuous idealism of youth, out of his determination to be independent, Stanton announced his conversion to the Jackson wing of the party.*

But this third act of independence had an effect on his fortunes. Back in Steubenville, people commented sorrowfully that "He has gone over to Jackson"; and Guardian Daniel Collier wrote to say that there was no more money for college.

II

IT DOES not seem to have been true. Although Collier's books have not been preserved for audit, he was a reasonably prosperous attorney, who a little later found means to support the young man for two whole years. Moreover, just about the time Edwin Stanton left Kenyon, the Steubenville house was sold for enough to send Lucy Norman Stanton to Virginia and to keep her there comfortably. The immediate result was that just before the nullification quarrel reached its most exciting climax with Jackson's fighting proclamation, Stanton left Kenyon "for a year or two" to make money. Mr. Turnbull was glad to have his bookstore clerk back, and even to promote him to the managership of a branch store in Columbus, at a salary of $250 a year, with sleeping quarters on the premises and meals taken at the home of a Mr. Howard, who exercised the mysterious profession of "steam doctor."

This boardinghouse connection led to a grim little passage. There was a cholera epidemic in Columbus that year, 1833. Returning to the Howards' for tea one afternoon, Stanton found that Anna, the daughter of the house, with whom he

* Stanton may have shared Jackson's economic and bank views at the time, but there is not the slightest evidence that he wrote, spoke, or even thought about them until later; he rather accepted them with the rest in the view that it was impossible to be less than completely a member of a party.

had eaten dinner that noon, had contracted the disease, died of it, and had been hustled into the ground by authorities fearful of contagion—all within the space of some five hours. The thought leaped to his mind that she might have been buried alive; he procured a spade, hurried to the burying ground, and dug her up to make certain.

Otherwise the Columbus interlude was a happy and a busy period. The eighteen-year-old bookstore manager's taste for debate led him to decide on the law as a profession. He found the law-reading that he did in every free hour as fascinating as anything he had known, and attendance on the proceedings of the state legislature he found delightful. He was popular in the town and well spoken of for his courage in the Anna Howard business, had fallen in love, and had begun to raise a beard.

The girl was Mary Lamson, an orphan living with her married sister; they decided to get married as soon as Stanton had passed his bar and hung out his shingle. Meanwhile, the date for the third-quarter payment of his salary came round and the young man found that his predecessor, as manager, had received more money for doing less work, and with less personal expense involved. He considered that Turnbull had practiced on him something not far from fraud, and said as much in a letter to his guardian. Collier, whose feeling toward Jackson and Jacksonites appears to have been considerably softened by the President's handling of the nullification crisis, replied that if Stanton would come back to Steubenville, he should have a residence in the Collier home and continue his legal studies in the Collier office.

Stanton accepted; the next two years were an unremarkable and unromantic procession of keeping accounts, making collections, and appearing in court as a junior to check citations and take down testimony, since court stenographers were called for only the most important cases in those days. His beard assumed the shape of a chin fringe. He wore heavy suits, tight-fitting around the legs, slept in a wooden bed big enough for three, acquired the habit of smoking an occasional cigar, and learned to write rapidly, almost as fast as a person could talk.

The only thing noted of him during this period was that he was present at an antislavery lecture given by Theodore Weld, the Massachusetts abolitionist, and was the first to spring to his feet at the speaker's call that all who believed it was the duty of the South to extinguish the institution should rise. In August, 1835, he passed his bar examination with honors at St. Clairsville, and that fall tried his first case.

The surviving records do not disclose whether he won it or not. Probably he did, for the story is that he went after the opposition's witnesses so fiercely that one of their counsel was moved to protest against the presence of this prematurely bearded youth on the ground that he was under age, not yet formally admitted to the bar, and was unfit to practice. Collier, who had been sitting at the back of the court to keep an eye on his young tiger, rose with: "Your Honor, this young man is as well qualified to practice law as myself or any other attorney of this bar; he has passed the examination; he is the son of a poor widow and should be allowed to go on." Without even waiting for a ruling, Stanton turned and continued his questioning; the judge only looked at him in a manner described as "quizzical."

On December 27 came the official notice of his election to the bar. Five days later, on New Year's Day, 1836, Edwin M. Stanton, attorney-at-law, left Steubenville for Cadiz, some twenty-three miles away by road, where he was beginning his profession as junior partner to one Chauncey Dewey. He made an instant and sensational success; exactly one year later found him on "the brightest, sweetest journey of my life," returning from Columbus by stage sleigh with Mrs. Edwin M. Stanton, née Mary A. Lamson, and every reasonable assurance that his future was secure. We do not know what the bride wore; probably a bonnet turned up in front and a ribbon cape with knots and streamers, as they were popular that year.

A few months later, at the age of twenty-two, Stanton was elected prosecuting attorney of Harrison County, upsetting a normal Whig majority, after a canvas in which he visited every home in the district with his wife by his side.

III

THE supporting incidents of this success story line out a picture of a young man with a passionate intensity of feeling, a formidable will-to-success, and an almost frightening capacity to support his ambition by toil that would break the health or destroy the nervous system of anyone else. He never seems to know the need of sleep; it is nothing for him to sit up till dawn studying his case and to present the argument at ten in the morning. He works all day Sunday and draws a gentle protest from the churchgoing Mary Stanton.

All the adjectives in this part of the story are superlatives. He walks twenty miles of the distance to claim his bride through an Ohio December, on roads that still have stumps in them. His brother Darwin visits Cadiz and goes hunting with a mutual acquaintance, but "Ed Stanton never hunted a day in his life." He has no time for such trivial matters as niceties of dress, or personal controversy, but carries "in a beautiful sheath on the inside of his vest, a fine dagger seven inches in length."

There is hardly a case of the period in the counties of Harrison, Jefferson, Carroll, Columbiana, Belmont, or Tuscarawas in which he does not appear, on one side or the other, always as presenting attorney in those strange little backwoods courts, where the décor was unpainted boards and judges in homespun consulted their private spittoons. He makes his points so vigorously that judges frequently tell him to sit down—a proceeding attended by futility, for it was noted that although he always sat obediently, he would be up five minutes later, with his objection framed in another form. He would come from court "with his collar broken down and his linen wet with perspiration"; and "it was impossible, after his character became known, to get weak or crooked witnesses to take the stand against him."

The lightning-fast, closely applied mind, the utter devotion to the cause in which he was engaged, gave Stanton a power of repartee that was feared and famous. He was trying a case against a lawyer named Roderick Moodey, who remonstrated with Stanton about his manner of examining a witness.

Stanton: "Make your appeals to the court, and quit whining."

Moodey: "I don't think a whine is any worse than a bark."

Stanton: "Oh, yes, Mr. Moodey, there is a difference—dogs bark and puppies whine."

The court: "We will take an adjournment."

A man named Thomas was accused of murder by poison. Stanton for the defense studied anatomy half the night for a couple of weeks and climaxed his study by taking some of the poison himself in the presence of the sheriff. Quick dosage with emetics was all that saved his life; but during the trial he made the prosecution's expert medical witnesses contradict each other so badly that they looked like ignoramuses, got his client a verdict in the second degree, and saved his life.

The Thomas case provides a clue to the basic thinking and method of approach, which are further illuminated by two other famous Stanton cases, one from four years later, one from ten. A Mrs. John Gaddis was found dying, her skull cracked in by half a brick. Before she went out, she said her husband did it. Gaddis had no money, but agreed to deed his home to Stanton in lieu of a fee. In spite of the fact that a deathbed declaration is regarded by all courts as the strongest possible evidence in a homicide case, Stanton brought off an acquittal that was for years the talk of legal Ohio. Mr. Gaddis, less impressed than the lawyers, complained that he "might as well have been hanged as deprived of his property and left to starve."

"You deserve to starve, since I have saved you from hanging, for you are guilty," said Stanton, sold the Gaddis place, and pocketed $500.

The other case was one of those slander actions in which early Ohio abounded, brought by a Miss Rectina McKinley against a certain Dr. Mears of Steubenville, who told people he had delivered her of a child. Stanton for the complainant induced the jury to decide that her reputation had been damaged $1,000 worth, whereupon one William Ralston hastily married the girl and came around to collect the money.

"Billie, you now have a good wife," said the attorney. "I have proved to the world that she is without a blemish. I charge only a thousand dollars for sending her out of court with a good character. A judgment of a thousand dollars as bait to catch a good husband, such as I believe you to be, is cheap, cheap as dirt." And he kept the money.

Obviously, there is hardly a trace here of the English tradition of jurisprudence: that a court is a forum for the discovery of objective facts, in accordance with which judgment shall be rendered. But it is important to realize that the departure was not Stanton's alone. This is the developing, strictly American idea of a court as an arena and a trial as a contest, in which points are awarded less for being right in accordance with some abstract ideal of justice than for fancy footwork and a good left hook.

Stanton himself certainly found the ethical difficulties raised by this approach to be troublesome at times. The Mansfield case, for instance. A miller of that name left his coat with $200 in it hanging on a hook, found the money gone when he retrieved the garment, and accused one of the men about the place of taking it. The theft could not be proved; the man sued for slander and, with Stanton as his attorney, won a judgment for $800. But when Mansfield came to pay, the young lawyer told him to make out the check for $400 and gave him a receipt for the whole. The balance represented the legal fee on the case, and Stanton was not sure but that the miller had been right.

The whole system of life was one in which it was extremely difficult to bring any simple ethical criteria to bear on cases that reached the courts. In the new states beyond the Alleghanies, the law itself was still in the process of formation. There was no body of statute and precedent stretching back to colonial days, as along the Atlantic seaboard. Most cases had to be tried under English common law; but English common

law, developed over many centuries in a stable and tightly organized community, was singularly ill-adapted to the new,
fast-moving society which was still fumbling out its ultimate
form.

Moreover, when the English common law reached the
American West, it encountered a series of abrasive influences
arising from the quite different constitutional background. In
the land of its origin there was nothing like the American division of the governmental function by subjects, so that national, state, and local municipal rules all applied directly to
the same individual, depending upon the activity in which he
was engaged. There was nothing like the theory which had
spread from the Constitution throughout the whole American
legal system, that every power is accompanied by limitations,
checks, and balances; and, for that matter, nothing like the
theory that a law or a governmental act may be voided as
unconstitutional. To meet such conditions, the English common law had to pass through a sea change.

The work of adaptation was in progress, under the leadership of Peter Hitchcock, who occupied the Ohio supreme
bench for twenty-one years, and who may be said to have
essentially completed his task by 1852. Meanwhile most cases
were in equity; that is, the courts themselves were determining
where the ethical line lay in a given type of case.

At this point Edwin M. Stanton was not merely struggling
to get a judgment for a client. That was a primary motive, to
be sure; lawyers win cases for clients, both to gather future
fees and to enhance their own importance. But there was
always somewhere in Stanton's mind the ideal of Cicero: that
human law can never be better than a reflection of divine law,
and that the more clearly the former is stated, the more nearly
it approaches the latter.

He lived in a time of legal flux and was anxious to have the
general principles of law, a department of ethics, traced out—
with advantage to his client, if possible. He claimed whatever
he could for a client, and if the judgment went against him,
filed it for future guidance. In a Pittsburgh case, later, he persuaded a judge to take the matter away from the jury and

render an *ex parte* decision from the bench. The upper courts reversed the decision, and Stanton never tried that one again.

There is also the peculiarly combative character taken by the Western revision of English common law. This may be traced to the locale in which the revision was conducted. The new elements flow from the frontier, which was so basically militant that it must make a battle out of everything that impinged about it, even religion. Phrases about "whipping that old devil" clamored through all the sermons of the time; one did not clear a field but "beat the forest" out of a piece of ground. One may debate about the origins of this frontier militancy,* but there is very little doubt that it early became embedded among the permanent characteristics of the race that still turns out a hundred thousand people to watch Notre Dame do battle with Army, and has provoked one of the acutest of military critics to remark that the failure of Adolf Hitler lay in not realizing that beneath the veneer of American official pacifism lay a profound and far-reaching spirit of combat. That spirit was in the atmosphere before Mr. Attorney Stanton passed his bar examination; he differed from his contemporaries only in the thoroughness with which he applied it and the energy with which he gave it expression.

Where did that energy come from? He was nearsighted, so that at an early age he had to wear glasses; he was shorter than most men, and subject to occasional paralyzing attacks of asthma. But the doctrine of compensation will hardly do, any more than the assumption that his replies to John Gaddis and Billie Ralston were dictated by a narrow cynicism. The law and good morals allowed Gaddis—and Thomas, the poisoner —their trials, with a champion on their side in the lists. Stanton, having accepted that championship, felt bound by a kind of legal Hippocratic oath to give his services to the limit of his ability. But he did not feel bound to give his personal sympathy to such clients, any more than does a prison doctor,

* Ellsworth Huntington, for instance, thinks it came about as the result of a process of selection, in which the more aggressive characters of European and colonial society were drawn off to the westward.

charged with saving a murderer's life so that he can be properly and legally hanged.

Moreover, the fighting attorney, who could tear a lying witness to pieces and who toiled so terribly, lived anything but a cheerless life. Every contemporary account speaks of his friendliness, the sweetness of his disposition, the sincerity of his religion, his kindness. He is named trustee for the estate of a feeble-minded girl who had been left a large wood lot as provision for her support, and promptly puts it on a ninety-nine-year lease that will place her income beyond the reach of anyone who has designs on it, charging no fee. His fees generally were low; he made money rapidly because of the vast number of cases he handled. He did not merely love his wife, he adored her with a passionate devotion that, although expressed in homespun terms, made Romeo of Montague look shallow and childish.

Out of this grew tragedy. In 1840 she bore him a daughter, named Lucy, who died in the following year to the accompaniment of intense grief, somewhat assuaged by the birth of a son in 1842, Edwin Lamson Stanton. But on March 13, 1844, Mary Stanton died suddenly in childbirth. "He threw her wedding rings and other jewels into the coffin and wanted her letters buried with her too." "He could not work and could not be consoled. He walked the floor incessantly, crying and moaning. At night he placed her night cap and gown on his pillow and cried and cried for his dear Mary. After her burial he himself put white stones around the grave and visited it every morning to see if a single one had been removed and also to place flowers on his beloved one's breast." "Where formerly he met everybody with hearty and cheerful greeting he now moved about in silence and gloom, with head bowed and hands clasped behind."

Long later, when he was about to marry for the second time, and considered it only honorable to burn Mary's letters, he put them in the fireplace but could not apply the match; a friend, eyes also misting, had to perform that office for him.

BACKDROP

Ohio Monitor

NEW INDIAN TREATY. Messrs. J. B. Gardiner, Special Commissioner, John M'Elvain, of this town, Indian Agent for this state, signed a treaty with the chiefs and warriors of the Seneca and Shawnee band of Indians in the Lewistown Reserve, in the county of Logan on the 20th ult. Forty thousand acres of land are acquired to the United States Government by this treaty and the county of Logan is cleared of Indian title. The Indians receive a tract of land of some greater extent west of Missouri and Arkansas, together with some other presents, and the expenses of their removal, which it is expected, the Government will perform for them next summer.

Charleston Mercury

TWENTY-FIVE DOLLARS REWARD. Absconded from the subscriber on the 2nd day of August last, my Mulatto Girl SELINA, 25 years of age, about 5 feet 4 or 5 inches high, no visible marks, of genteel appearance, and very plausible. Her dress cannot be described, as she took a quantity of clothing with her. She will no doubt attempt to pass as free. She had been hired out in this city for a number of years, and at the time of her departure was in the employ of one Dederich Feldtman, who, I understand, arrived here from New Orleans. He departed from the city at the same time, and it is supposed they went together.—E. F. Gitsinger

Ohio Atlas & Elyria Advertiser

STEAMBOAT ACCIDENT. As the steamboat *Beaver* was descending the river from Pittsburgh to Steubenville, she was run into at midships, by the steamboat *Plough Boy*, a few miles above the latter place, and sunk. The *Beaver* had been chartered by the Pittsburgh Guards, all of whom we understand were on board, for the purpose of conveying them to the grand Military Parade, which was to take place at Steubenville. We have not learned whether any lives were lost, or any personal injury sustained—but we presume there was not.

The subscriber would just like to say that for reasons not necessary to mention, that he must settle and collect his debts without delay.—E. L. Goodrich

Unsigned Memoir of the Campaign of 1840

Presently a couple of stragglers came up, stopped at the bar and were accosted with, "Well, how did you find the Genl.? did you get any hard cider?" and various other questions. They gave a very flattering account of their reception, but added, looking significantly at the same time, "We had some of the best wine that was ever drunk—it was sent to the Genl. from Europe." "From Europe" burst out several voices at once, "and does the log cabin candidate receive presents from Europe?" was echoed by the favorers of the administration.

Mary Conclin to Elizabeth Richards

Perhaps you would like to hear something in regard to the fashions. They are very gay & indeed the ladies cannot find anything bright enough. Frock coats are all the *ton* for winter. They are made something like a wrapper, plain waist and open sleeves. They are rather shorter than the dress, and wadded throughout. Some wear a large cape, others do not. The material is left to the taste and fancy of the wearer, but the most elegant are silk velvet. The handsomest dresses are the Cashmeres. Tabby velvets are worn by a great many, but they are not considered by persons of taste to be pretty.

Savannah Georgian

PLANTATION AND NEGROES FOR SALE. The Plantation, called Oakland, containing about five hundred and fifty acres, seven miles from town, on the Ogeechee road, with about ninety negroes, belonging to the estate of James Forrest, Esq., deceased, for sale. The negroes are a fine gang, and long accustomed to cotton planting on the place, which is well known to produce as fine crops of cotton as any in the neighborhood.— Rob't Mitchell, Exec'r.

3

THE WIDER STAGE

THE position Edwin M. Stanton had attained as an attorney is adequately pictured by the fact that no court could be held in Jefferson County during the term of his wife's death, because the prostrated lawyer was due to appear in every case on the calendar. By this date he was back in Steubenville, leaving Harrison County in 1838, even before his term as its prosecuting attorney expired, to take up a partnership with Judge Benjamin Tappan.

The Judge was an important Ohio character, with no hair on the top of his head and a great deal of it on the back of his neck; bushy eyebrows, a deeply etched face, and a slow, rolling, oratorical voice. He had known Stanton for a long time; the younger man had spent a week or so at his home with Mary on the wedding journey from Columbus. At the time of the partnership the Judge was expecting to be elected to the United States Senate. He wanted a trustworthy man of energy to hold down the office, while on Stanton's side, a partnership with a senator offered a far better opportunity than a minor elective post.

Two months after the formation of the new law firm, the Judge was duly sent to Washington, and the whole work of the office devolved on Stanton. It was not enough for him. He formed a whole series of other partnerships—with two men named Umbstaetter and Wallace at New Lisbon, with Colonel George McCook at Steubenville (which partnership became very nearly permanent and a friendship as well), with Daniel Peck at St. Clairsville, and occasionally with others on a temporary basis.

The arrangement sounds odd to our age when the courts sit simultaneously in several jurisdictions and a firm that has a case in a distant town needs the services of a local lawyer to conduct proceedings. But in Ohio of the 1840s, the judges rode circuit. When the calendar at Steubenville was cleared, jurists, attorneys, and clerks would ride off to New Lisbon in the same stage, spitting tobacco juice out the windows as they discussed appreciatively the manner in which a point had been brought out or an examination conducted. As a specialist in trial work, Stanton was a part of this traveling circus in every respect but as a tobacco chewer—perhaps because he felt it relaxed tensions, while his whole effort before a jury was to build them up. But he needed partners in various places to prepare the way before him—draw and serve papers, examine witnesses, arrange exhibits.

He accepted nearly every case that was offered him, took in several students not much younger than himself to handle details, and by the date of his wife's death, when not quite thirty, he was already leaving local contests in the hands of subordinates and confining his own efforts to appeal cases, the State Supreme Courts, and the Federal District Courts.

Money was no longer a factor; people were calling him "the king of Steubenville"; his income was one of the largest in town, and he used part of it to send his brother Darwin through Harvard, from which the young man was graduated with a medical degree. After Mary's death, Stanton sold the house where they had lived together and took a long lease on the largest and finest house in town; he bought out and tore down a glass factory that annoyed him by obstructing his view of the river. In place of the vanished industry he set out a fine garden plot, where apples, peaches, quinces, plums, cherries, pears, and grapes grew in rich profusion; the master of this manse could often be seen fondling his blooded cattle or helping the hands pitch hay. His mother was living with him now, and the place was full of children—those of Stanton's divorced sister, those of his sister-in-law, as well as his own son and a couple of orphans he had "hired" as houseboys, all of them so well provided for and supplied with pocket money that the neighbors grumbled over giving the young such luxury, as a poor way to prepare them for the rigors of life.

They might more profitably have given some thought to the example afforded by the labors through which this largesse was obtained. One of the houseboys remembered in later years how often, at ten or eleven of an evening, he was called to get out the cart and drive down to the office to help Stanton fetch a load of law books. The attorney would study them all night, eyes owlish behind his big glasses, rising from time to time to pace the floor as he thought on what he had read and how it might be used. This application, rather than courtroom oratory or the cross examinations in which Stanton took so much pleasure, emerges as the basic reason for his success. The first of the really big cases, which fell in the March term of 1845, just after Stanton had moved into the new house, shows the process very clearly.

This was the "Pork Case," which went back to a deal made on New Year's Day of 1836 by three men named William Talbot, William Thoms, and Aaron Gano to corner the Western market in pork and lard—a proceeding regarded in those days as a highly moral example of legitimate business enterprise. Gano and Thoms were wealthy men, but they put nothing into the operation except their credit. Talbot, the actual operator, went down the Ohio to the pork-raising lands of Illinois and Indiana, bought the meat with cash which he raised on notes of hand, shipped it to markets in Pittsburgh and New Orleans, and, with the money realized from sales, began a new cycle. The panic of 1837 knocked the bottom out of the pork market; Talbot had to sell at losses that wiped out the firm's bank account, and left it in debt. The principal, and almost the only creditor, was named John Moore. He readily obtained a judgment against Talbot for $23,000, but the other two partners dodged service of the papers and Talbot had no more money than a rabbit, and so Moore was left holding the bag.

He sued to have Thoms and Gano joined in the judgment.

The court found that the loans which made up the $23,000 were personal loans from Moore to Talbot, and had not been used for the purchase of pork; that Talbot had no authority to pledge the credit of his partners; that the date of the largest of Moore's several loans had been misstated in the papers, a fatal variance from the facts; that Moore had been largely paid off in pork, which he took for his own account. The judge gave a charge which threw out most of Moore's evidence and practically directed a verdict against him. It was rendered.

Enter Stanton on Moore's side. It did not occur to him to find it a serious drawback that the last round in the case was four years dead and decided when the matter came to him. "I must succeed," he said, "or my client will be ruined." He traveled to Indiana and Illinois, where the pork had been bought; to Pittsburgh and New Orleans, where it had been sold; to Philadelphia, where some of the brokerage transactions had taken place; and on the basis of new evidence and the improper charge of the judge, he secured a new trial.

When it was called, Stanton appeared in court with a series of formidable manuscript books. One contained the partnership agreement, which clearly authorized Talbot to pledge the credit of the three, with all the transactions under the agreement itemized and analyzed; another showed the purchases, which eyewitness evidence proved had been made by Talbot with money that Moore handed him; another showed the sales, demonstrating that Moore had not been paid in pork or anything else, since every pound of pork was accounted for. Still other books contained the testimony of every person who had dealt with the partnership during its existence, and all the laws and previous decisions that would apply in such a case. Opposing counsel were appalled by this mass of evidence; judge and jury found that when they wanted information on any part of the transaction, they had to get it from Stanton's books. They ended by accepting his view of the case as well as his facts.

He walked the square in front of the courthouse all night with a plug hat on the back of his head, waiting for the verdict to come in, and when it did, rejoicing even more than his client, he plunged into another of the great cases, the first of a series that carried the king of Steubenville beyond the frontiers of his realm. The clerk of the House of Representatives in Washington was named Caleb McNulty. He came from Mount Vernon, Ohio, and was well known to Judge and Senator Tappan, who was one of his bondsmen. While Stanton was arguing the Pork Case, a default of $44,500 was found in McNulty's department. The House dismissed him by unanimous vote; he was indicted and, as the Whigs were disposed to make political capital out of the affair, there were lusty demands from the Democratic newspapers that McNulty be rushed to prison and his bondsmen pay up to save the party honor. Tappan saw the accused man in jail, held without bail and very despondent over the fact that his counsel had told him the case was hopeless.

"Send for Stanton," said the Senator. The young lawyer reached Washington late on December 9, 1836, to find that the trial was to be held in the morning. He set to work at once on the statutes and rules governing the areas of McNulty's responsibility. By four o'clock in the morning he had discovered enough to make him certain that the indictment was not sound in law, so he slept for a couple of hours, had a decent breakfast, and went round to call on the Washington attorney in the case.

He was not out of bed; Stanton returned to his law books and studied on until ten, then waited on the Washington counsel with his proposition. They were lugubrious but willing to let him try. He stepped into the court without a brief and offered a motion to quash the indictment. The court was not very happy about the idea, taking it for an effort at obstruction. Stanton launched into one of his impassioned pleas, telling how he had spent the night and asking only one day more in which to prepare his argument, with the stipulation that if he were overruled the trial should begin at once. This seemed so reasonable that the District Attorney agreed; but that was the end of his case, for after Stanton had spoken for two hours on the following morning, the indictment was quashed and the prisoner was released.

II

SHORTLY before the McNulty case, another traveler made the journey between Washington to Ohio—reversing Stanton's course—and jotted down his impressions of Stanton's world in words that set America quivering with indignation. Mr. Charles Dickens found the capital a city of magnificent intentions, with streets looking as though they had been freshly ploughed; beset with tornadoes of dust. He saw a few clumps of small, mean wooden houses with green blinds, one white and one red curtain at each window. The decorum and politeness of a Presidential Levee (from nine to twelve in the evening) impressed him, but not the halls of Congress, where he was bored by the repetitiousness of the speeches and disgusted by the manner in which honorable members continually spat on the carpets. "Washington may be called the headquarters of tobacco-tinctured saliva."

The trip westward was made by canalboat, in a cabin so low that it was impossible to stand erect. At six, tables were spread, on which appeared liberal supplies of salmon, shad, liver, steak, ham, chops, sausage, potatoes, pickles, tea, coffee, bread, and black pudding. At night shelves were let down from the walls —just wide enough for a man, if he disposed himself on one side and remained motionless.

In the morning the passengers shared a large tin dipper, with which they dipped water from the canal into a tin basin on deck, before drying themselves with a community jack towel. The water was dirty to start with and most passengers did not bother to use it. The proceedings were not infrequently interrupted by the towboy's cry of "Low bridge!" Whereupon they had to lie down on deck. At eight the breakfast tables were laid with the same items that had been served the previous evening, to which was added a species of small wild game from the beds.

There were stumps in the abundant wheat fields, and along the banks as many log cabins as frame houses, each with an attendant outdoor clay oven, and all pretty widely separated.

In many places forest had simply been burned to clear the land, a procedure which shocked Mr. Dickens. The journey was enlivened by a series of quite incomprehensible threats about something rather dreadful, from a person who described himself as "a brown forester of Mississippi" and carried a knife.

At the mountains the canal gave place to a "railroad" on which the cars were pulled up one slope by a stationary engine and line, crossed flatter places behind horses, and descended the opposite grade by gravity. Pittsburgh lay under a pall of smoke and its music was the clamor of forges; the hotel was good.

It took four days to find a steamboat for the journey down the Ohio; on advice, Mr. Dickens secured a stateroom at the stern, since "when these craft blow up, as they do at the rate of one or two a week, the explosion generally takes place forward." It was even more difficult to get water for washing than on the canal, nor was the table as well set, the food consisting mainly of roast pork, with small dishes of beet root, Indian corn, pumpkin, and preserves. The passengers bolted these viands in gloomy silence, and did not appear to share Mr. Dickens' appreciation of the beautiful scenery and many islands along the stream. He was struck by the rarity of buildings, and so came at last to Cincinnati, a cheerful town of clean red and white houses, well-paved streets and footways of bright tile.

III

IT IS probable that Stanton's coup in the McNulty case did not altogether endear him to some of his political associates. A good many of his procedures did not, for he was an extremely poor hand at party discipline, the earlier uncritical partisanship having yielded to the family tendency toward independent thinking where a matter involved principle. Yet he was so telling a speaker, so indefatigable an organizer, that the Democratic party in eastern Ohio found it difficult to do without him— not to mention that there must have been something pleasing about having on hand a wheel-horse party worker, who wanted neither elective nor appointive favors for himself, only to have his fingers on the levers of the machine.

Thus, as early as 1840, he demonstrated in politics the same ability he displayed in court for exasperating opponents into betraying themselves. That was the Tippecanoe and Tyler Too year, when the Whigs discovered that hard cider and high jinks were a good substitute for ideas in dealing with an electorate that had few basic discontents. They staged a monster three-state parade and rally at Steubenville; Stanton promptly organized a counterrally. As the Whig parade passed his office, rolling one of their gigantic balls and doubtless in a state of some exhilaration, they found a big tombstone in front of it, pasted all over with the bills of the defunct Bank of Steubenville, whose officers were the very men leading the Whig meeting. With yells of rage their march broke up and hurried to the Democratic grandstand, where there was a lovely riot, with several people injured.

The following year Stanton was at the Democratic state convention, charged with drafting the plank against a revival of the United States Bank, and deploring the repeal of the independent treasury. But the year after that he spent the campaign across the river in Wheeling, Virginia, helping Dr. Darwin Stanton win election to the House of Delegates on the Whig ticket in a district normally Democratic. Eighteen hundred forty-three was an off year, but in 1844, Edwin Stanton was back at the state convention, once more drafting an anti-Bank resolution, but refusing to have anything to do with an "Address to the People" which declared for free trade, and using his skill as a manager to obtain delegates to the national convention who would be firmly for Martin Van Buren.

Now, with regard to every issue that meant anything in 1844, this combination of ideas and actions places Stanton solidly with the Locofoco, heretical wing of the party—the "radicals," as they have been called by people to whom anything with that name smells sweet. The United States Bank question had been killed by Andrew Jackson, and was buried when a Whig majority in Congress failed to get a bill for its revival past President Tyler's veto. It was included in the platform chiefly as a reminder to the voters that the Democrats had carried out a reform program without bringing down the economic rafters of the country.

Free trade was more a convenient noisemaking device than a realizable program. In Western minds it was bound up with a complex of such other postpioneer ideas as practically unlimited internal improvements paid for by the government, and state banks issuing clouds of lightly secured greenbacks. All postpioneer communities want the government to make the capital investment necessary for providing roads, bridges, dams, canals; all of them want easy money and lots of it. The West had supported Old Hickory in the quite mistaken belief that he was ardent for such a program. Western men assumed that Jackson's struggle with the United States Bank was undertaken, not in the interests of deflation, but to provide far easier and freer credit, exempt from Eastern banking controls.

Free trade appeared to fit into this structure; and, at the same time, it was a convenient rallying cry, for it represented the only ideological common ground between the Democrats of the West and the Southern party members of the Calhoun persuasion—except, of course, the idea of remaining in office. Banks of any kind, not merely the United States Bank, made Calhoun positively ill; in his mind, internal improvements were not only evil in themselves, but also in conflict with the narrow construction he gave the Constitution. But free trade was a part of his program, and he could work with people who believed in it.

Stanton pronounced free trade "absurd and a tendency toward direct taxation." And as though further to accentuate the complete alienation of thought between the Northern and Southern wings of the party, which was to grow into the Great Schism of 1860, both he and his friend and partner, the cadaverous Senator Tappan, were for Van Buren. Van Buren had pronounced himself opposed to the annexation of the Republic of Texas; and that annexation, with expansion into Mexico to provide still more territory for slavery, was precisely the issue on which the dominant Southern leaders of the party proposed to make the campaign of 1844.

They succeeded both in this and in keeping Van Buren out of the Presidency by means of the famous convention rule that no nominee should be adopted who did not receive the approval of two-thirds of the delegates. But they also succeeded in stirring up Edwin M. Stanton—which was not a very safe thing to do. But it is not likely that any of the Southern leaders thought that the emotions of a local Ohio politician would be important. For the present, Stanton only pulled out of active participation in politics, writing to one of his congressman friends: "There is too much inclination among Northern Men to submit in silence to the insolent demands of the South, and one of the chief duties that will devolve upon us as citizens of free and independent States will be to curb that spirit of domination that has been too long suffered to prevail."

He stuck to the party to the extent of drawing resolutions in favor of the Mexican War when it began, but in 1848 he went all through the state, organizing sentiment in favor of Van Buren's rump Free Soil ticket, and rejoiced when it drew enough votes to beat Lewis Cass, who, better than any man in American history, deserved the name of "doughface." There would be further annotations later; for the present Stanton ceased to be a political animal.

IV

IN SPITE of the fact that all faithful Millerites crowded to camps and hilltops in their ascension robes, the world failed to come to an end on the assigned date of April 23, 1843, and even failed to keep the postponed appointment on October 21, 1844. Yet without divine interposition a world was ending and one was beginning in those years when the young attorney Stanton reached out from Steubenville toward the conquest of a wider world.

For it was now 1846, the year of decision, when Morton

demonstrated the use of anesthetics, Colt established his fire-arms factory, and the new reduced rates trebled post-office business while changing its deficit toward a surplus. *Godey's* deplored any circumstance that might hamper feminine deli-cacy or draw a woman from the sacred sphere of the home; but "Oh, Susanna!" was the song of the hour, and there were women as well as men in those long ribbons of wagons moving out across the western plains, bound for the fabulous Oregon —which might turn out to be British territory.

Somewhat north of their route, moving more cautiously, with halts to raise crops, were the solidly organized trains of the Mormons. Unlike the settlers who followed the Oregon Trail, the Mormons sought a new land not because they thought it was American but because they knew it was not; Mexico would give them the freedom to conduct their peculiar com-munity that Illinois had denied them. Yet even as they held their prayers under the captains of tens, history was deceiving them. For in Washington, Congress had recognized the exist-ence of a state of war with the Mexican republic, and in Steu-benville, Ohio, lawyer Stanton, having drawn the wills of the local company of Grays, was watching them take the first steps of the long walk to Mexico that would turn the United States into a continental power.

Stanton wanted to join that march. Chronic asthma was assigned as the reason why he did not, but there was another and more tragic reason for his exclusion from the main stream of the electric year. Dr. Darwin Stanton, who had become assistant clerk of the national House of Representatives, came home in August with a fever, and took to his bed in a house on the Virginia side of the river. The illness became intense; in a paroxysm of pain, he snatched up one of his own lancets, severed an artery and bled to death. Edwin Stanton, arriving too late, wandered off into the woods without hat or coat, where a couple of friends found him in such a state that the attending doctor ordered them not to let him out of their sight.

It was such another spiritual crisis as that attending the death of his beloved Mary. He drew more within himself; people noted that the old affability, the instant lighting of the eye, were gone. A friend who had returned with some forgotten detail after a call once found him, for no discernible reason, seated at his desk in tears, head buried in his hands. His pleasure in the swift give-and-take of personal relations that constitutes politics was dead. The brief foray of 1848 in favor of Van Buren seems to have been conducted more because Judge and Senator Tappan wanted him to do it than for any interest he himself had in the cause.

Of course, Edwin Stanton reacted too swiftly to any human contact to become a cloistered personality, but his activities tended to seek the form of a closer application to his legal work. At the same time, his sensational success in the McNulty and Pork cases, widely talked about in the river community, brought him to the attention of the rising industrial world of Pittsburgh. There was a lawyer in that city named Charles Shaler, a former judge who had retired from the bench to share in the big cases and big fees provided by a region where business and its profits were expanding gigantically, while the legal framework within which business operated was not yet established. This Shaler had the necessary business, political and social connections, but needed a good court man to work with him. He offered a partnership to Stanton, and the Steubenville attorney was launched into a series of cases that fundamentally affected both the law and the industrial development of the nation.

The case of the Wheeling Bridge was the first. Ever since 1816, Ohio and Virginia had joined in trying to persuade Congress to bridge the Ohio River at Wheeling, and ever since the same date there had been objections from Pennsylvania. It was the era when steamers carried skyscraping smokestacks; the bridge would very likely stop all boats at the Virginia city, depriving Pittsburgh of its position as head of navigation and a port of entry—in fact, tending to drain away its industry toward Wheeling, for rail and road transportation were still far more expensive and less reliable than that by water. In 1847 private enterprise took a hand in the bridge question, and, as usual when it sticks its finger into politics, got action at once.

The Virginia state legislature chartered the Wheeling and Belmont Bridge Company to put a structure across the river, a thousand feet long over the central span, ninety feet above low-water level, the largest suspension bridge in the world. Ohio agreed.

There was an agonized buzzing among the Pittsburgh river men, for though the rapidly rising bridge was immense, it was still not high enough to let many of the 250 river packets pass. Yet what could they do, with the states on both sides of the stream favoring the structure? They could apply to Edwin M. Stanton; he knew most of them personally, and a year before had done them an important service in the matter of wharfage dues charged by towns along the river. The wharfs were owned by the towns, but the charges made for their use were often so heavy that they more than ate up the value of the business for which the ships put in.

"If the boats will pay me $2,000, I will agree to rid them of this wharfage," Stanton told one of the captains. They took up a collection and gave him his fee. He told them simply to stop paying wharfage, and when the town of Wellsville sued to collect from two of the ships, Stanton filed an answer, saying that wharfage on boats passing from one state to another was essentially a tax on commerce between states, therefore a plain violation of the Constitution.

Wellsville dropped its suit without a trial, and when the bridge problem came up, the steamboaters took their trouble to Stanton. A thorny one it was, for the Virginia courts were most unlikely to hear a complaint against the state itself from citizens of another commonwealth. The Federal Courts? Two separate districts of the United States Circuit Court were involved, the river being the boundary between them. This would make slow process, with loss to Stanton's clients through delays and appeals; and at the end of the street there was visible the inevitable reluctance of any court to interfere with a well-established institution that served some part of the public. "He gave it much thought," and decided to go straight to the United States Supreme Court in original jurisdiction, seeking an injunction to abate the bridge as a public nuisance.

To obtain his paper, three things were necessary. First, actual damage must be shown. Stanton boarded the steamer *Hibernian No. 2* and ordered her captain to take her down the regular channel between the bridge piles. The bridge knocked off her smokestacks and demolished the superstructure; splendid. Second, it must be demonstrated that nothing but an injunction would prevent the damage continuing. Stanton made a series of experiments, scientific investigations conducted by expert engineer witnesses, with different types of fuels, high and low drafts, short and tall funnels. He visited every town along the river down to Cairo, Illinois, collecting statistics on the relative costs of rail, road, and boat transportation, on the nature of the last, and on its importance to the economic life of the country. While on this junket, he fell down the companionway of the steamer *Isaac Newton* and sustained a compound fracture of the knee that kept him helpless for weeks and left him with a gimp that lasted all his life. He only called it a lucky accident and had law books brought to his bedside, saying that he might learn something about his business if convalescence were sufficiently delayed.

Perhaps it was a lucky accident; while lying on his bed, Stanton developed the third necessity of his case, the legal and logical reasons why the Supreme Court should intervene. He based his suit on two lines of reasoning, persuading the state of Pennsylvania to bring the action; first on the doctrine that a state has the right to ask the high court to protect its citizens from the oppressive actions of another state. The Supreme Court rejected this doctrine at the time, but came back and picked it up later; this concept is now a fixed point in constitutional law, and Stanton's argument is usually quoted. His second line was that Pennsylvania, as a state, had an interest in its own system of roads and canals, the revenue from which would be diminished by the bridge. Moreover, an injunction was the only remedy, since the injury was a continuing one, and no payment of damages would ever cure it.

On these grounds the Supreme Court agreed to hear Stanton. He appeared before it for the first time to begin argument on February 25, 1850. The bridge company's defense was that the whole question was a state matter; the Supreme Court had no jurisdiction. Stanton had been expecting that line of defense and was ready for it; he brought up Article 1, Section 8, of the Constitution: "The Congress shall have power . . . to regulate commerce among the several States." From this he derived the doctrine that if Congress had power to regulate commerce among the states, the state legislatures lacked that power; and as navigable waters were means of commerce among states, Congress had exclusive power over such waters. If the bridge did obstruct navigation, Pennsylvania was being deprived of a constitutional right by the action of other states.

The argument was so well supported, so lucid and forceful, that three of the judges took the unusual step of thanking Stanton for bringing it before them. It was the Roger B. Taney court which, under the influence of that old Jacksonian opponent of vested property, had been guilty of some deviationalism with regard to the commerce clause, but in answer to Stanton's plea, it now affirmed federal jurisdiction in words that might have been used by John Marshall. The constitutional question was never again in doubt; the court agreed to hear testimony on the facts. Here, too, Stanton was abundantly prepared, and in May, 1852, the court ordered a full judgment, with costs, for Stanton's side.

He had achieved a doubly important contribution to constitutional law, not only in establishing federal powers over navigable waters, but also because he had for the first time invoked the jurisdiction of the high court in an equity action. But he did not succeed in getting rid of the bridge. As soon as the Supreme Court decided it would hear the testimony on the facts, the owners of the structure trotted to their friends in the Virginia legislature, and persuaded that body to declare the route over the bridge a post road. When the final judgment came down in 1852, the Virginia delegation in Congress demanded that the bridge be made a national post road because the state Senate had said it was one.

This was right in the middle of the "don't-be-beastly-to-States'-Rights-men" period, following the last of the great compromises with the slaveholders. As a post road between states was something over which the court had just declared the authority of Congress absolute, the latter body declared that Virginia's law held good. The stacks of steamboats had to be cut down; and another item was added to the bill the South was running up in the mind of E. M. Stanton.

BACKDROP

Pittsburgh Morning Post

A Whig lecturer in Boston suggests that none should be allowed to vote but those who have gone through a certain course of literary education. We would be better satisfied with this if they would also require them to be possessed of an ordinary share of common sense. Under such a rule Whig voters would be scarce.

The Book of Courtship, or Hymeneal Perceptor, a preparatory love school for young ladies and gntlemen; also *The Lover's Own Book, or Mirror of the Soul,* by Amator. These books are handsomely printed on white paper and put in a neat cover. No young lady or gentleman should be without them, as much valuable information may be gathered from their pages on the all important subject of Courtship.

Pittsburgh Daily Aurora

IMPORTANT ARREST. Deputy U.S. Marshal O'Neill arrived here on Tuesday morning from Philadelphia, with Geo. W. Henderson, the counterfeiter, in his custody, and committed him to prison for trial.

Henderson's house, in Grant street, was searched some months ago, and counterfeit coin and machinery for making it were found, but the bird had flown. He was arrested a few days ago in Freed's Avenue, Philadelphia, and sent on here. Mr. O'Neill is an energetic officer—the same one who took charge of Watson, the Treasury Note Robber, arrested in Philadelphia and sent in his charge to New Orleans. We understand that he put neither of his prisoners in irons.

JUDGE PATTON. The incompetency of this man for the station he occupies, is notorious. If the whole bar were placed upon their oaths, nine tenths of them would be qualified to the fact of his imbecility—and his position is a melancholy proof of the unfortunate results which follow the system of placing lawyers upon the Bench, who have not sufficient ability to earn a subsistence at the Bar. As a practising lawyer, neither Patton nor Grier could obtain a livelihood; yet strange as it may appear, this very fact contributed to their appointment. The greedy thirst of the latter for an increase of his salary, was as disgraceful to the Judiciary, as it was disgusting in his private intercourse. Money, money, money! is the cry of this learned Judge; who says he cannot live upon $2,000 per year of the people's money.

ABOLITION BANNER. "I know there is a visionary dogma, which holds that negro slaves cannot be the subjects of property. I shall not dwell long upon this speculative abstraction. That is property which the law declares to be property. Two hundred years have sanctioned and sanctified negro slaves as property." Clay's Speech in the Senate, Feb. 7, 1840.

THE POLICE. The Chronicle has some well-timed remarks relative to the City Police. The watch is too feeble—they cannot suppress a row where six or eight are concerned—are unable to keep a proper watch on the stores from the great extent of their beats, and have scarce sufficient force to carry a drunken fellow to the watch-house.

New Orleans Picayune

NEGROES, NEGROES. Just received and for sale at No. 7 Moreau street, Third Municipality, the largest and likeliest lot of Negroes ever imported by the subscriber, consisting of Field Hands, House servants and Mechanics. Will be receiving new lots regularly during the season.—Wm. F. Talbott

SLAVES FOR SALE. The subscriber has on hand a large and valuable lot of SLAVES containing superior cooks, washers and ironers, seamstresses, carpenters, masons and servants of every capacity; field hands. He is offering these Slaves at terms and prices to suit the views of buyers and purchasers, who are requested to call and examine before making their bargains elsewhere.—New Orleans Slave Depot, 156 Common St., Elihu Creswell.

4

THE CONTROLLING CASES

THE law offices of Stanton and Shaler were on the ground floor of their own building, on Fourth Avenue, near Wood Street, in the heart of the Golden Triangle. All round them was a booming town, filled with the exhilarating tinkle of big money on the make; at the theatre people ate pork chops in the gallery and tossed the bones into the pit. The partners made enormous fees and never knew where their business stood financially, for their bookkeeping was conducted on the somewhat Gothic lines of having one partner draw his checks and enter his receipts in black ink, while the other used red—at least until Theobald Umbstaetter, the New Lisbon partner, came in to systematize methods, and to take care of things while one of the partners was away.

This was increasingly the case, for after the single major trial of 1848, the firm became more and more involved in corporate matters that took Stanton eastward or down river. That case itself, falling just at the time when he was organizing Van Buren sentiment in Ohio, may have had some influence on Stanton's evident, if unexpressed, decision that he could not succeed both as a lawyer and as a politician.

It grew out of one of the earliest pieces of American labor legislation, a law which provided that employers in the textile and paper industries could not compel their mill hands to work more than ten hours a day, instead of the twelve common to that era. Pittsburgh and Allegheny were cotton-milling centers; the owners said, with a certain amount of justification, that with a ten-hour day they could not meet the competition of the New England twelve-hour mills. They opened the offensive against the new law by closing down simultaneously; then thought better of this form of business suicide, opened the doors, rang the mill bells, and offered work to all who would stay for twelve hours.

There were a couple of riots, accompanied by some smashing, before owners and laborers took the eminently sensible step of putting pay for mill work on an hourly instead of a daily basis. Meanwhile, the Allegheny "operators," as the workers were called, brought charges of conspiracy against the mill owners and Stanton was retained for the defense.

The case was tried in an atmosphere of intense emotionalism, for the *Pittsburgh Post* had been running a campaign against the "cotton kings" and their "slave mills," * and most people, even in those days, were agreed that the conditions under which the girl mill hands labored were close to intolerable. This did not make the owners guilty of the criminal act of conspiracy, however; and, as Stanton pointed out, the evidence ran decidedly against any theory of concerted action. The attempts to reopen had been made by several individual mills over a spread of weeks, and there was no showing of concerted action. Two of the establishments widely anticipated the rest in making the new setup of hourly wages which accepted the ten-hour law.

Nevertheless, it quickly became evident that the case was being tried before a hanging judge, who thought that because the mill owners had done something for which they could not be punished, they should be found guilty of something they had not done. Stanton took exceptions to the judicial rulings at every step, and after His Honor had charged the jury, marched to the bar with a paper. "I demand that these instructions be read to the jury," he said.

* Simultaneously with one in favor of Lewis Cass for President, on a platform that substantially favored protecting human chattel slavery in the states and extending it to the territories; a dichotomy which the Democratic "liberals" of the period found no difficulty in accepting.

It was an outrageous violation of procedure, for which the lawyer might well have been found in contempt. But a glance at the paper told the judge that Stanton was perfectly right; he would not only draw a reversal, but a rebuke from the court of appeal unless the attorney's points were made. He withdrew his own charge and read Stanton's; it was practically one for acquittal, and that was the verdict—a verdict which brought him an intense, if temporary unpopularity that turned any thought of entering Pennsylvania politics to futility.

II

THE first of the great commercial cases reached its climax in 1852, the year of the Wheeling Bridge decision. It grew out of the fact that in the early decades of the century nobody knew exactly what a railroad was, though everybody was quite certain that it was a very good thing. In Pennsylvania, the state authorities thought it might be something like a canal. They built with public funds a line stretching westward from Philadelphia—the Philadelphia and Columbia—and placed it under jurisdiction of the State Canal Commission. The Commission was empowered by law to lease the use of the tracks to persons desiring to operate cars on them.

This had not been going on for very long before it was discovered that, unlike a canal, a railroad had to be controlled from a central office, with trains running on close, regular schedules, and that the only way this could be accomplished was for a single firm to have a monopoly of the use of a given set of tracks. The other railroads were chartered as private companies; among them was the Pennsylvania Railroad, whose charter covered a line running across the mountains from Pittsburgh to Harrisburg. From that point, cars for Philadelphia passed over a short independent line—which the Pennsylvania presently acquired on a long-term lease that was practically a purchase—to Lancaster, where they were switched to the state-owned tracks of the Philadelphia and Columbia.

Under a special act, the Pennsylvania was permitted to build its own station in West Philadelphia. Trains were made up there for transit westward over the same route by which they entered the city. Everything went along smoothly until the summer of 1852, when the Pennsylvania was notified that a new firm had been placed in charge as operator of the state-owned line. This was followed in August by the refusal of the Canal Commission at Philadelphia to accept one of the Pennsylvania's trains for transit to Lancaster. The railroad promptly sued for a writ of mandamus, to compel the Commission to haul its cars.

Now apparently the railroad was suffering from the high-handed acts of a couple of bureaucrats. Actually the Pennsylvania was merely beginning early on the pursuit which has characterized much of its long history. The real ache was that it wanted to be awarded the operation of the Philadelphia and Columbia; part of the complaint in the suit said that the act setting up the state line authorized "individuals" to run cars on the Philadelphia and Columbia, and since the Pennsylvania Railroad corporation was an individual, it had as good a right to run cars over those tracks as anyone else. Behind this lay a burning desire to have the tolls for the use of the state-owned tracks drastically reduced or altogether eliminated. Another part of the complaint said these tolls were too high; and the specific reason why the Commission had refused the Pennsylvania's train was because the road refused to meet the Commission's charges.

Stanton, in defense of the Canal Commissioners, analyzed the whole theory of the relations between that comparatively novel entity, the corporation, and the state that had created it. Corporations, he readily admitted, had some of the characteristics of individuals before the law. But a corporation was an android, an artificial person, created for a special purpose; the state had merely delegated to it a part of its sovereignty for the performance of certain specific acts. Corporate powers thus cannot be created by implication, nor extended by the construction of phrases in a charter. The Pennsylvania itself had admitted as much, by securing special legislation authorizing it to buy land in West Philadelphia and to erect a station there. The act carried with it no privilege of using the state's tracks to reach the station; it meant exactly what it said, and no more.

The Pennsylvania's original charter did indeed allow it to run cars over a road connected with it; but the Philadelphia and Columbia was not connected with the Pennsylvania, for the latter's terminal was at Harrisburg, and between that point and Lancaster the leased short line intervened. If the Pennsylvania were allowed to establish "connection" through intervening lines, it might use the tracks of almost any railroad in the United States.

Nor does the act authorizing the Canal Commissioners to permit individuals to use the state tracks give the Pennsylvania any rights in this respect. The privileges of the corporate individual are described in the charter calling that individual into existence, and this particular privilege is not in the railroad's charter.

Much of this, indeed, went back to the Warren Bridge decision of 1837, when the United States Supreme Court, under Roger B. Taney's leadership, held that no rights were granted by a corporation charter except those specifically mentioned. But that decision had been rather narrow and negative in its application, turning on the point of whether the charter of a private toll-bridge company had been impaired by the erection of a paralleling free public bridge. In *Pennsylvania Railroad vs. Canal Commissioners* the question was not one of a corporation merely trying to hold a privileged position already gained, but whether it might extend its privileges without the consent of the public. Stanton argued his case so closely, from so broad a basis, that State Chief Justice Jeremiah Black quoted him almost exactly in handing down a decision in favor of the Canal Commissioners.

This was defining the relations between corporation and state by limiting the ambit of the former. The next of the great cases found Stanton preserving the corporate institution against the arbitrary destructive powers of the state. This was also a railroad case, known as the "Erie Railroad War," owing to its origin in that rising city on the lake. The road that ultimately became the Lake Shore reached the town from two directions and, as not infrequently happened in those freehand days of railroading, the engineers of the two sections worked on different theories without consulting each other. The result was that trains from Buffalo to Erie ran on tracks six feet wide, while those from Erie to Cleveland were on the standard four-foot-ten-inch gauge. This was extremely annoying and expensive for the railroad, which had to transfer all its freight and passengers from one set of tracks to the other; but perfectly splendid for the city of Erie, which benefited to the extent of construction on storage buildings, taxes, employment of the men who transshipped the freight, and hotel accommodations for layover passengers.

In the fall of 1853, the railroad decided to make the broad-gauge section conform with the rest of the line. The city took umbrage and, with the immemorial rabble-rouser's bleat against technical improvement—that it takes the bread out of someone's mouth—passed an ordinance that a railroad of any other gauge than six feet was a public nuisance in Erie. In December the railroad went ahead and changed its gauge anyway. The city sent out gangs who tore up all the tracks within its limits and destroyed the bridges. The railroad relaid the tracks and placed them under guard. The city commissioned as many deputy sheriffs as it needed and ripped up the rails again.

The company then went to court, but it got little comfort there, for the court decided that the company had forfeited its franchise by illegal acts. Just to make things certain, the western members in the state legislature pushed through a bill repealing the Lake Shore's charter, and directing the governor to seize road and rolling stock in the name of the state. The engines and cars had been moved out of the state when the "war" began, but in every other respect the railroad's case was desperate when Stanton was called in, in 1856.

It was a State Supreme Court case. Stanton's line of argument was that although the railroad company's charter contained a specific provision for repeal in case the franchise were abused, the question of what constituted abuse was one for judicial determination by due process of law, not for arbitrary action by one party to the contract. For that matter, even forfeiture of the franchise carried with it no right for the state to seize the company's property. "State pride is the true basis of national glory," replied the court, and held against the railroad.

Stanton was by no means done. In fact, the very line on which he had sustained the defeat opened his path to a request for a new argument. He pointed out that this was more than a state matter; that the rolling stock used in Pennsylvania was owned by other states; that the development of long lines of communication transcended local interests into the national field; that contracts to carry the United States mail were involved. In case the state courts refused to grant his client relief, he proposed to ask the Supreme Court of the United States for an injunction on the constitutional ground that the obligation of contract had been doubly impaired—by the cancellation of a corporate charter, and by preventing the Lake Shore from carrying out its contractual obligation to the United States to carry the mails.

The state court knew exactly how it would fare if such an action were brought, for the doctrine that a charter is an inviolable contract had stood like the Rock of Gibraltar ever since John Marshall handed down his famous decision in the Dartmouth College case. Judge Black decided to hear the reargument, and after hearing it, the court suspended its own writ of execution against the railroad's franchise, and warned the city of Erie; while the legislature thought better of its hasty action and granted a new charter.

The important point in these cases is not that Stanton won them. He won others also, and lost a few, and was rebuked by judges. What made his cases remarkable, what made him almost unique as an attorney, was the combination of two features in his pleadings. One was the prodigious preparation he devoted to them, both on the law and the facts. "Now I shall have to work," said A. W. Loomis, one of the best-known trial lawyers of Pittsburgh, when he heard that the Steubenville attorney was coming to his city. "Stanton will study my side of the case as thoroughly as his own, and will know as much as I do of it." And after Stanton had delivered his argument in a case where canon law and church custom were involved, one of the pastors, present as a witness, asked Stanton what church he had studied for, and where.

The other striking feature of a Stanton trial was his ability, perhaps fully shared by John Marshall alone, to begin a line of argument with a broad, fully admitted, universal principle, leading step by logical step to the specific application, so producing a structure that stood firm, not only in the case he was handling, but as a controlling precedent in all others of similar type.

III

THIS last ability led Stanton through the greatest of all the commercial cases, one which laid down law in a field never touched before. On the records it is known as *McCormick vs. Talcott, et al., survivors of John H. Manny*, though Manny himself was still alive when the case began, in the fall of 1854.

The roots of that famous case ran deep, and it spread into a tree that filled the sky. Cyrus H. McCormick, one of the men whose actions really have changed the face of the earth, in 1831 invented a practical machine for reaping grain on his father's farm in Virginia. Before he built it, the cradle scythe was the best available reaping instrument. A man could not cut much more than half an acre a day with it, which meant that during the brief ripening season—ten days at most for such a cereal as wheat—five acres was all the production a single man could handle. Five acres of wheat leaves only a small exchangeable surplus not needed by the farm family, and increasing the number of laborers only increased the number of mouths to be fed from the crop. Wheat had thus always been a subsistence crop, except in areas like the Nile Valley, which produces twice a year, or where it was garnered by debased slave labor, as in the Roman colonies of North Africa.

Even McCormick's first imperfect model cut down seven acres of grain in a day. By 1844, he was selling over 200 reapers a year that could cut a guaranteed sixteen, and the ideal grain-growing territory in the flatlands of the Midwest was opening up like a flower under the influence of a type of agriculture never before seen in the world's history. But in 1848 competition began to enter the reaper field; for McCormick's patent, dated 1834, had now expired. Its renewal had been refused by the Board of Extension of patents, which consisted of the United States Commissioner of Patents, the Secretary of State, and the Solicitor of the Treasury.

McCormick, quite as good a businessman as he was an inventor, kept a very close eye on this competition. When the output and income of the firm headed by John H. Manny of Wisconsin began to approach his own, he sued the man for infringement of patent in the United States Circuit Court, Cincinnati district. The basis of the suit was not the original, expired patent of 1834—McCormick was willing to let anyone make the obsolete type of reaper it covered—but three improvements which McCormick had patented in 1847 and which, he claimed, Manny had copied from his later model reaper.

Only one of the three features had any real importance. This was the divider, a part at the end of the cutting bar, which separated the grain to be cut from that left standing. Without any divider at all, the grain quickly clogged the end of the bar and the machine became inoperative, so that all reapers had some kind of divider. The point on which McCormick and his lawyers based their suit was that on both the Manny and the 1847 McCormick machine, the divider had an upward curve. They spoke for a wide interpretation of patent rights, urging that even if someone else entirely had invented the curved divider earlier than 1847, the fact that it appeared on both reapers made Manny a violator, since his patent on a reaping machine had not been issued until 1851.

What was the law, and what the precedents in such a case? There were none, but the question instantly became one of national interest. Practically every farmer in the booming West felt himself involved, since not only was McCormick suing for $400,000 in damages but he also was asking the court to prevent the manufacture and use of any other reaper. It

would not only give him a monopoly but bring about the confiscation of many a reaper long in service.

McCormick retained E. M. Dickerson, with Reverdy Johnson of Maryland, whose Supreme Court practice probably
exceeded that of any other lawyer, and who was supposed to
be the best court speaker extant. Peter H. Watson had charge
of the defense; he chose George Harding of Philadelphia to
handle the mechanical features of the case and Stanton for the
legal aspects, while to meet the redoubtable Johnson in foren-
sics, there was a backwoods lawyer from Illinois who had
gained considerable reputation as an orator—Abraham Lincoln.

The four defense attorneys met for the first time at the
Burnett House in Cincinnati in the fall of 1855, a historic gathering. Lincoln had carefully studied the testimony and was
full of eagerness for his contest with the great Reverdy Johnson; he had written out the argument he proposed to make.
This excited the derision of Stanton, who always made notes
on little slips of paper and talked *ex tempore*, watching the
members of the court and suiting his method and line of argument to their reaction. This had given him a rather astonishing
reputation for urbanity among the more dignified appeals
judges who sat without juries, though the fire of his normal
type of expression burnt hotly as ever underneath, a fact which
became apparent when the conferences began.

For there was a difficulty. Dickerson and Johnson refused
to allow three lawyers to appear for the defense unless they
were together permitted to make the same number of arguments, Dickerson speaking twice. This was a plan which by no
means commended itself to chief defense attorney Watson.
On his second appearance, Dickerson could quite clearly introduce new technical matters which his special opponent, Harding, would not then be able to refute. There could thus be only
two speeches for the defense, and as Harding's technical argument was necessary, the choice for the other place lay between
Stanton and Lincoln.

The little dynamo from Steubenville had already been informed that Lincoln would make the closing argument, a place

usually reserved for him, and had greeted the Illinoisan's appearance with, "Where did that long-armed baboon come from?"—with sundry other remarks about the heavy boots, farmerish clothes, and dirty linen duster, whose back was splotched with perspiration, "like the map of a continent." He had put in more time on the case than Lincoln himself, studying every feature of law and fact, and was elaborately prepared. When he heard that his own argument might not be delivered, he burst out: "If that giraffe appears in the case, I will throw up my brief and leave."

A legal matter, and Stanton was the better lawyer; Watson reluctantly told Lincoln that he would have to give way. The disappointed man from Springfield turned his undelivered speech over to Harding (who promptly turned it over to the wastebasket), but decided to stay on, since he was not only interested in the outcome but had formed a quick friendship with a young man named Ralph Emerson, who was connected with the Manny firm.

To Emerson the McCormicks presently came with a compromise offer. "Will they yield all you want?" asked Stanton, when the matter was broached.

"No," said Emerson.

Stanton lifted one arm. "Then I know of but one way to compromise, and that is with sword in hand; to smite and keep on smiting."

Smite he did when it came his day in court. "At times the court regarded him in amazement, so extraordinary were his memory and power of analysis." The interpretation of patent rights, he said, must be regarded "in the light of the state of the art at the time of the invention patented." In this light the main, almost the sole question of fact was whether a divider on a harvesting machine had been in existence before 1847. If so, then both the Manny divider and that on the 1847 McCormick must be regarded as modifications on an idea independently available to both men. It made no difference that the modifications had assumed a similar form so long as the similarity were not an identity, which it admittedly was not.

It was a prodigious argument, striking into virgin territory from ground already traveled; so closely knit, so logical, so accurately bringing past precedent to the solution of current problems, that the courtroom had the impression that Reverdy Johnson, the great orator, had offered them nothing but agreeable sounds, while here were the facts. As Stanton progressed, the rejected Lincoln could not conceal his excitement; he stood up and walked back and forth at the rear of the court, eyes fixed on the speaker, taking in every word. That night, walking with his young friend from the Manny company, he suddenly burst out: "Emerson, it would have been a great mistake if I had spoken in this case; I did not fully apprehend it."

Emerson said nothing; there was a long silence save for the sound of footsteps on the turf. Said Lincoln: "Emerson, I am going home to study—to study law. You know that for any rough-and-tumble case (and a pretty good one, too) I am enough for any man we have out in that country. But these college-trained men are coming west. They have all the advantages of a lifelong training in the law, plenty of time to study, and everything, perhaps, to fit them. Soon they will be in Illinois and I must meet them. I am just going home to study law, and, when they appear, I will be ready."

He was to be abundantly ready, if not altogether through the study of law, a profession on which he refused to answer Ralph Emerson's question as to whether or not a man could be a lawyer and still live by the Golden Rule—thereby knocking on the head Emerson's half-formed intention of becoming an attorney. In the meanwhile, Justices McLean and Drummond filed their decision, fully agreeing with Stanton on all points and, as usual, quoting his argument.

The McCormicks promptly appealed to the United States Supreme Court. By this time they realized what they were up against and had so many counsel that half the hotels in Washington filled up with men in straw plug hats, carrying carpetbags full of papers. When they appeared in court, the judges had to limit the time each might take on argument, in order to keep the case from running for weeks. Stanton was given something less than an hour. He had been speaking for perhaps five minutes when Judge McLean leaned forward and asked whether the address was reduced to writing. "It is not," said the attorney.

"That is to be regretted," said the justice, and begged Stanton to desist, while he sent a deputy around for a "phonographer" to take down the words spoken for the guidance of the court. A little later, as the speaker leaned over and whispered to Watson a couple of times, one of the justices asked the reason why he was interrupting himself, and was told it was only an inquiry as to how much time he had left.

Chief Justice Taney looked along the bench, and yielded to that inner excitement that seldom failed to grip any legal mind when it came in contact with Stanton's reasoning. "Finish your argument in your own time, regardless of the rules we have fixed," he said.

After that, it was almost an anticlimax that the court should unanimously affirm the verdict of the lower body in favor of Stanton's clients.

5

DUSTY WASHINGTON; GOLDEN CALIFORNIA

B Y the date of the McCormick Reaper case appeal, Stanton had moved to Washington, a house in the 300 block of C Street. The old, old wounds of the deaths of Mary and his brother had cicatrized over; he had taken a new wife, a tall, fair girl from Pittsburgh named Ellen Hutchinson, sixteen years younger than himself, a pleasant person who liked social conversation and outings, and laughed at him when he suggested that they pass the time during their engagement in reading the Greek tragedies and philosophers. The engagement itself took place late in 1855, something over a year after he had broken a decade of abstention from all female society by expressing admiration for and a desire to make the acquaintance of an actress named Jean Davenport. The second Mrs. Stanton was calm and rather wise; her husband wrote her letters full of descriptions of surroundings and doings, which not only show their mutual tastes, but something of the life through which they moved:

By 10 o'clock [he writes about an outing near Steubenville] the children and myself reached a wild glen a few miles from town— Mother and my sister and Mrs. [Darwin] Stanton reached there shortly afterwards. There, on the side of a hill, stretched on a moss covered rock, the birds singing, the stream rippling gently below and leaves rustling in the wind, Eddie and I spent a couple of hours talking, reciting poetry and enjoying the day, while the rest were strolling in the woods or fishing in the stream.

Stanton to Ellen, Washington, December 6, 1856

This day has been spent in the Court House and in the Law Library. At Washington each day is much like any other. Breakfast at nine, go to the Court Room in the Capitol at 11, and remain until three—dine at 4, and from then until bed time as it may happen. My argument here is set for next Monday and I am busily engaged in preparation. The Supreme Court room is one of the places visited by strangers at Washington. It is a small room in the basement of the Capitol, immediately under the Senate chamber. There the nine judges sit in their silk robes and hear every case argued. Everything is quiet, so that you might hear a pin drop. The floor handsomely carpeted, the furniture of the best kind, with sofas on each side for ladies and other visitors.

Stanton to Ellen, Washington, April 11, 1856

Having an invitation this evening to a bridal party given to a daughter of Secretary Guthrie, I thought if you were here you would have me go. So in order to conform to your wishes I went. The company was not large, but very pleasant. Several fine looking ladies elegantly dressed were present. Among the most distinguished in appearance were Mrs. Slidell, Mrs. Weller and Mrs. Pugh. The gentlemen were composed of Judges, lawyers, Senators and Politicians. Both ladies and gentlemen were chiefly from the South and very agreeable. Mrs. Miller, wife of the Senator from California, was perhaps the most richly dressed lady present, and as she is a fine dashing looking woman, it became her very well. Mrs. Pugh is from Cincinnati, was married last fall to an old acquaintance of mine and had the reputation of being one (if not altogether) of the most beautiful women in the Country. I had much curiosity to see her and regret my disappointment.

After the wedding in June of the previous year, a long honeymoon trip from Niagara Falls down the St. Lawrence and through the White Mountains, and the birth of a daughter, while Mrs. Stanton was in the north:

Stanton to Ellen, September 18, 1857

Here I am at our own home writing to you from my own desk,— the first time I ever wrote to you from here, isn't it? I left Philadelphia yesterday on the 10 o'clock train, and had occasion to rejoice before reaching here, that you and baby were not along. The cars were very much crowded, the Southern people flocking home from the North. The weather was pleasant at Philadelphia, but by the time we got as far south as Baltimore the difference of climate became very apparent and oppressive. At Baltimore, we were packed thick as we could stand in the Rail Road omnibus, men, women and children, and on reaching the depot the cars were already full. Hot, dusty, tired we made rather a miserable picture.

A little after 7 o'clock we reached Washington; the weather seemed to grow hotter as we neared home. It was dark when I reached 365 C Street. Nobody but Lizzy was at home—I was as hungry as a wolf, having had nothing since morning. No ice—no meat—not an egg in the house—Lizzie had not expected me until today. The rooms were shut up—not a breath of air stirring. But after a while David and Catherine came home—a bath, a good cup of tea, some ice water, a glass of wine, and an excellent dish of oyster soup made things more comfortable. I sat on my steps smoking a cigar, looking at the stars, thinking of you, dear Ellen, and dear baby.

This morning at 7 o'clock, 80°. And getting hotter every hour. I had breakfast in the dining room—chops, corn bread, eggs, coffee.

II

LESS than a month after writing this letter, Stanton received one that formed the second event in the series which began when Lincoln stayed over in Cincinnati to hear him speak in the McCormick Reaper case. The missive was from Jeremiah Black, sometime Chief Justice of Pennsylvania, now Attorney-General of the United States, and it prayed Stanton to go to California to handle a little matter for the government.

This Jeremiah Black was one of the otherwise unremarkable men who are thrust into key spots at the crises of history; it is time to introduce him. A tall man with a bad temper, a craggy face, and a great mass of black hair; a vigorous controversialist, who actually believed in the Ten Commandments as a sufficient rule of life. Also a somewhat political judge, a great personal friend of President James Buchanan, and an important wheel in the machine which elevated that elderly functionary to the Presidency. When a new constitution gave the Pennsylvania Supreme Court its first elective judges in 1851, Black was one of the five chosen to office; a drawing of lots conferred on him the shortest of the five terms and with it the Chief Justiceship. Eighteen fifty-four, when he came up for reelection, was the year when the antiforeigner, anti-Catholic, Know Nothing Party swept the Pennsylvania polls. Black was the only Democrat on the ticket to survive the landslide, which made him a marked man. When Buchanan, having accepted the advice of the party bosses on every other place in his Cabinet, was allowed to choose one man of his own, he made the Judge his Attorney-General.

Black had not long been in office when he began to receive letters from a certain Auguste Jouan, a California adventurer now in Cincinnati, who said he knew something about the Limantour grant. Now this Limantour grant was precisely one of the things most disturbing to Attorney-General Black, both as a conscientious man and as a government official. It was one, the most important one, of a series of 803 claims that had been brought forward as a result of the 1848 peace treaty with Mexico, which provided that grants of land made under Mexican rule should "preserve the legal value" they had when California was ceded. Mexican methods had been rather haphazard, and the whole problem was new to American jurisprudence; Congress set up a special board of land commissioners for the examination of claims, with the right of appeal from their rulings to the United States District Court and thence to the Supreme Court in cases where the claims were not settled on a basis mutually satisfactory to claimant and government.

To these commissioners one José Y. Limantour, a merchant of Monterey, presented claims for 958 square miles of land, not quite as much as the state of Rhode Island. They turned him down on 924 square miles of this putative barony, but the rest of the claim was admitted as fair legal title. It included the entire city of San Francisco, all the islands in the bay, and the ground at Point Tiburon where the United States government was erecting two million dollars' worth of forts and lighthouses, so the mess it would make if the claims stood up can be imagined. In fact, at the date of the Jouan letters, Limantour had already collected $300,000 in quitclaims.

Those letters from Jouan, increasingly specific, reinforced Black's determination to appeal the action of the commissioners. But when he examined the thousand-page record of their hearings, it became evident that this appeal would be a very difficult matter. Here was a letter from Micheltorana, sometime Mexican Governor of California, requesting financial aid in return for land grants; a petition from Limantour, setting forth the land he desired. The latter paper bore an indorsement from the governor, inquiring as to the condition of the land desired; then a letter from the governor's secretary, again describing the land, and saying that he intended to grant it. The first grant was dated February 27, 1843; was written on the special stamped paper of the Mexican government, and countersigned by Bocanegra, Minister of Exterior Relations in the Mexican government. Here was a letter from Micheltorana to Bocanegra, inclosing Limantour's petition, and a letter from the minister to the governor, approving the first grant and allowing Micheltorana to make others. Here was a copy of Bocanegra's minute, ordering the letter to be written; it came from the archives in Mexico City. Here were two letters from the President of Mexico, to the President of the Board of Commissioners and to the Governor of California, recommending Limantour's claim to their special indulgent attention. Micheltorana was dead, but witnesses had testified that Limantour had made him the advances in money and goods, and clerks in his office testified that they had drawn the papers and seen him sign them.

That is, Limantour had an impregnable case, and an appeal was hopeless, in spite of Auguste Jouan. Black turned to the only man he knew who was in the habit of winning hopeless cases, the man he himself had pronounced the greatest lawyer in America after Stanton had persuaded his own court to reverse itself in the matter of the Erie Railroad War. Stanton accepted, and on February 21, 1858, having just finished his argument in *McCormick vs. Talcott, et al.*, he sailed aboard the steamer *Star of the West*, with a Spanish grammar in his baggage and his son Edwin as a companion. His assistant was a diminutive and very active lawyer from New Orleans, named Judah P. Benjamin. He expected to be in California for four months.

III

Stanton to Ellen, February 24, 1858

We now feel this morning a milder climate. It is still raining—the sea runs high, and everything on board presents a miserable condition—sick men, sick women—sick children. To any body that enjoyed the discomfort of their fellow beings, a crowded packet on a rough sea would be the very place to indulge their humor. Yesterday evening I had an attack of asthma, and have been suffering much all day. From this circumstance I am afraid I shall not derive all the benefit I had hoped from a sea voyage. We are now this afternoon running along the southern coast of Georgia. The weather is warm and pleasant, the sea quieted, and if I could get free from the asthma I should begin to enjoy the voyage.

Stanton to Ellen, February 25, 1858

I feel quite well—rested comfortably all night without any coughing. The events of the voyage are so few that each day may be chonicled in the words of the log—ran so many miles the last 24 hours—and are now in such a latitude and such a longitude. And it is well, for the conveniences of writing are even less than the occasions to write. A stool on which I sit and another stool on the top of which my valise and Eddie's are placed for a writing desk, fill the whole space of my State Room.

After a stop at Kingston in Jamaica and a visit to a church there:

Stanton to Ellen, March 1, 1858

The congregation was very aristocratic—chiefly colored persons—and was one of the most fashionably dressed, well-behaved, devout-looking assemblages I ever saw. Some of the ladies, quadroons, were dressed with great richness and very handsome. Whites and blacks sit together in the same pews. But the Military and Naval officers and official authorities have an elevated platform.

Stanton to Ellen, Panama, March 4, 1858

Panama is an ancient Spanish town, once one of the chief cities of the New World, distinguished for its strong fortifications, the splendor of its churches, and the wealth, luxury, and vices of its inhabitants. The streets are narrow and paved, the principal buildings of stone, the second story overhanging the side walk. But everything presents the appearance of dilapidation and decay, and bears witness to the degradation of the people. The battlements are in ruins, the gates are gone, the ditch that surrounds the walls is nearly filled up, turkey buzzards were perching on the towers. Two large stone churches are in ruins; and the Cathedral once one of the richest and most famous buildings of the world, is mouldy, damp and dirty, grass growing in the windows and on the roof. Naked children and more than half-naked women sit in the doorways and comb their hair in the streets. At a French Restaurant we got a very good dinner.

Stanton to Ellen During the Trip North on the Steamer Sonora

I have had the good luck to secure the only state room on the upper deck which is much superior to any other on account of the fresh air. I get out of my berth about sunrise, six in the morning—spend a couple of hours in bathing and toilet—eat an orange and stroll on the upper deck until breakfast ½ past eight. After a smoke and a stroll on deck I go to my room and write and read until twelve, when lunch is served in our room. Reading, talking, or sleeping fill up the time until dinner at ½ past four o'clock. After dinner until nine o'clock on deck—at nine a cup of good tea is brought to my room—and then we sit on the guards until 11 or 12 o'clock when sleepiness sends us to our berths. This is the way in which each day is spent, and one is just like another.

With deepest love, dear Ellen, I am yours ever.

IV

Jouan said that, as Limantour's assistant, he had accompanied that worthy on a trip to Mexico City in 1852, where the latter bought up eighty blank petitions and grants, which the obliging ex-governor Micheltorana signed, to have them filled in later with dates and descriptions. Seven of these signed blanks were still in Jouan's possession. This was a good start, but a rogue turned state's evidence is not the best of witnesses, and the opposition had a man named Costenares, one of Micheltorana's former clerks, to swear that Jouan was a liar and a forger. Neither was there anything in the records of the land commission to indicate the existence of any documents beyond those establishing Limantour's claims.

Yet it seemed to Stanton that grants of this importance could hardly have been made without leaving some official record. He began inquiring: but this was the roaring San Francisco of the 1850s, of the Vigilantes, the Bella Union, and the El Dorado, where men openly drove prostitutes out in fine barouches and hotel rooms cost $250 a month. Looting of various sorts was part of the contemporary moral system and the attorney encountered resistance or obstruction from a good many people not anxious to have records found. Almost his first move, then, was to draw an act making production of Mexican land papers compulsory, and another punishing the fabrication of claims, both of which were sent to Judge Black for passage by Congress. In the meanwhile, Stanton amused himself by collecting all Spanish and Mexican land laws and court decisions, having them translated and bound, with photographic copies of the official and undoubted seals and signatures necessary to the validation of documents.

Congress passed his bills in May. Now armed with sub-poenas, Stanton began his search again and quickly discovered that instead of being haphazard about keeping their records, the Mexicans had preserved every scrap of paper with formidable, antlike industry. The only trouble was that the records themselves had been scattered from hell to breakfast in the breakdown of civil government following the revolt of the American settlers. The biggest batch of papers were in a lumber room in the United States Surveyor's office at San Francisco, tumbled loosely into boxes; there were more at Benicia, and more still in every town and pueblo that had been the seat of any kind of Spanish or Mexican local government. Stanton's health had come back in the boon climate of the coast; he collected and went through all the papers, rising at seven each morning, pausing only for meals or when Edwin, Jr., would order him to bed, just before midnight.

"On Monday," he wrote, "I shall close the evidence in the Limantour case for which I came. And after that there will remain very little more to be done than count the dead and bury them. For the last few years a set of Mexicans has been plundering the United States at the rate of a million a year without any questions being asked. Having determined to throw a brick at them, I shall stay to see where it hits."

He might well write so, for he had achieved the greatest and most crushing of all the Stanton presentations. It was in four hundred folio volumes, and contained not only every law and decision relating to land in California since Spanish days, but also a complete record of every land grant either government had made. The name of Limantour appeared nowhere among the grantees. The specially stamped paper on which Limantour's grants were written had not been made until years after the grants. Micheltorana's account books were present; they showed he had never received the money or goods in return for which the grants were supposed to have been made. The seals on those grants were forgeries. So were the documents signed with the name of his secretary and Bocanegra. Full biographies of his witnesses were presented to show that they had never worked in Micheltorana's office, but, on the contrary, had made a profession of being land witnesses, and had appeared in many other cases. Records brought from Mexico City showed that Bocanegra had never countersigned the Limantour grants, and had never corresponded with Micheltorana about them. A carefully documented history of the ex-governor demonstrated that he had brought comfort to his old age by providing land claimants with predated official papers.

The proofs were so devastating that before the case was complete Limantour's attorneys threw up their briefs, and he himself fled the country. Nor did the matter end there, for Stanton's records, indexes, and biographies of perjured witnesses were now turned by the government against others and others and others of the claimants, including some prodigious fish, like the swindlers who laid claim to the fabulously rich New Almaden quicksilver mine.

Black's Report to Congress

The value of the lands claimed under grants ascertained to be forged is probably not less than $150,000,000. More than two-thirds of them in value have already been exposed and defeated. The preservation of all this property to the Government, and the honest settlers deriving their titles from the United States is of course a matter of great importance; but the moral effect of them will prove to be still more beneficent. These frauds operated like a curse and scourge upon the most magnificent portions of the American empire. Their confirmation would have retarded its growth, blighted its prosperity, and extinguished in the midst of the people all respect for the Federal Government.

Black to Stanton

There is a rumor which annoys me sometimes, about you coming home suddenly. This is a thing that won't do to think of as long as there remains anything you can do for the great cause you are engaged in. There is no other man living on this round earth for whom I would have assumed the responsibility which I have taken with you. You must succeed, or be able to prove that success is utterly impossible. It is true that I can't float unless I ride on the wave of your reputation, and I want it to roll high. When you make up your mind to come home, you must give me due and timely notice of it. All this I have said in consequence of the opinion which divers persons have expressed with great confidence, that you would return.

The pressure to return to Washington was there all right. Ellen's letters to her husband are not extant, but one of the replies is.

Stanton to Ellen, August 17, 1858

In your letter you say you want me 'to love my child' and enjoy with you her little winning ways and to sympathize with you in her ailments; and you express the fear that as time passes and cares press upon me these feelings may be blunted. Dear Ellen, if I know my own heart your wish is gratified. I do love our child and enjoy her little ways, and sympathize with her ailments, and expect to do so all my life. No length of time, no distance, no cares can blunt the feelings of love with which I worship the wife of my bosom and regard her child. Short as has been our wedded life it has been so full of happiness for me, that nothing else in life can be balanced against it. Like other mortals I may yield to the necessities of life, must bear its burdens, and struggle with its cares, and perform its duties, but for all this the love of my wife and child will be the only and sweetest reward. Nor do I ask you, dear Ellen, to forget your love in your ambition—your love is the *substance* of my life, all else is hollow. That love, if I know my own heart, I would not neglect or sacrifice for all that the world can offer.

BACKDROP

Washington Intelligencer

It again falls to our lot to record another murder in our streets. About three o'clock yesterday afternoon three young men, somewhat flushed with drink—of whom John Essex, a powerfully built stalwart stone cutter was one—were walking eastward along the north sidewalk of Pennsylvania avenue where it crosses 9th street. As they passed the curb stone they were met by a single person. When about ten feet from the three, the individual, whose name was Owen Quigley, cried "Hurrah for Magruder" whereupon Essex dealt Quigley a tremendous blow on the weasand, felling him to the ground, and followed the blow by three violent kicks upon the face of Quigley, rendering him insensible. Quigley lived only from ten to fifteen minutes after the blow. Essex escaped and, as we hear, quickly left the city.

By Telegraph from Cincinnati. The Convention re-assembled at 9 o'clock this morning and resumed balloting for a Presidential candidate. On the third ballot (the 17th counting those of yesterday) the Hon. James Buchanan of Pennsylvania, received 296 votes, the unanimous vote of the Convention, and was accordingly declared the nominee of the Convention for the Presidency of the United States. On the second ballot the Hon. John C. Breckinridge of Kentucky was unanimously chosen.

London Times

Mr. Buchanan has been the most ductile and flexible of politicians. He has been a Federalist and is now a Democrat, Pro-Free Trade and Anti-Free-Trade, pro and anti almost everything about which parties in America have warmly disputed. He is not a man of great resolution or violent counsels but he possesses a peculiar facility of effacing himself and yielding implicitly to the influence of those who surround him, often persons of inferior judgement to his own. He is a thorough-paced demagogue and unscrupulous partisan, and, though unexceptionable in private life, has grown gray among all manner of intrigues and maneuvers.

Washington Intelligencer

GIBBS' WIG, HALF WIG, BRAID AND CURL Manufactory, Penn. ave. between 9th and 10th streets, upstairs—The above articles in every variety constantly on hand or made to order, and repaired at the shortest notice. Also, Toilet articles of all descriptions, comprising Tuck, Side, Dressing and other Combs, Brushes.

N.B. Hair work repaired or taken in exchange.

The celebration yesterday in Washington and Georgetown in honor of the successful laying of the Telegraphic Cable between the old and new worlds was not undertaken under any public authority; nor was it at all general; yet a few citizens took it upon themselves to place the great achieved triumph of the age before the minds of the people. The morning was ushered in by the firing of a national salute in Georgetown and by the ringing of a bell, usually rung on festive occasions, and the display of the national flag. In Washington Messrs. Wall, Stephens & Co., took the lead by the display on the front of their tall and handsome establishment of the stars and stripes, with the British national banner on the same staff.

$200 REWARD—Ran away from the subscriber, on the evening of the 1st instant, a Negro woman, belonging to the

estate of Mrs. Sophie H. Peerie, deceased, named Cornelia
Diggs, about twenty five years of age, five feet five or ten
inches high, of a bright mulatto color, and is a very well made
woman. I will give the above reward if taken in the District
or State of Maryland, or $400 if taken in a non-slaveholding
State and secured in jail so that I can get her again.—G. Waters

New York Tribune

We have lost the battle. The Bunker Hill of the new struggle
for Freedom is past; the Saratoga and Yorktown are yet to be
achieved. A party of yesterday, without organization, without official power, without prestige and latterly, almost without hope, has now overborne the oldest party in the country,
with its hundred thousand office-holders, its 80 millions of
annual expenditures, its million and a half voters trained by
the habits of a lifetime to vote without question or hesitation
whatever bears its label. The Republican Party, called into
being by the Nebraska Iniquity of 1854, having a substantive
existence in but 16 states, has beaten one of the rival parties
which boast of their compact organizations in all the States
but has failed to beat the other in its first Presidential canvass.
James Buchanan is our next president and John C. Breckinridge, vice president and the Free State men of Kansas are
temporarily delivered over to the tender mercies of the Border
Ruffians.

United States Supreme Court, December Term, 1856

In the case of DRED SCOTT vs. JOHN A. SANFORD: The plaintiff
was, with his wife and children, held as slaves by the defendant in the State of Missouri, and he brought this action to assert the title of himself and his family to freedom.

In considering this part of the controversy, two questions
arise:

1. Was he, together with his family, free in Missouri, by
reason of the stay in the territory of the United States?
2. If they were not, was Scott himself free by reason of his
removal to Rock Island, in the state of Illinois?

The Act of Congress upon which the plaintiff relies, declares that slavery shall be forever prohibited in that part of the territory ceded by France which lies north of 36 degrees 30 minutes north latitude, and not included within the limits of Missouri.

It is the opinion of the Court that the Act of Congress which prohibited a citizen from holding and owning property of this kind in the territory of the United States, is not warranted, and is therefore void.

It is contended, on the part of the plaintiff, that he is made free by being taken to Rock Island. Our notice of this part of the case will be very brief. As Scott was a slave when taken into the State of Illinois by his owner, and was held there as such, and brought back in that character, his status depended on the laws of Missouri, and not of Illinois.—Taney, Ch. J.

Chicago Press and Tribune

From sunrise till high noon on Saturday Ottawa was deluged in dust. The first of the seven great debates which Douglas had consented to hold with Lincoln, had started La Salle, Will, Kendall and other surrounding counties, in unwonted commotion. Before breakfast Ottawa was beleaguered with a multiplying host from all points of the compass. Teams, trains and processions poured in from every direction like an army with banners. Military companies and bands of music monopolized the throughfares around the Court house and the public square. Two brass twelve pounders banged away in the center of the city.

Shortly after 12 o'clock, the special train from Chicago, Joliet etc., came in *with seventeen cars*. When it reached the depot, three deafening cheers went up for Abraham Lincoln. The Douglas procession moved down the Peru road to Buffalo Rock, where they met the Pro-Slavery champion, whom they escorted to the Geiger House.

At 1 o'clock the crowd commenced pouring into the public square. The rush was literally tremendous. Two or three times the surge of people on the platform nearly drove the reporters off.

Ottawa, Saturday evening, Aug. 21, 1858. The Republicans of Ottawa are in high glee. The triumphant manner in which Lincoln handled Douglas this afternoon filled them with spirit and confidence, and while I write the town is alive with excitement, bonfires are blazing on every corner, and a magnificent torchlight procession, accompanied by two bands of music, is parading the streets, and everywhere the cry is Hurrah for Lincoln!

Washington Intelligencer

Enamelled Shirt Collars, Patented
Elegant and entire new—Gentlemen are
requested to call and see the Patent
Enamelled Shirt Collars.

Stevens's

6

BACKGROUND BECOMES
FOREGROUND

STANTON reached Washington and the wife to whom he wrote those letters with their deep-toned bell of affection, in the early days of February, 1859. As might be expected, there were cases waiting—another reaper patent infringement matter, the appeals to the Supreme Court in the California land frauds by men who thought they had covered their tracks more carefully than Limantour, a case in which he forced a municipality to pay some construction bonds it had guaranteed. But all these were shifted into the background by an event which took place on the morning of Sunday, February 27, 1859.

On that day Mr. Philip Barton Key, six feet of elegance in frock coat, silk hat, walked past the home of Congressman Daniel E. Sickles, twirling alternately a gold-headed cane and the tips of his blonde mustachios. He was observed to draw a handkerchief from his pocket and wave it toward the building. A moment or two later, the Congressman ran rapidly out, shouted, "Key, you scoundrel, you have dishonored my home; you must die!"—and fired a shot into him.

"Don't shoot! Don't murder me!" exclaimed Mr. Key, and being provided with no other weapon, produced a pair of opera glasses from his breast-pocket and threw them at his assailant. Sickles did shoot again, this time bringing down his buck; and as men poured out of a nearby club to pick up the corpse, walked calmly to the house of Attorney-General Black and asked that a magistrate be summoned inasmuch as he had just killed a man.

The fact that the killer chose Judge Black's home as the place to give himself up is a good indication of how far this was removed from the ordinary affair of adultery-and-revenge —which was, in any case, not very ordinary in the moralistic 1850s. It was a cream of society business. The elegant Mr. Key was a United States attorney, son of the author of the "Star Spangled Banner," captain in the Montgomery Guards, the best seat on a horse in the city. His sister was married to "Gentleman George" Pendleton, a politically powerful congressman from Ohio; his father's sister to the Chief Justice of the Supreme Court. He was so big a pot, indeed, that hardly anybody below the status of Congressman Daniel E. Sickles would have dared to shoot him.

For Sickles himself was no inconsiderable pot; member of the General Committee of Tammany Hall, architect of the devices by which that organization intrenched itself in the New York City government for an uninterrupted generation and a half, President Buchanan's secretary of legation in London during two of the years while that old gentleman was preparing for his high office by occupying a position that would keep his name in the newspapers without requiring him to have any opinions on what was happening at home. Sickles was one of Buchanan's managers at the 1856 nominating convention, the only man below senatorial rank in the little group that met at the Barlow House to haggle their candidate into position over the apparently irresistible forces arrayed for Stephen A. Douglas and Franklin Pierce.

Naturally, he brought down the famous New York criminal lawyer, James R. Brady, as chief counsel for the defense. Quite as naturally, Judge Black's friend Stanton joined Brady at the counsel table. It was a deliciously sensational trial, with ladies in treble-soled boots and crinoline crowding the courtroom to clutch at every word about the fallen sister; for nearly a month the papers almost forgot the news from Kansas, the doings of the Mormons, and the scandal in the Philadelphia post office. They were encouraged to do so, chiefly by Stanton, who did little of the court work, such as examining witnesses, but saved himself up for a grand effort in the closing speech and stage-managed the whole affair.

The newspapers were encouraged to gloat over every detail of the background—how Sickles first met his wife at the home of his guardian, he a law student then, she a child of four, Teresa Bagioli, daughter of the Gran Maestro of the Montressor Grand Opera Company—how he married her when she was sixteen, a singularly beautiful girl with dark, melting eyes. She was the outstanding social success of Buchanan's London ministry, and could have been one of the most brilliant hostesses of his administration.

But a year before the shooting, a junior clerk of the House named S. K. Beekman began telling a story about a visit to the Grosvenor Inn on the post road outside Washington one rainy day. Key and Teresa Sickles, out riding together, were marooned at the place by a storm, he said; Mrs. Sickles took off her wet riding habit, and the two spent an hour together. Sickles got hold of this tale and questioned Key, who indignantly denied any wrong-doing, and continued to be a frequent visitor at the Congressman's house; but by this time he and his paramour had already found a highly satisfactory arrangement in the form of a room in a house on 15th Street, which he rented from a Negro named Gray. Teresa used to repair thither so frequently in answer to his signals that even Sickles' servants knew of the affair. "Here comes Disgust to see Disgrace," they would say on Key's appearance. Sickles himself learned of the house of rendezvous through an anonymous letter on the Thursday preceding the shooting. He sent a friend named George Wooldridge to watch the place and, having learned that it was frequented by a woman whose dress and description left no doubt that she was Teresa, confronted her with the evidence. She wrote and signed a confession—a lush document:

I have been to a house on 15th Street with Mr. Key. How many times I don't know. Usually stayed an hour or more. I did what is usual for a wicked woman to do. Had nothing to eat or drink there. The room was warmed by a wood fire. Mr. Key generally goes first. Was there on Wednesday last, between 2 and 3. Went in the back gate. Went to the same bedroom, and there an improper interview was held. I undressed myself. Mr. Key undressed also. Mr. Key has kissed me in this house a number of times. I do not deny that we have had connection in this house, last spring a year ago, in the parlor on the sofa.

Now the point was that this is good evidence of adultery, but the trial was for murder, and most of this information could not legally be received as evidence in the case at issue. The court, indeed, specifically, and correctly rejected the fair and frail Teresa's confession when it was offered. But Stanton was far less interested in what went on in the courtroom than in how events there were reported outside; that is, for better or worse, he was introducing a custom that has become an established feature of American practical jurisprudence—the custom of trying his case in the newspapers.

Thus, from the very moment when the selection of talesmen began, the case was handled to create the impression that Judge Crawford—the same Crawford who quashed the McNulty indictment on Stanton's first Washington plea, now a quiet old jurist who dealt mainly in civil cases—was a hanging judge, engaged with Prosecutor Robert Ould in a kind of unacknowledged combination to send a man to the gallows. Maryland common law ruled in the District; it required that for jury service a man must show that he owned $800 worth of property beyond his debts. The provision had actually been a dead letter for many years, but Stanton made an issue of it, and forced the judge to rule against him, on the basis of an outworn and undemocratic law. He tried to bring in the testimony of the Negro, Gray, who rented the house of assignation to Key, and was, of course, overruled. He offered Wooldridge's report on his researches at the house "as tending to prove Sickles' state of mind at the time," and, when Prosecutor Ould objected, was overruled again—whereupon Stanton accused Ould of "malignantly seeking for blood," said he did not have the honor of the prosecutor's acquaintance, and did not wish to have it. (Stamping of feet in the courtroom.)

Technically, the defense was on a line never before taken in an American court, and only once, nearly a century and a half before, in England—temporary insanity. There was a great deal of evidence to show that on the fateful Sunday morning Sickles was "in an agony of despair; his screams were of the most frightful character." But this was only to give the jury a legal excuse for an acquittal. The actual line, offered by one of the junior counsel in an opening speech and driven home by Stanton in a long summation greatly admired at the time, was that there were no laws against adultery because society considered that every man should protect himself and his home against it. Therefore Sickles had acted substantially in self-defense.

At the end of twenty days the defendant wept, the jury knelt in prayer, and then acquitted him—and there was one more addition to the series of precedents written into American legal practice by the hand of E. M. Stanton.

II

IT WAS the last.

On May 2, 1860, the Democratic National Convention in flowered and steaming Charleston adjourned for six weeks, and what Senator Seward of New York described as "the irrepressible conflict" entered its active phase.

The adjournment represented the last attempt of the Democratic party, North, to make the Southern brethren see reason. The party had come within an ace of losing the 1856 election, only succeeding through heroic efforts and a vast outpouring of funds in the pivotal state of Pennsylvania, and because Stephen A. Douglas, the Little Giant of the West, had brought Illinois and Indiana into line. By 1860 things looked very bad for the Democracy in Pennsylvania; there was a factional fight on in the party, with the controlling elements opposed to the administration. Boss Forney had bolted the ticket during the previous year; the Republicans captured the legislature, and under the astute and farseeing management of Simon Cameron, that new antislavery party seemed very likely to carry the state for Seward, the probable nominee.

New England, New York, Ohio, and New Jersey were almost certain to go Republican as well, which would give Seward 106 electoral votes out of the total 303. All the slave states together counted only 120 electoral votes; the only hope for the Democrats lay in carrying them and adding to them some of the states of the great Northwestern bloc—Indiana, Illinois, Iowa, Wisconsin, Michigan, Minnesota—which together had 43 electoral votes.

Only one man in the Democratic party stood any chance of winning the necessary states in this region, and that man was Douglas, five feet two inches of dynamo, with bright blue eyes and booming bass voice, the inspired sophist, who insisted that the only way to settle the irrepressible conflict was to pretend it did not exist. The free states (he said) would remain forever free and the slave states might maintain slavery forever. There was no danger that any slaveholder would lose his property; the Supreme Court's decision in the case of Dred Scott proved it. New territories coming into the Union should settle for themselves where they wished to stand.

The Compromise of 1850 had settled all questions; the Kansas-Nebraska Act of 1854 was a logical extension of that compromise. "Neither to legislate slavery into a territory nor to exclude it therefrom, but to leave the people perfectly free to form and regulate their domestic institutions in their own way—that is popular sovereignty," he said. It sounded good, it sounded democratic and logical. In the name of that doctrine of self-determination the party had swept to victory in 1852 and 1856; to abandon it now would be to split the party in half and turn the government over to the Republicans.

The trouble was that the doctrine of popular sovereignty (or "squatter sovereignty" as they called it), which had been so very acceptable to the Southern leaders in 1850 and even in 1856, when a plank in favor of it went into the platform, was no longer anywhere near enough for them in 1860. The Southerners came to the Charleston convention demanding that the new platform include a resolution by Senator Albert Brown of Mississippi: "Neither Congress nor territorial legislatures, whether by direct legislation or legislation of an indirect and unfriendly nature, possesses the power to annul or impede the constitutional right of a citizen of the United States to take his slave property into the common Territories. The first time that they might decide whether slavery was to exist there or not was when they rightfully formed a constitution to be admitted as a state."

Just what this meant had been appallingly demonstrated in the case of Kansas which, under Douglas' masterpiece, the Kansas-Nebraska Act, had been allowed to decide whether it would be slave or free on applying for admission to the Union. By a combination of some of the most obvious ballot-box stuffing ever seen in America and the arrival of some thousands of Missourians for election day only, a proslavery legislature had been elected in Kansas, certified by a proslavery governor appointed from Washington, and had called a proslavery constitutional convention. Assembling in 1857 at Lecompton, it drew a constitution and directed its submission to the voters. They were to decide, not whether the constitution should be accepted, but whether it should be accepted "with slavery" or "without slavery"; but if the vote went to the "without" side, slaveholders in the state were to be protected in the possession of their human property and in the progeny of that property.

In spite of feverish efforts to promote Southern colonization, the Kansas plains were so unfriendly to the slave-grown crops of cotton and tobacco that the free-state men were greatly in the majority in the electorate. They refused to vote at all on the rigged proposition offered them by the convention, especially since they had recently captured the legislature. It ordered a second referendum on the question of accepting or rejecting the Lecompton constitution. This time the slaveholders stayed away from the polls, claiming that acceptance "with slavery" had already been decided at the first referendum; but now, nine days after that vote, rejection of the constitution carried by a vote which demonstrated the true strength of the two parties.

The Southern Democrats of Congress—who had control of the party machinery, a working majority, and the support of the Buchanan administration—decided to treat the second referendum as illegal on the ground that the Lecompton constitution had already been accepted and that it contained a provision prohibiting amendment before 1864. They intended to accept Kansas as a slave state; that is, they meant to have more slave territory and more proslavery senators, by whatever means, over whatever objections.

But here they encountered the squat, powerful figure of Stephen A. Douglas. He was personally ambitious, and knew very well that he would never again have any hope of victory in his great Northwestern barony, if it were demonstrated that the doctrine of popular sovereignty worked out into so monstrous a fraud as the Lecompton constitution. It is possible that he was also personally honest, and no little disturbed on the moral side at the rigging of the referendum and reports of the Lecompton proceedings—that fifteen of Kansas' thirty-four counties had not been represented at all at the constitutional convention, that the delegates who appeared were a singularly raffish lot who seldom bothered to attend meetings, and, when they did come, were normally so drunk that they had to be nudged into sufficient consciousness to register assent to the propositions placed before them.

Douglas denounced the Lecompton constitution, and led the fight against it so effectively that, after some maneuvering, the acceptance of Kansas under it was beaten. No Southerner could forgive him; and what was even worse, the little senator, in one of the debates with Abraham Lincoln when both were running for the Senate in 1858, pronounced the "Freeport heresy." His opponent asked him a series of questions; in answer to one of them, Douglas said, yes, a territorial legislature had a clear, legal right to exclude slavery before the territory came into the Union.

The Buchanan administration, whose whole theory was

that Democrats and democracy could only be held together by giving the South everything it asked, tried to read Douglas out of the party for these acts of insubordination; while the South announced that it would never, never, never see the Illinois senator in control of the party machinery. To the warning that rejection of Douglas would split the party, they were perfectly indifferent; if they failed to obtain their "rights," they meant to split not merely the party, but the Union. Many of them thought this would be a good idea in any case.

Thus, as far back as the glorious Compromise of 1850, Governor Collier of Alabama, William Yancey of the same state, and Senator Robert Barnwell Rhett of South Carolina, all called for the secession of their states because the compromise itself did not concede enough to the South. That compromise was an omnibus action which included the Fugitive Slave Law, a fairly iniquitous and far-reaching piece of legislation, providing that commissioners attached to United States Circuit Courts should order the return to servitude of a claimed fugitive after a summary process, in which the black man was forbidden jury trial, the right to testify in his own behalf, or to produce witnesses. It was not enough. The compromise also included prohibition of the slave trade in the District of Columbia and the admission of California as a free state, and the South regarded both these acts as aggressions against the territory marked out for their peculiar institution. They could think of no solution but a nation that was all slaveholding.

Since 1850 the drive for downright secession had steadily gathered steam. "A Southern republic is the only safety," said Yancey when he received the news that the Republicans had carried New York in the midterm election of 1858; and J. L. M. Curry wrote to Washington while on a visit to his Alabama district: "I have been amazed to find the growth of the disunion sentiment among our people. Many absolutely desire such an event, while nearly all seem to regard it as a question of time." Men who thought along these lines did not hold the intellectual leadership of their section, to be sure. That rested with Jefferson Davis of Mississippi, Howell Cobb, and Alexander H. Stephens, the splendid little fragment of a man from

Georgia. They thought that more could be gained by remaining within the organization—the party, the Union.

But even these logicians accepted unquestionably John C. Calhoun's doctrine that the Union was a dissolvable alliance. They could thus bring no argument but expediency against secession; and expediency is the weakest possible ground during a period of tension, when the masses are drifting steadily leftward under leaders who express emotion rather than thought.

At the Charleston convention, the Southern extremists adopted the strategy of beating Douglas by outflanking him through the platform, which they tried to load with some form of Brown's resolution making the territories safe for slavery. The Little Giant would obviously find this so unacceptable that he could not run on it. The strategy failed; the Douglas men had a clean majority in the convention, and would not accept the most watered-down version of a plank in opposition to their candidate's squatter sovereignty doctrine.

The Southern leaders still had votes enough to prevent Douglas' nomination under the two-thirds rule, but in the humid heat of Charleston, with the galleries wildly applauding every outburst of perfervid Dixie oratory, the end had now become confused with the means. Yancey led the Alabama delegation solemnly from the convention floor and, as men cheered and ladies fluttered handkerchiefs, was followed by the delegations of Mississippi, Louisiana, South Carolina, Florida, and Texas. Most of Georgia, all of Arkansas, followed on the next day; in a theatre where the backdrop was a painting of the Borgia Palace the seceders drew a platform declaring it was the duty of Congress to protect slavery in the territories, and sat down to wait until the Douglas leaders had eaten their humble pie.

The Douglas leaders did nothing of the kind; instead they adjourned the convention to Baltimore, where there would be less pressure from the galleries, and to June 18, which would give them time to make deals, particularly with those statesmen of the South who did not belong to the "fire-eater" faction—as the Rhett-Yancey crowd were called. The deals were made all right, but the best results the Douglas men could get were sets of contesting delegates from Georgia, Alabama, Louisiana, and Arkansas, along with all the bolters save those from South Carolina. The row at Baltimore accordingly hinged on the question of which groups of delegates should be seated. The solid Douglas majority voted a report which accepted the old delegations from Georgia and Arkansas, but insisted upon the new, pro-Douglas men from Alabama and Louisiana. Now the bolters bolted again, accompanied by so many from other states that they numbered 105 out of an original total of 303.

The rump comfortably nominated Douglas. The seceders moved to another hall and proceeded to nominate John C. Breckinridge of Kentucky, the jolly, kindly Vice-President of the Buchanan administration, who had once been a Douglas man himself—and the Democratic party was split down the middle. This was indeed handing the election to the Republicans, for they had by-passed Seward, against whose career some pretty stiff objections could be brought, in favor of the wholly unexceptionable Lincoln.

The only other candidate in the field was John Bell of Tennessee, who had been nominated by a group of moribund old gentlemen with frilled shirt fronts, still calling themselves Whigs, on a platform which consisted solely of "The Constitution of the Country, the Union of the States, and the Enforcement of its Laws."

The result was what everyone expected, in spite of a whirlwind campaign by Douglas who, in the effort to get the election thrown into the House, summoned the last ounces of energy remaining in an ill and breaking body to take him on a speaking tour from New England to Virginia and Baltimore to Chicago. Lincoln had only 39 per cent of the total popular vote, but he had more than anyone else, carried every free state save for three of the New Jersey electors, and obtained a crushing electoral college majority over the combination of Bell (Virginia, Kentucky, Tennessee), Douglas (three New Jersey electors and nine in Missouri), and Breckinridge, who took the remaining Southern states.

In South Carolina the Presidential electors were not chosen by popular vote, but by the legislature. In convoking that body, Governor William H. Gist said the probability of the election of a sectional president by a sectional party was wrong, and if that party carried out the policy to which it was committed, the Southern states would become mere provinces of a consolidated despotism, hostile to their institutions and bent on their ruin. He advised honorable legislators to remain in session, so that they might call a convention "to consider means of redress," should the election of Lincoln become a fact. The legislators ordered an election to the convention on December 6. South Carolina's senators and Federal judges resigned, and on the twentieth of the month, while all the church bells rang, cannon fired salutes, and citizens wearing blue cockades organized impromptu processions of joy, South Carolina declared herself an independent commonwealth.

III

WHAT was Edwin M. Stanton doing during this tremendous parade of events?

Chiefly he was minding his own business as a legist, a non-political animal living in a jurisdiction where he had no vote. Politics was part of that dead world left behind with Mary and his brother. He attended Congress not infrequently, but it seems to have been more out of technical interest in the performance of the speakers than out of any deep concern with what they said. There is record of his congratulating Jefferson Davis on one of the latter's speeches, but it was for the logic of the argument, and anyone at all could reasonably congratulate Davis for that, since he was one of the closest reasoners from false premises that the Senate has ever seen.

The nearest the little attorney came to the vortex during that hectic year was in the spring. A committee of the Republican-dominated House, headed by John Covode of Pennsylvania, began digging around in the garbage cans of the administration in the hope of finding something smelly enough to affect the election. They turned up an excellent instrument in the person of one Cornelius Wendell, subcontractor for the job of doing the public printing, who knew exactly how the appropriations for producing public documents had been maneuvered into the coffers of the Democratic party. He had fallen out with Buchanan and showed no hesitation in telling everything he knew, and perhaps a bit more. Judge Black had Stanton go over Wendell's preliminary testimony and draw up a series of questions by means of which an administration man on the Covode committee could demonstrate that Wendell was a liar of exceptionably inaccurate memory. Nothing came of the committee's investigations except the establishment of the Government Printing Office; other issues rushed on so fast and loud that they made the printing scandal look picayune.

On those other issues, as a man close to the administration (which detested the very name of Douglas), and as a frequent caller at the perpetual open house kept in Minnesota Row by the convivial Breckinridge, Stanton was for the ticket of the Southern branch of the Democracy. But without trumpets or fireworks; there was no letter-writing, interviewing, or effort, merely an opinion expressed in conversation that the best method of preserving the Union would be to elect Breckinridge. Even this was conventional; everyone talked of preserving the Union by electing the party candidate, with the exception of the muttering fire-eaters.

After the voting was over, Stanton remained one of the nameless figures of Washington life until December 20, 1860, the day South Carolina seceded, when he was suddenly appointed Attorney-General of the United States. He was forty-six years old.

BACKDROP

Washington Intelligencer

DISSOLUTION OF THE UNION—To such as believe this dissolution certain, at an early day, I hereby offer to exchange any amount of real property that I may own in Virginia, Illinois, Iowa and the City of St. Louis, Mo., for improved or unimproved real estate in the City of Washington.—B. Milburn.

SPECIAL NOTICES. New Lecture by Rev. Henry Ward Beecher at 16th Baptist Church. Tickets $.25.

Madame Lola Montez, Countess of Landsfeld, will give her amusing and laughable Lecture for the 1st time in New York entitled "Fashion" at Mozart Hall. Tickets $.25.

Should the weather be cold and the jacket be thin;
Just take a wee toothful of Morris's Gin.
Should you feel at a loss what to take at an Inn;
Just call for a glassful of Morris's Gin.
Should you e'er be perplexed how to rake up the bin;
Just sit down to a bottle of Morris's Gin.
Should a party of friends for an evening drop in;
Just send for a dozen of Morris's Gin.
Should you wish the consent of Nell's daddy to win;
Just send him a puncheon of Morris's Gin.
Should ever the earth be flooded again;
Let us all hope the rain will be Morris's Gin.

CAMELS. Since the introduction of camels a few years since and the full and complete establishment of their adaptability to our Southern clime, various experiments have been made in regard to their usefullness as substitutes for the horse and mule. Recently in Montgomery, Ala., quite a crowd assembled near the capitol to witness a camel ploughing match. To test the comparative strength of the camel and mule, one of the latter was obtained, and the contest became quite spirited and exciting. The result in this particular case was decidedly in favor of the camel; but whether or not it is more serviceable for plantation purposes can hardly be decided yet.

$100 REWARD. Ran away from subscriber on Monday morning, Jan. 2, a Negro man, Isaac Galloway, a bright mulatto. His height, as near as I can guess, is 5 feet six, eight or ten inches; full suit of hair and very likely when dressed up. He had on, when he left me, a country suit of Grey Fulled Linsey, but I have no doubt he has changed his clothes.

I will give the above reward if taken in the District of Columbia or any of the free states and $50 if taken in Maryland; in either case to be secured in jail so that I can get him again. He has a sister in Georgetown, D.C. belonging to Dr. Grafton Tyler of that place.—ABSALON A. HALL

New York Tribune

DEPARTURE OF THE BENICIA BOY. Among the passengers of the steamship *City of Washington*, which left on Saturday for Europe was John C. Heenan, alias "Benicia Boy" who goes out to fight Sayers, the English champion. A crowd of sporting men accompanied Heenan to the steamer and waved enthusiastic adieus as the steamer moved from the dock. Heenan expresses his entire confidence in being able to win the match. Shortly after the steamer had left, two Buffalo officers came running up the wharf in hot haste to arrest him; but the bird had flown.

7

THE TORTURED HOURS

IT was Black's appointment.
Buchanan's Cabinet was collapsing round him, a symbol of the dissolving Federal Union, while the poor old man, who had climbed this far up the ladder by genteel intrigue, could do nothing but wring irresolute hands and sustain himself with alternate dosages of prayer and Monongahela whiskey.

The strong man of Buchanan's entourage, so far as it had one, was undoubtedly his Treasury man—Howell Cobb of Georgia —jolly, witty, rich. He was the most effective public speaker the administration possessed; had joined Alexander H. Stephens and Robert Toombs in organizing the Constitutional Union party in their state at the time of the Compromise of 1850, and administered the fire-eaters a sound beating. In 1856 he toured the North, a Southern man in favor of the Union, and made a great impression. By 1860 things had changed; he went to New York to campaign for Breckinridge, and told everybody he met that the South could never afford to submit to the election of Lincoln.

Yet Cobb really believed in Buchanan as "the truest friend to the South that ever sat in the Presidential chair," and thought his own line of duty lay in standing by the President's side— partly out of sincere friendship, for he was a friendly man; partly to see that no legal barriers were thrown in the way of secession before March 4. But by the beginning of December, the pressure of telegrams and letters from home became intolerable; Cobb prepared a pamphlet urging the people of Georgia to secede on inauguration day, and, on December 8, sent a copy of the still-damp proofs to Buchanan with his resignation.

The Secretary of State, old Lewis Cass, followed one week later—seventy-four now, corpulent and flabby, whatever faculties he once possessed so rotted by age and strong waters that he could come to no decision, conduct no business, and only barely sign the diplomatic papers which Buchanan himself and the Assistant Secretary prepared. He had long been a dead weight in the Cabinet, and the President was heartily glad to see him go. It was the issue on which he resigned that hurt; Buchanan's refusal to reinforce the weak forts at Charleston harbor, the only place where the national flag still flew in seceded South Carolina.

But reinforcing was the one thing the President could not possibly do, in spite of the advice of General Scott, head of the army. His guiding principle was that there should be no "effusion of blood" during the remaining weeks of his administration —peace in our time. To that end he had asked Mr. Jefferson Davis of Mississippi to help him revise his December message to Congress. Under Davis' guidance, Buchanan put into it the statement that though the election of Lincoln was no just cause for dissolving the Union, the southern states had a right to demand the repeal of the northern Personal Liberty Acts, which interfered with the operation of the Fugitive Slave Law. "Should it be refused, then the Constitution, to which all the States are parties, will have been willfully violated by one portion of them."

To the same peacemaking end, Buchanan secured from Attorney-General Black on November 20 an opinion on the question of whether military force could legally be used in a state where there were no federal judges or marshals to call for it. The request was probably rigged into a form that would comfort the old man by leaving him no legal alternative but the peace he desired, for the South Carolina federal judges and marshals had resigned. But Black gave him the desired "NO."

"If [troops] are sent to aid the courts and marshals, there must be courts and marshals to be aided. Without the exercise of these functions the laws cannot be executed in any event. Under such circumstances to send military force into any State would be simply making war."

Moreover, the insurrection-suppressing powers granted by the Constitution to the executive cease at the state line: federal government has no authority to use violence except at the request of a state. "War cannot be declared by the central government against a State." An attempt to do so would be, *ipso facto*, an expulsion of such state from the Union. "Congress possesses many means of preserving [the Union] by conciliation, but the sword was not placed in their hands to preserve it by force."

Very clear, and only the day before the question of the Charleston forts came up in Cabinet, on December 10, there had waited upon Buchanan the resigned congressmen from South Carolina, who already considered themselves the commissioners of a foreign power. They wanted the forts; the President did not see how he could give away federal property without laying himself open to impeachment, and only wanted peace in his own time.

With each party trying to overreach the other by the use of carefully chosen phrases, they reached a nice little agreement, which should have kept the whole question in a state of suspended animation until Lincoln. Mr. Buchanan thought he had diddled the ex-congressmen into promising that no action would be taken against the forts until the new administration had been granted time to negotiate for their surrender; but the Carolinians thought they had the President's promise that no change in the status of the forts would be made unless hostile action were taken against them. So Buchanan refused to reinforce, and Lewis Cass could resign on an issue that reminded people for the record that he had been Andrew Jackson's Secretary of War in the old heroic days of the struggle against Nullification.

Others were not so careful of the record—for example, Jacob Thompson of Mississippi, the black-browed, humorless

Secretary of the Interior, with the sunken cheeks, burning ambition, and lovely wife. He came to Buchanan just after Cass resigned, on a day when Washington lay blanketed with one of its rare falls of snow, and offered a novel proposition. The governor of his own state wanted him to go to North Carolina as an ambassador "to express the earnest hope of Mississippi that North Carolina will co-operate with her in the adoption of efficient measures for the common defense of the South."

Thompson thought he ought to do it; told the President that the proposition of acting in concert with North Carolina would give the go-slow elements in Mississippi a handhold by which they could postpone secession until March 4, give time for conciliation, and permit the President to end his administration with most of the states still in the Union. Buchanan did not like it, but still less did he like the thought of losing permanently from his social life the vivacious Mrs. Thompson and from his councils the cold, calculating brain of his Secretary of the Interior. Go, then, in God's name. *203901*

Isaac Toucey, Secretary of the Navy, did nothing but wait to see what Buchanan would do, and then agree that it was the best course, a poor counsellor for a man who found it difficult to do anything. John B. Floyd, the Secretary of War, was so incompetent and so addicted to playing favorites among contractors that already during the summer Congress had haltered him with a civil appropriations bill which forbade him to buy marble from one man and bade him to put another, specifically named, in charge of an aqueduct. The Cabinet contained no one, no one on whom poor Buchanan could rely except Judge Black, and he begged the judge to move into the vacant chair of the Secretary of State.

Black refused to accept unless the man he had named the greatest lawyer in America brought his acute legal mind to the Cabinet at a time when all laws seemed collapsing. This was how Stanton became Attorney-General.

II

JUDGE Black said long later that he insisted upon Stanton's appointment because the two were "in perfect accord on all questions, whether of law or policy." But between the 20th of November, 1862, when the Judge wrote his official opinion that an attempt to preserve the Union by force would itself dissolve the Union, and the 20th of December, when the new Cabinet member was sworn in, there was a remarkable transaction somewhere along the line. On a day "early in December" that was certainly after the Presidential message to Congress of December 3, Black laid before Buchanan a memorandum for his private use:

The Union is necessarily perpetual. No state can lawfully withdraw or be expelled from it. The Federal Constitution is as much a part of the constitution of every State as if it had been textually inserted therein. The federal government is sovereign within its own sphere, and acts directly upon the citizens of every State. Within these limits its coercive power is ample to defend itself, its laws, and its property. It can suppress insurrections, fight battles, conquer armies, disperse hostile combinations, and punish any of its enemies.

The hand of Esau, but the voice of Jacob. Clear as a clang, that memorandum, so different in expression and spirit from Black's opinion which preceded it. Both the memorandum and the message to Congress which followed it sprang from the heart and mind of Edwin Stanton,* the man who had changed his party when South Carolina first threatened secession twenty-nine years before. His chance to drive home exactly what he meant came at the first full-dress Cabinet meeting he attended; but before that, and leading up to it, the singular transactions of Mr. Secretary of War Floyd began to crawl out of the woodwork.

This Floyd was a Virginia gentleman, a states' rights man

* The reasons for thinking so are rather intricate and some of the points are debatable. All are set forth on pages 461–466.

but theoretically opposed to secession, who lived in a high and florid style, and behaved officially according to the same pattern. In the early days of the administration, Congress fell on a wrangle and missed passing a deficiency appropriation bill. The contractors, by whom Floyd was surrounded as soon as he took office, represented that the government's failure to pay cruelly deprived them of cash with which to meet their own bills. Floyd cooked up with them an ingenious expedient, by which he endorsed their bills as valid; the banks loaned money against these acceptances and collected when the appropriation came through.

The arrangement offered such conveniences, by allowing Floyd to contract for anything he chose without bothering Congress for money until the whole transaction was a *fait accompli*, that it speedily became the normal method of doing business with the War Department; and as that department had charge of a great deal of construction in Washington, the amount of business was large. Not even an admonition from President Buchanan, who only learned of the procedure after it had been going on for a year, could make Floyd stop. The contractors were such good friends, they pressed him so, and it could not be demonstrated that there was anything illegal about the method.

But there was something worse than illegality; there was a law of diminishing return. At some date early in 1860, the whole money market became flooded with over $5,000,000 worth of Floyd-endorsed bills. The banks refused to discount any more, questioning whether Congress would ever furnish funds to dig the War Department out from under this snow-drift of paper.

This was peculiarly bad news for one of the biggest contractors of all, William H. Russell, who had spread himself so thin that unless he soon obtained some cash, he would break. He had met in Washington social circles, however, an official of the Interior Department, a man named Godard Bailey, vaguely related to Mrs. Floyd. He was the black sheep of an important South Carolina family; had been given his government job by Secretary Thompson because no one was able to find anything else the man was competent to do. Bailey had the keys of a strongbox in which was kept the Indian Trust Fund of $3,000,000 in unregistered negotiable securities; he often mentioned this treasure to Russell.

When the banks refused any more Floyd paper, Russell told Bailey that the honor of the Secretary and the family were involved. The only salvation (suggested the contractor) was to exchange some of the bills endorsed by Floyd for the bonds in the Indian Trust Fund, allowing him, Russell, to meet his need for cash by marketing the securities. Of course, as soon as Floyd got his appropriations, the bills would be paid, the bonds replaced, and no one would ever know of the transaction. Bailey agreed; that fall it was observed in Washington society that he seemed to have struck it rich; he was setting up drinks and buying cigars for everybody. The strongbox was presently short to the extent of $875,000 worth of bonds.

But when the December session came, Congress became so busy with secession that Floyd could do nothing whatever about getting an appropriation to meet the bills. Late in the month, the day before South Carolina seceded, Bailey realized that within less than two weeks the Treasury auditors would be calling for the coupons on the bonds. He wrote a confession, which reached Floyd on a sickbed that night.

When Buchanan learned of the matter three days later, he asked Floyd's resignation. The Secretary indignantly refused to quit until his own name had been cleared. But this was three days after; Floyd's more immediate reaction to the confession was curious, and leaves some doubt about the sincerity of his theoretical objections to secession. On the morning after he learned of Bailey's defalcation, the day South Carolina seceded, he issued verbal orders that 124 heavy cannon be shipped from the arsenal at Pittsburgh to Texas "to complete the forts there."

It was not the first time Secretary Floyd had sent arms southward. As far back as the closing weeks of October, 1860, he was in touch with an agent of South Carolina, who wanted to buy 10,000 rifles for the state. In November, Floyd was writing to Governor Gist that no rifles were available, but he had the right number of smoothbore muskets at Watervliet arsenal; South Carolina had better take them as they were, since a year would be required to rifle them, while in their present state they were good guns that would send a charge of buckshot "spitefully through an inch plank at 200 yards." In fact, all through the later months of his administration, Mr. Floyd displayed a truly wonderful solicitude about bringing up to quota the federal allotments of small arms to the Southern states for the suppression of a possible servile rebellion. By the date of the Bailey affair, 150,000 stand had been sent south.

Perhaps worst of all was that Stanton knew all about the Pittsburgh cannon shipment and Floyd knew that he knew it; a telegram had come from the new Attorney-General's law partner, Judge Shaler, and a mass meeting of indignation had been held in Pittsburgh. The bedeviled Secretary of War was thus in a mental state where no Virginia gentleman ought to find himself when a full Cabinet meeting was called for the afternoon of December 27. But fortune favored Floyd with an issue on which he could take a high heroic line and bury any criticism of himself under an avalanche of graver issues.

That morning the President was preparing to grant an audience to a new set of South Carolina commissioners (with considerable doubt as to the wisdom of the step) when there entered to him Senator R. M. T. Hunter of Virginia, and Jefferson Davis, still Senator from Mississippi, both with somber faces.

"Have you received any intelligence from Charleston in the last few hours?" asked Davis.

"None," said Buchanan.

"Then I have a great calamity to announce to you," said the Senator, and told how during the previous night, Major Anderson, commanding the Charleston forts, had spiked the guns of not-easily-defensible Fort Moultrie, burned their carriages, and retired with all his forces to Fort Sumter, which rose sheer from the water on an island in the center of the harbor. "And now, Mr. President, you are surrounded with blood and dishonor on all sides."

Buchanan sat down. "My God," he said, "are calamities never

to come singly? I call God to witness, you gentlemen, better than anybody, know it is not only without but against my orders. It is against my policy."

(How different was all this from the days, less than a year gone, when all three as gentlemen and friends, sat down to dine with the first Japanese delegation to visit the United States, or sailed through calm summer airs down the Potomac to visit the giant steamship *Great Eastern!*) Davis said solemnly that, yes, this alteration in the status of the forts would be productive of discontent and very likely lead to a collision. The only way of avoiding mischief was to pull the garrison out of Charleston harbor altogether. Buchanan could not quite see that, and he had the obstinacy of a weak man. He pronounced that it was his duty to preserve and protect the property of the United States.

Davis said, well then, why not a compromise? Let an ordnance sergeant and a caretaker detail be left in Sumter—and while he was about it, in Fort Pickens at Pensacola as well—until the matter could be adjusted with the seceding states. He would have to consult his Cabinet, Buchanan replied, and having eaten a light dinner, proceeded to do so, while every bar in the city filled up with men tumultuously discussing the news.

Floyd opened the Cabinet meeting in a high and boisterous voice, by launching a diatribe against Major Anderson for having violated his express orders. He demanded the Major be sent back to Moultrie at once. Judge Black contradicted Floyd to his face about the orders, and sent for the War Department files. There it was in black and white; on December 7, 1860, Floyd had sent Major Don Carlos Buell to Moultrie with verbal instructions, which being delivered, Buell cleared his own record by writing a report. He said he had told Anderson to act on his own discretion, withdrawing to the stronger fort if necessary. The report bore a signed endorsement by Floyd: "This is in conformity with my instructions to Major Buell."

This evidence of a double game did not in the least discourage Floyd, who kept pressing his demand for the abandonment of Sumter. Buchanan was rather inclined to agree with him that the fort should be evacuated, and Floyd tried to clinch things with a paper: "It is evident now from the action of the commander at Fort Moultrie, that the solemn pledges of the government have been violated by Major Anderson. In my judgement but one remedy is now left by which to vindicate our honor and to prevent civil war; that is, to withdraw the garrison from the harbor altogether. I hope the President will allow me to make that order at once."

Black snapped at Floyd that if a minister of England had advised surrendering an effective fortress he would have been sent to the block. But Thompson had returned from his trip; he brushed the historical reference aside, and Buchanan was clearly inclining to the viewpoint of the two Southerners.

Stanton, newest man in the Cabinet, could stand it no longer. He lashed out that as the President's legal adviser it was his duty to say that the surrender of Fort Sumter by the government would be a crime equal to the crime of Arnold, and all who participated in it should be hung like André; a President of the United States who made such an order would be guilty of treason.

Up leaped Floyd, his face suffused with blood; pale, glaring Thompson rose with him, gesturing as though he meant to strike the Attorney-General, and Buchanan raised both hands, saying deprecatingly; "Oh, no! Not so bad as that! Not so bad as that!"

Things came back to the discussion level, but senators kept calling on the President with protests against Anderson's move, or merely to discuss it with him, and the Cabinet broke up with no line of action definitely decided.

Next morning Buchanan gave the postponed audience to the South Carolina commissioners. They pushed him hard, along the line of Floyd's paper, that his personal honor was involved, he had pledged that nothing about the forts should be changed, and the pledge was now violated. He must order Anderson back to Moultrie at once, or better, evacuate the harbor altogether.

"You are pressing me too importunately," bleated the President. "You don't give me time to consider; you don't give me time to say my prayers. I always say my prayers when required to act upon any great state affair." Then he protested that he had given no pledge, and as for ordering Anderson back to Moultrie, South Carolina herself had rendered the step impossible, for the morning telegraph brought the news that the state had seized the abandoned fort.

After a long argument, the commissioners retired glumly, one of them recording the opinion that Buchanan would have redeemed his pledge if he had not been "previously screwed up and terrorized by Mr. Stanton, his new Attorney-General." That night there was another Cabinet meeting; Stanton came with his written resignation in his pocket, ready to produce it if Buchanan approved the evacuation order. Black and Joseph Holt, the Postmaster-General, were ready to do the same; they had been talking during the day. The President would have to choose between them and John B. Floyd.

The discussion was even more movemented than on the evening before, Floyd hammering away at the pledge until Stanton reminded him that he had "millions of dollars in fraudulent acceptances afloat." The Virginia gentleman found it necessary to recline on a sofa.

Thompson and Philip F. Thomas of Maryland, who had replaced Howell Cobb in the Treasury, took over for the be-kind-to-Carolina movement, the former basing a new plea to give up the fort on the ground of generosity. South Carolina is a small state with a sparse white population—we, on the other hand, are a great and powerful people, who can afford to say: "See, we will withdraw the garrison as an evidence that we mean you no harm."

That triggered Stanton again. "Mr. President," he said, "the proposal to be generous implies that the government is strong, and that we, as the public servants, have the confidence of the people. I think that is a mistake. No administration has ever suffered the loss of public confidence and support as this has done. Only the other day it was announced that a million of dollars had been stolen from Mr. Thompson's department. The bonds were found to have been taken from the vault where they should have been kept and the notes of Mr. Floyd were substituted for them. Now it is proposed to give up Sumter.

All I have to say is that no Administration, much less this one, can afford to lose a million of money and a fort in the same week."

Floyd answered no word, but next morning he sent round to the White House a letter, declaring he could not stay in a government that had lost its honor.

III

But disposing of the peculiar Secretary of War was not disposing of Fort Sumter, as Black and Stanton discovered the next evening, December 29, when Buchanan read to his Cabinet a letter which he proposed as the reply to one left by the South Carolina commissioners at the close of the aborted interview the day before. Toucey, of course, thought it a marvelously statesmanlike document and just what the occasion required; Thompson and Thomas clung savagely to the view that the fort ought to be given up, while Black, Holt, and Stanton protested against having anything more to do with the commissioners.

"These gentlemen claim to be ambassadors," the Attorney-General burst out. "It is preposterous. They cannot be ambassadors; they are lawbreakers. They should be arrested. You cannot negotiate with them; and yet it seems by this paper that you have been doing that very thing. Mr. President, I must say that the Attorney-General, under his oath of office, dares not be cognizant of the pending proceedings."

There was another long argument, ending in a vacuum. Black could not sleep that night, and next morning, December 30, a Sunday raw and chill, he rounded up Stanton and Holt. The three agreed to resign if the Presidential letter were sent to the commissioners as written, and dispatched a messenger to say so. Meanwhile, Benjamin F. Butler of Massachusetts, who was so good an administration Democrat that he had helped nominate Breckinridge and then campaigned for him, saw Stanton, then Black and the President, offering his services gratis to prosecute the commissioners if they were arrested and indicted. These events so worked on the soft but tenacious metal of the Presidential mind that Black and Stanton were called to the White House. Buchanan told them that he "could have no further disruption of his official household," and handed them the draft letter, with a request to prepare any legal objections they might have to its clauses.

The two men took this, quite correctly, as a polite license to shift the ideology of the document toward their own. Stanton drafted his suggestions for changes and showed the paper to Holt, who approved every word of it, then hurried to Black, who added two points to the five the Attorney-General had made, and took the document to Buchanan.

This was the "Memorandum of December 30," later famous. It objected to Buchanan's draft on the ground that at two points it acknowledged South Carolina's right to diplomatic representation before the government of the United States, and thereby implied that the state had acquired the rights and powers of a separate nation by "the mere ordinance of secession." It asked Buchanan to strike out an expression of regret "that the commissioners are unwilling to proceed with the negotiations, since it is very clear that there can be no negotiations with them." It asked him to delete from the record any intimation that the government was willing to negotiate with anybody about the possession of a military post belonging to it. It requested the elimination of a clause about "coercing a state by force of arms to remain in the Union, a power that I do not believe the Constitution has conferred on Congress." Buchanan was asked to substitute for his implied assent to the doctrine of a pledge on the status of the forts given by him, a strong and flat denial that any pledge had been given or intended. It asked the deletion of every word that suggested the least criticism of Major Anderson's action. It requested the insertion of a statement that no wrong was committed against South Carolina by the movement from Fort Moultrie to Fort Sumter. "It is a strange assumption," said the memo, "of right on the part of one state to say that the United States troops must remain in the weakest position they can find in the harbor. It is not a menace of

South Carolina or of Charleston or any menace at all. It is simple self defense."

In short, that memo of December 30 was the voice of sovereignty, speaking in tones as ringing as Alexander Hamilton's, putting an end for good to any possibility that secession by consent of the government would become an established precedent. The letter that resulted was so utterly different in tone from Buchanan's message of December 3 that the Carolina commissioners could hardly believe they were dealing with the same man. They were flatly told that the federal government would turn over no property under any conditions, and that it intended to maintain its garrisons where they stood.

The commissioners were shocked, and so were all the prosecessionist circles, through which the news spread rapidly on the last day of the year. Many came to the White House reception on New Year's Day, sporting the blue cockade of the South, and turned up their noses at the hand which the President extended to them in greeting; and, the day following, the commissioners replied in a letter denouncing Buchanan as a dishonorable liar.

IV

THE diplomatic missive from the Southern commissioners reached the White House to find the Cabinet once more in session, with Jacob Thompson, now a lone voice, crying against the idea of reinforcing Sumter. Black and Stanton kept pushing it forward as the only possible course, while fat, gouty old Winfield Scott, commander of the army, kept on urging it. Buchanan indorsed the commissioners' letter to the effect that it was of such a nature that he could not receive it, and sent it back to them; then said: "Reinforcements must now be sent."

They were sent, aboard the steamer *Star of the West*, which had carried Stanton to Panama, sliding out across the New York harbor bar under a cloudy sky on the evening of January 5. Jacob Thompson did not find out they had gone until three days later, when he promptly resigned, on the ground that the step had been taken without notice to him, a member of the Cabinet. The Cabinet record shows no dissent to the President's remark; back in Mississippi, Thompson told a crowd that he had not heard Buchanan say reinforcements would be sent, which is a little odd, as everyone else at the meeting heard it. Perhaps the explanation was that advanced by the *Chicago Tribune*, that at the meeting the President offered everybody whisky and took some himself. Perhaps it was the one later put forth by Judge Black: "Thompson was not meant to hear." In any event, Thompson finished his Mississippi speech by boasting to his hearers that as soon as he learned of the sailing, he telegraphed Charleston, so that the batteries would be ready to beat off the relief ship—which they duly accomplished on January 9.

By this date, Buchanan had put his "official household" in reasonable order, with Holt moving over to the War Department, where he instantly canceled Floyd's order for the shipment of the Pittsburgh guns. The ineffective Thomas was about to leave the Treasury in favor of John A. Dix of New York, a businessman and silk-stocking political operator, who had straightened out the howling mess in the New York post office, when its head was discovered to be $160,000 short in his accounts.

But it was a household on caretaker status; neither the President nor anyone in his administration any longer had the power to influence events: the tides were running fast and deep, the papers that carried the news of the firing on the *Star of the West* also announced that Florida, Alabama, and Mississippi had seceded, Georgia and Louisiana would be gone before the month was out, Texas before the end of another, there would be conventions in North Carolina, Arkansas, Missouri, and Virginia. Already calls were running for a convention where the Southern states could form a new union, nearer their hearts' desire; the troops were drilling; each day came news that some new fort had been seized—Pulaski by Georgia; Marion, Barrancas, and McRae by Florida; Morgan and Gaines by Alabama. In Texas, General Daniel Twiggs surrendered all the posts of the state and 2,500 soldiers to the new authority; in New York, Mayor Fernando Wood was urging the city council to secede from the Union as a free city, at peace with both the sectional republics.

"Let the erring sisters go," said Horace Greeley's *New York Tribune*, which so many people regarded as the voice of the Republican party that the statement was taken as the policy of the incoming administration. Congress did little but trot from one plan of compromise to another, trying to seduce the erring sisters back into the Union. There was a committee of thirty-three in the House, one man from each state; there was a committee of thirteen in the Senate, after the House committee found itself unable to produce anything more constructive than eight separate and mutually contradictory reports.

Proposed: that a general constitutional convention of all the states be held. Proposed: that the ex-Presidents (there would be five on March 4, more than at any time in American history) mediate the whole dispute. Proposed by John J. Crittenden of Kentucky, the state of compromise, which had given Henry Clay and his great series of adjustments to the Union: that the 36-30 line dividing slave territory from free be extended to the Pacific, and Congress be deprived by Constitutional amendment of the power to legislate against slavery where it existed— with a variety of sub-proposals on fugitive slaves and the slave trade.

No proposals acceptable. The least the slavery men would take during those weeks when the old nation was shattering and the new one being formed was an immovable provision, by law or amendment, for slavery in all the territories. The most the incoming administration would give was that slavery should not be interfered with where it was established. Senator Seward went to see the President-elect and brought back his word: on slavery in the territories, no.

Yet Senator Seward remained genial, confident, smiling— obviously destined to be the real head of the new administration under the titular Presidency of the inexperienced Lincoln. The Senator was personally intimate with Jefferson Davis, and held long talks with the Mississippian, sitting by the bedside where the latter lay, face gaunt with the pain of the inflamed eye, whose sight he was to lose, before Davis pronounced his solemn speech of farewell. He went off to Montgomery to be somewhat surprisingly elected President of the new Confederacy, when the Georgia delegation could not agree on which of the three leading men from their state should have the place. Seward was still intimate with the Virginia congressmen, especially Senator Hunter; saw them daily, and by this contact was held responsible for the opinion running through the hall of rumors that the Confederacy formed at Montgomery was never intended to be permanent; that as soon as the new administration came to power at Washington, there would be a peace conference, with the old Mother of Presidents in the saddle, compromising all differences.

Seward remained perfectly bland, mildly amused at such tales as the one that a riot would be staged to prevent the counting of the electoral vote; that 200 Texans with bowie knives and pistols were coming to assassinate the new Chief Magistrate before he could take office. He even laughed at the perfectly genuine story that Senator Wigfall of Texas, the scarfaced duelist with the pirate eye, had worked out a plan to kidnap Buchanan and so make Breckinridge President. Seward was the only man in the capital who seemed to be keeping his head in that exotic atmosphere, the only one who did not seem to realize that Washington might turn out to be the capital of the new Confederacy.

Well, he had reason for calm. He was probably the best-informed man in the city during the last hours of the Buchanan administration. He himself was the leader of the Republican councils; his sly gossip, Thurlow Weed, had spent two days with Lincoln, and brought back a report on how the new President stood with regard to everything at all important. In addition, the Senator knew that eight companies of regular troops were on their way to protect the capital and the inauguration. He knew that the city was full of clever New York detectives, who had tracked down every plot. He knew that the D.C. militia would be purged of all disloyalists; he knew that the Southern Confederacy was not yet ready to take any overt action.

He knew all these things because he was getting daily precise reports on everything that went on in Buchanan's Cabinet from E. M. Stanton.

It could be considered an outrageous breach of confidence on the Attorney-General's part, a kind of treason to the President who had appointed him, and who not unnaturally expected that the inner workings of the government would be kept secret unless permission were given to release. The moral question is one for philosophers. Stanton held that his brief was from the Union. "I am willing to perish if thereby the Union may be saved," he wrote in a passionate flash from Vergniaud, on the day when *Star of the West* failed, simultaneously with the secession of Florida, Alabama, and Mississippi.

Buchanan complained that he lacked power to do more than send one unarmed ship. A select committee of the House, headed by Henry J. Dawes of Massachusetts, produced a bill giving the President express authority to call out the militia to defend or recover federal property. Buchanan did nothing to push it and it failed; Buchanan did nothing about anything. He would not even listen when Stanton proposed that senators and representatives from the states already seceded should be placed under arrest; it took the combined efforts of Black, Stanton, and Holt to persuade the old man to do so much as allow the eight companies of troops to come to Washington. Peace in my time.

The world was crashing down, while the amiable dodderer tinkered with schemes for conciliating men who wanted no conciliation. Stanton even discussed with the Dawes committee the basis on which impeachment proceedings might be drawn. No, that was no good, either; impeachment is for positive wrongs, not merely the absence of anything right; there was no hope for the Republic but in the new power, and to that power Stanton gave his adhesion. "*Que mon nom soit flétri; que la patrie soit sauvé!*"

BACKDROP

Washington Intelligencer

Mr. Lassie, a French Gentleman now on a visit to this country, will exhibit a small model of a balloon invented and constructed by him in the hall of the Patent Office. The balloon differs from other constructions of this sort in that it enables the aeronaut to propel his vessel through the atmosphere in any direction and with certainty and safety.

EDICT AGAINST LYNCHING. The frequent lynchings in Savannah have at last attracted the official attention of the Mayor and City Council of that place, who denounce such proceedings as lawless and subversive of good order and security. A reward of one hundred dollars is offered for the apprehension and conviction of parties implicated in such outrages. The Savannah Republican approved of the proclamation and says that the oldest, wisest and best citizens of Savannah condemn the course of the vigilance committees.

Mr. Huyer, the postmaster at Charleston, has forwarded an order to the Post office Dept. for $440 worth of postage stamps for the use of the Charleston office.

The Department postpones the filling of the order for the present. Only twelve postmasters have resigned in South Carolina. No contractor for carrying the mails has yet intimated a wish to throw up his contract.

TOM, The Blind Negro Boy Pianist, The Wonder of the World, The Marvel of the Age. A living miracle, blind from birth, without one moment's instruction, not even knowing the name of a single key upon the fingerboard, or the shape of a piano, yet master of the piano, playing from the operas of Lucrezia Borgia, Norma, Linda, Somnabula, Trovatore, Traviata, Daughter of the Regiment and others with a master's hand and a master's touch. A Negro child, only ten years old, raised upon a plantation, simple-minded, a child in all his wishes and wants, yet master of one of the greatest sciences, playing two pieces of music at once, and conversing at the same time, reproducing the most difficult pieces after once hearing them, playing the second to any piece without even hearing it once, then exchanging seats and reproducing the piece correctly, performs with his back to the instrument and sings in French and German without understanding either language.

Concert at the Assembly Rooms commencing Tuesday evening. Doors open at 6½ o'clock. Concert at 7½.

Admission 50 cents, children 25.

8

IN TRANSIT;
DISSATISFACTION

ON the afternoon of March 4, 1861, bleak and chilly after a fine morning, Abraham Lincoln rode to the Capitol through streets lined with weaponed men. From a temporary balcony there he told the world that "the Union of these States is perpetual"; that "no state on its own mere motion can lawfully get out of the Union"; that he meant to enforce the national laws in every part of the states, and that "in your hands, my dissatisfied fellow-countrymen, and not in mine, is the momentous issue of civil war."

The papers were not quite sure whether it was a fighting speech or not, and while they waited to find out, Washington passed into a state of suspended animation, punctuated by office seekers. They pullulated; all day long an endless procession of them marched up the White House steps, clutching the papers that proved how worthy the holder was of a post office, an Indian agency, or at the very least, a clerkship. They filled the corridors of the building, and waylaid the President when he left his office to get a meal; they held up his carriage on the street to thrust documents at him. Except for them (as Dr. Gwin, the fire-eating Southerner who had become a senator from California, wrote to some South Carolina friends), "Washington has become a realization of Goldsmith's Deserted Village."

For with the disappearance of the slaveholding aristocracy

who, if they could arrive at no formula for arranging the affairs of a nation, understood so perfectly how to arrange a dinner table, social life had taken on an air of genteel vulgarity, of the tasteless splendors of the backwoods. It was said of Mr. Lincoln that he had actually worn black gloves to the opera; it was known of Mrs. Lincoln that she spoke of the Secretary of State as a "dirty abolition sneak," and would not speak to the wife of the senior senator from Illinois at all. At the ball following the inauguration a scandalous number of people had their hats and overcoats stolen; it was whispered that the new Vice-President had a dash of the tarbrush.

Meanwhile the new power was doing nothing or worse than nothing to arrest the disintegration of a nation. When Congressman Sherman of Ohio brought to Lincoln his brother, a retired army captain who had been superintendent of a military school in Louisiana, to explain the seriousness of the situation there, the President only grinned and said: "Oh, well! I guess we'll manage to keep house"—which so disgusted the retired captain that he departed Washington in a red cloud of fury and took a job with a streetcar company in St. Louis. The supple Mr. Seward was known to be in communication with a new set of Confederate commissioners who had come to Washington; had, in fact, assured them through old Justice Campbell of the Supreme Court, that Fort Sumter would be given up peaceably—after all that effort in Buchanan's Cabinet.

Stanton to ex-President Buchanan, March 14, 1861

There is no doubt of Sumter being evacuated; report says the order has gone out, but that I think is doubtful. You will have noticed the resolution introduced yesterday by Mr. Douglas in the Senate. It looks like a comprehensive platform for relinquishing everything in the seceded States, and even those who sympathize with them. To me it seems like the first steps toward a strictly Northern non-slave-holding confederacy. Lincoln will probably (if his Administration continues four years) make a change that will affect the constitutional doctrines of the Court. The pressure for offices continues unabated. Every department is overrun, and by time all the patronage is distributed, the Republican Party will be dissolved.

Old General Scott, who had been so strong for reinforcing Sumter in the Buchanan days, had swung around to the opposite view, after hearing how strong were the Carolina batteries, how short on supplies and ammunition was the garrison. It would take 20,000 men to relieve the fort, he said; no such force existed or could be raised, and he had adopted Greeley's phrase about letting the erring sisters depart, with a few modifications of his own. At the Cabinet meeting on March 15, only two members were found to disagree with the General, but no decision was taken. Nobody knew who was or would be a secessionist next while all the border slave states—Delaware, Maryland, Virginia, North Carolina, Kentucky, Tennessee, Missouri, and Arkansas—hung irresolute between the old government and the new, and senators from Texas still sat in the Capitol.

"Wanted—a Policy!" cried the leading editorial of the *New York Times*; "Come to the Point!" shouted Greeley from the *Tribune;* and Mr. Stanton was preparing a brief for the extension of the McCormick reaper patents, in which he set forth the remarkable doctrine that, owing to the reaper, American wheat had become more important to Europe than American cotton.

A certain Captain Gustavus Vasa Fox of the navy, who had prepared a plan for the relief of Sumter in December, went through Carolina to the place under a pass, saw Major Anderson, and reported that the plan would still work. Lincoln's former law partner, Ward Hill Lamon, also went down and reported in an exactly opposite sense, but "My policy is to have no policy," Lincoln told his secretary. How could he have one? He was not even sure of controlling Congress, the united wings of the Democratic party were in the majority against him in the country as a whole, and with the Southern influence removed from Congress, the Democracy was guided by the sharpest political critic of the age—Stephen A. Douglas.

General Scott's advice to evacuate was rejected in the Cabinet, but there was still no group decision on relieving; and on April 1, Mr. Seward wrote the President a memo, saying: "We are at the end of a month's administration, and yet without a policy, either domestic or foreign." He told his wife that he had assumed a kind of dictatorship, and continued the letter to the President by proposing to make demands on Spain, France, and England that would rouse the patriotism of both sections for a foreign war. A policy must be adopted and prosecuted with energy (he said); either the President himself must do it, "or devolve it upon some member of the Cabinet." Lincoln quietly replied: "If this must be done, I must do it"; and the clever Mr. Seward, shaking his head, perceived that he was not, after all, prime minister to a fainéant king. But this correspondence was hidden from any eyes but those of the two.

Stanton to ex-President Buchanan, April 3, 1861

Although a considerable period has elapsed since the date of my last letter to you, nothing has transpired here of interest but what is fully detailed in the newspapers. I have not had any intercourse with any of the present Cabinet except for a few brief interviews with Mr. Bates, the Attorney General, on business connected with his department. Mr. Lincoln I have not seen. He is said to be very much broken down with the pressure that is on him in respect to appointments.

The policy of the Administration in respect to the seceding States remains in obscurity. There has been a rumor for the last two or three days that, notwithstanding all that has been said, there will be an effort to reinforce Fort Sumter. But I do not believe a word of it. The special messenger, Colonel Lamon, told me that he was satisfied it could not be done.

The new tariff bill seems to give the Administration great trouble; and luckily it is a measure of their own. The first month of the Administration seems to have furnished an ample vindication of your policy, and to have rendered all occasion of other defense needless. The rumors from Richmond are very threatening; secession is rapidly gaining strength there.

But the rumor about reinforcing Sumter was perfectly true. The adroit Secretary of State wrote orders for ships and troops to go both there and to Fort Pickens at Pensacola, and slipped them in among some other papers the President was signing—

a piece of chicane whose impact on the Navy Secretary, Gideon Welles (who looked like Father Christmas and thought like Old Scrooge), was such as to send him into a rage against Seward from which he never recovered. But the ships were made ready, the ships steamed out of New York harbor, and old Justice Campbell wrote Seward an angry letter, accusing the Secretary of bad faith, then resigned and went back to the South from which he had come. The District militia was called into service; a little fewer than half of them refused to take the oath.

Stanton to ex-President Buchanan, April 11, 1861

There is great "soldiering" in town the last two days. The yard in front of the War Office is crowded with the district militia, who are being mustered into service. The feeling of loyalty to the government has greatly diminished in this city. The administration has not acquired the respect and confidence of the people here. Not one of the Cabinet or principal officers has taken a house or brought his family here. Seward rented a house "while he should continue in the Cabinet" but has not opened it, nor has his family come. They all act as though they meant to be ready to "cut and run" at a minute's notice. And besides, a strong feeling of distrust in the candor and sincerity of President Lincoln and of his Cabinet has sprung up. If they had been merely silent or secret there might have been no ground of complaint. But assurances are said to have been given and declarations made in conflict with the facts now transpiring in respect to the South, so that no one speaks of Lincoln or of any member of his Cabinet with any respect or regard.

It is believed that a secession ordinance will be passed by the Virginia convention today.

On the last point the correspondent was wrong; it was April 17 before Virginia went out of the Union, five days after the hour when, at four o'clock in the morning, the first shell screamed across Charleston harbor toward Fort Sumter, and all the citizens ran out into the streets to congratulate each other under joyfully caroling bells.

Stanton to ex-President Buchanan, April 12, 1861

We have the war upon us. The telegraphic news of this morning you will have seen before this reaches you. The impression here is held by many—

1. That the effort to reinforce will be a failure.
2. That in less than 24 hours from this time Anderson will have surrendered.
3. That in less than thirty days Davis will be in possession of Washington.

It was not until two days later that there began to come to a confused and dubious Washington, where secession badges were still sold in the street, the news of that instant and glorious phenomenon, the uprising of the North. "At dead of night, at news from the South" all doubts and differences disappeared; there were no longer Republicans, Democrats, or Whigs, only voices that cried for the old flag and the Union. Stephen A. Douglas, a dying man, made a speaking pilgrimage through the Middle West; to an immense audience in the hall where Lincoln had been nominated, he flung: "Before God, it is the duty of every American citizen to rally around the flag of his country."

In New York, where so lately they had discussed the secession of the city, 200,000 people met in Union Square to shout for the Union; the Irish formed four regiments, and the dandy Seventh marched down Broadway through a lane of cheering two miles long. The St. Louis Germans gathered in their Turner halls and enlisted to a man; all the lamp posts of Pittsburgh were decorated with ropes for hanging traitors; Ohio offered three times as many men as Lincoln requested from her. Every township in Massachusetts held a meeting to speak loyalty, and, before sunset of the first day, 3,000 men joined the colors in Boston; throughout Philadelphia impromptu mass meetings in the streets merged into a vast demonstration under the leadership of veterans of 1812; judge and jury walked from a Milwaukee court to enlist together.

Then came the doubts, the terrible business of learning that most of war is anxiety and heartsick waiting. It did not take eyes that could see through a grindstone to perceive that with Virginia out of the Union and Maryland likely to follow, Washington might easily be the capital of the Confederacy. Social life was dead; all places of amusement closed. "Why don't the troops come?" was the only word that passed from man to man. On April 18 a Virginia army of 6,000 took the great arsenal at Harpers Ferry without a fight—or what was left of the great arsenal, for the forty-five guardsmen burned and blew it up before they left. The Baltimore and Ohio was severed, Washington cut off from the West. On April 20 the navy yard at Norfolk went up in a tempest of fire, and with it, four warships. "Why don't they come? Why don't they come?" said Lincoln, looking from the window after pacing the floor for an hour.

On the nineteenth the first of them did come, the Massachusetts Sixth Regiment—but they came bedraggled and bearing their dead on stretchers, after fighting their way through riotous prosecessionist Baltimore. That night the telegraph wires went down, the railroad bridges were burned, Washington was an isolated city, practically a besieged city, from which men fled in wagons or pushing wheelbarrows piled with their belongings. A week of this tension—then the troops really did begin to come from Annapolis, which they had reached by water; the New York Seventh; and Ben Butler with more men from Massachusetts. They camped in the Capitol and baked bread in its basement. More followed; Rhode Islanders with their governor leading them and the New York Fire Zouaves, hard men who growled that they had not been sent through Baltimore to give that angry town a taste of its own medicine.

The capital began to look like a camp, with drumtaps and marching in the spring dusk, and President Lincoln suspended the writ of *habeas corpus* on the line from Washington to Philadelphia.

Stanton to ex-President Buchanan, May 11, 1861

On the 24th of April, the day after the Baltimore riot, and again on Blue Tuesday, I wrote to you. These letters will probably reach you some time.*

The negotiations carried on by Mr. Seward with the Confederate Commissioners through Judge Campbell and Judge Nelson will some day, perhaps, be brought to light, and, if they are as has been represented to me, Mr. Seward and the Lincoln Administration will not be in a position to make sneering observations respecting any negotiations during your Administration. It was in reference to these that Jefferson Davis, in his message, spoke with so much severity. The state of affairs is tolerably well-detailed in the public prints. But no description could convey to you the panic that prevailed here for several days after the Baltimore riots. This was increased by reports of the trepidation of Lincoln that were circulating through the streets. Women and children were sent away in great numbers; provisions advanced to famine prices. In a great measure the alarm has passed away, but there is still a deep apprehension that before long the city is doomed to be the scene of battle and carnage. In respect to the military operations going on or contemplated, little is known until the results are announced in the newspapers. General Scott seems to have *carte blanche*. He is, in fact, the Government, and, if his health continues, vigorous measures are anticipated. I have been moving my family, my former residence being made unpleasant by troops and hospitals surrounding me. Marching and drilling are going on all day in the street. The troops that have arrived here are in general fine-looking, able-bodied, active men, well equipped, and apparently ready and willing for the service in which they are engaged.

On May 13 the railroads through Baltimore began operating again, and the next thing was that Butler, now a general, was in charge of the mutinous city, with troops to make his orders stick. The new enlistments were to be for three years instead of the three months of the first call. Maryland balanced, balanced perilously, and then by legislative act decided that state had no power to quit the Union; Kentucky proclaimed neutrality, and everybody and his brother came to

* They never did.

Washington to look for contracts, in a visitation which made
the descent of the office seekers seem puny. The only star rose
over the western counties of Virginia, which had refused to
ratify the ordinance of secession. Virginia sent troops; so did
Ohio, under a young officer named George B. McClellan,
who had invented a new type of saddle and written a brilliant
survey of the Crimean campaign. There were a couple of fights;
the Virginians were driven through the mountains in prone
rout, and behind McClellan's guns, a new state was made for
the Union.

Stanton to ex-President Buchanan, June 6, 1861

While every patriotic heart has rejoiced at the enthusiastic spirit
with which the nation has aroused to maintain its existence and
honor, the peculation and fraud that immediately sprang up to
prey upon the volunteers and grasp public money as plunder and
spoil has created a strong feeling of loathing and disgust. And no
sooner had the appearance of imminent danger passed away, and
the administration recovered from its panic, than a determination
became manifest to give a strictly party direction to the great
national movement.

General Dix informs me that he has been so badly treated by
Cameron that he intends immediately to resign. This will be followed by a withdrawal of financial confidence and support to a
great extent. The military movements, or rather inaction, also ex-
cite great apprehension. It is believed that Davis and Beauregard
are both in this vicinity, and that they can concentrate over 60,000
troops. Our whole force does not exceed 45,000. It is also reported
that discord exists between the Cabinet and General Scott in respect to important points of strategy. Our condition, therefore,
seems to be one of greater danger than at any former period.

Stanton to General John A. Dix, June 11, 1861

No one can imagine the deplorable condition of this city, and
the hazard of the Government who did not witness the weakness
and panic of the Administration and the painful imbecility of
Lincoln. We looked to New York in that dark hour for our only
deliverance under Providence, and, thank God, it came.

The action of your city especially filled me with admiration, and proved the right of New York to be called the Empire City. But the picture has a dark side—dark and terrible—from the corruption that surrounds the War Department, and seems to poison with venomous breath the very atmosphere.

On every side the Government and the soldiers are pillaged. Arms, clothing, transportation, provisions, are each and all the subjects of speculation and spoil.

Mr. Attorney Stanton was not the only man who chafed over military inaction. Horace Greeley pinned "FORWARD TO RICHMOND!" at the masthead of the *New York Tribune*, and half a hundred other papers took up the cry. Congress met; gazed curiously at drunken officers in the Willard's bar, ratified Lincoln's quite illegal calls for troops and use of funds, and began crying for "sudden, bold, forward, determined war."

The pressure became intolerable; on June 29, the Cabinet called in General Irvin McDowell, who had been placed in charge of the field forces based on Washington, and told him to prepare a forward movement. He was a handsome man with a pointed iron-gray beard, much devoted to architecture and landscape gardening, whose French military education made him obviously superior to every other officer for the post, even if General Scott didn't think so; besides, he was a personal friend of Secretary of the Treasury Salmon P. Chase. Not one of his officers had commanded as much as a brigade before, and his divisional organization was homemade for the occasion. But Lincoln said that if his troops were green, so were the enemy. Let him go forward by July 9; strike the 25,000 rebels at Manassas with his 30,000, according to plan.

Of course, the date could not be met. It was the sixteenth before the column of loose regiments, who did not even know the names of their own higher officers, straggled across the Long Bridge and down into the Virginia countryside. They moved to the cheering news that General McClellan had gained another brilliant victory (the adjective was his own) in West Virginia, and they moved with the help of pretty ladies in crinoline, carrying picnic lunches in their gigs, and a cloud of congressmen, including six senators. The troops straggled

and picked blackberries, joked and sang; an alfresco war until July 21, when the guns began to shoot. Then a Union victory was checked when Thomas J. Jackson of the Confederacy
stood like a stone wall; reinforcements to the rebels unexpectedly came from the Shenandoah Valley onto McDowell's
flank; the Union victory became a frightful defeat, and everybody ran away, leaving behind many dead and some prisoners,
including a live congressman.

Stanton to C. P. Wolcott of Steubenville, July 24, 1861

Affairs in Washington are to some degree recovered from the
horrible confusion exhibited on Monday and Tuesday—the dis-
organized rabble of destitute soldiers is being cleared from the
streets by slow degrees, the army officers are not swarming so
thickly in the hotels and taverns and are perhaps beginning to join
their men. The enemy have advanced to Fairfax, and their pickets
extend some miles this side—but their movements are as unpene-
trated a mystery as before. Why they do not take possession of the
city, as they might have done without serious resistance on Monday
and Tuesday is a marvel.

Stanton to ex-President Buchanan, July 26, 1861

The dreadful disaster of Sunday can scarcely be mentioned.

The imbecility of the Administration culminated in that catas-
trophe; an irretrievable misfortune and national disgrace never to
be forgotten are to be added to the ruin of all peaceful pursuits
and national bankruptcy, as the result of Lincoln's "running the
machine" for five months.

You perceive that Bennett * is now for a change in the Cabinet,
and proposes for one of the new Cabinet Mr. Holt, whose opposition to Bennett's appointment was bitter and intensely hostile. It
it not unlikely that some changes in the War and Navy Departments may take place, but none beyond these two Departments
until Jeff Davis turns out the whole concern. The capture of Washington seems now to be inevitable; during the whole of Monday
and Tuesday it might have been taken without any resistance. The
rout, overthrow and utter demoralization of the whole army is

---

* James Gordon Bennett, editor of the *New York Herald*, who wanted
to be Minister to France.

complete. While Lincoln, Scott and the Cabinet are disputing who are to blame, the city is unguarded and the enemy at hand.

General McClellan reached here last evening, but if he had the ability of Caesar, Alexander or Napoleon, what can he accomplish? Will not Scott's jealousy, Cabinet intrigues and Republican interference thwart him at every step?

II

THIS was the last of the Buchanan letters. The Old Public Functionary had replied to them only with notes resembling the vaguely friendly noises of a companionable dog, and Stanton doubtless felt that correspondence with him was a good deal like telling secrets to a hole in the ground. It is rather a pity the series did not continue; the letters make one of the best diary accounts of Washington events during the period, so accurate in the description of things seen, heard or sensed, so inaccurate in prediction.

For if General McClellan was not Alexander, Caesar, or Napoleon (though a good many people called him by the last name, prefixing it with "Little"), there was much that he could and did accomplish. A thousand regulars were formed into a provost guard; they cleared the streets of drunken soldiers and the taverns of roughs in blue, who were in the habit of eating dinners for sixteen and charging them to the Confederate States' government. The troops went under canvas south of the river, where they really drilled—not as companies, but as regiments, brigades, divisions, with the General likely to turn up for an inspection at any moment, in his French style képi, surrounded by aides with European names.

He gave the men enough to eat, he saw to it that they had all the creature comforts soldiers can have. He equipped them with guns that would shoot and adequate ambulances, and, when a regiment mutinied, he sent sixty-five of its men to the Dry Tortugas. A great belt of forts began to ring Washington; there was no longer any chance the rebels would take the city. "McClellan's our leader, he's gallant and strong," the men sang to the best march tune since *La Marseillaise*, a matter of no mean importance. "Little Mac!" they shouted among the reddening leaves of autumn at reviews which they began to run through with something approaching military precision.

It was the fact that he was *Little* Mac that dripped gall into a cup almost overflowing with the sweetness of being cheered by a hundred thousand marching men as they obeyed his orders, of having two princes of France on his staff, of being the central figure at a series of magnificent champagne parties, where men from Wormley, the caterer, opened oysters for hours. It was unpleasant for a man of McClellan's size to be seen with the immense, glittering, and barely mobile Scott; it was still more unpleasant to be outranked by the old man, who did not in the least agree with the McClellan concept of strategy.

Early in August, the commander of the Army of the Potomac—he himself devised the name—was already reporting to his wife that he "had a row with General Scott," who was "the great obstacle." A few days later, Scott was "the most dangerous antagonist I have," and by October, McClellan was "firmly determined to force the issue with General Scott" by persuading senators to have the hero of Lundy's Lane retired by legislative action.

The trouble was that General Scott cherished the insane delusion that the Army of the Potomac ought to do something beside blow bugles and hold parades. It was perfectly clear to General McClellan that Washington stood in deadly peril from the 150,000 "strong, well-drilled, and equipped" rebels in northern Virginia. The personal reports he was receiving from Alan Pinkerton, the Chicago detective whose bureau had been transformed into an espionage agency, said so. It made no difference that Prince Napoleon, after a visit to the Confederacy, reported their army at Manassas as consisting of 60,000 men, "ragged, dirty, and half-starved." It made no difference that deserters, Negro refugees, and letters through the lines, all pictured the prince's estimate of Confederate numbers as rather high. Or that the compilation of the Ordnance Bureau showed the Confederacy did not have weapons for more than 150,000 men, armies of the east and west put together. "I am leaving nothing undone to increase our force; but the old General always comes in the way. He understands nothing, appreciates nothing."

Little Mac was far too expert an operator to allow such an incubus to hamper him for long. By the end of October he had made the snubs and pressures so unendurable that old General Scott asked to be placed on the retired list, and was shipped out of the capital in pouring rain at four o'clock on a pitch-dark morning. The obstacle was now removed; General McClellan was commissioned as General-in-Chief of the Army of the United States. He fully appreciated this apotheosis, as he demonstrated a few nights later, when the President and Secretary of State Seward came to his fine house on Jackson Square on some business. The General was at a wedding when they arrived, so they sat down to wait. They heard the servant announce their presence as McClellan came in, but he went on upstairs and a little later sent down word that he had gone to bed. The next evening the men of Blenker's German division held a grand torchlight procession and a display of fireworks for their leader.

A few days later, the news ran in of a remarkable proceeding off the Bahamas. On November 8 the United States sloop-of-war *San Jacinto* halted the British mail packet *Trent* with a shot across her bows, sent a boarding party, and took out two of her passengers. They were John Slidell, ex-Senator from Louisiana, now commissioner of the Confederate government before the Court of France, and James M. Mason, ex-Senator from Virginia, who had a similar mission to England —two of the stiffest of the secesh lot, whose capture occasioned a perfect outburst of banquets, speeches, cheering, and congratulatory resolutions for Captain Charles Wilkes of the sloop.

But was it a legal act? Seward, Cameron of the War Department, Welles of the Navy, even Attorney-General Bates, thought that it was, and that the inevitable indignant protest from Britain should be gracefully but firmly rejected. They called in the General-in-Chief of the army; and McClellan, who had already told reporters that he was in favor of holding the two prisoners at any cost, wanted to be sure of the legal point. He asked S. L. M. Barlow of New York, a big, florid, Tammany politician-lawyer with down-sweeping mustaches whose acquaintance he had made during the summer. Barlow said the question was complex; he would like a consulting opinion from someone who understood how to find a way through mazes where there was no brightly lighted lamp of legal precedent to guide.

"Whom would you go to?" asked the General, and being told, "Mr. Stanton," approved him at once, as a fellow Democrat, and as a lawyer with a reputation for winning cases. The two attorneys consulted all morning and reached the conclusion that the capture of the Confederate commissioners was so thoroughly illegal that England would be quite right in demanding their release at the point of the sword. McClellan, who seldom accepted any opinion that did not coincide with his own, did not care for this one, but he did like Stanton, whom Barlow brought around for an introduction in the evening.

The question of the commissioners not having been decided in Cabinet that day, there were more consultations, and an intimacy quickly sprang up between the officer of the army and the officer of the law. They were in perfect agreement on the subject of the President, whom Stanton referred to as "the original gorilla," remarking that if DuChaillu had known his business, he would have gone to Springfield, Illinois, instead of to Africa to conduct his researches in anthropology. McClellan was convulsed by the wit of such remarks, and began to be a frequent visitor at the home of his new friend, from which he wrote to his wife late in November: "I have not been at home for some three hours, but am concealed at Stanton's to dodge all enemies in the shape of 'browsing' Presidents, etc."

That "etc." covered wounds. It was not only Mr. Lincoln who pestered the General by interfering in affairs that were none of his business, but the members of the Cabinet, who "bored and annoyed" General McClellan by their requests for information and other importunities. There were "some of the greatest geese in the Cabinet I have ever seen." "I have a set of men to deal with, unscrupulous and false; if possible they will throw whatever blame there is upon my shoulders." The exception was Simon Cameron of the War Department, who sensibly occupied himself with contracts and political contacts, and stopped issuing orders from his own office, so that everything relating to the American army, down to the most insignificant details of recruiting procedure, bore the signature "By command of Major General McClellan."

It was enough to drive the young General to a sickbed (and it did) to have his one friend in the Cabinet fall under a cloud just at this juncture. There was a Congressional Committee on the Conduct of the War. Like all congressional committees, the first duty of this one was to assert the supremacy of the legislative, so they went hunting for smells, and they found a good many of them in Mr. Cameron's department.

There was the matter of the Hall's carbines: sold by the department as useless junk at $2.00 apiece, repurchased by the government at $15.00, condemned and sold again at $3.50, slightly repaired and repurchased at $12.00, then found useless after all. There was the Pennsylvania cavalry command, which reached Louisville in such shape that nearly half its horses (which cost the government $58,200) had to be condemned before the regiment took the field. There was the Pennsylvania Railroad, which charged the government for transporting soldiers nearly double what it charged anyone else, made no allowance for baggage, and then shipped the men in boxcars. There was the fact that when the Senate passed resolutions calling for information on contracts and payments of money, Cameron did not even answer, while weeks and months went by.

To be sure, a certain proportion of this outcry was merely odor chasing. When a delegation of New York and Boston bankers was challenged by Lincoln to produce one single proved case of the Secretary's personal dishonesty, they could do nothing of the kind. But this did not alter the facts that Cameron had no system for running his department, probably failed to answer the Senate's requests for information because he did not have it and was without any means of obtaining it, and was surrounded by the set of beings whose rapacity aroused Stanton's comments as early as mid-June. Which is to say that Simon Cameron had been unable to make the perilous passage from politics to statesmanship; used his office after the manner of a master of the former art to pay for past services and to provide for future ones.

Lincoln loyally stuck by the only member of his Cabinet he had not wished to appoint, but he was uncomfortable about it and it was clear that Cameron constituted a weakness. Then in November Cameron solved the problem by cutting off his own head. His annual report as Secretary of War was due; into it he inserted a clause recommending that the slaves of rebels be armed, and nailed it down with a paragraph of legal argument, which Stanton, as his attorney, put into words:

Those who make war against the Government justly forfeit all rights of property, privilege and security derived from the Constitution and laws against which they are in armed rebellion; and as the labor and service of their slaves constitute the chief property of the rebels, such property should share the common fate of war to which they have devoted the property of loyal citizens. It is as clearly the right of the Government to arm slaves when it may become necessary as it is to use gunpowder or guns taken from the enemy.

This, thought the intricate Cameron, would surely take the more radical abolitionists of Congress off his neck by making him a member of the lodge. But there was a difficulty. The Secretary knew perfectly well that such a statement would never get past Lincoln, who had just dismissed John C. Frémont, general commanding in the West, for putting exactly the same thing into a proclamation. It was nice to conciliate the Radicals; but Kentucky was still uncertain; Missouri, Maryland, and Tennessee had thousands of slaveholding Union men who would very likely tumble into the other camp over the obvious threat of servile war contained in the document. So the old master of political strategy outflanked the President by having the report printed before Lincoln even saw it, sending advance copies to all the newspapers and then to every post office in the country for general distribution.

The plan succeeded in one respect, for the papers printed the report, and everyone learned what Cameron intended to say in it. But Lincoln, no mean strategist himself, recalled the post-office copies telegraphically, cut the offending remarks from the report before sending it to Congress, and wrote Simon Cameron a little note:

"As you have more than once expressed a desire for a change of position I can now gratify you with my view of the public interest. I therefore propose nominating you to the Senate next Monday as Minister to Russia."

Two days later, on January 13, 1862, President Lincoln sent to the Senate the nomination of Edwin M. Stanton as Secretary of War.

"What will you do?" asked the new Secretary's friend, Donn Piatt, when he called that evening.

"Do? I intend to accomplish three things. I will make Abe Lincoln President of the United States. I will force this man McClellan to fight or throw up; and last but not least, I will pick Lorenzo Thomas up with a pair of tongs and drop him from the nearest window."

Lorenzo Thomas was the Adjutant-General.

III

THE question of why Lincoln appointed to one of the most important offices under the United States a man who had attacked and practically villified him is not infrequently asked.*

At the time of the appointment, Lincoln regarded devotion to the Union as one of the highest forms of morality ("I hope I have God on my side, but I must have Kentucky"); and there could be no possible question about Stanton's devotion. Lincoln can hardly have been ignorant of Stanton's communications to Seward while the former Attorney-General was still a member of Buchanan's Cabinet, and this devotion, without

* See also the Appendix, IV: Stanton's Appointment.

regard to its effect on Stanton's private reputation for morality, cannot have failed to impress the President.

In the second place, it was a politically highly desirable step to have a genuine Breckinridge Democrat in the Cabinet just after John C. Breckinridge himself had "gone South." The Douglas Democrats were for the Union and the war, but a good many of the Breckinridge men still needed to be brought in.

This is perhaps of minor weight, and so is the factor of Stanton's acquaintance with McClellan and his position as McClellan's attorney, though it is by no means improbable that Lincoln thought that if anyone could persuade McClellan to move, Stanton would be that man. Of quite another order of importance, however, is Stanton's well-established reputation for incorruptibility. Washington, then as now, was a whispering gallery; very few people can have been ignorant of Thad Stevens' remark that he had said Cameron would not steal a red-hot stove, but he would be glad to retract. By substituting Stanton for Cameron, Lincoln was fully aware that he was strengthening his administration at its weakest point, the one where it had been most under attack. Whatever the new Secretary did, he would do in honesty.

Most decisive of all, he would do it in competence. The War Office demanded a prodigious grasp of detail, and an ability to co-ordinate this detail into a relevant whole. Lincoln had had an impressive demonstration of this in the McCormick Reaper case. (For the moment, never mind the President's wide charity, his ability to forget even insults in view of the end to be achieved; these lie on the surface.) It is perfectly clear that Lincoln never forgot the way in which the details of that case were assembled by Stanton into a coherent pattern. It is quite as clear that he knew all about the California land cases, in which Stanton showed precisely the same qualities.

It would seem, then, that there is little mystery in why the President should appoint to the War Office one of the strongest Union men in Washington, a Breckinridge Democrat, a friend of McClellan, an incorruptible, and a man of unlimited drive and capacity to handle detail. He may have expected that Stanton would be difficult to handle, but some of the men he had already—for instance, Seward, Blair, and Welles—were not exactly putty to the touch.

BACKDROP

Washington Intelligencer

Franklin (Mo.), Aug. 11. Advices from Springfield to Thursday morning last have been received here. No battle has yet been fought since Gen. Lyon took up his position at that point, but one was hourly expected. Five hundred cavalry were ready to move against the enemy on Thursday morning. The Home Guards were also in motion, but the regulars remained in position. The rebels were encamped on Wilson Creek, twelve miles from Springfield (20,000 strong.)

General John C. Frémont to War Department

St. Louis, Aug. 11, 1861. General Lyon's Aid reports an engagement with severe loss on both sides. Gen. Lyon was killed. Col. Sigel is in command. He is moving back in good order from Springfield towards Rolla.

Washington Intelligencer

WAR RUMORS FROM ENGLAND. New York, Dec. 15. The steamship *City of Washington* has arrived with later dates than those brought by the *Europa*. She left Queenstown on the 5th.

The excitement growing out of the seizure of Mason and Slidell was unabated.

The Paris *Temps* repeats the statement that the Emperor

Napoleon has tendered his offices as mediator in the affairs of America.

It is rumored that the steamer *Persia* has been chartered to carry troops to Canada but this is pronounced premature.

BOOK II

The Realization

9

SETTING UP HOUSEKEEPING

H ENRY DAWES of the Dawes Committee dropped in on the President after the appointment was announced to congratulate him on getting such a man as Stanton for his Cabinet, in the next breath making some remark that led Lincoln to say, yes, there were those who had warned him that the new Secretary of War would run away with the whole concern. "We may have to treat him as they are sometimes obliged to treat a Methodist minister I know of out West. He gets wrought up to so high a pitch of excitement in his prayers and exhortations that they are obliged to put bricks in his pockets to keep him down. We may be obliged to serve Stanton in the same way, but I guess we'll let him jump a while first. Besides, bricks in his pockets would be better than bricks in his hat."

Stanton himself would never have approved this method of approval; he submitted to the Presidential jokes with patient resignation, congratulating himself that he "could feel a deep, *earnest* feeling growing up" in the Cabinet. Very likely; there would be some earnest feelings at any table where Stanton sat beside Montgomery Blair, the Postmaster, who detested his politics, and Gideon Welles, who despised the War Secretary's hair-trigger process of thought, instantly translated into action. The grandfatherly Navy man interpreted Stanton's dynamism as evidence of a shallow mind, his ability to work in harness as hypocrisy, and could find no point of contact with a personality that was utterly uninterested in who received credit for an accomplishment. "Blair says he is dishonest," wrote Welles, "that he has taken bribes, and that he is a double dealer. I doubt his sincerity always. He is industrious and driving, but devises nothing, shuns responsibility."

The patriarch of the Cabinet kept these thoughts to his diary—a good plan, since he was so much of an expert at minding his own business that he had not bothered to find out what kind of jumping was going on in that War Department, where Secretary Cameron used to dodder around, borrowing from one man a piece of paper to make a note, from another a pencil to make it with, then putting both in his pocket to be forgotten.

Mr. Welles might have been enlightened if he had spoken with the head of the Washington arsenal, for instance—the day after that gentleman had received from Stanton an order to send to Harpers Ferry some heavy guns, requested by telegraph. In the evening it occurred to the new Secretary of War that the arsenal man was a Cameron appointee; he went round to the building, found it locked and silent, dug up an assistant who said the guns had not gone. No one had the keys; Stanton mobilized a working party, broke down the doors, personally helped haul out the guns, and trucked them to the station. Next morning the official dropped in on Stanton on his way to work. "It was inconvenient, Mr. Secretary, to dispatch those guns yesterday, but if you think it is at all urgent, I will attend to it this morning." Stanton gave him a look: "The guns are now at Harpers Ferry, and you, sir, are no longer in the service of the United States government."

Order Posted in the War Department, January 20, 1862

The War Department will be closed Tuesdays, Wednesdays, Thursdays and Fridays against all business except that which relates to active operations in the field. Saturdays will be devoted to the business of Senators and Representatives; Mondays to the business of the public.

No private interviews, not even with one of Stanton's law partners, who called at his home one evening, and was told to come around at one of the morning hours at the Department, which became so famous. At eleven precisely, the door of the reception room opened, the Secretary came in, walking with quick, catlike steps to a dais where stood a tall desk, and began to ask applicants: "What brings you here?"

Everything brought them there; there were "contractors, claimants, sick, wounded, cranks with inventions, office-seekers, Cyprians after passes, sorrowing widows, brokenhearted fathers, convicts, deserters, dismissed or suspended officers." They presented their cases to the Secretary, who disposed of all with a celerity and ruthless snap judgment wonderful to behold. "He flew at me like a tiger," one of them would report; "He was wonderfully quick and kind," said another.

He could tear up a contract and fling the pieces in the contractor's face; he could pass a white-haired father through to the bedside of his wounded son; he could twit the president of the Wheeling Bridge Company on their old opposition, while approving a claim the bridge man brought; he could also stand with stony face and turn away the parents of a soldier condemned to be shot for desertion. He was the man of war in the place of war.

Lincoln soon heard of what went on at these morning hours and often, when business permitted, with the remark that he was "going to see old Mars quell disturbances," he would stroll over to the War Office to stand silently, watching the human drama flow past.

After the morning hour was over, Stanton washed his face, sprayed cologne into his beard to remove the traces of the unpleasant breaths that had been blown at him, then usually retired to the telegraph office he had established in the library of the Department. There he spent the time until urgent physical necessity for food or sleep forced him to leave—reading messages or reports, writing, telegraphing to governors, officers of the various commands, factories. If Lincoln were not present, Stanton would carry some important communication over to the White House two or three times daily; but more frequently as the war went on, the President came over to sit in the same office, fingering over the sheets of yellow flimsy, sometimes talking and telling stories with the cipher operators, sometimes when things were going badly, lying silent on the couch, waiting for news or daylight.

II

IT WAS in that office that the first brick dropped. There was a man named Thomas T. Eckert, a telegraphic expert, commissioned a captain, and assigned to McClellan's headquarters in the big house on Jackson Square. Reports of operations passed through his hands for delivery to the head of the army. On October 21, 1861, Eckert received a message of unusual importance. A detachment of Union troops had crossed the upper Potomac for an advance toward Leesburg; were ambushed, surrounded, and nearly all cut down.

Among those who fell was Colonel E. D. Baker, whose loss gave the incident its unusual importance; for this Baker was no ordinary colonel, but Abraham Lincoln's intimate friend, eloquent, handsome, intelligent, one of the brightest spirits of the new regime. As Senator from Oregon, he had done much to hold the Pacific coast secure for the Union; speaking in uniform, with his sword across his Senate desk, he denounced John C. Breckinridge's opposition to war measures in terms that led the former Vice-President to leave his Senate seat and join the Confederate army. And now Ned Baker was shot dead; Eckert thought the message announcing his loss was so important that he followed McClellan to the White House and handed it to the general as the President stood by. McClellan glanced over the telegram, stuck it in his pocket, and went on talking about something else.

It was several hours later when Lincoln stopped in at the headquarters telegraphic office on his way to see McClellan and asked Eckert if there were any late dispatches from the front. There were none in the files, said the telegrapher, acutely embarrassed, but unwilling to give the President the death message, when the general who was his immediate superior had not seen fit to do so. Lincoln went on in to McClellan and there received the news that brought him out a moment later with tears rolling down his face. "He almost fell as he stepped into the street."

The President never blamed Eckert in any way, doubtless accepting the delay of the message as just one of McClellan's little ways of putting browsing presidents in their place; but when the Little Napoleon tried a similar assertion of superiority on Stanton, there began to be difficulties. It may be said to have commenced on the day after Stanton's confirmation, when he went round to Jackson Square to open his term in office by a conference with the commanding general. It happened that McClellan was just preparing for his "morning levee" upstairs when Stanton's card came; he went right ahead with the function, which consisted as usual in exchanging compliments with the various aides and the two French princes. Stanton was kept waiting for an hour.

The Secretary was reported as "incensed," and when the ranking officers of the regular army came on their official call the next day, he made them a little speech: "I do not attempt to conceal the pleasure I feel at meeting so fine and capable a body of men; yet we are not here for personal pleasure or gratification, but for a great and holy purpose. Our government is assailed and our country is in peril. We have been called upon to save them and we must, we shall, be equal to the call. It is my work to furnish the means, the instruments, for prosecuting the war for the Union and putting down the rebellion against it. It is your duty to use those instruments, and mine to see that you do use them."

McClellan found the suggestion that his army ought to be moving "offensive," and said so, fearing that he might have "serious difficulties" with this new Secretary, who unlike the satisfactory Cameron, did not leave the management of the war to the man who really understood the business. He would have been still more disturbed if he had known that Stanton was writing to his friend Charles A. Dana of the *New York Tribune:* "This army has got to fight or run away; and while men are striving nobly in the West, the champagne and oysters on the Potomac must be stopped."

The western reference was to the news that came in on the morning after Stanton's speech to the officers, January 21. General George H. Thomas, commanding a small army for the Union in eastern Kentucky, had been attacked in his camp at Mill Spring by Confederate General Zollicoffer and turned on his opponent so fiercely that Zollicoffer was killed and his entire command broken up. A minor victory; but of enormous strategic importance, and the first real triumph the Union had won in the field. Stanton got out a bulletin about it, signing it "by order of the President," which omission of his own name made McClellan morose. But the action point was that the Secretary of War learned of Thomas' victory through the newspapers, McClellan not having bothered to send over the dispatch he received from telegrapher Eckert.

When this sort of thing happened two or three more times, Stanton suspected leaks from McClellan's office to the press, and had one of his new assistant secretaries, Peter H. Watson, make an investigation. Watson reported that Eckert was probably neglecting his duties and certainly withholding important military dispatches from President and Secretary. Stanton sent for Edward S. Sanford, president of the American Telegraph Company, to take over the place and wrote an order for Eckert's dismissal, but Eckert and Sanford were good friends, and so the American Telegraph man persuaded the Secretary to see Eckert and perhaps let him resign instead of sending him out of the service in disgrace. They found Stanton bristling, with a pile of telegrams on his desk. Why had they not been delivered to the Secretary of War when received?

Because he had been ordered to give all military telegrams to the commanding general and to no one else, said Eckert.

One more of McClellan's little games, and this man was apparently one of McClellan's pets. "Well, why have you neglected your duties by absenting yourself from the office so frequently?" Stanton snapped.

This was a harder one to answer; Eckert was just protesting that it was not true in the least, but if Stanton thought so, he begged permission to resign, indeed must be allowed to resign, when he felt an arm over his shoulders, and looked up to see Abraham Lincoln, President of the United States.

Lincoln: "Mr. Secretary, I think you must be mistaken about this young man neglecting his duties, for I have been a daily caller at General McClellan's headquarters for the last three or four months, and I have always found Eckert at his post. I have been there often before breakfast, and in the evening as well, and frequently late at night, and several times before daylight to get the latest news from the army. Eckert was always there, and I never observed any reporters or outsiders in the office."

Stanton looked at his visitor for one moment, then picked out a paper from the pile before him. "I believe this is your resignation, is it not, sir?" he said, and tore it into pieces which drifted to the floor. "I owe you an apology, Captain, for not having gone to General McClellan's office and seen for myself the situation of affairs. You are no longer Captain Eckert; I shall appoint you a major as soon as your commission can be made out."

It was made out by the following day; with it came an order transferring Eckert, with assistants and instruments, to the new telegraph office in the War Department, and directing that only business which concerned the commanding General should be routed through to Jackson Square.

McClellan was appalled, but Eckert's telegraph service speedily became one of the most efficient departments of the service, with wires from each division to Army, from Army to War Department, and an independent corps of linemen, who laid lines whenever the troops moved. Stanton gave orders that the cipher keys should remain in the hands of operators alone, not even generals having the right to see them.

The most characteristic of Lincoln's bricks was the one he dropped in Stanton's pocket over the business of war prisoners. Some of them wanted to get out of their prison pens into Union blue; Lincoln, persuaded that it was a good idea to accept them, issued an order to do so. As soon as Stanton heard of it, he trotted over to the White House with the Provost-Marshal-General, James B. Fry, and began explaining: a procedure unrecognized in international law would subject the men to trial as deserters if captured, with a variety of other reasons against it. "Now, Mr. President, those are the facts and you must see that your order cannot be executed."

But Lincoln had promised—to the men themselves, among others. He sat on the sofa with his long legs crossed, looked solemn, and said: "Mr. Secretary, I reckon you will have to execute that order."

Stanton: "Mr. President, I cannot do it."

Lincoln's voice went a trifle hard. "Mr. Secretary, it will have to be done."

Fry tiptoed out. Just as he reached his own office, so did a messenger with a chit from Stanton: execute the order.

The relations between President and Secretary developed along lines determined by the subordinate's demoniac energy and almost savage devotion to the cause he was serving and the chief's forebearance and trust. Stanton would icily refuse an appeal by the mother of a condemned soldier, then be found in his office, tearfully praying: "Oh, God, help me to do my duty"; but Lincoln would commute the sentence.

The two were so much together that the intellectual and ceremonious Welles agreed with McClellan in suspecting "intrigues" on the Secretary's part, without specifying how an intrigue—which must essentially be based on the withholding or falsification of information—could be operated against a President who was so very accessible to anyone with a complaint or a plea.

There were intrigues occasionally, but only on the level of the Hassler case, and usually by Lincoln. J. J. C. Hassler, a man well known in the Northwest and an acquaintance of several congressmen, was a captain of volunteers who wished to transfer to the regular army. Now under the peculiar system which developed by itself during the war, regular army appointments were held out as rewards instead of the decorations normal in other countries. Even McDowell, in command of the Union forces at Bull Run, was only a brigadier in the regular service, and Henry W. Halleck, commanding all the forces in the West, was a colonel of regulars though a major-general of volunteers. Stanton had refused a transfer into the regulars to his own nephew; when Lincoln came with a delegation of congressmen to present Hassler's request, the Secretary said no and no again, and turned to other business.

Lincoln went back to the White House, told the Captain to resign from the volunteer service, walk across the street and enlist as a private of regulars; then had his commission made out for a promotion to a captaincy. When the papers were brought to Stanton, he "gave the man one of those through-and-through looks"—but he signed.

III

MORE normally President and Secretary were co-operating in dropping bricks in other pockets. Stanton had not been in office a week before he was after Lincoln with a barrage of measures designed to clear up the mess Cameron had left, and the President pushed them rapidly through Congress. On January 22, 1862, a new law authorized the appointment of two assistant secretaries; Stanton chose Peter H. Watson, the lawyer who had been head of the counsel table in the Mc-Cormick Reaper case, and John Tucker, head of the Pennsylvania Railroad, the latter to have authority over contracts for steamers, transports, wagon-trains, and transportation in general. Just what this meant came out a week later, when Congress whipped through a law giving the President authority to take over railroad and telegraph lines when and as needed.

In accordance with this law, the censorship of telegraphic dispatches, which had been under the State Department, was shifted to War. E. S. Sanford, Eckert's friend, became a colonel and head of the activity—an able man, but a great frequenter of grogshops. He drove correspondents half mad by the way he turned their cherished prose into gibberish, and he persuaded Stanton to order the arrest of the editor of the *Sunday Morning Chronicle* for printing information about future military movements. The editor was a big pot and moreover the proprietor of the paper was John W. Forney, secretary of the Senate and Pennsylvania political boss, one of the few Buchanan Democrats who actively supported the war, and so Stanton had to let everybody off after obtaining apologies and promises of better behavior. But it became distinctly more difficult for the Confederates to make their plans on the basis of the Northern press.

D. C. McCallum was appointed military director and superintendent of railroads, "to take possession of all railroads, engines, cars, locomotives"; an appointment that cut almost as deeply as anything Stanton did during the weeks of reorganization, since he himself watched over the roads with the elaborate knowledge of their organization acquired during his preparation of the railroad cases.

Finally, on January 29 came another order which cut still deeper and had effects more lasting:

1st. That no further contracts be made by this department for any article of foreign manufacture that can be produced in the United States.

2d. All outstanding orders for the purchase of arms, clothing, or anything else, in foreign countries are hereby revoked.

3d. All persons claiming to have any contract, order, or authority of whatsoever nature, from this department for furnishing arms, clothing, equipment or anything else to the United States are required within fifteen days of this date to give written notice of such contract, with a statement in writing of what has been done under it.

4th. It is seldom that any necessity can prevent a contract from being reduced to writing, and even when made by telegraph its terms can be speedily written and signed; and every claim founded on any pretended contract, agreement or license now outstanding, of which notice and a copy is not filed in accordance with this order, shall be deemed fraudulent and void.

When this paper came up in Cabinet, Seward fell on the first two paragraphs: "It will complicate the foreign situation," which was the thing he had to think of, what with England still delicate over the *Trent* business, and Louis Napoleon in

France only waiting for a pretext to recognize the Confederacy and maybe try breaking Lincoln's blockade.

"It will have to be issued," answered Stanton, "or very soon there will be no situation to complicate."

He had been talking to Chase and was well buttressed with facts supplied by that ponderous but shrewd financial officer. The war was costing more than a million dollars a day, with a good part of this money flowing abroad in the form of gold; and so little to show for it in the direction of suppressing the rebellion that the price of gold on 'change was rising faster than even the outflow would justify. And what was this money buying? Shoes whose uppers pulled away from the soles after half a day's march, and shoddy clothing of many colors and weaves.

> "I, Lieutenant-Colonel Graham,
> Of the Twelfth, depose and say
> That the coats contractors gave us
> Were of shoddy cloth of grey;
> Only for a day we wore them,
> And they came to pieces then—"

—chanted *Vanity Fair* in recognition of the open scandal, and McClellan's inspectors had to condemn 25,000 infantry coats, which had cost the government $167,750, before anyone put them on.

In arms the situation was, if anything, worse. The great iron foundries of Pittsburgh were pouring out artillery as fast as needed, but the small arms that came to Washington with the first rush of citizen soldiers were so haphazard a lot that in one regiment there were thirty-three types of guns, and in nearly all regiments the really serviceable muskets had to be reserved for the men doing guard mount. Making good the obvious lack was one of the first pressures that fell on Cameron in April, 1861. He rushed agents to Europe to buy all the small arms in sight, which was a commendable display of energy.

But most of the agents were Cameron men, that is, gentlemen who understood everything about controlling the voters in a city ward, and practically nothing about ordnance. On top of this, they worked on commission, a percentage of the amount spent. The result was what might have been expected; the agents got into the minor German states that maintained private armies, and at fancy prices acquired one of the finest collections of antique arms ever assembled—smooth bores dating back to the French Revolution and even to Frederick the Great, guns that would not take American ammunition, or for which the powder had to be specially made.

Stanton's exposition of the situation carried Lincoln with him into approving the order, and there was inaugurated that prodigious process of military-industrial development which is America's chief contribution to the art of logistics. Government arsenals turned out standard arms by mass production methods and private manufacturers competed furiously to produce new designs of weapons, which would give them a certain, if temporary, advantage in an insatiable market.

But it was the last two paragraphs of the order that really caused flutterings in Washington parlors. At the outbreak of the rebellion Cameron had entrusted a character named Alexander Cummings, publisher of the *Philadelphia Bulletin* and the *New York World*, with $2,000,000 and authority to make contracts for more, then sent him to New York to expedite troops and supplies. Cummings' conduct had been singular and his explanations vague; $160,000 of the money turned up in his personal bank account; he had no vouchers. The House passed a resolution censuring Cameron for having trusted him, and though Lincoln defended his Secretary, Washington was still full of men with claims for this or that done on Cummings' sayso. Now they must submit their papers to Stanton, and the prospect made them shudder. But the army marched in good shoes and new blue uniforms and fought with good rifles for all the rest of that long war.

IV

THE new broom swept clean, but there was one corner it could never quite clear up. In it sat the figure of Charles P. Stone, with a face like that of an unhappy prince by Rembrandt. He was a West Pointer, long a resident of Maryland, with his social foot in the Southern camp, and a somewhat passionate man. He had served under Scott in Mexico and became a captain. The General sent for him when things began to look bad during the secession winter and placed him in charge of the District militia; it was Stone who purged the existing formations of secessionists, enlisted new men to the strength of nine companies, drilled them well, and arranged them with the regular troops to cover Lincoln's inauguration.

The influx of new men pushed Stone up rapidly; by the fall of 1861 he was a brigadier-general, at the head of a division on the upper Potomac. In October he was directed to make a demonstration from his camp at Poolesville on the Maryland side, toward the Confederate positions and camp at Leesburg. The division of General George A. McCall had been sent up the river along the Virginia bank as far as Dranesville to cover some mapping operations, and McClellan thought McCall's approach might cause the rebels to leave their Leesburg position.

Stone accordingly sent out a reconnaissance party, which found nothing that night; then followed by sending across the river the Fifteenth and Twentieth Massachusetts. But in the meanwhile McClellan had withdrawn McCall without telling Stone anything about it. The rebels discovered his absence; the two Massachusetts regiments were surrounded, heavily attacked, and wiped out, except for a few who got away by swimming or in a couple of leaky flatboats.

This was the affair of Ball's Bluff, the importance of which was triple. It fell at a time when very little was going on in the war to occupy the attention of honorable members of Congress; one of the most respected honorable members, E. D. Baker, was killed on the battlefield; and the two Massachusetts regiments were silk-stocking formations, largely composed of highly articulate Brahmins. A grandson of Paul Revere, a nephew of James Russell Lowell, and the son of Oliver Wendell Holmes were all hit, and two of them died.

The honorable members reacted and with vigor. It was perfectly evident to them that there had been cowardice, incompetence, or something worse at Ball's Bluff, and they rather felt that the blame lay with Brigadier-General Charles P. Stone. But they wanted positive evidence; so they set up an investigating committee, the Committee on the Conduct of the War, which became permanent, ubiquitous, and irritating. As its purpose was to heat things up, it quite naturally attracted the members of what Lincoln's private secretary used to call "the Jacobin Club"—the fire-eaters, the Radicals, "the infernals." There were four senators, Ben Wade of Ohio, Zachariah Chandler of Michigan, Andrew Johnson of Tennessee, Lyman Trumbull of Illinois; four representatives, D. W. Gooch of Massachusetts, John Covode of Pennsylvania, George W. Julian of Indiana, Moses F. Odell of New York.

Covode was the investigator who stuck so many banderillas in Buchanan's hide during the late administration, but the real leadership of the committee rested with Wade—barrel-chested, vulgar, shrewd, and violent, who kept a sawed-off shotgun in his desk during the secession winter and tried every means he knew to provoke some of the Southern fire-eaters into calling him out, for he was a deadly shot—and with tall, hard-faced Chandler, a Yankee who had made his million as a merchant in Detroit and gave $10,000 of it to buy rifles for the abolitionists in Kansas.

The appetite of this formidable committee was by no means decreased when Secretary Cameron refused to give any information on Ball's Bluff on the ground that it was "not deemed compatible with the public interest." While they were digging up testimony for themselves, the survivors of the battle were writing to Governor John A. Andrew of Massachusetts in a tone of anger and bitterness. They placed the blame for the defeat on Stone, more than suggesting that he had allowed them to be shot up because he did not care to help them. He had employed his troops in capturing fugitive slaves, they said; he had forwarded mail into the Confederate lines; had been warmly received at secessionist homes on both sides of the Potomac; had greeted in his own camp men who later turned out to be rebel officers.

Governor Andrew told his Massachusetts soldiers to disobey any future orders that sent them in pursuit of fugitive slaves. Stone replied with a hot protest against civilian interference in military matters. Andrew sent the correspondence to Senator Charles Sumner of his state, with the remark that Massachusetts would raise no more troops to serve under such officers. Sumner denounced Stone on the floor of the Senate, whereupon Stone was ill-advised enough to write the Senator a letter that practically invited a challenge to a duel and denounced all abolitionists, especially those from Massachusetts, as trouble-making fools.

It was now January; Stanton had become Secretary of War. Wade's committee thought they had in the letter to Sumner evidence of where Stone's true sentiments lay. They summoned him before them, questioned him sharply on the events leading up to Ball's Bluff and, in the manner of Congressional inquisitors, began to edge their remarks with innuendo about Stone's loyalty.

"This is one humiliation I hoped I should never be subjected to," Stone cried at them, furiously. "I raised all the volunteer troops that were here during the seven dark days of last winter. I could have surrendered Washington."

They could extract from him no admissions, and the evidence was too indefinite for formal charges; but Wade saw Stanton, Stanton saw McClellan, then had Stone arrested and sent to solitary confinement at Fort Lafayette in New York harbor. There were no charges. He stayed imprisoned for 189 days, then was released, still without charges and without explanation.

It was an act arbitrary to the point of cruelty, and even Senator Sumner, himself a fairly hard-boiled Radical, thought Stone should be confronted with his accusers. Yet Abraham Lincoln, surely one of the kindest and most just men in history, began writing a letter saying there were no real charges against Stone—then stopped, and never completed it.

For there were real charges, even though the mental pattern of the age could find no words in which to phrase them. At the very best, Stone had managed to make himself the representative of every type of conduct that could not be tolerated in this war. That the conflict could be conducted on the basis of certain courtesies among belligerents was perhaps true; but when these courtesies included social intercourse with disloyalty and the forwarding of mail (if Stone did forward it), the suspicion of espionage is aroused. Such a suspicion is nearly as bad as the thing itself when the object of it is a commanding officer whose military success has been something less than conspicuous.

Moreover, Massachusetts was an abolition state, the Massachusetts soldiers were abolitionists. A general who employed them in the pursuit of fugitive slaves (which Stone did in at least one case) and who denounced them as trouble-makers for objecting was in effect tampering with the loyalty of his own men. They were soldiers required to obey orders, but citizen-soldiers required to obey only military orders, not those which imposed a species of thought-control. Governor Andrew's remark about raising no more troops for such officers made the point with sufficient accuracy. In fact, Stone made the strongest case against himself very nicely by protesting against civilian control of the military.

It was his misfortune that the lines of permissible conduct for officers in a civil war had not been laid down at the time that Wade's committee called him in; and it took the arrest to draw them hard and fast for the rest of the war. But Stone was an unfortunate man, anyway. When he later served with troops again, he did well enough personally, but it was in a disastrous campaign west of the Mississippi which ruined the reputation of everyone in it; so he resigned the army and entered the service of the Khedive of Egypt.

Stanton's final comment was: "To hold one commander in prison untried is less harmful in times of great national distress than to withdraw several good officers from active battlefields to give him a trial. Individuals are nothing; we are contributing thousands of them to save the Union, and General Stone in Fort Lafayette is doing his share in that direction."

BACKDROP

Wool to Scott

Fort Monroe, Sept. 2, 1861. Agreeable to your instructions of the 12th and 21st August last, after consultation with Commodore Stringham, I prepared 860 men, under the command of Major-General Butler, to proceed with the commodore's expedition against some batteries at Hatteras Inlet, North Carolina.

Major-General Butler returned on Saturday morning, when he communicated verbally the following result, viz: captured at the inlet 715 prisoners, 1,000 stand of arms, 30 pieces of cannon, one 10-inch columbiad, a prize brig loaded with cotton, a sloop loaded with provisions and stores, two light-boats, a schooner in ballast, 5 stand of colors.

DuPont to Secretary Welles

Off Hilton Head, Port Royal, Nov. 8, 1861. I have the honor to inform you that yesterday I attacked the enemy's batteries on Bay Point and Hilton Head, and succeeded in silencing them after an engagement of four hours duration, and driving away the squadron of rebel steamers.

The action was begun on my part twenty-six minutes after 9, and at half-past 2 the American ensign was hoisted on the flagstaff of Fort Walker, and this morning at sunrise on Fort Beauregard.

Landing my marines and a company of seamen, I took possession of the deserted ground and held the forts on Hilton

Head till the arrival of General Sherman, to whom I had the honor to transfer its occupation.

General A. E. Burnside to McClellan

Roanoke Island, N.C., Feb. 10, 1862. I have the honor to report that a combined attack upon this Island was commenced on the morning of the 7th by the naval and military forces of this expedition, which has resulted in the capture of six forts, forty guns, over 2,000 prisoners, and upwards of 3,000 small arms.

General S. R. Curtis to War Department

Headquarters, Army of the Southwest, Pea Ridge, Ark., Mar. 9, 1862. On Thursday, the 6th instant, enemy commenced the attack on my right, assailing and following the rear guard of the detachment under General Sigel. During the night I became convinced he had moved to attack my right or rear. Therefore, early on the 7th, I ordered a change of front to the right. The enemy at 11 a.m. commenced an attack on my right. The fight continued during the day, the enemy being entirely repulsed with the loss of the commander, General McCulloch.

The plan of attack in the center was gallantly carried forward. Before the day closed I was convinced the enemy had concentrated his main effort on my right. I therefore commenced another change of front, so as to face the enemy. The change was fully in progress when at sunrise on the 8th my right and center renewed the firing, which was immediately answered by the enemy. My left, under General Sigel, moved close to the hills occupied by the enemy, driving him from the heights. I immediately ordered the center and right wing forward, the right turning in the left of the enemy. This final position inclosed the enemy in the arc of a circle. A charge of infantry extending throughout the whole line completely routed the whole rebel force.

10

THE MIND OF A SOLDIER

NO matter what else came up, the chief preoccupation of those early days of Stanton's secretaryship was with those "serious difficulties" McClellan had anticipated. The young General, who had almost gaily assumed the task of saving the country (he thought at one point that he might have to assume a military dictatorship, and after the saving had been completed, commit suicide to preserve liberty), was haunted by men who had not the slightest conception of military operations. "The people think me all-powerful," he wrote to his wife. "Never was there a greater mistake. I am thwarted and deceived by these incapables at every turn."

The incapables wanted him to clear out the batteries by which the rebels had closed the lower Potomac to navigation, for instance. The General explained that the batteries were merely there as an extension of Johnston's Confederate army at Manassas; as soon as Johnston was driven from his position, they would go away. The incapables could not seem to understand that this settled the matter; they only came back at him with requests to reopen the Baltimore and Ohio Railroad, where it had been cut at Harpers Ferry. McClellan explained, patiently, modestly, that this would involve a dispersion of forces.

Then they began prodding him to advance on Manassas; could not be made to see that the Virginia roads would be impassable for artillery or wagon trains before spring, and that in any case, the Confederates were waiting there with

200,000 men and hundreds of guns. The Pinkerton espionage organization made the researches which established this fact —a remarkable and efficient network set up by the Chicago

The Region West of Washington

detective, with lines to the highest quarters in Richmond, a secret organization of Negroes who met in cellars of the rebel capital, and a courier who had so worked himself into the confidence of the Confederate government that he was carrying their secret messages between Richmond and Baltimore. In short, the incapables simply could not be made to see that the country could only be saved by General McClellan and in a military way. They persisted in the absurd view that the demands of civil government and even of politics should have some influence on military decisions.

While the General lay sick in bed, refusing to let browsing Presidents visit him, Lincoln even had the temerity to go to Montgomery Meigs, Quartermaster-General of the army, with: "General, what shall I do? The people are impatient; Chase has no money, and he tells me he can raise no more; the General of the Army has typhoid fever. The bottom is out of the tub. What shall I do?"

Meigs sensibly advised that if the President could not see the General-in-Chief, he ought to call on some of the subordinates; and so Lincoln summoned McDowell and William B. Franklin, generals of division, who might be supposed to represent both sides of whatever military opinion there was, since Franklin was a good friend of McClellan's and McDowell was the man he had superseded.

The President remarked that if McClellan did not want to use the Army of the Potomac, he would like to borrow it, and asked the generals about the possibility of opening operations soon. McDowell thought the roads might permit a march against Johnston's position within three weeks; Franklin did not wish to talk, but being pressed, rather favored a plan to transfer the army by water to the mouth of the York River for direct operations against Richmond. Both officers agreed that the forces were strong enough to make some forward move; it was merely a question of which one.

The news of this interview, passed on to McClellan,* was a better physic than any the doctors could offer. Two days later the General was out of bed for another conference of commanders. Some of the Cabinet were present, but not Stanton, whose appointment did not go to the Senate until the next morning. Lincoln asked McDowell to repeat his remarks; McDowell did so, with an apology to McClellan for

---

* He says the news came through Stanton, but this is something more than doubtful. It was before Stanton's appointment, at a time when he was not in the secret of Presidential interviews of any kind.

the necessity of offering his opinion to the Commander-in-Chief of the Army.

"You are entitled to have any opinion you please," said McClellan, coldly. He could see the point now; there was a conspiracy to oust him from his command for the benefit of McDowell, the Chase man. This was promptly confirmed when Chase, in his usual peremptory tone, asked the General what he intended doing with the army, and when he intended doing it.

There was a long silence; McClellan said that a movement in Kentucky was to precede any from Washington. After another period of silence, during which everyone seemed waiting for more, the General added that he was unwilling to divulge his plans, always believing that in military matters, the fewer persons who knew them, the better. This was true enough to bite; those present all knew that the elegant hostess, Mrs. Rose Greenhow, was at that moment in Old Capitol prison for having passed on to the Confederates advance notice of McDowell's move toward Bull Run. Lincoln asked whether McClellan had counted on any particular time—not that he wanted to know what it was, but whether McClellan had a time in mind. McClellan said he did, and the meeting adjourned.

But this was not good enough for Meigs, who came around later to urge McClellan to speak out definitely before the Cabinet, giving plan and date. The Quartermaster was an extremely able man who, by the nature of his position, had a good deal of contact with Congress and the civilian polity generally, and he knew that the country was running a temperature. Affairs vis-à-vis England and France were still delicate, and the Confederacy must not be allowed to establish its independence by mere absence of action taken against it. McClellan said that if he told the President his plans they would be printed in the *New York Herald* the next morning, and began to talk about the conspiracy against himself.

But when the conference reassembled the next evening—Stanton still not present—here was Postmaster-General Montgomery Blair, who disliked Chase and the Radicals almost as much as McClellan did, urging the General to be more specific.

Unwilling to let down his best supporter in the Cabinet (now that Cameron was gone), McClellan exposed certain details. His plan was the one adumbrated by General Franklin—load the army aboard transports, take it down to Urbanna on the Rappahannock, and strike through to Richmond behind Johnston. This will make use of Union sea power, the Confederates would be forced into a hasty retreat from their powerful, fortified lines at Manassas, and the ensuing battle would be fought at the gates of Richmond, where it would be decisive.

When? As soon as the roads in southern Virginia had dried enough to take the weight of armies.

This silenced, if it did not altogether satisfy, the Cabinet. But it did nothing to smooth out those other incapables of the Committee on the Conduct of the War who, of course, were not informed of the plan. They hauled McClellan in and extracted from him the statement that there were only two bridges across the Potomac at Washington, whereas military strategy requires a commander to safeguard any retiring movement he may have to make while attacking an enemy.

Zach Chandler's traplike jaw sprang open. "General McClellan," he snapped, "if I understand you correctly, before you strike at the rebels you want to be sure of plenty of room so that you can run in case they strike back."

"Or in case you get scared," sneered Ben Wade from beside him.

It was a painful, a humiliating, an unbearable contrast to the cheers that greeted the young Napoleon whenever he moved through the camps, and it is perhaps not surprising that there should arise in the General's mind some itching doubt as to what would really happen when he put his glory to the proof —a doubt that could only be assuaged by demanding the means of certain, not probable, victory.

Under the circumstances, it was peculiarly cruel for McClellan that just as the Pinkerton reports showed that the force in Johnston's Manassas lines had grown to 240,000, the Secretary of War should have General Ben Butler compile a return on the strength of the rebel army from various sources, and that it pretended to prove that there were only 70,000 Confederates across the Potomac. Butler, of course, was merely one of the incapables near the center of gravity of the administration, but that Stanton had listened to him probably meant he had joined the conspiracy.

II

CHASE says it was Lincoln, on the urging of Stanton, who precipitated the next crisis by calling in his private secretary on January 27 and dictating "General War Order No. 1," which directed that the military and naval forces of the United States move on the enemy by February 22. Just what this meant appeared four days later, after McClellan had put his plan for a movement on Richmond via Urbanna into writing, and it had been disappointingly disapproved by the Cabinet. On January 31 the President issued a "Special War Order" for McClellan alone—"that all the disposable forces of the Army of the Potomac, after safely providing for the defense of Washington, be formed into an expedition for the immediate object of seizing and occupying a point upon the railroad, southwestward of Manassas Junction, all details to be at the discretion of the General-in-Chief, and the expedition to move before or on the twenty-second day of February."

McClellan thought he saw the hand of Stanton in this imposition, and he was probably right. But he stuck manfully to his task, working for three whole days on a long paper which explained how brilliant and unexpected his own proposed move would be. It drew a short reply:

Major-General McClellan:
    If you will give me satisfactory answers to the following questions, I shall gladly yield my plan to yours.
    1st. Does not your plan involve a greatly larger expenditure of *time* and *money* than mine?
    2d. Wherein is victory *more certain* by your plan than mine?
    3d. Wherein is victory *more valuable* by your plan than mine?
    4th. In fact, would it not be *less* valuable in this, that it would

break no great line of the enemy's communications, while mine would.

5th. In case of disaster, would not a retreat be more difficult by your plan than mine?

Yours truly,
A. Lincoln

Of course, such a communication from a man who was a civilian and therefore ignorant of the art of war had to be answered by another long essay, very educational. The General explained that the terrain of southern Virginia was far better than that in the north for offensive purposes, the roads in the first region being passable in all seasons, the soil more sandy, the ground more level, the woods less dense. He was "by no means certain" of beating the enemy at Manassas, but along his own line success was sure. "The worst coming to the worst," Fortress Monroe at the mouth of the James could be used as a base and we can "operate with complete security, although with less celerity and brilliance of results" than by Urbanna. As for Lincoln's complaints that Congress and the country were becoming impatient: "I believe that the mass of the people have entire confidence in us. I am sure of it. Let us then look only to the great result to be accomplished and disregard everything else."

The General regarded this document as a masterpiece and said long later that it had convinced Lincoln. He was happily spared further pressure from the Committee on the Conduct of the War by the fact that just at this juncture the Union river gunboats under Flag-Officer Foote shelled into submission Fort Henry on the Tennessee, while its land face was carried by some troops under an unknown brigadier named Grant. The dispatch announcing the event was read in Congress amid demonstrations of applause; New York was all hung with flags, men cheered on the streets of Philadelphia, and St. Louis reported that the drinking saloons were filled with Union men imbibing congratulatory cocktails.

But three days later, on February 9, the confounded Committee woke up again. It seemed that they had been nagging Stanton about the blockade of the lower Potomac and the continued interruption of the Baltimore and Ohio Railroad. The cloture of the river was not only an inconvenience; it was having a most unpleasant effect on the government's ability to obtain loans in Europe; the severance of the railroads made impossible direct communication between Washington and the West. Stanton told the Committee that there was never a night without his cheek's blushing with shame at this double disgrace upon the nation. He had already pressed the General pretty strongly about it, and McClellan had placed General Hooker's division, down opposite the rebel batteries, under preparatory orders to clear them from the river—but he would bring McClellan in and let him make his own explanation.

(As a matter of fact, Stanton had done more than press McClellan; the Baltimore and Ohio had become a particular project of his. Its president was a man named John W. Garrett, of Baltimore, wealthy and with strong social connections all through the South, smelling odoriferous of secession himself, but bearing the reputation of a not altogether unreasonable being. Stanton called him in soon after taking office and said: "Baltimore is largely a secession city, but it is being ruined and your railroad is being ruined by the rebels. Now I will rebuild the parts of the railroad which may be destroyed by the rebels and use the line if you will throw the weight of all your influence for the Union." They shook hands on it; Garrett was making good nicely on his part of the bargain, and now it was up to Stanton to be as exact.)

Before the Committee, McClellan demonstrated that he could learn a lesson as well as any other man by being soldierly, direct, and positive. He had just been seeing what could be done about those two matters, he said; their achievement was not a matter of weeks, but of days.

The Committee called the interview very satisfactory. They might have been somewhat less pleased had they known that when McClellan left their chambers, it was to send a telegram revoking Hooker's authority to cross the river and clean out the lower Potomac batteries. As to the Baltimore and Ohio project, Stanton's personal interest in it had become so acute that he very likely harried the young General about it in a manner the latter felt unable to resist. It took McClellan only eleven days—lightning speed for him—to work out a plan for a demonstration up the Shenandoah Valley by a reinforced division. After the movement the division would stand as a permanent outpost on the Virginia side, supported by a bridge built on canal boats from the Chesapeake and Ohio canal, which would be locked into the river at Harpers Ferry.

The plan was ready just in time to take McClellan away from the capital on February 22, and thus to avoid embarrassing questions about why he had not met the date named in "Special Order No. 1." He may not have had this in mind, though he can hardly have been ignorant of the little incident when he sent one of the glittering staff officers to explain to the President why it would be impossible to move on time. "Why?" asked Lincoln. "The pontoon trains are not ready," said the staff man, diplomatically. "Why in hell and damnation *ain't* they ready?" demanded the President, and went on with some writing that had been interrupted, driving his pen a little faster than usual.

In any case, the thundering piece of news that came off the wires on February 16 had once more taken the limelight off McClellan's doings. The unknown Grant had marched his men from Fort Henry across a neck of land to the great rebel stronghold of Fort Donelson on the Cumberland—so strong a hold that it had driven off the ironclads that took Henry, with guns dismounted and engines disabled. There was a battle across ground spotted with snow and frozen sleet; the rebels were driven into the works, some of the works taken. They asked for a parley: "No terms but immediate and unconditional surrender will be accepted. I propose to move immediately upon your works" were the words with which the Union general made himself a known Grant; and captured the fort with an army of 13,838 men.

Even a civilian could see by the map that the forward line of the Confederacy across Kentucky was broken. "Men embraced each other on the streets"; bands played through the streets of Trenton; in Milwaukee all the stores and offices closed; Stanton read the dispatch to the assembly at his morning hour and the room broke into cheering. Congress adjourned; in New York business stopped on the Merchants'

Exchange while the news was read and everybody sang "The
Star-Spangled Banner"; and Horace Greeley launched one of
his most flamboyant editorials:

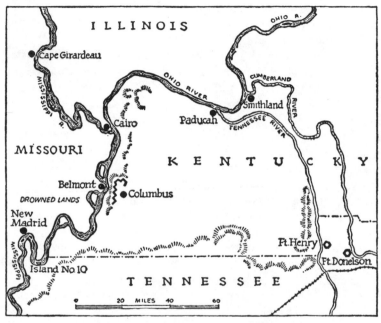

The Kentucky Campaign—February 1862

While every honest heart rises in gratitude to God for the victories which afford so glorious a guaranty of the national salvation,
let it not be forgotten that it is to Edwin M. Stanton, more than
to any other individual, that these auspicious events are now due.
Our generals in the field have done their duty with energy and
courage; our officers, and with them the noble democracy of the
ranks, have proved themselves worthy sons of the Republic; but it
is by the impassioned soul, the sleepless will and great practical
talents of the Secretary of War that the vast power of the United
States has now been hurled upon our treacherous and perjured
enemies to crush them to powder. We cannot overlook the fact
that, whereas the other day all was doubt, distrust and uncertainty;
the nation despairing almost of its restoration to life; Congress
the scene of bitter imputations and unsatisfactory apologies; the

army sluggish, discontented and decaying, and the abyss of ruin and disgrace yawning to swallow us; now all is inspiration, movement, victory and confidence. In one word the nation is saved; and while with ungrudging hands we heap garlands on the defenders, let a special tribute of affectionate admiration be paid to the minister who organized the victory which they have won.

Whatever others might think of this blare of off-key trumpets, it touched the object of the praises nearly:

Stanton to Greeley, for publication

Sir,—I cannot suffer undue merit to be ascribed to my official action. The glory of our recent victories belongs to the gallant soldiers and officers that fought the battles. No share of it belongs to me.

Much has recently been said of military combinations and "organizing victory." I hear such phrases with apprehension. They commenced in infidel France with the Italian campaign, and resulted in Waterloo. Who can organize victory? We owe our recent victories to the spirit of the Lord, that moved our soldiers to rush into battle, and filled the hearts of our enemies with terror and dismay. The inspiration that conquered in battle was in the hearts of the soldiers, and from on high; and wherever there is the same inspiration, there will be the same results. Patriotic spirit with resolute courage in officers and men is a military combination that never failed.

We may well rejoice at the recent victories, for they teach that battles are to be won now, and by us, in the same and only manner that they were ever won by any people, since the days of Joshua—by boldly pursuing and striking the foe. What, under the blessing of Providence, I conceive to be the true organization of victory and military combination to end this war was declared in a few words by General Grant's message to General Buckner,—"I propose to move immediately upon your works."

III

THUS came February 22, 1862, the day of the general offensive, and the only news on the Potomac was that Willie Lincoln, the President's little son, was dead of typhoid fever, and all celebration of the holiday canceled. But four days later, Stanton was pulled from bed by a telegram from General McClellan: a bridge had been "splendidly thrown" across the Potomac at Harpers Ferry; 8,500 infantry, 2 squadrons of cavalry, and 18 guns were on the Virginia side, "ready to resist an attack."

It may have occurred to Stanton to wonder why an invading army should want to resist an attack, but, before he could inquire into General McClellan's peculiar concept of offensive war, there was another telegram. The General had discovered that his carefully assembled canal boats were six inches too wide to pass the locks into the Potomac; as the detachment on the south bank would have no line of retreat without the permanent bridge, he had withdrawn the troops and called the whole enterprise off. The cost to the government was a million dollars; the sole result of the expedition was to give rise to the only witticism of which Salmon P. Chase was ever accused. He said the movement had died of lockjaw.

On February 25 Union gunboats, cruising far into the heart of the Confederacy, captured Nashville, but General McClellan wrote a memo saying he was well satisfied with what had been accomplished at Harpers Ferry, and understood Lincoln was, too. He remained satisfied until a rather painful interview with the President, early on the morning of March 8. Lincoln said he wished to talk about "a very ugly matter" and then hung fire. The more quickly approached, the better, said the General. Lincoln mentioned the Harpers Ferry fiasco, listened to McClellan's usual adroit and unconvincing explanations, pronounced himself at ease, since to have said anything else would only have produced more words, and turned to the ugly matter.

The big objection to the plan for moving the army down the bay, said the President, was that it would leave Washington uncovered. The enemy might seize the capital by a sudden thrust, and that would mean recognition of the Confederacy by the European powers and the end of everything. Now it was being suggested, by people whose suspicions had to be

taken into account, that McClellan was inviting the blow—
leaving the capital unprotected by treasonable design.

The little General sprang to his feet and, in a manner which
he himself later described as "not altogether decorous," shouted
that Lincoln would have to retract that statement; he would
never permit the word "treason" to be coupled with his name.
Lincoln said he did not believe a word of the rumor himself
and was making no accusations, merely telling McClellan what
other people were saying. After the General fizzed a bit more,
the President apologized, and McClellan left, wondering "how
a man of Lincoln's intelligence could give ear to such abominable nonsense." He was inclined to place the origin of the canard
with Stanton, but he was wrong; the Secretary had only taken
to Lincoln a letter giving an account of McClellan's initiation
into the pro-Confederate Knights of the Golden Circle, so cir-
cumstantial, so detailed, that it was worth examination, if only
to decide that it was a pack of lies.

Senator Browning, for one, had been asking the President
if he still believed in McClellan's fidelity; and he was not the
only one. Moreover, the General did not stop to consider that
the men who produced the abominable nonsense were the men
running the country that kept his army going, and they would
have to be satisfied somehow. But such a consideration would
have clashed with the theory by which the General had begun to account for his difficulties. Stanton had not only joined
the conspiracy against him, but had become the head of it;
working hand in glove with the Radicals of the Committee on
the Conduct of the War, he was poisoning the Presidential
mind. The Secretary's regular policy was "to prevent personal
interviews between the President and myself. He was thus
enabled to say one thing to the President and exactly the
opposite to me."

The General had been clever enough to outflank the objections to his plan of campaign by summoning a council of
war of his twelve division commanders to consider the matter.
It was meeting as he left the White House after the painful interview. Only two of the generals had ever heard of the pro-

posed movement by water, but as soon as it was broached, the group reacted in a manner quite satisfactory to McClellan. For the plan: H. M. Naglee (as deputy for Hooker, not present), W. F. Smith, Louis Blenker, George A. McCall, William B. Franklin, Fitz John Porter, Andrew Porter, E. D. Keyes; opposed: John G. Barnard, S. P. Heintzelman, Irvin McDowell, E. V. Sumner; total: eight to four. Naglee, as recorder, led the group around to report to the President, finding him "quite unwell and exceedingly nervous" after his talk with the General-in-Chief.

Lincoln seemed surprised at the weight of the vote in favor of the McClellan plan; Stanton came in and began cross-examining the generals, who became more and more uncomfortable as it appeared from his line of questioning that he was not only opposed to the maneuver, but well buttressed with reasons against it.

After the officers had gone, Lincoln said: "We can do nothing else than adopt this plan and discard all others; with eight out of twelve division commanders approving it we cannot reject it and adopt another without assuming all the responsibility in case of the failure of the one we adopt."

Stanton: "I agree with your conclusions, but I dissent from your arithmetic. The generals who dissented from the proposed plan of campaign are independent of the influence of the commanding general, while all the rest owe their positions to him and are especially under his influence, so that instead of eight to four there was but one against four. You, as a lawyer, in estimating the value of testimony, look not only to the words of the witness, but to his manner and all the surrounding circumstances. Now, who are the eight generals upon whose votes you are going to adopt the proposed plan of campaign? All made so since General McClellan assumed command, and upon his recommendation, influenced by his views, and subservient to his wishes."

Lincoln was silent for a while, considering. Then he said: "I admit the full force of your objections, but what can we do? We are civilians—we should justly be held accountable for any disasters if we set up our opinions against those of experienced military men in the practical management of a campaign. The campaign will have to go on as decided by the majority."

So McClellan won his usual victory in argument; but before the busy day was up, he learned that it had been accompanied by defeat on another issue. Ever since the previous fall Lincoln had been urging the General to organize the twelve unwieldy divisions of the Army of the Potomac into corps, instead of trying to run everything himself. No, no, said McClellan, I do not wish to promote generals to corps commands until they have proved themselves in battle at the head of divisions.

(Possibly it was because he could not bear to see any authority intervening between himself and the army he had come to regard almost as a personal possession; possibly out of that same preoccupation with the Napoleonic legend that led him to issue proclamations beginning "Soldiers!" Napoleon had neither made corps nor corps commanders until he had seen his men in the field.)

Now, as he reached the office in Jackson Square, General McClellan discovered an order, signed by the President, dividing the army into four corps of three divisions each. The General had not even been consulted on it, and to make things infinitely worse, the corps commanders named were McDowell, Sumner, Heintzelman, Keyes—three of them men who had voted against his plan of campaign in the council of war. For that matter Keyes had only approved it with the condition that the rebel batteries be first cleared from the lower Potomac.

General McClellan knew exactly where to place the blame for this overriding of his expressed wishes. He placed it on Stanton; and he was perfectly right.

IV

THE track now seemed to be cleared. That night a special order was issued for the move "down the Potomac, choosing a new base at Fortress Monroe or anywhere between here and there," with stipulations:

1. To leave in or about Washington such a force as would in the opinion of the General-in-Chief and the corps commanders give the city complete security. (Four days later McClellan met with the corps commanders, and the five men agreed that 40,000 to 55,000 men would serve this purpose.)

2. Not to move more than two corps until the Potomac should be unobstructed.

3. To begin by March 18.

But next day, the day on which the news arrived that a Confederate ironclad had destroyed two Union ships in Hampton Roads, as McClellan was working out the details of his move with Stanton and the President, there came from the telegraph tidings that threw everything open again. The Confederate batteries along the Potomac had been abandoned and Manassas was evacuated!

McClellan excused himself from the meeting and went across the river to verify the report. Before evening Stanton had a message from him: "The troops are in motion"—in pursuit of the retreating enemy. All next day the streets of Washington rumbled with wagons and artillery making for the Long Bridge, while bands blared through a pouring rain. Then the army was gone.

That "pursuit" had some peculiar results. For the soldiers it was a kind of ecstatic picnic down to Manassas and Centerville, where they found the place utterly desolate, stinking with blue and yellow smoke from the huge stores of bacon Johnston had burned. Local people and Negroes united in saying that the Confederates had never had more than 50,000 men in the place, and during the last three months, not over 30,000. There were correspondents with the army; they wandered around the famous plateau of the battle and discovered that most of the 300 field guns and 30 pieces of siege artillery, which the Pinkerton reports described as anchoring the rebel lines, were Quaker guns—wooden simulacra of cannon, painted black and mounted on carriage wheels. Or there were embrasures with "no platforms on which to work guns, nor any appearance of there having been any."

McClellan inveighed against "the ignorance which has led

some journals to trifle with the reputation of an army," but not very loudly, because he had other troubles. Not the least of them was the fact that on March 11, while he was still at Manassas, there came an order (obviously promoted by the sly Stanton) relieving him as General-in-Chief of the Army of the United States and restricting him to the command of the Army of the Potomac, now that he was actually in the field.

He felt it as a demotion. "I regret that the rascals are after me again," he wrote to his wife. "The idea of persecuting a man behind his back!"

One of the French princes met him on the bridge on the way back to Washington. The General was riding alone, and he looked anxious, one might have said not at all like a commander who had been conducting a pursuit. In fact, McClellan felt compelled to drop even the word "pursuit" when he made his report, saying the march "afforded a good intermediate step between the quiet and comparative comfort of the camps around Washington and the rigors of active operations."

But the active operations at last, at long last, were to begin. The troops started embarking on March 17, after the General had issued to them an address, in which he informed them that he would "demand of you great, heroic exertions, rapid and long marches, desperate combats, privations perhaps. We shall share all these together, and when this war is over we shall return to our homes, and feel that we can ask no higher honor than the consciousness that we belonged to the Army of the Potomac."

It was very well received and nobody noticed that it was practically a translation of one of Napoleon's proclamations to the Army of Italy.

11

I MUST HAVE MORE TROOPS

WHEN McClellan was relieved as General-in-Chief of the Army, Lincoln was all for letting a man worthy of the place develop. In the meanwhile, someone had to sign orders, so Stanton became the titular head, and as such, sat in on the detailed planning of the campaign. A special military advisor to President and Secretary was found in Ethan Allen Hitchcock, grandson of the hero of Vermont, a veteran general of forty years' service. His chief value was his knowledge of technical terms and procedures; he was not much interested in war or even the nation, having become one of those strange New England mystics, esoteric philosopher and metaphysician, author of books on alchemy and essays to prove that Shakespeare and Dante had a special order of knowledge, which they concealed from the vulgar in a species of cryptogram within their works.

The plan of campaign was rather complex, and was affected by a general military departmental reorganization which took place at the same time. Everything west of a north-and-south line through Knoxville, Tennessee, was erected into the Department of the Mississippi under General Henry W. Halleck who, as viewed from Washington in March, 1862, had been the organizer of the victories in the west. Everything east of the crests of the Alleghanies fell into the department of McClellan's Army of the Potomac. The territory between Potomac and West became the Mountain Department, commanded by General John Charles Frémont, "the Pathfinder," first presidential candidate of the Republican party, who had made such a fool of himself in St. Louis, but, by the same token, so much a hero to all good abolitionists that Lincoln simply had to find a command for him.

The Frémont force was to be used for a drive southwest along the valleys into eastern Tennessee, where Union sentiment was strong, and where also there was an important lateral railroad along the line Chattanooga-Knoxville-Lynchburg-Richmond. This command was to be strengthened by Blenker's division of Germans from the Army of the Potomac, men between whom and Frémont there lay a deep bond of *gemütlichkeit*. McClellan did not like the loss of a division, and especially of this one, which always received him at its headquarters by opening champagne, and he liked it still less when Lincoln said that political pressure made the shift necessary; wrote it down that the President was a poor thing, weak of will.

Out in the Shenandoah Valley, various formations had been assembled into a corps under General Nathaniel P. Banks, a tall former Governor of Massachusetts. There was not much rebel opposition in the valley, so Banks was instructed to send part of his men through the Blue Ridge to Manassas, in furtherance of a new stipulation that enough force be kept at that communications center to prevent its repossession by the Confederates.

Now that Johnston had retreated from Manassas to a point south of the Rappahannock, McClellan decided to give up the Urbanna project, which would no longer place him in the enemy's rear, and advance along the "less brilliant" line between the York and James rivers. Three corps would move by water; the other, 30,000 men under McDowell, would march cross-country to Fredericksburg, waiting McClellan's call—to join him on the peninsula, or to operate independently behind the Confederate flank while their main body faced the Union gross. McClellan wanted, and would have, between 100,000 and 140,000 men for his campaign.

On his table of organization these included part of the troops garrisoning Fortress Monroe, under General John E. Wool, a veteran of more than twice McClellan's age, who had fought with something more than credit in the Mexican War. From the beginning he co-operated heartily, waiving his seniority to take McClellan's orders, making all the arrangement for the debarkation and encampment at the fort. With his help the troops were quickly set ashore; the General joined them on April 2, and ordered that the advance on Richmond begin on April 5, in two columns moving up the parallel roads of the peninsula.

Then it began to rain, and General McClellan discovered that the roads he had praised as passable in all seasons, one of the main reasons for preferring his own plan of campaign, were not quite up to his advertisement. It was hard for the infantry to move; the wagons and artillery could not move in any practical sense, and this was particularly bad, since the Confederates "evinced a determination to hold Yorktown" (as the young General put it in his dispatch) by opening fire with cannon.

It also rained a series of messages which left General McClellan in despair. Before leaving Washington, he had found from the returns that General Wool's garrison amounted to 15,000 men; asked that 10,000 of them be organized into a division under General Joseph K. F. Mansfield and added to the Army of the Potomac, while Wool and his fortress should also fall under McClellan's orders. This was accorded, and Wool himself offered no objection. But the nasty question of the *Virginia* (ex-*Merrimac*) and Norfolk and her possible interruption of water communications kept coming up, and though the Navy Department thought she could be beaten in another fight, she remained a menace to the army. The logical step was to cut the base from under her by an amphibious expedition for the capture of Norfolk. But this could hardly be done by McClellan from behind his back, while campaigning up the peninsula; and the army's rear areas needed protection and control. So an order of April 3 made Wool independent again.

This left "me without any base of operations under my own control," said McClellan, without explaining why an army on the move needed a base of operations under its own control.

Worse yet; on the same day, he had the news that Stanton had stopped recruiting.

But these were pinpricks beside the thunderbolt that fell on the following morning.

General McClellan:
    By order of the President, General McDowell's army corps has been detached from the force under your immediate command and the General is ordered to report to the Secretary of War; letter by mail.

McClellan thought that taking McDowell away from him was "the most infamous thing that history has recorded." It was obvious to him that this was another piece of Stanton's machinations to make him fail; but actually, it all traced to a small battle and his own somewhat peculiar theories of military arithmetic.

On March 23, before McClellan took ship for the peninsula, Stonewall Jackson led 5,000 men down the Shenandoah Valley and attacked a brigade of Banks' command at Kernstown. The Confederate intelligence was faulty, the Yankees had twice as many men as they were expected to have, and Jackson was soundly beaten, for the first, last, and only time in his life, but he said: "The most essential fruits of the battle are ours"— and he was right. McClellan had a quick conference with Banks; the earlier plan was modified by leaving that officer's whole corps in the valley, while troops were drawn from the Washington forts to hold the Manassas outpost.

McClellan then went down to Fortress Monroe, and drew a return showing that he had met the stipulation about making Washington absolutely secure by leaving 73,846 men in and around the capital. This return reached Stanton on April 2; and the more he analyzed the figures, the less he was impressed. McClellan had included Banks' 35,000 in the Shenandoah, who were a good deal farther from Washington than was Johnston's army. He had included several regiments which were not in Washington at all, but back in the state capitals, where they were being organized. He had included Blenker's division, which was only in Washington while waiting for a train to take it to Frémont. He had included the 13,000 men currently in the forts, but Brigadier-General James S. Wadsworth, who commanded those forts, had already been to the War Department with a complaint that McClellan had drafted off all the trained troops for his campaign and replaced them with raw recruits from the north who were without discipline and did not know how to handle cannon. Stanton promptly tested this by having a general alarm given, as for an attack; it took three hours for 4,000 men to assemble, a good half of them without ammunition.

In fact, the real total of men in and around the capital totted up to only 28,000, even including Blenker, and many of these could only be called fighting men by some exercise of the imagination. In addition to the decision of the assembled corps commanders on the numbers required for the defense of the capital, there was in the files a report from McClellan himself, dated in January: it said that he could only undertake a forward movement with 75,000, because Washington would not be safe unless there were 58,000 left to defend it. Stanton took the relevant papers around to General Hitchcock and to Lorenzo Thomas, Adjutant-General of the Army (whom he had not yet succeeded in dropping out the window with a pair of tongs), and asked one question: Have the President's orders regarding the protection of Washington and Manassas been obeyed?

They reported instantly and positively that the orders had not been obeyed; as instantly, Lincoln ordered McDowell not to move from where he was, and created for him a new military department, Department of the Rappahannock.

At once the campaign descended into one of lower mathematics, in which most of the engagements were fought on paper. McClellan opened it with a long dispatch on the day after he received the order withholding McDowell, saying that he was reduced to frontal attack on a very strong line at Yorktown, and begging that if he could not have the whole of McDowell's corps, he might at least be granted General William B. Franklin and his division. Franklin had stood near the top of his class at the Academy; he was an engineer, cautious as a soldier, but of extraordinarily keen mind, and with no little power of self-expression. McClellan and he were warm friends.

This was followed by a document for the record, in which McClellan maintained that he would have only 85,000 troops when all en route reached him, but Lincoln had Stanton look up the papers, then wrote:

I have just obtained from the Secretary of War a statement, taken as he says from your own returns, making 108,000 men with you. You now say that you will have but 85,000 when all en route to you shall have reached you. How can the discrepancy of 23,000 be accounted for? And once more let me tell you, it is indispensible to you that you strike a blow. I am powerless to help this. The country will not fail to note, is now noting, that the present hesitation to move on an entrenched camp is but the story of Manassas repeated.

This was dated April 9, after McClellan had already spent four days in merely contemplating Yorktown, and it established a pattern that was repeated with only minor variations for almost a month more. McClellan wrote his wife that he was tempted to tell the President to come and break the enemy's lines himself; he managed to overlook the fact that on the day before, Brooks' brigade of Keyes actually had broken into the lines and was recalled—because the General held the follow-up too risky.

Now that he was not to have McDowell to cut in behind the Confederate position that ran from Yorktown to the marshy Warwick River, and so across the peninsula, the General felt himself reduced to the less brilliant operation of building siege works and reducing the mighty Confederate fortifications by bombardment, followed with assault. "Do not misunderstand the apparent inaction here," he pleaded. "Not a day, not an hour has been lost. Works have been constructed that may almost be called gigantic." But he would have to have Franklin, preferably at the head of his own division and McCall's as well; he would have to have a brigade of engineers; he needed Parrott rifled guns from the works at Washington.

What he did not have to have was interference, whether in

the form of urgings to attack or requests for accurate information. His reports were masterpieces of obfuscation. Stanton sent Hitchcock down to find out exactly how many men McClellan had, or at least how his force compared with the work before him; Hitchcock reported that the force was ample—and found himself added to the list of McClellan's persecutors. Stanton asked Wool to undertake a similar mission; by instruction, McClellan's commanders refused Wool precise information, and the General countered by another demand for Wool's troops, who were building roads in his rear areas at the moment. McClellan reported that he had only 68,000 men present for duty; that the Confederate lines held 30,000, and a few days later, that they held 58,000; that 45,000 men had been taken from him before operations began; that he had been deprived of 50,000.

Shields' division of Banks was sent to McDowell; over Lincoln's objection, Stanton released the desired division of Franklin to McClellan, and the latter kept them aboard transports, eating hardtack and skilly, for two weeks. McClellan reported that he had silenced a one-gun battery, and drew from the Secretary perhaps ironic congratulations: "Good for the first lick. Hurrah for Mott and the one-gun battery." He reported that the first parallel was finished, and, the next day, that it was "essentially finished," and, the day after that, that it was making good progress. He reported that "The time for opening fire is now rapidly approaching"; he reported that "You have not much longer to wait."

On the morning after that last report, Union pickets could no longer see the "Secesh" flag over Yorktown. When patrols advanced cautiously, they found that the Confederates had evacuated.

Manassas repeated. Long afterward, it was found that Confederate General John B. Magruder, a handsome fellow of much talent in amateur theatricals, had only 12,000 men in the Yorktown lines on the day McClellan reached them. He spent almost two weeks marching them round and round barns and woods, where they would be most visible. A good part of his guns were Quakers.

II

THE papers talked of McClellan's "splendid strategy," and the "glorious victory" it would soon produce at Yorktown—perhaps in time for tomorrow's edition. They announced that it was Stanton's fault that the victory had not come sooner; he was "running the campaign himself without even consulting the President," said the *Express;* he "aspired to be the General Commanding," according to the *World*, and was under the domination of the Radicals, according to the *Herald*, which added a long (and completely imaginative) account of a Cabinet meeting, in which Stanton violently opposed reinforcing McClellan.

Yorktown was the harder to bear because every wire from the West told how the flag was forward there. In March, while McClellan's council of generals was approving his move to the peninsula, the tiding came that at the corner of Arkansas, General S. R. Curtis and Franz Sigel with the Missouri Germans fought a hard four-day battle against double their number of rebels; drove them so far and fast that it was said afterward the state of Montana was populated by the fugitives. Missouri was set free; in London, the "ambassador" of the Confederacy, Mr. Mason, was reduced to explaining in society that his nation had always expected to lose the border states, that the war was now only beginning along the frontiers of the cotton kingdom.

In April, as McClellan was protesting that he could count on only 85,000 men, the news came from the Mississippi. At the border of Tennessee and Kentucky, where the river swings a great S curve, the rebels had built a fortress on Island No. 10, and to support it, held the eastern bank below with troops and batteries, the position so hemmed in on the rear by swamps that land approach was impossible. But the ironclad *Carondelet* ran past the fort by night and thunderstorm; General John Pope, a clever engineer who had once proposed making the Southwestern desert an earthly paradise by means of artesian wells, cut a canal through the peninsula behind the island and brought transports through, captured the batteries on the Kentucky shore under the guns of the ironclad, and isolated and took Island No. 10 with 7,000 prisoners.

Before this news was wholly digested, there came more from southern Tennessee, where General Grant was pushing up the rivers toward the main Confederate lateral rail line, with gunboats in support and the new three-division Army of the Cumberland swinging in behind, under General Don Carlos Buell, who as a major carried the message to Sumter, a thousand years ago. On Sunday, April 6, 1862, a swarm of rebels came yelling through the thickets against Grant's loosely ordered lines; drove him back and back, in fighting so savage that one could cross the field from side to side on the bodies of dead men; then were held with difficulty under a dying sun, just before Grant's whole army was gone. But Albert Sidney Johnston, considered the ablest soldier in the South, was dead, and his troops were badly used. That night under flaring torches Buell's steady battalions marched into the lines, and next morning, with red-haired Sherman, cap off and dirty, shouting, "Give them hell!" at the peak of the rally, the rebels had been driven from the field in prone rout.

It was a victory; but one that brought problems, that Battle of Shiloh. The nation and Europe learned with a shock that over 10,000 were casualties on either side in the greatest battle the New World had seen. It compared with the days of Napoleon for figures, and more than compared, for European armies usually broke under losses proportionately far less. Up to Shiloh, most men, North and South, thought that independence could be achieved, or the rebellion crushed, by one or two more resounding victories like Bull Run or Donelson; now there was no doubt of a dark and terrible war.

Nor were the problems merely psychic alone. There seemed to be something wrong with General Grant. Henry Wager Halleck, Commander of the Department of the Mississippi, said so; and Henry Wager Halleck knew more about military science than any man in America, perhaps any man in the world. He could have drilled a formation of Alexander the

Great's *argyrospides*, or commanded a division under Marshal Daun. He had lectured on war at Harvard, written a textbook on strategy and tactics, translated another from the French, and had capped all this by organizing California as a territory and writing its constitution as a state. Old General Scott had unlimited confidence in him; persuaded Lincoln to make him one of the four major-generals at the time of the first call for troops. McClellan, as commander of the army, sent him west to take charge of the whole area when it became necessary to pull Frémont out. Stanton did not particularly like the man. He had encountered him in San Francisco, when Halleck, retired from the army to take up a legal career, appeared as one of the attorneys for the malodorous Limantour. But it was a personal, not a professional antipathy; one had to admit that Halleck's correspondence was prompt, his returns accurate; he went about his business in a businesslike way, without the complaints and fits of temper that marked McClellan.

Also, in startling contrast to McClellan, Halleck's command produced results. He stayed at his headquarters in St. Louis, to be sure; but this was not too unreasonable in a co-ordinator who had to control several armies operating on a front across six hundred miles of latitude. When Stanton took office in January, one of his first steps had been to send Assistant Secretary Thomas Scott out to see this Halleck, and his report also was favorable—in fact, it led to Halleck's appointment to the general direction of the Western armies. Stanton coupled it with an expression of his desire to see the General take the field in person: "I am very much inclined to prefer field work rather than office work for successful military operations. The general who stands upon the field of battle and leads his forces in person is the one most likely to win the victory."

Halleck expressed the opinion that if he were given 50,000 men from the Army of the Potomac, he could drive through to Nashville. Such reinforcements were quite out of the question, of course, but Halleck never complained. Instead, the army under his general direction had taken Henry, Donelson, and then Nashville, well before the February 22, 1862, date set in Lincoln's General War Order No. 1. In return for this, Halleck had only asked that Grant and Pope be made major-generals; on the heels of which Pope promptly took Island No. 10, and Grant won a victory at Shiloh. That is, it was apparent that General Halleck had the gift of choosing the right kind of subordinates and getting them to do things.

He was therefore heard with respect when he began to express some dissatisfaction with Grant—now a major-general, but on Stanton's nomination the morning after the news of Donelson came, long before the arrival of Halleck's request for his promotion. Grant's "army seems to be as much demoralized by the victory at Fort Donelson as that of the Potomac by the defeat at Bull Run," Halleck wired McClellan. "It is hard to censure a successful general immediately after a victory, but I think he richly deserves it. I can get no returns, no reports, no information of any kind from him."

The story reached Halleck, and he passed it on to McClellan, that Grant was drunk a good deal of the time. "Do not hesitate to place Grant in arrest," McClellan wired back, and though Halleck did not quite do that, he turned the army over to General C. F. Smith, and kept Grant in a peculiar state of suspended animation at Fort Henry for nine days—or until Grant recovered his command by asking to be relieved if his conduct were not satisfactory, with a statement of the reason for his relief.

On the heels of this came Shiloh, with its many dead. A tide of criticism against Grant rolled in from the West, including the statement that he was so drunk he could not sit his horse on the day of the battle. The story was untrue; but the fact that it could spread and be believed was really the expression of the profound emotional shock Shiloh had produced; Illinois officers wrote their congressmen that Grant must go, he knew nothing about tactics, which amateurs of war always consider as a means of winning battles without bloodshed. The congressmen called on Stanton, got nowhere, and asked A. K. McClure (the publisher-politician, and a man of weight) to be their delegate before Lincoln. McClure called late at night to tell the President that the confidence of the country required the removal of Grant.

Lincoln heard the delegate out, sat silent for a while, and then said slowly: "I can't spare that man—he fights."

It was one of the great decisions of the war, and Stanton had nothing to do with it directly; one cannot say how deeply Lincoln was infected with the Secretary's violent prejudice in favor of generals who proposed to move immediately upon the enemy's works, for that was a matter of personal conversation between the two men, and Lincoln already had a certain streak of the same prejudice.

Yet even Shiloh was quickly masked by another piece of news that sent the dignified Charles Francis Adams, minister to the Court of St. James, capering around his drawing room. On the night of April 23, while McClellan was wiring for more Parrott guns, Admiral David Glasgow Farragut fought his way past the forts at the mouth of the Mississippi in a terrific night battle, destroyed the entire enemy squadron in the lower river, and captured New Orleans, largest and richest city of the Confederacy.

"Glorious news comes borne on every wind but the south wind," wrote young John Hay, the Presidential secretary. "The little Napoleon sits trembling before the handfull of men at Yorktown, afraid either to fight or run. Stanton feels devilish about it."

One earnest of that feeling was the fact that on April 19, while McClellan was begging for more heavy artillery, Stanton ordered a salute of a hundred guns to be fired by each army, while chaplains gave thanks to God for recent victories, the nation tendering its homage to Generals Curtis and Sigel and their troops for Pea Ridge; to Grant, Buell, and their forces for Shiloh; to Pope for Island No. 10—and to McClellan for nothing.

Next day (the day the transports bearing Franklin's division reached Hampton Roads) there was a conference between Stanton and the war committees—Military Affairs, Conduct of the War. Old Thaddeus Stevens was there, the gloomy, poker-playing ironmonger from Pennsylvania, with his club foot and brown wig; Fessenden of Maine was there, the hard-faced abolitionist; Zach Chandler, Ben Wade, and George Julian.

Thad Stevens said he was tired of hearing damned Republican cowards talk about the Constitution; he was in favor of stripping the rebels of all their rights and giving them a reconstruction that would stifle treason forever. "My policy," said Stanton, and they fell to denouncing slave-catching by the army, in memory of Charles P. Stone, McClellan's refusal to listen to information brought by Negroes, and his insupportable slowness. But as Ben Wade remarked, the General was still king, there was nothing anyone could do but hope he would fight, or that something would make him; and Stanton left the group to go fall on a quarrel with General Hitchcock, who then and there wrote out his resignation.

The Secretary was shocked. "If you send that paper," said he, "you will destroy me." Stanton apologized, begged pardon for the faults of a temper badly strained by events, spoke of the intolerable pressure upon him, and persuaded the military adviser to throw the document in the fire.

III

Stanton to McClellan, May 4, 1862

Accept my cordial congratulations upon your success at Yorktown, and I am rejoiced to hear that your forces are in active pursuit. I hope soon to hear of your arrival in Richmond.

The "active pursuit" (to which McClellan had referred in his own dispatch) was conducted by the army, while the General himself rode down to Fortress Monroe to supervise the debarkation of Franklin. At Williamsburg the pursuit made contact with the Confederates, and the Army of the Potomac fought its first battle—a scrambling, inconclusive rearguard action of amateur soldiers, conducted mainly by Hooker's and Kearny's divisions of Heintzelman, which ended in a rebel withdrawal at five o'clock, when McClellan arrived just in time to ride along the lines and let all the soldiers cheer him.

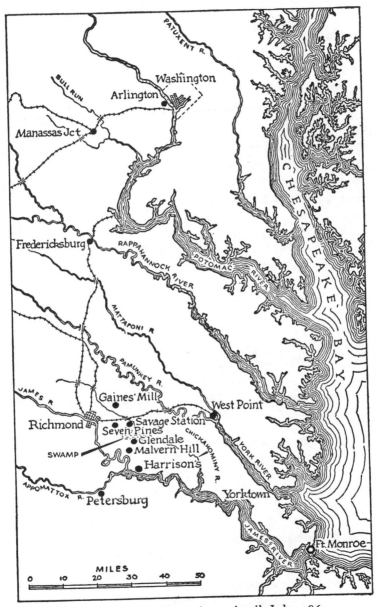

The Peninsular Campaign—April–July 1862

McClellan to His Wife

As soon as I came upon the field, the men cheered like fiends, and I saw at once that I could save the day. It would have been easy for me to have sacrificed 10,000 lives in taking Yorktown, and I presume the world would have thought it more brilliant. The Battle of Williamsburg was more bloody. Had I reached the field three hours earlier, I could have gained greater results, and have saved a thousand lives. It is perhaps well as it is, for officers and men feel that I saved the day.

McClellan to Stanton, May 5

I find Joe Johnston in front of me in strong force, probably greater a good deal than my own, and very strongly intrenched. I learned from prisoners that they intend disputing every step to Richmond. My entire force is undoubtedly considerably inferior to the rebels, who still fight well, but I will do all I can with the forces at my disposal.

General Wool (Transmitting Officer) to Stanton, May 6

The desponding tone of Major-General McClellan's dispatch of last evening more than surprises me. He says that his entire force is undoubtedly considerably inferior to that of the rebels. If such is the fact, I am still more surprised that they should have abandoned Yorktown.

That little fight left a hangover. McClellan asked, and received, authority to "inscribe the names of battles upon the banners" of his regiments, and immediately became involved in an argument at headquarters between Generals Sumner and Heintzelman. They were a pair of Old Army men, Indian fighters from the plains; Sumner tall, with an awe-inspiring manner, white mane and beard and a prodigious voice that earned him the name of "Bull"; Heintzelman, hard enough to have broken a sledge with his face, an ironclad disciplinarian; both of them by long experience and adaptation thoroughly competent to meet any situation in which they could personally speak to a hundred soldiers, and not very competent at anything else. It seems there had been a certain ambiguity in McClellan's orders for the advance; the two old warriors groused about whose duty it had been to lead and whose to support, and McClellan perceived that their wrangle gave him an admirable opportunity to set right one of the wrongs that had been done him.

McClellan to Stanton, May 9

I respectfully ask permission to reorganize the army corps. I am not willing to be held responsible for the present arrangement, experience having proved it very bad, and it nearly resulted in a disastrous defeat. I wish either to return to organization by divisions or else to be authorized to relieve incompetent commanders of army corps. Had I been half an hour later on the field on the 5th we would have been routed and lost everything. I found there the utmost confusion and incompetency, the utmost discourage-ment on the part of the men. At least a thousand lives were sacrificed . the organization into corps.

Where McClellan got the figure of a thousand lives sacrificed at Williamsburg was a mystery to Washington; he had reported (correctly) only 450 dead in the action. But President and Secretary were as vulnerable on the point of responsibility as they had been when the matter came up with regard to the plan of campaign. They had a long conference; Stanton telegraphed McClellan that he might suspend the corps organization or any of his generals if he wished, and helped the President compose a letter:

Lincoln to McClellan, May 9

I now think it indispensible for you to know how your struggle against [the corps organization] is received in quarters which we cannot entirely neglect. It is looked upon as merely an effort to pamper one or two pets and to persecute and degrade their supposed rivals. I have had no word from Sumner, Heintzelman or Keyes. I am constantly told that you have no consultation or communication with them; that you consult and communicate with nobody but General Fitz John Porter and perhaps General Franklin. When you relieved General Hamilton * the other day, you thereby lost one of your best friends in the Senate. Are you strong enough—are you strong enough, even with my help—to set your foot upon the necks of Sumner, Heintzelman, and Keyes, all at once?

No, McClellan decided, he was not quite strong enough for that. But he could and did outflank the incapables in Washington and the incompetents with the army at a single blow, by drawing a division each from Heintzelman and Keyes, using the new division of Franklin and the reserve division of Sykes to make two new corps—the VI for Franklin and the V for Porter. The latter, as Lincoln had learned, had become a great friend of McClellan's. He was stocky, handsome, black-bearded; like all the members of that predominantly naval family, high-minded, quick-tempered, and arrogant toward anyone who did not belong to the sacred lodge of the military profession; like most of the Porters, he thought clearly and talked intelligently when the pillars of the lodge were set. The young Napoleon differed from the old one in preferring this intellectual type, and distrusted the brains of mere driving fighters, like generals of division Hooker and Phil Kearny.

McClellan was too much occupied, he wrote, to leave his command even for an hour and go meet the President and Stanton, who came down to Fortress Monroe on May 9th, the day of the renewed corps organization squabble, in an effort at harrying McClellan into speeding his advance. This left the Presidential party, which also included Chase, high and dry; and as there had been some slightly wistful discussion about Lincoln taking the field in person, Stanton suggested it be tried now, the President leading General Wool's command across the Roads to clear out Norfolk. The experiment was made on the morning of May 11, and all three officers of the government behaved in a highly characteristic manner. "As soon as

---

* In the case of C. F. Hamilton, at least, McClellan seems to have been perfectly right. He could get along with neither superiors nor brother officers, nor those under him. Later he went west and commanded a division under Rosecrans, who found him equally intolerable; finally, he decided his talents were insufficiently recognized and resigned from the service.

Stanton heard firing in every direction where there were rebel forces, his delight knew no bounds"; Chase issued orders to everybody in a manner that reminded spectators of the Duke of Wellington; Lincoln became so annoyed over the general confusion of military affairs that he threw his hat on the ground and decided he did not want to be a general.

But Norfolk was taken, the Confederates blew up their fearsome ironclad, and Union gunboats could ascend the James to cover McClellan's left flank. He was now moving slowly up the peninsula, chiefly by the right, because he had on his left the wide swamps of the Chickahominy, which he had quite forgotten to mention when discoursing on the advantages of the peninsular plan, partly because he would not abandon hope of having McDowell's corps placed under his orders again. Or if not McDowell, troops from somewhere, anywhere, but more troops.

McClellan to Stanton, May 8

I think the time has arrived to bring all the troops in eastern Virginia into perfect cooperation. I expect to fight another and very severe battle before reaching Richmond, and therefore should have all the reinforcements that can be given me. All the troops on the Rappahannock, and if possible, those in the Shenandoah, should take part in the approaching battle. We ought immediately to concentrate everything and not run the risk of engaging a desperate enemy with inferior force.

McClellan to Stanton, May 12

I respectfully apply to be furnished with two or at least one additional regiments to furnish the garrisons for Yorktown, Gloucester and Williamsburg. It is extremely embarrassing to break into the existing brigade organizations, as I am compelled to do, to supply these garrisons.

It was becoming clear to General McClellan that the reason he could not obtain these absolutely necessary reinforcements was that Stanton must be up to his old trick of "saying one thing to the President and exactly the opposite to me."

McClellan to Lincoln, by Telegraph, May 14

I have more than once telegraphed the Secretary of War, stating that in my opinion the enemy were concentrating all their available force to fight this army in front of Richmond, and I have received no reply whatever to these telegrams. I beg leave to repeat their substance to Your Excellency. I cannot bring into battle more than 80,000 men at the utmost, and with them, I attack in position, probably entrenched, a much larger force, probably double my numbers.

Stanton was tied to his room with a bad case of ophthalmia when this priceless missive arrived, but Lincoln replied for him that he had seen all telegrams and both he and the Secretary were doing their best. Four days later, however, Washington yielded; McDowell was to act as McClellan's right wing, while "remaining in position to cover Washington." The Army of the Potomac edged forward, established a base at White House on the York, with a railroad running back to handle supply, and on May 25, Heintzelman's III Corps and Keyes's IV were across the Chickahominy and built bridges connecting them with the rest of the army. They were five miles from Richmond, and could hear the churchbells of the city ring. "Can you not get near enough to throw a few shells into the city?" asked Lincoln.

McClellan to Stanton, May 25

Situated as I am, I feel forced to take every possible precaution against disaster and to secure my flanks against the probable superior force in front of me.

However, "No time will be lost in bringing about a decisive battle," the General wired, two days later. He had 126,089 men, 98,000 of them in line. On May 31, General Joe Johnston, with 73,920 men, attacked him.

IV

THE question arises of why Lincoln and Stanton, two of the better analytical minds in the business, put up with this campaign of complaint and delay, big words and little deeds. One answer is, of course, that in spite of everything, McClellan remained to a large part of the country and to all of the Army of the Potomac, the shining hero who had saved Washington after Bull Run. He had done nothing; but nothing had happened to him, and relieving him could clearly have a disastrous effect on the morale of the army and the country. But the best answer was delivered by Lincoln himself, when Ben Wade called to demand that McClellan be thrown overboard.

"Whom would you put in his place?" asked the President.

"Anybody!"

"Wade, anybody will do for you, but I must have somebody."

Who else was there? Not the senior corps commanders, clearly not up to McClellan's mark, and the juniors were his men, made in his image, while McClellan had demonstrated that he could drill an army and move it with precision.

BACKDROP

Grant to War Department, April 9, 1862

It becomes my duty to report another battle between two great armies, one contending for the maintenance of the best government ever devised, the other for its destruction. It is pleasant to record the success of the army contending for the former principle.

. . . During the night all was quiet, and feeling that a great moral advantage would be gained by becoming the attacking party, an advance was ordered as soon as day dawned. The result was the gradual repulse of the enemy.

I feel it a duty to a gallant and able officer, Brig.-Gen. W. T. Sherman, to make a special mention. He not only was with his command during the entire two days action, but displayed great judgement and skill in the management of his men.

Washington Intelligencer

We understand that the Hon. Caleb B. Smith, Secretary of the Interior, has authorized Mr. Newton, Superintendent of the Agricultural Division, to use the ground along the Ninth Street front of the Patent office building in experimenting with the culture of cotton. This will be interesting to the curious.

LAUGHING GAS. Dr. Colton will continue his lectures and exhibitions of the laughing gas at the Washington Theater.

Twelve gentlemen of the first respectability will inhale the gas on each evening.

New York Times

Having a note for Secretary Stanton, your correspondent called to see him on Saturday. Standing at the desk in an ante-room, I found a very pleasant-looking gentleman conversing with several around him. Scrupulously neat in his appearance, of heavy frame, and immense black beard, with intelligent eye and business manner, he looked for all the world like the photographs which represent him. While awaiting my turn, the following conversation ensued between him and a dealer of glue of the City.

Mr. X: Secretary Stanton, I have some letters for you. I am a glue dealer of New York. I wish, sir, to have permission to gather up the carcasses of dead horses at Bull Run for the purpose of using them in my business. Can I be accommodated?

Mr. S: Yes, sir. I will give you a note to the Quartermaster to furnish you with transportation, as I regard it as a sanitary measure. Is that all, sir?

Mr. X: No, sir. (asks to have a friend, a colonel, appointed Brigadier).

Mr. S: Has he been in any battles?

Mr. X: No, sir, but he has strong political influence.

Mr. S: I cannot appoint him, sir. I have hundreds of such applications. We have meritorious men who have suffered, who have been in action, and these must be attended to first.

The others came in, some wanting one favor, some another. Mr. Stanton receives them all with the courtesy that distinguishes him, never getting excited, always patiently listening, noting each case and disposing of it quietly and rapidly.

New York Commercial Advertiser

The Secretary of War has certainly committed grave errors since he took charge of the department, and we have reason to believe that the President is far from satisfied with the Secretary's treatment of General McClellan. It is even said that after the general commanding went to Yorktown, the President felt it his duty to interfere peremptorily for his protection, and sent troops to him that Stanton had witheld; and we believe that such is a fact. Various reasons are assigned for the behavior of the Secretary of War to General McClellan, the most common of which is that the Secretary has seen visions of a White House that will want an occupant in 1865.

Stanton to the Reverend Herman Dyer

Yours of the 10th is welcome as an evidence of the continued regard of one whose esteem I have always been anxious to possess.

I have been very well aware of the calumnies busily circulated against me in New York and elsewhere respecting my relations to General McClellan, but am compelled from public considerations to withold the proofs that would stamp the falsity of the accusations.

When I entered the Cabinet I was and had been for months the sincere and devoted friend of General McClellan, and to support him and, so far as I might, aid and assist him in bringing the war to a close, was a chief inducement for me to sacrifice my personal happiness to a sense of public duty.

I went into the cabinet about the 20th of January. On the 27th, the President made his Order No. 1, requiring the Army of the Potomac to move. It is not necessary, nor perhaps proper, to state all the causes which led to that order, but it is enough to know that the Government was on the verge of bankruptcy, and at the rate of expenditures the armies must move or the Government perish. The 22d of February was the day fixed for the movement, and when it arrived there was no more sign of movement on the Potomac than there had been for three months before.

Between the 22d of February and the 8th of March the President had again interfered, and the movement on Winchester and to clear the blockade of the Potomac was promised, commenced and abandoned.

On the 8th of March the President again interfered, ordered the Army of the Potomac to be organized into army corps, and that operations should commence.

Two lines of operation were open—one moving directly on the enemy at Manassas and forcing him back to Richmond, beating and destroying him by superior force, and all the time keeping the capital secure by lying between it and the enemy. This was the plan favored by the President. The other plan was to transfer the troops by water to some point on the lower Chesapeake, and thence advance to Richmond. This was General McClellan's plan. The President yielded his own views, although they were supported by some of the best military men in the country. But by a written order he imposed a special condition that the army should not be removed without leaving a sufficient force in and around Washington to make the capital perfectly secure.

When a large part of General McClellan's force had been transferred to Fortress Monroe, information was given to me that there was great reason to fear that no adequate force had been left to defend the capital. I ordered a report of the force left. It was reported by the commander to be less than 20,000 raw recruits, with not a single organized brigade.

These reports were submitted to the President, who also consulted General Totten, General Taylor, General Meigs and General Ripley. They agreed in the opinion that the capital was not safe. I directed McDowell to remain with his command. And the order was approved by the President.

Down to this period there has never been a shadow of difference between General McClellan and myself. It is true that I thought his plan of operations objectionable; but I was not a military man, and while he was in command I would not interfere with his plan, and gave him every aid to execute it. But when the case had assumed the form it had done by his disregard of the President's orders, I was bound to act.

When this order was communicated to General McClellan, it of course provoked his wrath, and the wrath of his friends was directed upon me because I was the agent of its execution.

Now, one word as to the political motives: What motive can I have to thwart General McClellan? I am not now, never have been, and never will be a candidate for any office. I hold my present post at the request of the President.

I knew that everything I cherish and hold dear would be sacrificed by accepting office. But I thought I might help to save the country, and for that I was willing to perish. If I wanted to be a politician or a candidate for office, would I stand between the Treasury and the robbers who are howling around me? Would I provoke and stand up against the whole newspaper gang in the country who, to sell news, would imperil a battle? I was never taken for a fool, but there could be no greater madness than for a man to encounter what I do for anything less than motives that overleap time and look forward to eternity.

I believe that God Almighty founded this Government, and for my acts in the effort to maintain it I expect to stand before Him in judgment.

You will pardon this long explanation, which has been made to no one else. It was done to you, who was my friend when I was a poor boy at school and had no claim upon your confidence and kindness.

The official records will at the proper time fully prove:

First—that I have employed the whole power of the Government unsparingly to support General McClellan's operations:

Second—that I have not interfered with nor thwarted him in any particular:

Third—that the force retained from this expedition was not needed and could not have been employed by him.

Fourth—that between the President and myself there never has been the slightest shadow of difference on any point, save the detachment of Franklin's force, and the President yielded only to an anxious desire to avoid complaint, declaring at the same time his belief that the force was not needed by General McClellan.

12

SEARCH FOR A REMEDY

ON May 23, the day that Keyes's IV Corps crossed the Chickahominy, Washington had sudden bad news from the Shenandoah; a regiment of infantry and two companies of cavalry were wiped out by overwhelming force at Front Royal. The regiment was the 1st Maryland, from Baltimore, and that town went into a fury which caused Stanton no little trouble, but the salient feature of the event was the fact that the attack had been made by Stonewall Jackson's command, 15,000 or 20,000 strong by the estimates, and still moving when heard of. Jackson might now go westward to strike Banks, who lay at Strasburg with only 6,000 men; or north to weakly garrisoned Harpers Ferry; or (as Quartermaster Meigs surmised) slip through the Blue Ridge for a blow at Washington.

McClellan thought the move was merely a demonstration against the Capitol to keep him from being reinforced, and said so in a characteristic telegram asking for more troops. But it was less what Jackson would do than the opportunity of cutting a leg off the Confederate army that drew the attention of Lincoln and his War Secretary. Defensive precautions first: a wire to McDowell, whether the rebels could cross the Potomac below Harpers Ferry?—with transport ordered to Acquia Creek to bring a I Corps division to Washington if such a crossing were possible. (It was not, and McDowell did not send the division.) Several batteries of artillery to Harpers Ferry, and a reassuring telegram to the commander there, who seemed in a state of funk: "Whatever you do will be cordially approved, be the result what it may."

Now, the counterstroke. The force nearest Jackson was McDowell, who had been reinforced by Shields's division from the valley, bringing him up to over 20,000. His head of column was eight miles beyond Fredericksburg, marching to fall in on McClellan's right wing. There were also Frémont's 20,000, at Franklin in western Virginia, over the mountains from the Shenandoah. These two commands (and Banks's also) belonged to units whose only overlord was Washington, and so the campaign had to be co-ordinated from the War Department.

McDowell's march was checked by a telegram, and a few hours later he was ordered to the valley by way of Front Royal, while Frémont was to "move against Jackson at Harrisonburg [which is in the upper valley] and operate against the enemy in such a way as to relieve Banks. You must not stop for supplies, but seize what you need and push rapidly; the object being to cut off and capture the rebel forces in the Shenandoah."

This would seem clear enough, but it was not clear enough for John Charles Frémont, who marched his troops northward instead of south or east, and on the twenty-seventh reported from Moorfield, having taken a route that would bring him to the lower valley. His excuse was that this would more quickly enable him to reach Banks at Strasburg, and also that he was desperately in need of supplies. For one of the few times in the war, there seems to have been something really wrong with the Union quartermaster service, since Frémont's surgeon reported many men weak from lack of food; but the idea of supporting Banks along such a line only revealed the extent of Frémont's capacity for military thinking. Before he had reached Moorfield, Banks was already at Harpers Ferry, after a fine retreat, in which he saved his command and his artillery with only insignificant loss.

Well, go to Strasburg, then (Stanton wired Frémont repeatedly) "by the best route you can" and "without delay."

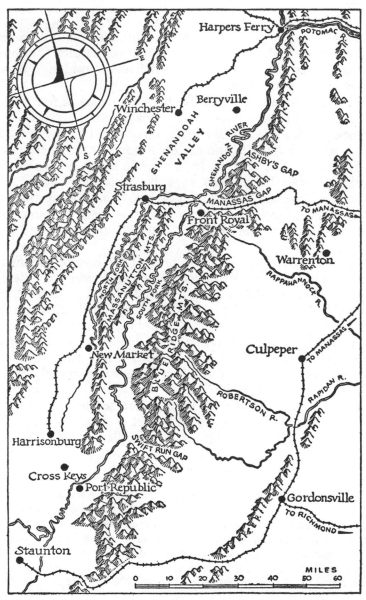

The Shenandoah Valley

But Frémont dawdled along, complaining that Jackson had 30,000 to 60,000 (which must have produced an unpleasant recollection of McClellan), and that he would reach Strasburg on the thirty-first and "take up a defensive position" (which must have produced another).

Shields's division of McDowell's Corps made a fine march through Front Royal on that day, but he could not very well attack Jackson's 15,000 alone, the other two I Corps divisions were well behind him, and the only word from Frémont was that he had been held up by a terrible storm, in which the hailstones were big as hens' eggs. Next morning, June 1, the Confederates marched through Strasburg and on up the valley, while Lincoln and Stanton waited many hours into the night for news of the battle they thought they had prepared.

Then it was wait again, for news of the double pursuit up the sides of the Massanutton Range, which divides the valley in half, Frémont's column on the west, McDowell's on the east. The tidings came on the ninth from Port Republic, where the roads unite, and they were bad. On the previous day Jackson had thrown his full strength against the half of Frémont that had reached the ground, and smashed it in a battle at Cross Keys; that afternoon of the ninth he swung round to give Shields also a hard stroke. To Lincoln and Stanton, sitting at the end of the ticking telegraph, there seemed no point in bringing further units up to be beaten in detail by a concentrated opponent; both columns were recalled.

McClellan to Stanton, May 28

There is no doubt that the enemy are concentrating everything in Richmond. I will do my best to cut off Jackson, but am doubtful whether I can. The real issue is the battle about to be fought in front of Richmond. All our available troops should be collected here—not raw regiments, but the well-drilled troops. It cannot be ignored that a desperate battle is before us; if any regiments of good troops remain unemployed it will be an irreparable fault committed.

On the day this dispatch was written, Stuart of the Confederate cavalry reported that McDowell was definitely gone north and west; Johnston planned his attack on McClellan, a quick smash at the right wing of the Union army, north of the Chickahominy. But the night of May 29 it came on to rain like the flood of Noah and many bridges went out, while the Chickahominy turned from a river thirty feet wide and four feet deep to a torrent of sixty feet by ten. Johnston shifted plans to strike the two Union corps south of the stream, and on the morning of May 31, rain over but river still in spate, he delivered his blow.

It was a bad battle on both sides. Johnston intended a double envelopment of Keyes's IV Corps, which lay jutted forward between Fair Oaks and Seven Pines (the conflict appears in the records under both names), using twenty-three of his twenty-seven brigades, something like 60,000 men. But his orders were not very precise, the country was confused by timber and swamps, the roads heavy; the formations that were to flank Keyes's right and cut him off from the bridges never got out far enough, and only flanked successive brigades. The attackers on the opposite wing were hung up on bad roads, and instead of making a flank attack, had a frontal fight with a division of Heintzelman led by Phil Kearny, "the one-armed devil."

On the Union side, there was a good deal of cracking under pressure in the early stages. "Casey's division, which was in the first line, gave way unaccountably and discreditably," said McClellan in his telegraphed report, a remark apparently made on the basis of what the first eyewitnesses arriving at headquarters said, for the General retracted it when he reached the field after the battle was over and found out what had really happened. Keyes and Heintzelman were carried back a mile or more, then stabilized in the twilight, and were joined by Sumner with his II Corps, which crossed on bridges whose underpinning was gone, and where water stood to men's waists. "Impossible, sir? I am ordered!" the Bull roared at one of his staff.

Next morning the Confederates tried again, but found lines partly dug in, more solid, and well supported by artillery;

could accomplish nothing, and pulled out with some 6,000 casualties against the Union 5,000 for the two days. Joe Johnston was badly wounded on the first evening; his successor was Robert E. Lee of Virginia, who filed for future reference the fact that McClellan had made no effort at counterattack, nor any to use the V and VI Corps, north of the river. When the news of the battle came to Washington, Zach Chandler got drunk in the bar at Willard's and delivered a short address to the convivial companions present—subject: McClellan is a liar and a coward.

McClellan to His Wife, June 2

It is certain that we have gained a glorious victory. I am tired of the sickening sight of the battlefield, with its mangled corpses and poor suffering wounded! Victory has no charms for me when purchased at such cost. I shall be only too glad when it is all over and I can return where I best love to be.

McClellan to Stanton, June 4

Please inform me at once on what reinforcements, if any, I can count on having at Fortress Monroe or White House, within the next three days, and when each regiment will arrive.

Stanton to McClellan, June 5

I will send you five regiments as fast as transportation can take them; the first to start tomorrow from Baltimore. I intend sending you a part of McDowell's force as soon as it can return from its trip to Front Royal, probably as many as you want.

McClellan to Stanton, June 10

I will attack as soon as the weather and the ground will permit; but there will be a delay, the extent of which no one can foresee, because the season is altogether abnormal. I present for your consideration the propriety of detaching largely from Halleck's army to strengthen this; for it would seem that Halleck has now no large organized force in front of him, while we have.

II

ACTUALLY, it was ten regiments, not five, that joined McClellan as humming June rose over the tidewater lands—plus McCall's whole division from McDowell, which brought the Army of the Potomac in line of battle up to 105,000 men, while its total was only 2,000 less than it had been in the days of the camps before Washington. This was all and more than all McClellan had asked (were it not for his high figures in absentees, which had begun to worry Stanton a little); but now the old game began again, while all the army except Porter's Corps was moved to the south bank of the Chickahominy. McClellan intoned that there were 200,000 Confederates in Richmond, and they were entrenching rapidly; Beauregard and many of his troops had reached the Confederate capital from the west; McClellan regretted his inferiority in numbers.

But the weather improved and on June 19: "We shall await only a favorable condition of the earth and sky and the completion of some necessary preliminaries." Four days later, one of those necessary preliminaries had become the possession of three batteries of a new type gun, invented by one General James—to which Stanton replied that there was no General James who manufactured ordnance, and no record of any such guns having been offered to the War Department.

McClellan to His Wife, June 22

By an arrival from Washington today I learn that Stanton and Chase have fallen out; that McDowell has deserted his friend C. and taken to S. Alas! my poor country that should have such rulers. I tremble for my country when I think of these things. When I see such insane folly behind me, I feel that the final salvation of the country demands the utmost prudence on my part, and that I must not run the slightest risk of disaster, for if anything happened to this army our cause would be lost.

Yet he had planned (the General said later) a general attack for June 26. Unfortunately, this was the date when Lee, having brought the Confederate strength to nearly 90,000 by drawing Jackson in from the Valley, attacked him.

III

IT WAS not, like the raid up the Shenandoah, a complete surprise. In fact, it should not have been a surprise at all, for Jackson and Lee had embarked upon the perilous task of laying evidence intended to deceive under the eyes of one of the acutest analysts of evidence the country ever saw. They began their campaign of rumor-spreading soon after June 15, when Stuart of the Confederate cavalry, having ridden right around the Union Army, reported Porter's V Corps as isolated on the north bank of the river, with its right wing in air. The plan was to pin this corps under a frontal attack from the main body of Lee's army, while Jackson should take it in flank and rear, crumple it up, and sever McClellan's communications with his base at White House.

No inkling of this reached McClellan through his Pinkerton men, but on the twenty-fourth he had a deserter from Jackson's force, who said that Stonewall had been at Gordonsville on the twenty-first with fifteen brigades, and would attack McClellan's right rear on the twenty-eighth. "Where is Jackson?" McClellan asked Stanton.

Stanton to McClellan, June 25

We have no definite information as to the number or position of Jackson's force. General King yesterday reported a deserter's statement that Jackson's force was, nine days ago, 40,000 men. Some reports place 10,000 rebels under Jackson at Gordonsville; others, that his force is at Port Republic, Harrisonburg and Luray. Frémont yesterday reported rumors that western Virginia was threatened, and General Kelley that Ewell was advancing to New Creek, where Frémont has his depots. The last telegram from Frémont contradicts this rumor. The last telegram from Banks says the enemy's pickets are strong in advance at Luray. The people decline to give any information of his whereabouts. Within the last two

days the evidence is strong that for some purpose the enemy is
circulating rumors of Jackson's advance in various directions, with
a view to concealing the real point of attack. Neither McDowell,
who is at Manassas, nor Banks and Frémont, who are at Middletown, appear to have any accurate knowledge of the subject. A
letter transmitted to the Department yesterday, purporting to be
dated Gordonsville on the 14th instant, stated that the actual attack
was designed for Washington and Baltimore as soon as you attack
Richmond, but that the report was to be circulated that Jackson
had gone to Richmond, in order to mislead. This letter looked very
much like a blind, and induces me to suspect that Jackson's real
movement is now toward Richmond. It came from Alexandria,
and is certainly designed, like the numerous rumors put afloat, to
mislead. I think, therefore, that while the warning of the deserter
to you may also be a blind, it could not be safely disregarded. I
will transmit to you any further information on this subject that
may be received here.

In this model of an intelligence summary, it is noteworthy
that the Secretary is not in the least worried about Washington or Baltimore; also the result was that McClellan was not
in the least worried about his right flank. "If I had another
good division, I could laugh at Jackson," he wired back.
Porter was duly attacked at Beaver Dam on the twenty-sixth,
and without warning. But Jackson, the Confederate hurri-
cane, was inexplicably late; A. P. Hill's division of Lee, 14,000
strong, came too early, flung itself frontally against Porter's
45,000, and only succeeded in finding out how good the Union
artillery was.

The night after the battle, McClellan visited Porter's headquarters; he found his friend in excellent spirits, expecting to
be attacked again next morning, but confident that he could
hold against anything if only slightly reinforced, and urging
his commander to strike hard against Richmond south of the
Chickahominy. The rebel lines there must be very weakly
held. (They were.) But the neurotic Napoleon with the mania
for martyrdom was not thinking in such terms. He left Porter's
tent and telegraphed his quartermaster-general to send all the
supplies that could be moved from White House to Savage

Station, south of the Chickahominy, in preparation for a shift of base to the James. The remaining supplies were to be burned. That is, he was going to retreat; and it was with this thought in mind that he telegraphed Stanton not to worry, even if he heard that Yorktown was in possession of the enemy—also that he needed more troops.

Stanton to McClellan, 11:20 P.M., June 26

The circumstances that have hitherto rendered it impossible for the government to send you any more reinforcements than has been done have been so distinctly stated to you by the President that it is needless for me to repeat. Every effort has been made by the President and myself to strengthen you. King's division has reached Falmouth; Shields' division and Ricketts' division are at Manassas. The President designs to send a part of that force to aid you as speedily as it can be done.

During the night, Porter was drawn back to a crescent around Gaines' Mill and the bridges, but McClellan sent him no reinforcements. At dawn Lee struck again, now with the full strength of the Confederate army, while dramatist Magruder made a terrific noise in the Richmond lines, with firing on pickets, cannonade, and officers in the woods shouting orders to imaginary troops. McClellan stayed all day at his headquarters, reading the messages in which Porter told how desperately he was pressed; finally sent two brigades to the north bank, and was nobly prepared for the news of the afternoon— that the V Corps was broken, two regiments captured entire, with all the heavy artillery, after a fight as savage as Shiloh.

McClellan to Stanton, June 27

Have had a terrible contest. Attacked by greatly superior numbers in all directions on this side; we still hold our own, though a very heavy fire is still kept up on the left bank of the Chickahominy. The odds have been immense. We hold our own very nearly. I may be forced to give up my position during the night, but will not if it is possible to avoid it. Had I 20,000 fresh and good troops we would be sure of a splendid victory tomorrow.

Well, he had 60,000 fresh and good troops south of the river, who had done nothing all day but listen to Porter catching hell on the north bank. He also had Hooker and Kearny, who came to headquarters late at night with corps commander Heintzelman to demand that instead of retreating to the James, they be allowed to attack, break through the lines into Richmond. With their two divisions alone they would do it, they said, and Heintzelman thought they could do it; though Sumner and Franklin thought the rebels very strong on their fronts, taking the Pinkerton reports as gospel. McClellan only listened while Kearny denounced his commanding general in terms that led the others to expect him to be ordered before a court-martial. After midnight, when the unit commanders had gone, it occurred to the little Napoleon that he had not made his position sufficiently clear, and so he composed another dispatch.

McClellan to Stanton, 12:20 A.M., June 28

Had I 20,000 or even 10,000 fresh troops for use tomorrow, I could take Richmond; but I have not a man in reserve, and shall be glad to cover my retreat. You must send me very large reinforcements, and send them at once. More men would have changed this battle from a defeat into a victory. As it is, the government must not and cannot hold me responsible for the result.

If I save this army now, I tell you plainly that I owe no thanks to you or to any other person in Washington.

You have done your best to sacrifice this army.

McClellan was afterward immensely proud of this appalling missive and of the fact that Stanton and Lincoln accepted it in a silence which proved their guilt. He did not know that it had raised the hair of Sanford in the War Department telegraphic office, who found the last two sentences so near the line of treason that he quietly deleted them before showing the dispatch to the Secretary.

In the meanwhile, the retreat to the James was on, with the long trains of wagons (how many were there? 2,600? 4,300? 5,000?—all these figures appear in various of McClellan's reports, but from the line of march, the smallest is the most likely) rolling along; the Army of the Potomac deploying to cover them, and Lee striking and striking in the repeated effort to break the tortured serpent as it crossed the swamps. On the twenty-ninth there was a hot fight at Savage Station; Sumner, Heintzelman, and Franklin held off the rebels all day, with no one in command, because McClellan was directing the march of retreat.

Next day, an even heavier battle at Frayser's Farm; the rebels against Heintzelman, Franklin, and McCall's division of Porter—a near thing, a desperate thing, and a good part of the Union army was gone but for Jackson's second failure to move in time. July 1 brought the Army of the Potomac to Malvern Hill, with easy access to Harrison's Landing on the James; McClellan saw all tight, turned over his command to Porter, and went aboard a gunboat. Lee attacked disjointedly because his staff work was bad; the rebels ran into long ranks of the magnificent Union artillery and their army was simply torn to tatters. They had lost 15,000 men in the campaign; McClellan, 10,000.

Kearny once more wanted to counterattack, but the retreat was on; the soldiers cheered McClellan when he rode through the crowded and dirty camp at the landing, and they hunted lice in their clothes, while reinforcements came in from the north, and Burnside's IX Corps reached Fortress Monroe from the Carolina sounds.

McClellan to Stanton, July 1

I need 50,000 more men, and with them I will retrieve our fortunes.

IV

AMID all this—amid the anxieties, the hopes deferred, and bitter disappointments (for thirty-six hours on June 29–30, the air at the War Department was electric with the news brought by a correspondent that Gaines' Mill was according to plan, and McClellan was fighting his way into Richmond)—through it all, the outer office at the War Department was crowded with visitors each morning at eleven, and there were snap decisions to make.

For instance, it was quickly evident that the cessation of recruiting in April had been a mistake; Stanton used Jackson's valley campaign to set things going again, by telegraphing thirteen governors: "The enemy in great force are advancing on Washington. You will please organize and forward immediately all the volunteer and militia forces of your state"—and was abused for falling in a panic. When Jackson turned back south, Stanton canceled the militia call and persuaded the diplomatic Seward to persuade the governors to offer new men instead of making a call for them—public sentiment being so touchy on more calls for troops. A big camp of instruction was set up near Annapolis with General Wool in charge. Just whose idea it was to offer hundred dollar bounties for new enlistments is not clear; Stanton certainly had to go into the details of this plan and approve it. Some of the states spoke of drafting men to fill their quotas—the first time the word had been mentioned, though nothing was done about it then.

For instance again, there was still the question of contracts, over which Cameron stumbled so badly. Stanton could not go into every one himself, but he appointed a special commission, consisting of his old fellow-Cabinet-member, Joseph Holt, with Robert Dale Owen of Indiana; they brought in a report on July 1, the day of Malvern Hill, and, after that, new rifles cost the government $4 less apiece than they had cost before. Or another case: on June 22 Stanton wired McDowell that he has learned that fifty miles of telegraph wire have been abandoned during the pursuit of Jackson. "I think that some effort should be made to get it."

There was a barrage of difficulties with the press, which had sent out clouds of correspondents, who insisted on publishing accounts of strength and plans of campaign in a highly uninhibited manner. As early as his first month in office, Stanton had to put out an order that anyone obtaining military information from any other source than the War Office should be "deemed a spy"; and in March he showed he meant it by seizing the plant of the Washington *Sunday Chronicle* and arresting all the printers for publishing an unfortunately accurate strength report on the Army of the Potomac. But this by no means ended the matter; the papers constantly groused and sniped about the inadequacy of the battle reports given out by Assistant-Secretary Watson, and were bitter about the way Sanford, whose office made him censor of telegraphic dispatches, turned the purple prose of their correspondents into nonsense. Sanford certainly lacked finesse; and to make matters worse, Stanton was more than once forced to ask field commanders to keep their officers from writing letters home, full of the very details he was trying to keep off the wires.

There was a complaint that a Captain Hatch had seized some supplies at Cairo, Illinois; there was a letter from Colonel Ned Baker's daughter, asking for the "vindication" of her father's memory; there was the question of a military governor for Tennessee (Andrew Johnson got the post); there were troubles in New Orleans, where General Ben Butler had embroiled himself with the foreign consuls.

There were long conferences with Chase over soldiers' pay, which had been made in specie, and so tended to find its way into Confederate treasuries. Make it greenbacks thenceforth, was the decision, with fractional shinplaster notes, bearing the denominations of several postage stamps linked together, without perforations or gum on the backs.

There was a visit (in March) from an engineer named Charles Ellet, with soulful eyes and long ringlets of hair. He had been blessed with an idea which both the tsar of Russia and Secretary Welles rejected—why not build a new class of ships on the western rivers, very fast and fitted with sharp beaks of iron, but without guns except for a few small arms, so that their captains would be compelled to use them as rams only? Stanton knew this Ellet; he had built the Wheeling bridge as well as the one at Niagara, and his judgment commanded respect. Try the rams, try anything, he said; and sent Ellet to Pittsburgh, New Albany, and Cincinnati, telegraphing to the mayors to give him help and credit.

Ellet built several of his queer ships and, commissioned a colonel, took four of them down the Mississippi in person. As might be expected, there were some fairly sharp objections to the presence of an army fleet on the river from Flag Officer Charles H. Davis, who commanded the Union squadron of ironclad gunboats. This began a long serial argument between Stanton and Welles, whose ultimate result was a victory for the latter, when he had all the rams transferred to navy control. In the meanwhile, Stanton telegraphed Ellet to fight the enemy where he found them, whether the navy liked it or not. This turned out to be a good idea, for on June 6, the very day after this wire, the rebel river squadron met the Union fleet off Memphis in the only general naval action of the war. Ellet's rams arrived earliest; aboard *Queen of the West,* he nearly cut the Confederate flagship in half, and two more of the rebel craft disabled each other when they tried to attack one of the fast Union rams from both sides at once and missed her. The heavy Union ironclads destroyed three more Confederate vessels; the remaining three fled downstream, but Ellet's rams caught two of them, and Memphis surrendered without a shot on land.

The Colonel himself was severely (and it turned out, mortally) wounded in the battle; that night, in spite of the cares of the current valley campaign, the Secretary of War found time to carry the news to Ellet's wife and daughter at Georgetown Heights. He found Mrs. Ellet terrified, drew the daughter aside and, with tears in his eyes, besought her to be of good cheer, that everything would be done for her mother. Next morning there was a carriage at the Ellet door with passes that would carry the pair westward to their dying man by the most rapid route.

There was the matter of army transport, which had been one of the scandals of the Cameron regime. Stanton was thoroughly at home in this field; as early as February 20, he summoned a conference of railroad presidents and managers at his office and told them that any more charges like the one the Pennsylvania had made * would result in their lines being

* See page 131.

seized: "But the better way is for the railways themselves to operate in the public interest, and I expect, of course, you will do so." They appointed a standing committee to confer with the Secretary, and cut rates for soldier transportation 10 per cent below schedule. But when the peninsular campaign began, it became evident that all was not yet perfect. The advancing armies slowed up in proportion as they moved beyond rail-head, Frémont ran short of supplies in western Virginia, and McDowell's march to Fredericksburg was delayed because rail transport could not keep up his supplies.

Stanton hit upon the device of creating a new, government-operated railroad system in the zone of the armies, and to head it up, summoned one Hermann Haupt. He was a West Pointer, a railroad man and engineer, then busy constructing the Hoosac Tunnel through the Berkshire massif between Boston and Albany—a work since overshadowed by greater tunnels, but not until Haupt taught other people how to build them. It was one of the Secretary's happiest inspirations; Haupt was a big, handsome, blond-bearded man, as arbitrary and efficient as Stanton himself, a strange chick for West Point to hatch, essentially a builder who abhorred the ways of destruction. He began by demanding that he should have no rank, title, or uniform, no compensation beyond his expenses, and that he could go back to his tunnel after the campaign was over. The conditions he set wore away under the tooth of time; Haupt did not see his tunnel again until nearly the close of the war, when he retired as a general.

In the meanwhile, he recruited his own labor force, built railroads and bridges furiously, and told military officers to go to hell. The railroad down to Fredericksburg had been destroyed and its ties torn out; he rebuilt it complete in twenty days, including a bridge 400 feet long and 90 feet high, whose timbers came right out of the surrounding woods. Lincoln went down to see it, and came back to tell the Committee on the Conduct of the War: "That man Haupt has built a bridge across Potomac Creek on which loaded trains are passing every hour, and upon my word, gentlemen, there is nothing in it but cornstalks and bean-poles." Haupt also set up a courier service for military news along his rights of way, and sent telegraphers with pocket instruments to make observations at the fighting front; Stanton came to depend so much on the accuracy of these reports that he made an order that Haupt's messengers should be admitted to him at any hour of day or night, and it was due to them that the Secretary often had a knowledge of what was really going on that was uncanny—and unpleasant —to some of the field officers.

V

By July 3 McClellan had hiked the number of reinforcements necessary to "retrieve our fortunes" up to 100,000 men, and on the fifth his Chief-of-Staff and father-in-law, General Randolph Marcy, came to Washington for a personal interview. Stanton informed the General that nine or ten thousand men were being drawn from the commands of Generals Burnside and Hunter to be sent to McClellan. He only wanted to be of service to McClellan and "would be willing to lie down in the gutter and allow him to stand on my body for hours." (Marcy's account.)

Marcy said—what? Major A. E. H. Johnson, who was present, says he said that unless McClellan were allowed greater independence (which presumably meant he was not to be hounded about attacking any more) and enlarged resources, he might find it necessary to surrender his army to Lee. No one has confirmed this, but Marcy certainly said something very serious, for:

Stanton to McClellan, July 5

I have talked to General Marcy and meant to have written to you by him, but I am called to the country, where Mrs. Stanton is with her children, to see one of them die.

I can therefore only say, my dear general, in this brief moment, that there is no cause in my heart or conduct for the cloud which wicked men have raised between us for their own selfish purposes.

No man ever had a truer friend than I have been to you and

shall continue to be. You are seldom absent from my thoughts, and I am ready to make any sacrifice to aid you. Time allows me to say no more than that I pray Almighty God to deliver you and your army from all peril and lead you to victory.

McClellan to His Wife

Stanton is the most unmitigated scoundrel, the most depraved hypocrite and villain. I think that (I do not wish to be irreverent) had he lived in the time of the Saviour, Judas Iscariot would have remained a respected member of the fraternity of Apostles, and that the magnificent treachery of E. M. Stanton would have caused Judas to have raised his arms in holy horror. Enough of the creature!

The subject of Marcy's visit was also serious enough to send Lincoln down to Harrison's Landing on July 8, the day of the death of Stanton's infant son, James. President and General talked, and McClellan favored Lincoln with a long letter which he had spent several days in composing. It advised the President that the effort to obtain requisite forces for putting down the rebellion would be hopeless unless the policies of the government with regard to slavery and the protection of private property were changed radically, and instructed him just how and in what manner they should be changed. There was even a suggestion that the army would not fight for the suppression of slavery, and as this was McClellan's army, the one he had trained, and which cheered him every day on parade, he presumably knew what he was talking about. Lincoln only said, "Thank you," for this advice on how to run the government and put the letter in his pocket, but it probably triggered the reaction that came three days later.

General Halleck was summoned from the West to be General-in-Chief of the armies.

Something like this had been brewing for quite a while—in fact, ever since Jackson's quick campaign down the Shenandoah and the effort to trap him had demonstrated the necessity of having in Washington a good military head who could combine the movements of armies and extract from the combination the kind of results Stanton and Lincoln had failed to get when they tried to direct three separate forces onto Jackson's rear. Also someone who could meet McClellan's complaints and arguments about inferiority with replies on quite as good military ground, or else give him peremptory orders from a position where General McClellan would not be able to shift responsibility to a vulnerable civilian authority for not having his own way.

The first step in reorganization was the obvious one of putting under a single command the three forces whose co-operation against Jackson had been managed from Washington. For this purpose, General John Pope, who had done so well at Island No. 10, was brought out of the West. There is no record of Stanton's having a particular attitude toward him; Montgomery Blair had, though, denouncing the man as "a liar and a trickster; all the Popes are so." But Lincoln had known Pope's father, and, while admitting his capacity for deception, thought the quality might not be useless to a military commander. After all, was not Grant accused of drinking?

So Pope took command of the newly designated Army of Virginia during the early days of the Seven Days' Battles, and began to reorganize in a manner that showed a certain capacity. Frémont refused to serve under him, on the technical ground that he outranked Pope on the army list, and it was a pleasure to Stanton and Lincoln to replace him with Franz Sigel, who was quite as popular with the Germans, and had made a good fighting record at Pea Ridge.

The question of the top command remained after this, however, and for this purpose Hitchcock, the nearest man, was clearly impossible. He only proposed schemes there were no troops to carry out, and kept asking to be allowed to retire to "the tranquillity of hermetic speculation"—a man so deep in philosophy that the affairs of the material world had become a vulgar bore. After the Seven Days, he was allowed to go back to his metaphysics.

As for Halleck, Assistant Secretary Thomas Scott's reports spoke well of him. It was true that after Stanton urged him into the field command, his advance from Shiloh had been exasperatingly slow, with long lines of forts and trenches, but he had ended that advance on May 28 by taking the communications center at Corinth, Mississippi, and severing one of the two lateral railroads across the Confederacy. Perhaps an office commander instead of a field man after all; but an office commander was the specific need.

When McClellan got into trouble at Gaines' Mill, Lincoln made a flying trip up to West Point to see old General Winfield Scott; found the elder statesman of the army had not changed his original opinion that Halleck was one of the soldiers best fitted to command armies. At the same time, Stanton sent Halleck an order to prepare 25,000 men for movement east in case McClellan's difficulties should turn grave, and Senator Sprague of Rhode Island went out to see the commander of the West.

This Sprague was William Sprague, the same who, as governor, had marched into Washington at the head of the first troop contingent; a close friend of Chase, whose daughter he was to marry, and a source of much influence. Lincoln and Stanton trusted him as an observer. He had independently conceived the idea of bringing some of Halleck's men east, and secured a letter of introduction from Lincoln to the General, and was a kind of unofficial ambassador and observer; reported very favorably on Halleck, which meant that the new General-in-Chief would have important political support. Stanton himself apparently did not like the idea at first—at least he told Pope so—but was soon talked round by Pope, who wanted a higher military command in Washington. Thus Halleck.

McClellan to His Wife

In all these things the President and those around him have acted so as to make the matter as offensive as possible. He has not shown the slightest gentlemanly or friendly feeling, and I cannot regard him as in any respect my friend—I feel confident that he would relieve me tomorrow if he dared to do so. His cowardice alone prevents it. I can never regard him with any other feelings than those of contempt.

Halleck, having split his western command between Grant and Buell, and having given them instructions, arrived on July 23. Washington saw a tall man in a uniform so tight it seemed about to burst, with big pop eyes and a smooth-shaven face surrounded by a fringe of beard; slovenly in appearance, fond of scratching his elbows, who remarked at his first meeting with the Cabinet: "I confess I do not think much of the Negro." He went down to Harrison's Landing on the twenty-fifth and had a long conference with McClellan. Halleck told him that unless the Army of the Potomac could at once attack Richmond, sound military principle required that it be concentrated with Pope's force in an area where it could simultaneously cover Washington and operate against the Confederate capital. Impossible, said McClellan, to move forward without 30,000 reinforcements. Halleck said the President authorized him to offer 20,000; if these were not enough, the army must be withdrawn from the James. McClellan said the army would be demoralized by such a withdrawal, and the two men parted.

There were more conferences at Washington—Lincoln, Stanton, Halleck, and Pope. On July 29 McClellan received an order to send away his sick, and on August 3 a peremptory order to evacuate the army from the peninsula to Acquia Creek. He protested, but this time he was dealing with a man who could and did accept the responsibility as his own.

Halleck to McClellan

I find the forces divided, I wish to unite them. Only one feasible plan has been presented for doing this. If you or anyone else had presented a better plan I certainly would have adopted it. But all of your plans require reinforcements which it is impossible to give you.

Jackson, fortified by two divisions from Lee's main army, was already moving against Pope.

13

REMEDY STILL TO BE FOUND

WITH the coming of Halleck in July, 1862, the movement changes. Stanton becomes the invisible man so far as operations are concerned; there are no more intelligence summaries like that before the Seven Days, not so much that he failed to make them as that he made them verbally and they failed to get into the record except as emissions from the new General-in-Chief. Halleck himself quickly slipped into function as the secretarial member of the triple-headed executive managing the war. His mind was slow and pedantic, and after the first brief flash, he almost made a fetish of not giving orders that would involve him in responsibility; but he furnished military phraseology for ideas developed by Lincoln and Stanton, supported their judgments with military reasons, and only rarely interposed a military objection.

Between those other two, the relations had grown very close; Welles complained that the administration was departmentalized, that there were no regular Cabinet meetings, and that the President was more often with Stanton or Seward, both of whom the naval man regarded as sly. Around the co-operation between President and War Secretary anecdotes clustered like May bees around a bole. Anecdote of the speculator who brought irresistible political pressure on Lincoln for a pass through the lines to buy cotton, took it to Stanton to have it countersigned, and presently returned with the indignant report that the Secretary had torn the Presidential paper to pieces, thrown them on the floor, and stamped on them. Lincoln opened his eyes wide, and said calmly: "Well, you go back and tell Stanton that I will tear up of a dozen of his papers before Saturday."

Anecdote of the Coles County riots,* when some Southern sympathizers set on furloughed Union soldiers at Charleston, Illinois, and killed or wounded eleven of them. Fifteen men were arrested and lodged in a fort; a delegation came to ask Lincoln for their release, headed by the President's cousin and boyhood friend, Ned Hanks. Stanton was brought in with the papers and the fierce statement that the fifteen were criminals and "Every damned one of them should be hung." Lincoln asked: "If these men should return home and become good citizens, who would be hurt?" After the Secretary left, Hanks remarked: "Abe, if I's as big as you, I'd take that little feller over my knee and spank him"; but only drew a laugh and the remark that Stanton was a bigger man than he looked, maybe bigger than he himself.

Anecdote of the mother who wanted the release on parole of her wounded son, a prisoner in Fort Meyer; explained that he had not even enlisted voluntarily in the Confederate Army, and received from Stanton only a hard refusal, but from Lincoln an order of release. Or most famous and burlesque of all the anecdotes, the correspondence carried to and fro between President and Secretary by a would-be chaplain:

Dear Stanton:
    Appoint this man a chaplain in the army.

                                            A. Lincoln

Dear Mr. Lincoln:
    He is not a preacher.

                                            E. M. Stanton

Dear Stanton:
    He is now.

                                            A. Lincoln

* In December of this year, 1862, but belonging here ideologically.

Dear Mr. Lincoln:
  There is no vacancy.

                                          E. M. Stanton

Dear Stanton:
  Appoint him chaplain-at-large.

                                          A. Lincoln

Dear Mr. Lincoln:
  There is no warrant in law for this.

                                          E. M. Stanton

Dear Stanton:
  Appoint him anyhow.

                                          A. Lincoln

Dear Mr. Lincoln:
  I will not.

                                          E. M. Stanton

This time Stanton won, but not infrequently he was out-flanked, as in the case of Pennsylvania's draft to fill her troop quota in 1862. Cass township of Schuylkill County, under the domination of the malodorous Molly Maguires, refused to furnish a man. A. K. McClure, Lincoln's publisher friend, was technical head of the draft; when he reported the refusal to Stanton, the Secretary placed two regiments at his disposal and told him to enforce and be damned to the consequences. But McClure did not like the prospective results, and neither did Governor Curtin, when the matter was taken to him. They wired Lincoln; Lincoln wired back: "Say to McClure that it might be well in an extreme emergency with the appearance of executing the laws; I think McClure will understand." McClure did; he got affidavits that Cass township had already filled its quota by volunteering, and Stanton never knew of the deception.

President and Secretary had in fact worked out a method, which Lincoln summed up by saying: "I cannot always know whether a permit ought to be granted, and I want to oblige everybody when I can; and Stanton and I have an understanding that if I send an order to him that cannot be consistently granted, he is to refuse it, which he sometimes does. And that led to a remark which I made to a man the other day who complained of Stanton, that I hadn't much influence with this administration, but hoped to have more with the next."

The "understanding" was never reduced to writing and probably never to words. Lincoln merely used the incorruptibility, the burning intensity, and ruthlessness of his Secretary to protect himself from the effects of politics, only intervening when it was a question of the humanities—or of that species of humanity which is also politics, as in the case of the Coles County riots. The President had constantly to think of how many votes an act would cost or gain, not for himself, but for the prosecution of the war. Even peoples' opinion of him as a President was part of this complex; his government was necessarily founded on being obliging to the point of complacency. Not that Lincoln lacked moral courage, or feared any disagreeable duty; but it made for a more efficient and popular government that he should appear in the role of pardoner, while his subordinate wore the mantle of severity.

Stanton not only entered the combination as careless of what people said or thought of him as he was in the days of the Pittsburgh "cotton kings"; he was by the nature of the unwritten understanding assigned to the cat-belling tasks which Lincoln found difficult. For the President, there were issues moral, ethical, and political; his very preoccupation with them set the Secretary free to devote all his terrible energy to the single objective of restoring the Union. And as time went on, as the two men fitted more snugly into their roles, this contributed to develop both farther along the line tacitly adopted.

II

Pope began badly, with a proclamation that he had come from the West, "where we have always seen the backs of our enemies; from an army whose business has been to seek the adversary and to beat him when he was found; whose policy has been attack and not defense." This was followed by an announcement that his headquarters would be in the saddle, which provoked the obvious witticism that this was the place for his hindquarters; and then one that the army should live off the country as far as practicable; and then another that an oath of allegiance should be exacted of all "disloyal male citizens" within the lines

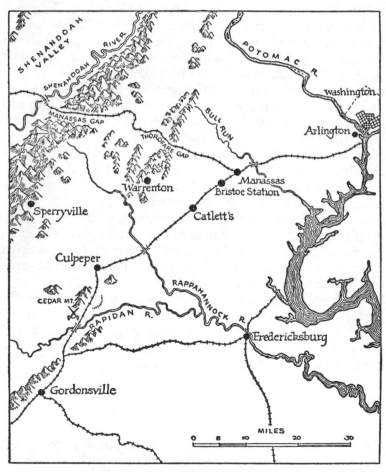

Pope's Campaign—August 1862

of the army, on violating which they would be shot. The last, of course, was clearly illegal, since oaths under duress have no binding force, and no one knew it better than Stanton; but he was letting Halleck do the talking, since he was letting the new General-in-Chief do all the talking in the direction of the army.

Much of the talking during those early days of August was devoted to getting McClellan's army out of the peninsula. The General, who had so easily and quickly embarked for the move to Fortress Monroe, now encountered incredible difficulties in placing the troops aboard ship for the return. He protested, complained that the army "cannot possibly reach Washington in time to do any good," spoke of hoping "to be ready to move tomorrow afternoon in the direction of Richmond," and ran out a week without sending a man to the transports—and late at night of August 9, the War Department wires began to carry word of a battle fought far out under the shadow of the Blue Ridge, at Cedar Mountain on the Rapidan.

Banks's Corps was in it, and as night came down, a division of McDowell's, with Pope in person leading toward the end. It came out afterward that there had been a good deal of bungling, orders badly written and misunderstood, and that Pope was already writing that "Sigel's Corps, though composed of the best fighting material, will never do much service under that officer." But the picture as Washington had it that night was that the Army of Virginia had taken the offensive and not done badly, remained in possession of the field, and gave as good as it took from superior numbers.

The trouble lay in those superior numbers, and that more might soon join them, undeterred by McClellan. (As a matter of fact, more were on the way; on August 7, when a Union outpost on Malvern Hill was withdrawn, Lee decided that McClellan would keep McClellan's army immobilized for long enough to permit the destruction of Pope; his movement westward by rail began on the tenth.) A reserve division was being organized under General Samuel Sturgis from the troops around Washington, but it would not be ready for the field until three weeks were gone. Another division of 8,000 under

J. D. Cox had been assigned to the Pope command, but it was out on the Gaulay River in western Virginia, 425 miles from Washington, and the Baltimore and Ohio, over which it would have to travel, had all its cars busy hauling 4,000 or 5,000 men a day between Baltimore and Washington. Burnside and his IX Corps reached Fredericksburg on August 1, but without wagons, artillery, ambulances, or cavalry, and could hardly be considered in shape to give much help. "Please make McClellan do something to prevent reinforcements from being sent here," wired Pope.

Halleck shot off another and very peremptory order to McClellan to get moving. Stanton reached President Garrett of the B & O, found he had some gondolas available, and rushed them out to bring in Cox, who had to make a ninety-mile march and a trip in steamboats before he could reach railhead, but the Secretary co-ordinated him so smoothly that there was no delay. Cox actually reached Washington three days after the gondolas reached him, a highly creditable performance, but one in a vacuum, since the division arrived too late to be of any help to Pope. Twelve regiments of Burnside were sent forward from Fredericksburg at once along the north bank of the Rappahannock under General J. L. Reno; they could draw supplies down from Washington, and Pope had retired to that stream, making junction easy. Burnside himself was dispatched as ambassador to McClellan, an office for which he was admirably qualified, both because he was personally on good terms with the General, and because everyone testified to his singularly winning personality.

He did a good job; McClellan wrote to his wife that Halleck was really his friend, that when the armies were united, he expected to have command of both; and for a few days he really pushed matters. Porter and the V Corps began debarking at Acquia Creek on the twentieth, and took up the march for Fredericksburg at once. Heintzelman and the III Corps also moved with dispatch, but they came in deep-draft ships, and the water at Acquia was shallow, so they were brought round to Alexandria, to be shipped down Haupt's railroad to Manassas. The first elements of the corps reached Pope on the twenty-third; at this date Franklin was already on the tide with the VI

Corps. He would be in Alexandria on the twenty-fourth.

Pope had reorganized his cavalry under a big, slow-moving, sagacious man from the Inspector-General's department, named John Buford, of whom a great deal more would be heard. On the eighteenth Buford's troopers clashed with Confederate Stuart, and removed any doubt about the rebels' purposes by capturing an adjutant with a letter in his pocket, which set forth Lee's plan to crush Pope before he could be reinforced. The questions were how strong he was, and what was the detail of his intentions?—for his cavalry had been raiding on the Union left across the Rappahannock, and there were movements of heavy columns in the valley toward Pope's right.

This was the news of the twenty-fifth, a tense day in the sticky heat of Washington. Pope had been detaining railroad cars at his end of the line, as convenient temporary store-houses for his supplies, while the last of Heintzelman's men and the first of Cox's were waiting at Alexandria for transportation, and the cars had to be extracted. A Confederate cavalry raid on Catlett's Station burned a couple of trains and left some question about the bridge there. Then General Sturgis of the reserve division decided he would be needing transport, though his troops were not ready to move, and to obtain it, seized a section of the railroad west of Alexandria, and refused to allow trains to pass over it in either direction. When the dynamic Haupt arrived to straighten the complex mess out, Sturgis received him with drunken gravity and the immortal words: "I don't care for John Pope one pinch of owl dung." Hours were lost before Haupt could get stern orders from Halleck for the release of the road.

Pope had been expecting the General-in-Chief to come forward in person to co-ordinate things between the Army of the Potomac and the Army of Virginia, and this seems to have been the intention, but on the night of the twenty-third the wires began to burn with a problem of quite another order, and it pinned Halleck to his desk. Out in the west, General Buell had concentrated his Army of the Cumberland around Nashville, expecting that Confederate Bragg, who had assembled his forces at Chattanooga, would make a try for the recovery of central Tennessee. There was a range of mountains between the two; the news that hit Washington on the twenty-third was that behind the screen of the ridges, Bragg had flung a whole corps through Cumberland Gap into Kentucky, and was now out of the mountains into the blue grass himself, with a couple hundred miles start on Buell.

It presently developed that this was largely Buell's own fault; he had rejected the advice of his number-one man, Thomas, who wanted to close up to the ridges and attack Bragg as soon as he poked his nose out. That settled it; Buell must go, in spite of Halleck's plea to give his old subordinate "a little more time." The command was given to Thomas; but the peculiar Virginian confused things by not finding it honorable to supersede his chief, and there was no time to send anyone else in the midst of a campaign, so Buell had to be restored.

But Louisville, Lexington, Cincinnati, lay open to the rebel rush. There were only some scattered new regiments without any training, or even proper weapons, on the north side of the Ohio, and governors, municipal authorities—everybody—were screaming frantically to the War Department for help. Once more Washington was the only co-ordinating authority: "Just think of the immense amount of telegraphing I have to do," Halleck wired to Pope on the morning of the twenty-sixth, "and then say whether I can be expected to give you any details of the movements of others, even when I know them."

This was in reply to a request for news of Franklin and Cox, who had, in fact, been ordered through Manassas to join Pope at Warrenton that day. But McClellan was now at Alexandria; Franklin would not move without the orders of his immediate superior, and he did not get those orders. That night at eight o'clock, the telegraph operator at Manassas wired that some Confederate cavalry were in the town; then the line went dead.

(It was Stonewall Jackson with 23,000 men, after one of the heroic marches of history; the long lines tramping through heat and dust, munching green corn and apples picked in the bordering fields. "Close up! Close up, men!" from the officers and jingling harness the only sounds, until with a yell they rushed into Manassas under the twilight and feasted half the night on delicacies from the vast Union storehouses before setting fire to everything that could not be eaten or drunk.)

By the following morning, Pope had a fair idea of the situation; wired through Burnside at Fredericksburg that he was concentrating to attack the enemy, but both the III and V Corps had no trains and very little ammunition, and the III Corps no artillery; wanted a strong force sent to Manassas at once, with a construction crew to repair broken bridges, and trainloads of powder and bullets. Halleck wired to McClellan about Franklin again; McClellan replied that Franklin had been ordered "to prepare to move," and that he thought the proper policy was to make the defenses of Washington perfectly safe, for which purpose a couple of new corps should be mobilized. He had a report that the Confederates were moving on Washington and Baltimore with 120,000 men. That night McClellan crossed the river for a conference with Halleck, and everything seemed to be settled about rushing more troops to Pope, but the next afternoon, the twenty-eighth, after Sumner had arrived to add his corps to the troops at Alexandria, there was another dispatch:

McClellan to Halleck, August 28

Neither Franklin's nor Sumner's corps is now in condition to move or fight a battle. It would be a sacrifice to send them out now.

Of course, a copy of this went to Stanton, as all major messages did, and with it came one from Pope, that he was in contact with the enemy and fighting a battle. Up to this time the Secretary's contacts with Halleck had been purely verbal; now he corresponded, and for the record:

Stanton to Halleck, August 28, late

I desire you to furnish me information on the following points:—
1st. At what date you first ordered the general commanding the Army of the Potomac to move from the James River.

232 THE REALIZATION: 1861–1865

2nd. Whether that order was or was not obeyed according to its purport with a promptness which, in your judgment, the national safety required, and at what date the movement commenced.

3rd. What order had been given recently for the movement of Franklin's corps, and whether it was obeyed as promptly as the national safety required.

4th. You will furnish me copies of the orders referred to in the foregoing paragraphs.

Halleck replied that he had ordered McClellan to send away his sick on July 30, and received neither reply nor action; repeated the order on August 2; that he had directed McClellan to move the Army of the Potomac on August 3; that the move had not actually begun until August 14, and not with the promptness he had expected or that the national safety demanded; that he had repeatedly ordered Franklin's corps forward and received only excuses. The documents bore him out.

This reply and its enclosures apparently did not reach Stanton until very late that night, or early on the morning of the twenty-ninth. That same morning McClellan wired that Franklin was in motion, but by early afternoon, there was another McClellan dispatch, saying the corps had halted some seven miles out of Alexandria and did not think it ought to go farther. Halleck replied exasperatedly that he wanted Franklin to go far enough to find out something about the enemy.

That night the President and Secretary Hay had dinner with Stanton and his pretty, pale wife. Hay thought she looked as though it hurt her to smile, and it probably did; she had buried her baby only six weeks before, and the doctors gave her little chance of having another. The Secretary of War was "loud about the McClellan business," and after they rose from table there came a message from Pope that he had fought a heavy battle, suffered 8,000 casualties, but more than held his ground. He asked for Franklin, Cox, Sturgis, and provisions, and commented that he had a dispatch from McClellan, which said that wagons and cars would be loaded with food as soon as Pope sent a cavalry escort to Alexandria to pick them up. "Such a request, when Alexandria is full of troops and we fighting the enemy, needs no comment." At the same time came one more message from McClellan, asking for "distinct orders in reference to Franklin's movements for tomorrow."

He got distinct orders, and finally, at 11:00 A.M. of the thirtieth, ordered Franklin and Sumner forward to link up with Pope. Neither actually moved before 1:30 P.M., and when they did move, it was only in time to meet the stragglers and wounded coming back from the bloody and dreadful defeat of Second Bull Run. For it was not Jackson alone, but Lee's whole army that Pope faced on the two days. On the first, he had been held when one wing could not drive through a prepared position and the other wing never fought at all; and on the second, he had been counterattacked and driven from the field by forces that were really, not imaginatively, superior—in good order, covering his retreat, but driven. He had lost 14,000 men and Phil Kearny, killed in a brush at Chantilly during the retirement.

That day of the thirtieth Stanton had an inspiration that was something less than happy, end product of a series of bickerings that circled around the Surgeon-General's office in a highly unedifying manner. When the Secretary came in, he found Dr. Clement A. Finley occupying the post—a nice old bewhiskered gentleman from Philadelphia, opposed to female nurses, who not only did very little work himself, but also hampered the work of the civilian Sanitary Commission—a volunteer organization which was making a fine record in caring for sick and wounded soldiers. Finley placed a doctor named John Neill in charge of the Washington military hospitals. Presently Stanton had a letter accusing Neill of hopeless inefficiency and peculation, which he forwarded to Finley for report or action. But Finley regarded Neill as a fellow-member of the union, and sent the letter to him instead; there was a libel suit, and Stanton furiously exiled Finley to duty in Boston, from whence he resigned.

This was in April. The Sanitary Commission, by now very influential, secured the appointment of Dr. William A. Hammond, a big, powerful man, as positive as the Secretary, with whom he at once began to spark over the issue of setting up a separate ambulance corps. Halleck said such a corps was unmilitary, the quartermasters had always handled ambulances; Stanton backed the General, on the ground that the army trains were already too large, but the issue was not dead.

The reflux of Second Bull Run was the chance to prove the ambulance service unnecessary; in notices posted at the Treasury and in all hotels, Stanton asked for volunteer surgeons and male nurses to go to the battlefield. There was no transportation; the provost-marshal seized a wild collection of "omnibuses, cabs, market wagons, old family coaches, hay wagons, dog carts, rockaways, sulkies, and gigs," with horses from the livery stables. To fill them a raffish mob from Lord-knows-where began to gather in the evening. A good many of them were drunk, and the rest proceeded to get that way before the night was up. Some of them never reached the conveyances, and many of those who did fell off. Of one contingent of a thousand, only seventy-five reached the army. After this, Dr. Hammond was given his head about the ambulance service; it became a credit to the Union and the model of all future military medicine.

A bad, black day, August 30; if the battle and the nurses were not enough, there came from the west the news that General William Nelson, with a pickup force of raw regiments and local militia, had been heavily defeated and scattered at Richmond, Kentucky; Lexington would be gone in the next few hours, Louisville and Cincinnati were open, and the Ohio River states frantic. Chase waited on Gideon Welles with a paper, the product of Stanton's inquiry to Halleck on the twenty-eighth:

Mr. President,—The undersigned feel compelled by a profound sense of duty to the government and the people of the United States, and to yourself as your constitutional advisors, respectfully to recommend the immediate removal of George B. McClellan from any command in the Armies of the United States. We are constrained to urge this by the conviction that after a sad and humiliating trial of twelve months and by the frightful and useless sacrifice of the lives of many thousand brave men, and the waste of many millions of national means, he has proved to be incompetent for any important military command, and also because by recent disobedience of superior orders and inactivity, he has twice imperilled the fate of the army commanded by General Pope, and while he continues to command will daily hazard the fate of our armies and our national existence, exhibiting no sign of a disposition or capacity to restore by courage and diligence the national honor that has been so deeply tarnished in the eyes of the world by his military failures. We are unwilling to be accessory to the destruction of our armies, the protraction of the war, the waste of our natural resources, and the overthrow of the government, which we believe must be the inevitable consequence of George B. McClellan being in command, and seek therefore, by his prompt removal to afford an opportunity to capable officers under God's providence to preserve our national existence.

It was in Stanton's handwriting (and for that matter, it bears the earmarks of his style); the idea was that a united Cabinet should sign it and give it to Lincoln. Chase, Bates, the Postmaster-General, and Stanton himself had already signed, Smith of the Interior said he would, too. Welles agreed that McClellan was a menace, but he declined to add his name; the paper was disrespectful and improper. After another effort on the following day, the petition idea was dropped.

At the same time, Lincoln was saying to young John Hay: "He has acted badly toward Pope; he really wanted him to fail."

Even the President did not know that as early as his arrival at Alexandria, the Commander of the Army of the Potomac had been writing to his wife:

I take it for granted that my orders will be as disagreeable as it is possible to make them, unless Pope is beaten, in which event they will want me to save Washington. Nothing but their fears will induce them to give me any command of importance, or to treat me otherwise than with discourtesy.

III

THERE was a formal Cabinet meeting on September 2. Stanton came when the others were already there and very excited, saying that he had just heard from Halleck that the President had consolidated the Army of Virginia with the Army of the Potomac and placed McClellan at the head of both. Even Welles found this news alarming; when Lincoln presently entered and confirmed it, burly Chase went right at him with the remark that giving that man command was equivalent to giving Washington to the rebels. Stanton backed him up. Lincoln replied that it distressed him exceedingly to differ from them, but "There is no one in the army who can man these fortifications and lick these troops into shape half as well as he can."

This much was probably true; as soon as the tired, dispirited ,oldiers who came pouring into town with the drunken nurses heard that their favorite general was in the saddle again, they began to feel better. The announcement was cheered whenever it was made; overnight the mob that had shown signs of degenerating into a rabble became an army again, its duties precisely performed, the men in position, the officers going about their business with snap. Supplies of lint, bandages, and surgeons, for which Stanton had called on the northern cities, began to arrive on every train; the bags of cement which had barricaded the Treasury building were taken down, and the files of official papers, which the War Secretary had packed for shipment north, were unpacked again.

The General's restoration was clearly necessary, for though Lincoln did not know what McClellan was thinking, writing to his wife, or saying to Porter, he could and did know that a horrible black effluvium of mistrust was rising from the defeated army; it blamed, it was suspicious of, absolutely everyone but its favorite general. Pope had lost, he was a liar and a braggart, possibly disloyal; but that was not all. The colonel of the First Michigan Cavalry wrote from his deathbed that he was a victim of Pope's imbecility and McDowell's treason, and the letter was published. "Traitor! Scoundrel!" the troops shouted at the cold, unpopular corps commander as they marched past him.

It was unjust, it was unreasonable; pure moonshine and imagination, for McDowell had done as well as any officer could. But there it was, a factor in that morale which it is as important that soldiers should take into battle as their bullets. So McDowell had to be relieved (the dynamic Hooker received his corps), and McClellan reinstated. Yet even so, Lincoln's step was less taken in the military field than in that region of high political strategy, where he never hesitated to overrule his Secretary of War.

For as long ago as the day when the President and Welles rode back from the cemetery where little James Stanton had been laid to rest, Lincoln brought up the subject of a proclamation freeing slaves within the rebel lines. The matter was quite thoroughly aired at a Cabinet meeting on July 22, while McClellan was still at Harrison's and Halleck just about to take up the reins of war.

The discussion was described as acrimonious; only Chase and Stanton were strongly for the idea, and Blair was vehemently opposed. Seward thought it might cause foreign governments to break the blockade and maintain slavery for the sake of cotton, which was a measure of how well Seward could read the Continental mind; but also that with military affairs in their current condition, it would "be viewed as the last maneuver of an exhausted government, a cry for help." The last point carried so much weight that Lincoln agreed to defer the whole matter until there was a victory on which to issue the proclamation.

Even this did not quite satisfy Stanton; as early as that May of 1862, he had prepared a proclamation of his own, declaring the slaves of rebel owners forfeited to the United States and, since the state could not hold slaves, therefore free. Lincoln persuaded him not to issue it, but slaves kept pouring into the Union lines, especially in the Department of the South, which consisted of the seized outposts along the Atlantic coast. Stanton asked Congress for legal authority to free them by confiscation. Lincoln intended to veto the bill if it reached him, and even had his veto message written, on the ground that Congress had no authority to legislate on slavery within the states. Stanton thereupon consulted with his Congressional friends, and they put through an explanatory rider, saying that the act was intended to confiscate no more than the rebels' life interest in their property, which removed the ground for the veto, whereupon the bill went through.

But that was in May; now the time had come (the President felt and said) when the purpose of the North must be made absolutely clear before the world, even in the face of defeat—especially in the face of defeats that might persuade Europe to recognize the Confederacy, unless that recognition appeared to entail approval and support of human slavery; the constitutional monarchies could not afford that. "This step is a necessity; in delaying it so long we have given dissatisfaction if not offense to many whose support we cannot afford to lose; and we shall have been condoning a moral wrong." Lincoln would wait only for the victory; but he would not let Chase and Stanton hurry him into it.

What Stanton failed to see, but what Lincoln perceived with the greatest clarity, was that the proclamation required a counterweight, to assure the conservative pro-Union elements, of whom Montgomery Blair was the representative in the Cabinet, that the administration had not capitulated to the Radicals; that although the Confederacy might be conducting a war in favor of slavery, the federal government was not fighting against that debatable institution. Four states of the Union were still slaveholding states, and Bragg's invasion (in which he carried arms for the 10,000 recruits he expected to gather in Kentucky) made one of them an area of peculiar sensitivity just at this time. None of the slaveholding Union states had shown the slightest interest in the bill passed by Congress in April, offering federal financial help to any state that wished to set up a plan for compensated emancipation.

The fall elections were also hurrying on, and Lincoln could not and did not miss the indications that, all across the sweep of the North, there was a reaction in favor of conservatism.

Now McClellan was, on the opposite side, as much of a politician as John C. Frémont. He wrote letters to the papers from the peninsula; he talked freely to people who would get his views into the papers; he had received at his headquarters the disreputable, but indisputably powerful Democrat, Fernando Wood, mayor of New York. He was for protecting the rights of Southern property, even slaves. He was the darling of the conservative press, which had a vague, but substantially accurate, idea that the Radical Chase and the assimilated Radical Stanton wanted to get rid of him.

Returning McClellan to the command of the army was not only a military step which could not possibly do much harm while the strategic purpose was the defense of Washington; it was also a political measure which made use of McClellan's politics for a purpose McClellan never would have approved —that of rallying the nation behind the proclamation that would be issued with the next victory.

BACKDROP

New York Evening Express

Secretary Stanton, from the start, began to intrigue against Genl. McClellan, in order to take from the General the command of the Army of the Potomac and concentrate it upon himself. The President is in his power—in the same way as a merchant is in the power of a confidential clerk. The President has to act upon the facts as presented by the Secretary of War.

New York Herald

The Popular Excitement is vindictive against Secretary Stanton and the abolition traitors of whom he is the tool. The members of the cabinet who ought to be changed are the Secretary of War, the Secretary of the Navy and the Secretary of the Treasury. No one wants to see Secretary Seward disturbed. Already, the people of Philadelphia hoot Stanton's name in the streets and declare that no more men will enlist while he remains in office.

14

TWO HEROES

THIRTY-FIVE new regiments joined the army that marched cheering past McClellan's residence and out of the city, north and west, to face victorious Lee. Pope's report on Banks's rashness in bringing on the Cedar Mountain battle was so stiff that the General-Governor was relieved of field command and brought in to take over the defenses of Washington; his corps was numerated the XII, and given to old General Mansfield of New Hampshire, with the white beard. The organization was tightened along the line; among the troops the atmosphere became almost as electric as in those brave days a year gone; and on September 6, late, the tidings were that they marched to battle, for the Army of Northern Virginia was across the Potomac, north of Leesburg.

McClellan rode out the next morning, surrounded by his staff and a regiment of regular cavalry; from field headquarters he reported that Lee had 120,000 men, and was probably bound for Baltimore. The General wanted reinforcements, particularly Porter's V Corps, more of the troops from the Washington defenses, and that part of Keyes's IV Corps which was still in the peninsula; but he was pushing forward with what he had. Porter was placed on the march to join him at once, and the Department forwarded reports collected partly by Governor Curtin of Pennsylvania, partly by officers from General Wool's Baltimore staff, which estimated the rebel host as not over 50,000 and said positively that it had marched through Frederick, complete with trains, in sixteen hours. This would make the 50,000 estimate almost exactly right.

McClellan made no comment on these figures; the map showed him pushing forward at the rate of six miles a day, while he cleaned up organizational details as he went. On September 13 he was in Frederick, being pelted with flowers from the windows, where some of his officers heard the beginnings of the story that developed into the legend of Barbara Frietchie. That morning he had an incredible piece of good fortune; a private of the 27th Indiana found on an abandoned Confederate campground, wrapped around some cigars, a paper signed by Lee's personal adjutant. It was the Southern commander's Special Order No. 191, setting forth his plan of campaign in detail—and it was a plan of campaign that offered McClellan an unrivaled opportunity to destroy the Confederate army.

Lee himself, with two of the big Confederate divisions, was at Hagerstown or near it; Jackson, with all the rest, had turned westward to capture the Union force covering the important B & O bridge at Harpers Ferry. To put the matter in nongeographical terms, the Confederate army was split in two, and the Army of the Potomac was nearer either part than they were to each other. The news reached Washington in a rather cryptic telegram from the General to the President: "I have all the plans of the rebels, and will catch them in their own trap if my men are equal to the emergency"; together with word from Curtin of Pennsylvania that many of the Confederates were ragged, hatless, barefoot, and the Marylanders were showing no enthusiasm whatever over being rescued from the despot's heel.

The next day there was a more detailed dispatch to Halleck, speaking of finding one of Lee's orders; then on the evening of the fifteenth an outline battle report. McClellan had forced Crampton's and Turner's gaps in South Mountain; he said Lee had told somebody "that he must admit they had been shockingly whipped" and placed his own loss at 15,000 men. Brave, soldierly Reno, who had taken over the IX Corps while Burnside served as McClellan's second-in-command, was killed. That same day old General Scott got a telegram of self-

congratulation from McClellan, and the word came that
Harpers Ferry had surrendered with 12,000 men and considerable stores, but in revenge, the cavalry of the command had
escaped, and, in making their way out of the trap, captured
Longstreet's reserve ammunition train.

The sixteenth was without news; early on the morning of
the seventeenth McClellan wired that he had found the enemy
in position around Sharpsburg, behind Antietam Creek, and
was waiting for a ground fog to lift before attacking. The day
dragged until five in the evening; then a message from the
field:

We are in the midst of the most terrible battle of the war, perhaps of history. Thus far it looks well, but I had great odds against
me. Hurry up all the troops possible. Our loss has been terrific, but
we have gained much ground. I have thrown the mass of the army
on the left flank. Burnside is now attacking the right, and I hold
my small reserve consisting of Porter's corps, ready to attack the
center as soon as the flank movements are developed.

This looked better than any previous field dispatch of Mc-
Clellan's. It was presently followed by a request for ammunition, especially artillery ammunition, to be sent to Hagerstown.
Stanton had bowed himself out of direct contact with the army
after McClellan's restoration, not even mentioning the General
to his fellow Cabinet members, and only grunting when they
brought up the matter, letting Halleck handle all the correspondence. His only intervention had been an order detaching
the stately General John Reynolds to Pennsylvania to organize
the state's reserves at the urgent request of Governor Curtin.
But the ammunition represented an emergency; the Secretary
sat up all night to get McClellan his bullets past the mess caused
by the fact that Lee's advancing troops had destroyed thirty-
six miles of railroad track and twenty-three bridges, with the
shops at Martinsburg, and a not inconsiderable number of
trains.

A special train was loaded with ammunition at once and
dispatched via Baltimore and Harrisburg to Hagerstown, with
orders signed by Stanton to the three different railroads

involved: "[This train] must have the right of way through-out, as General McClellan needs the ammunition, to be used in the battle to be fought tomorrow. It is expected that you will use every possible effort to expedite this train." A duplicate trainload of ammunition was sent forward to Frederick; and a wagon convoy of 414 loads followed by road. So did a newly organized division of 8,000 under General A. A. Humphreys.

But the ammunition was never unloaded, for no battle was fought on that morrow, the nineteenth bringing from McClellan only: "Our victory is complete; the enemy is driven back into Virginia," and the twentieth a request that cavalry from the Washington defenses should embarrass Lee's operation. After the high hopes this looked so little good that Halleck had to reply: "We are still left entirely in the dark in regard to your own movements and those of the enemy. You should keep us advised of both as far as you know them."

McClellan replied with regrets that the General-in-Chief had to do so much fault-finding and had "not found leisure to say one word of commendation of the recent achievements of this army, or even to allude to them." He followed this up crisply with a call for twenty new regiments, but by the date he did so, officers, correspondents, and wounded were filtering back into Washington, and the story of the Antietam campaign and its tragically lost opportunities was becoming clear.

It had been a heavy battle all right—as heavy as Shiloh: 12,000 casualties for the Union side, 13,000 for the Confederates, after as dreadful a day as any seen on the continent. But the more one examined the maps, the more one went over the details of the campaign, the more the why's piled up. McClellan had spent the day of the battle on the porch of a house on a hill which gave a good view of the whole field; why had he left the I and XII Corps to fight on the Union right for four hours, without putting in another man? Why had he let Sumner and the II Corps fight a furious battle on the right-center until well past the meridian, while Franklin's V Corps only supported without helping—thus allowing the battered rebels to shift men from one part of the line to another? Why had McClellan only sent Burnside and the IX Corps in on the left when the battle was all over elsewhere, except for some can-

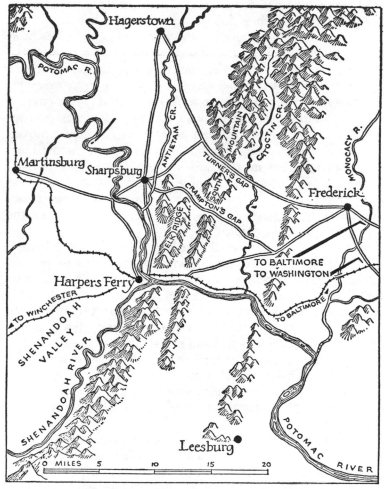

The Antietam Campaign—September 1862

nonading? Why had Porter's V Corps stayed under the General's eye, sitting around on the ground all day while the others fought? The Humphreys division joined Porter that night, bringing him up to 21,000; why, in heaven's name, had not these strong fresh troops been used for a renewal of the attack on the eighteenth? This is what Grant did at Shiloh, and here at Antietam, Lee had a river at his back, could not retreat or even scatter as the rebels did from the western battle.

And while one was about it, why had the Confederates been allowed to unite their separated wings? It appeared that Franklin's corps had the lead of the march on the night Lee's order was found; from where he stood it was seventeen miles by road to Harpers Ferry; but it took him two days to cover a third of this distance, and to push through what was only an outpost line at Crampton's Gap. In fact, he had never moved at all until the morning of the fourteenth, and neither had McClellan with the main guard, though the records showed he had Lee's lost order in his hands at least by early afternoon of the thirteenth. Why? Why? Why? It did not make sense; or rather, it made sense only in one sense. "McClellan has the slows," said Lincoln dolefully.

Yet to remove him now, on the heels of a victory, even if a disappointing and strangely incomplete one, was to remove the much-desired occasion for the Emancipation Proclamation, and God alone knew when there would be another such chance for that document. McClellan with his slows was not likely to provide one soon; nor Buell, crawling toward Bragg across the map of Kentucky at an equally snaillike pace. And though there came from the army farther west the news that on September 19 and 20, at Iuka, Mississippi, General W. S. Rosecrans had beaten off a Confederate attack in the most handsome manner, there was no news of a pursuit, or of the rebels badly hurt.

Antietam would have to serve as the moment for the proclamation; on September 22 Lincoln called a formal Cabinet meeting, and as Stanton sat in frozen silence, read a passage from Artemus Ward, laughed heartily, then said he would issue the proclamation at once; had called them together only to see whether the text might be revised with advantage.

It was in the papers two days later. When McClellan read it in the *Baltimore Sun*, he threw the paper in the corner and stamped his foot. "There! Look at that outrage!" he cried. "I shall resign my commission tomorrow!"—and wrote his wife that this "with the continuation of Stanton and Halleck in office, render it almost impossible for me to retain my commission and my self-respect at the same time."

II

APPARENTLY he beat his self-respect into line, for he made no motion toward resigning; he stayed where he was, and told Halleck, who arrived the next day in a fruitless attempt to wring a plan of campaign out of him by personal interview, that he needed large reinforcements and was prepared to attack Lee if the Confederates should again cross into Maryland. Stanton had no part in this mission; he was extremely busy, not only with the daily details, but also with a conference of state governors, which met at Altoona, Pennsylvania, the twenty-fifth "to take measures for the more active support of the government," which was technically a way of saying that the agenda would be concerned with methods of raising more troops. Morgan of New York refused to come, on the ground that his state was already in excess of its quota.

He may have suspected that any conference summoned by Pennsylvania's Curtin, and Tod of Ohio (who were the promoters), and in which this pair, with Andrew of Massachusetts, were the moving spirits, would have quite other objectives than the straightening out of the recruitment business. He would have been perfectly right. Andrew and Curtin had made themselves a steering committee to lay two proposals before the conference—how to get rid of McClellan and how to persuade Lincoln to do something positive on the subject of slavery. The news the governors found in their papers on the day before the conference assembled took all the steam out of the second proposal, and there were too many Democrats present for anything to be done with the first, so Stanton tried to coax them into giving the conference some meaning by a pronouncement in favor of using new recruits to fill up the old regiments already in service. But this was a sacred cow; every time a new regiment was formed, a governor could appoint a new colonel. Thus the conference only drank whisky, listened to some speeches, voted approval of Lincoln's proclamation (the slave states and New Jersey dissenting), and, after a trip to Washington to shake hands with the President, wandered homeward in an atmosphere of futility.

They were closely followed to the capital by a singular character named J. Wesley Greene, a writer for the new *Chicago Times*, which carried its opposition to the war so far that many generals refused to allow its sale within the area of their commands. He had been in Richmond, he said; brought with him terms of peace given verbally by Jefferson Davis, which included a general amnesty for political offenses, restoration of all fugitive slaves, and each of the high contending parties to be responsible for its own debts. Lincoln called Stanton in; there were several hours of talk that day and on the two following, but that, too, ended in futility, with the Secretary's giving Greene $100 and an order on the railroads for his transportation to Chicago.

Halleck came back from his visit to McClellan baffled by his inability to get anything positive out of the man, and much worried over affairs in the West. He had left Grant with a front covering the lateral railroad from Memphis to the great bend of the Tennessee River, and instructions to keep the line operating. But the rebels were giving Grant a good deal of trouble with cavalry raids; he had been forced to send two divisions to help Buell against Bragg's northern invasion, and although Iuka was a handsome victory, it showed that rebel forces were far out on the eastern end of the line, the most dangerous spot.

The Confederate commanders—old Pap Price, of the original Mississippi command, and Earl Van Dorn, who had been brought across the Mississippi, with the reconstituted relics of the army that had fought at Pea Ridge—might either slide up the corridor east of the Tennessee and join Bragg, or they might unite and smash a part of Grant's thinly distributed forces. Handling such a situation on the map was one of Halleck's favorite sports and he gave it all his time, telegraphing Grant two or three times a day.

Stanton himself could clearly accomplish nothing about

discovering McClellan's intentions—the General's correspondence with his wife remained private, but he said enough in public to leave no doubt about his feelings toward the Secretary—and so Lincoln in person went on to the Army of the Potomac's headquarters. The visit produced nothing but a photo of the two at a table where the American flag was being used as a tablecloth. The President stayed several days, returning to Washington just in time to learn that one of Halleck's alternatives had come true. On October 3 Price and Van Dorn united, and slashed viciously at Rosecrans' division of Grant around Corinth. The night wore on with doubtful news, but next day the wires told how Grant had hit back, and the two Confederates were driven from the field, considerably battered—a thing which, it was becoming increasingly apparent, was likely to happen to people who slashed at Grant.

There was a tripartite conference—President, Secretary, General-in-Chief—and on October 6, Halleck sent McClellan a peremptory order: "The President directs that you cross the Potomac and give battle to the enemy or drive him south. Your army must move now while the roads are good. The President advises the interior line between Washington and the enemy, but does not order it. You will immediately report what line you adopt, and when you intend to cross the river; also to what point reinforcements are to be sent. I may add that the Secretary of War and the General-in-Chief fully concur with the President in these instructions."

McClellan to His Wife, October 8

I received today a very handsome set of resolutions from the councils of Philadelphia, thanking me for the last campaign. The councils pitched into the government for not thanking me, most beautifully. The phrase about my having "organized victory" is a cut at Stanton, who last winter issued an order scouting the idea of "organizing victory" and rested on the sword of Gideon and Donnybrook Fair.

The Commander of the Army of the Potomac answered Halleck's order with a remark that he was pushing everything as rapidly as possible to get ready for the advance, but he found it necessary to go to Philadelphia to visit his wife, and savor the incense of the councils at first hand; and on the night of Thursday the ninth, confused accounts of a desperate battle at Perryville in Kentucky began to drift in.

The next day there was a hot debate in the Cabinet; Chase said that the people of Norfolk were suffering, and wanted permits to bring out some of their products in exchange for necessities. The kind-hearted President was inclined to agree that they should, in spite of the fact that the whole thing was rather obviously one of those deals for trade across the line, to the benefit of the financial men with whom Chase consorted. Welles and Stanton found themselves in the unusual position of agreeing perfectly; the Navy man said the object of a blockade was to cause suffering, and if it were raised for one place, it should be for all, while Stanton rapped out that Norfolk was hot with rebellion, and aid sent there would go straight to the relief of Richmond. Lincoln said he had not sufficiently considered that aspect; asking Chase to see what could be done.

Next morning came word that Confederate cavalry were in Chambersburg, Pennsylvania, and two days later the discouraging tidings that it was Stuart, with his whole command, and he had ridden completely around the Army of the Potomac for the second time, crossing the river scot-free between McClellan's army and Washington. McClellan complained that the War Department had not furnished his cavalry with enough horses to prevent such movements; he was getting only 150 remounts a week. The McClellan newspapers in the north picked up the charge with an alacrity which suggested a leak at headquarters.

Stanton to Quartermaster-General Meigs, October 13

General complaint is made by General McClellan of the inadequate supply of cavalry horses for his command. You will please report what efforts have been made and are now being made by your department for that purpose and whether any and what authority, aid or instructions can be given by the Secretary of War to accomplish this object.

Meigs replied promptly and with figures; from September 1 to October 11, McClellan had received 10,254 horses, more than Stuart had in his whole command, an average of 1,709 a week. The political campaign looked bad and there were complaints from Illinois about the number of refugee Negroes sent there; on the fourteenth Stanton stopped the movement, and McClellan protested that his army could not move for lack of shoes. To another request from Stanton, Meigs replied that every requisition of the Army of the Potomac for shoes and clothing had been met, and McClellan telegraphed that he needed more carbines and muskets. But at last, after another order from Halleck, on October 26, came word that the army was crossing the Potomac, east of the Blue Ridge. Lee was reported still in the valley; Lincoln told Hay, and probably Stanton as well, that he would make this a test case. If McClellan allowed the Army of Northern Virginia to interpose between him and Richmond without a battle, out he would go.

By this date the full reports from the battle at Perryville and its strategic sequel were in, and the jig was up for Halleck's friend, Buell. In the battle itself he had engaged only half his forces, and whatever was gained had been gained because a young brigadier named Sheridan counterattacked right into the teeth of a rebel advance against him, and tore the enemy center to pieces. After the battle, Buell had moved so mildly on the track of the retreating Confederates that they got away safely into the mountains—no more fighting, no more damage. Now Buell had no such political protective coloration as McClellan; indeed, when the Western governors called at the White House after the Altoona conference, they were pretty strong over the complaints they had received from soldiers of their states about his harsh discipline; and they had some remarks of their own about the dangers Buell's slowness had brought upon them.

So Buell must go; but who should be given the Army of the Cumberland? Stanton still wanted Thomas, the victor of Mill

Spring, who had made a wonderful march to join Buell at Mumfordville during the campaign, just when the Confederates appeared to have trapped the Union army. Chase was for Rosecrans, Grant's second; he was a Catholic and his appointment would have a happy effect on the elections, besides he was an Ohio man, while Thomas had refused the command once before. Stanton distrusted this Rosecrans, not liking the way he had let the rebels escape at Corinth when Grant set a trap that should have wiped them out. The two Cabinet members argued the thing out, with Lincoln as referee; finally he cocked his head on one side and said something about Thomas having had his chance: "Let the Virginian wait; we will try Rosecrans." Stanton went back to the War Department, dumped down in a chair, and said sourly to Piatt, whom he found waiting: "Well, you have your choice of idiots; now look out for frightful disaster!"

The Army of the Potomac slid slowly down the face of the Blue Ridge; on election day, November 4, McClellan reported that the head of his infantry column was in front of Ashby's Gap through the mountains, and resistance was expected. But next morning Stanton walked into the President's office with another telegram; Lee's main body had been located, and it was at Culpeper, behind the Rappahannock, between McClellan and Richmond.

"Mr. President, what do you think now?"

"As you do," said Lincoln, and without another word began to write.

General Order No. 182

By direction of the President of the United States, it is ordered that Major-General McClellan be relieved from the command of the Army of the Potomac, and that Major-General Burnside take command of that Army.

By order of the Secretary of War

III

THIS was not the end of the McClellan business; by no means the end of it. On November 10, General Fitz John Porter was relieved of the command of the V Corps; on November 17, he was placed in arrest and on November 27, he was ordered before a court-martial for trial. The charges were connected with the Second Bull Run campaign: that he had not moved in time to join Pope's main body, as ordered, by a night march on August 27; that he had violated an order issued to him and McDowell jointly, to move forward together on August 29; that he had disobeyed a very positive order to attack Jackson's right flank on the afternoon of the same day (this was later famous as "the 4:30 order"); that he had acted with unnecessary slowness on August 30, the day of the Union defeat, falling back prematurely afterward. The charges were not brought by Pope himself, who had only asked for a court of inquiry into the whole campaign, but by his inspector-general, Brigadier-General S. B. Roberts.

Behind all this lay another Charles P. Stone story. On that August 27, the date of the first disobedience charged against him, Porter wrote a letter to his friend Burnside: "The strategy is magnificent, and tactics in the inverse proportion. I do not doubt the enemy has large amounts of supplies provided for them and I believe they have a contempt for this Army of Virginia. I wish myself away from it, with all our old Army of the Potomac, and so do our companions. Most of this is private, but if you can get me away please do so. Make what use of this you choose, so it does good." Two days later, still without having been in action, he sent Burnside another letter: "I hope Mac is at work and will soon get us out of this." These documents expressed such singular feelings toward the general under whom Porter was supposed to be in action that Burnside found it necessary to lay them before Halleck and Lincoln; unquestionably Stanton knew of them, too. On September 1 the President called McClellan in and told him that he did not quite trust what Porter might do.

For answer McClellan produced a long letter that he himself had received from Porter that morning. "The men are without heart, but will fight if cornered," it said. It said Pope had held a council of his corps commanders, to whom he announced his intention of standing his ground and fighting, which disappointed them all. It said: "I do not wish to see the army back if it can be helped; but I fear it may be kept here at the will of the enemy, to cripple it so that when it does get back it will be so crippled that it cannot defend the forts against the powerful enemy. I expect to hear hourly of our rear being cut and our supplies and trains at Fairfax station being destroyed, as we are required to stay here and fight. The bearer will tell you much."

McClellan did not say what the bearer had told him, but he considered the letter a complete vindication of his friend; it was the sort of letter he himself might have written. Lincoln did not see it in quite the same light, and neither did Stanton. The President had McClellan send Porter a telegram asking him to give Pope his full support, which was all that could be done at the time; but on September 5, with the campaign over, an order was prepared relieving Porter, together with Franklin and Charles Griffin, one of the former's brigadiers, who had done a good deal of talking around Willard's. They were to go before a court of inquiry. But by September 5 McClellan was in the saddle again; he asked that the relief order be suspended, and in accordance with the policy of giving him anything within reason, it was suspended. But this did not quiet the stories, nor the accumulating evidence that Porter had so much loyalty for McClellan that there was very little left over for anyone or anything else; nor did it wipe out the fact that since he had been attacked at Gaines' Mill, he had done less fighting than any other corps commander.

At the trial, his defense on the charge of failure to make a night march, as ordered, to join Pope's main body was that the night was very dark, nothing would have been gained by starting his march at once instead of two hours later; and besides, the men were tired and hungry. As for the joint order of the twenty-ninth, it had been ambiguous; and Porter brought testimony contradicting McDowell's own that the two men had made arrangements to move forward together. More of the defense testimony tended to show that Pope's 4:30 P.M. order was received too late for any attack to be made, and that the ground was too rough for an attack; he had in fact sent forward a skirmish line of two regiments supported by two more. On the thirtieth, he had not really retreated, only written notes to McDowell and General King, who commanded the division next to the V Corps in line, saying that he was going to retreat, and they had better send their trains to the rear.

Now the delayed night march was no great thing in itself, only it went rather peculiarly with Porter's letter to Burnside of the same date, saying that he wanted to be away from Pope. There was no getting away from the record of the twenty-ninth, however; McDowell and Porter had started from approximately the same place, McDowell's corps had been in action and fought hotly, while Porter's had not fought at all, except for the two regiments in the skirmish line. Late in the afternoon, the positive attack order, the one of 4:30, found Porter talking to General Sykes, one of his division commanders. Porter did not mention what kind of an order he had received, or that he had received any; he did not send out a reconnaissance to discover whether the ground in his front were impassable or no. He simply did nothing; and on the next day, the thirtieth, likewise did nothing, though the sound of the fighting was plainly audible and some of the effects of it were visible. In a battle where he had one of the strongest corps present, his casualties were 1,678, most of them missing, out of a total Union loss of 14,662.

Reverdy Johnson, Stanton's old opponent in the McCormick Reaper case, was Porter's attorney. He summed up to the effect that the 4:30 order arrived so late it would have resulted in a night attack; that Porter could not have reached Jackson's flank because Longstreet's corps of Lee was in the way; and that anyway, the ground was too rough; as for the thirtieth, Porter had done nothing. This struck the court as rather thin; they founder Porter guilty and sentenced him to be cashiered from the army; Lincoln approved the findings.

15

EBB TIDE

NEW York City requested that General Frémont be sent there to raise and lead a corps of 50,000 men, and Stanton had to knock that idea on the head; General Curtis in Missouri sent some of his troops flying out on a tangent into Kansas with muskets for the local militia and Stanton had to slap him over the wrist for it; the governor of Vermont complained that a regiment from his state had been unfairly blamed for its performance in a fiasco at Baton Rouge, and he had to be soothed; there were papers to prepare in the case of a swindling boardinghouse keeper named Kohnstamm, who had collected $300,000 through false claims on the War Department; it appeared that, after all, the people of occupied Norfolk were hungry enough to justify some relaxation of the blockade rules, and the obstinate Welles had to be outmaneuvered—and there was the question of who should command the Army of the Potomac.

It is not recorded that Stanton had a candidate. Chase did —the handsome and militant Hooker, whom he had visited as the General lay in a bed at the Insane Asylum, with a foot wound received at Antietam. Burnside was the only other possible candidate among the corps commanders, with Mansfield and Reno killed in action, Sumner and Heintzelman clearly growing pretty old for field work, and Franklin touched with a suspicion of Porter's disease. But although he wanted Hooker, Chase could hardly object to Burnside, with whom he had some connection, the General being an intimate of Governor Sprague of Rhode Island, who was so close to Chase that he was to marry the Treasury Secretary's daughter.

Burnside's record was good; he had conducted a complex operation in the North Carolina sounds with success, taking 2,600 prisoners; moved with dispatch to Fortress Monroe when McClellan got into trouble during the Seven Days; moved with dispatch and cheerfulness again to the assistance of Pope. He was frank, loyal, and politically right, both in the army sense as a personal friend of McClellan's, able to tap some of the loyalty the soldiers held for that officer, and also as a member of the War Democrats, the civilian party it would be most desirable to have at the head of an army.

The last consideration was not without importance; even keeping McClellan in until the day after election (deliberately, said the antiadministration press) had not prevented a Democratic swing that was only one step removed from a disaster. Five states were lost, including pivotal New York, which elected Horatio Seymour as governor, frankly for peace with the Confederacy. The Lincoln men kept their control of Congress only by grace of the western frontier states and the Pacific coast.

Burnside to command, then. The new General began modestly, saying, as the flakes of a premature snow fell on his manly face and abundant whiskers, that he was not competent to command so large an army, and answering McClellan's congratulations on the appointment with: "That, sir, is the last thing upon which I wish to be congratulated." But he took hold as though he meant business, immediately wiring a tentative plan of campaign and some desired organizational changes to Halleck. The General-in-Chief went down to army headquarters at Warrenton on November 12 to talk things over. They agreed that the desideratum was to get between Lee and Richmond and force the Confederates to attack in defense of their supply lines and capital. Halleck thought this could best be done by a rapid advance through Culpeper and Gordonsville, along the line McClellan had been following so languidly. Burnside preferred a quick leftward slide to Fredericksburg, and an advance from that point, straight on the Confederate capital. If he stayed close to the Blue Ridge (he said), his communications would be lengthened and exposed to Confederate cavalry raids; the advance on the Fredericksburg line would allow him to be supported by water. Halleck revealed how much of a General-in-Chief he was by neither accepting Burnside's plan nor insisting upon his own, but took both back to Washington for consideration by Lincoln.

Stanton's approval should be part of that consideration, of course. But the western armies were always too far away for him to take any part in the planning phase, and McClellan was either planless or secretive, so that as things had fallen out, the War Secretary kept his hands off plans and confined himself to implementation and the choice of men. More in his line were Burnside's reorganization proposals. The army contained 113,-000 men in six corps, which the commander proposed to realign into three "grand divisions" of two corps each, under Sumner, Franklin, and Hooker. The corps commanders also were shuffled; Reynolds came back from Pennsylvania to take over the I Corps, and W. F. "Baldy" Smith to take the VI Corps in Franklin's Grand Division. George Stoneman, who had been on Steve Kearney's march to California with the famous Mormon Battalion in the old wars, and later commanded a division under Heintzelman, took the III Corps, and Daniel Butterfield, who had been a staff officer, received the V; these two were Hooker's Grand Division.

Sumner's corps commanders were Darius Couch of the II and Orlando B. Willcox, who had been captured at Bull Run and was just back on exchange, in charge of Burnside's old corps, the IX. Heintzelman was relieved of field service to take charge of the Washington defenses, and a place was found for the politically important Banks, as head of an expedition that was to work north from New Orleans against Port Hudson on the Mississippi.

The organizational changes were approved at once, but it took twenty-four hours to obtain Lincoln's assent to the plan of campaign, which he passed down through Halleck with a rider that he thought it would succeed "if you move rapidly

—otherwise not"—a Presidential way of saying, "Now, don't be a McClellan." There were rumors that Jackson was making another descent of the Shenandoah, and President Garrett of the Baltimore and Ohio telegraphed Stanton apprehensively about it, but Stanton never even bothered transmitting the worry to Burnside, while Burnside, confident that his eastward movement would draw the whole Army of Northern Virginia after him, started his march.

On November 19 he reported personally from Falmouth, opposite Fredericksburg, that Sumner's Grand Division was there, Franklin some eight miles north, near Acquia Landing, Hooker six miles west. The pontoon train, expected by water from Washington, had not arrived. The next morning Stanton had a remarkable letter from Joe Hooker; that officer wanted to take his Grand Division across the Rappahannock, and move in behind Fredericksburg to some point on the railroad connecting that place with Richmond; inquired whether rations could be sent him directly from Washington up the mouth of the river. There is no information on what the Secretary thought of this spectacle of a subordinate commander making his own plan of campaign without reference to his commander, and expecting to be supported by the War Department. He merely showed the letter to Lincoln and chalked up a black mark against Hooker in his own mind.

On the day when the Burnside dispatch and the Hooker letter were written, it came on to rain, very heavily and cold, swelling the Rappahannock so that even the upper fords became impassable to anything but cavalry. Burnside explained this in another dispatch of the twenty-second, which also carried the discouraging news that all his troops were still on the north bank, the pontoons for the bridges still being missing; Longstreet's Corps of Lee had reached Fredericksburg.

This did not look much like getting between Lee and Richmond, and when, on the twenty-fifth, another Burnside dispatch reached Washington to say that only one pontoon train had arrived, and that without full equipment, Lincoln and Stanton both went down to Acquia to see Burnside and find out what was wrong. They arrived on the twenty-sixth, to discover the General in good health and spirits, not too cast down over the failure of the pontoons, nor disposed to blame other people, as McClellan had done; determined to force his way through the Fredericksburg line. His contact reports gave Lee's army 85,000 men, which checked well with other sources, and was a welcome relief from McClellan's "Oriental estimates" of Confederate force. President and Secretary returned, well satisfied, and since Burnside had all the enemy before him, drew Heintzelman and 15,000 men from the Washington defenses to move down to Acquia as a reserve for the main army.

II

Parenthetical. The story of the slow-moving pontoons did not come out until much later, and it was this: Halleck, with his usual talent for writing something out and then assuming that the task was performed, bungled the instructions, and the commander of the Washington Engineer Brigade, Brigadier-General Daniel Woodbury, was too lazy to leave his comfortable bed in the city. The pontoons had been at Harpers Ferry; on the day of his Warrenton conference with Burnside, Halleck telegraphed to Woodbury that they should be sent to Washington, but treated the whole matter as routine business, putting into the wire no sense that the pontoons were in urgent demand. Then he forgot about the matter.

On November 16, Woodbury telegraphed Burnside that one pontoon train would start that day by road, while the second would come by water. But the first train did not actually start until the nineteenth; Woodbury held them at Washington to fit the train with new horses, and the horses with new harness. This train ran into the storm which began the day it moved, and was so mired and so lacking in anyone to drive things through that the water-borne train, leaving much later, was the first to reach Acquia. When this train did arrive, there were no horses or wagons to take the pontoons the eleven miles cross country to Fredericksburg.

Woodbury later told the Committee on the Conduct of the War that the real trouble lay with Burnside; he should have waited five days more at Warrenton before beginning his march—which is to say that the commander of the army should suit his operations to the engineer officer's convenience. Stanton never forgave Woodbury after he learned the facts, and if, after this, he sometimes took similar movements into his own hands, it was because the Antietam ammunition reached McClellan in plenty of time, while the pontoons reached Burnside too late.

Actually, the opportunity to make anything of the campaign went out the window on the twenty-second, when Longstreet's men began lining Marye's Heights, behind Fredericksburg. Up to the seventeenth, Lee had been completely deceived as to the purpose of Burnside's march, and on the nineteenth he was still contemplating no more than a holding action at Fredericksburg, with a main defense position behind the next river, the North Anna.

But now he had the heights in strength, and Burnside's decision to persist had become a frightful mistake, with the enemy well intrenched and plentifully supplied with artillery. Persistence may be a military virtue; it may also indicate paucity of resource. The civilians who visited Burnside were not only still too much amateurs of the business of war to suspect this fact; they were also in the grip of pressures from the constituencies which had just elected so many men who called the war a failure. In a military sense, the right thing was to maneuver upstream again, or to abandon such a campaign altogether and go into winter quarters. Everyone, even Burnside, particularly Burnside with his political connections, knew that such a step would be fatal after McClellan's removal for lack of aggressiveness.

The string had to be played out; and, while it was being played out, the singular J. Wesley Greene published in the *Chicago Times* his account of his interviews with Jefferson Davis, Lincoln, and Stanton, describing the President as "the highest type of despot" and the Secretary as revealing so much "semi-fiendish vindictiveness" that he, Greene, would not use an order for free transportation back to Chicago, because he feared Stanton would have him assassinated en route.

III

On the night of December 11, 1862, Haupt's information service brought the news that Union troops were in Fredericksburg, while Sigel, with the new XI Corps, which had been covering Washington from the region of Manassas, and Slocum, with the new XII, which had been at Harpers Ferry, were on the march to support Burnside. The news of December 12 was still cheerful: Burnside across the river in force and preparing to attack. The thirteenth being a Saturday, Secretary Welles laid aside work in his own department, being concerned over the results of the fighting, and stepped around to the War Department. He did not see Stanton; someone told him that the troops had done well, and Burnside and our generals were in good spirits. He noted a certain "shuffling over of papers and maps, and a far-reaching vacant gaze at something undefined and indescribable" which filled him with apprehension.

The fact was that at this time nobody knew much more than Welles. It was not until dawn on Sunday that a memo report from Burnside said all his troops were south of the river, had taken the first ridge outside the town in spite of heavy losses —"about 5,000"—and hoped to gain the dominating crest that day. But then less gladsome messages began to run along the lines, and toward evening dispatches from some of the correspondents that confirmed Welles's worst fears. The losses were not 5,000, but over 12,000, more than at bloody Antietam, and with nothing—absolutely nothing—to show for it, for the men had been spent in suicidal head-on assaults against steep hills covered with artillery and stone fences lined with riflemen. The Confederates on their crests had hardly been hurt at all; the rather hysterical Henry Villard of the *New York Tribune* doubted whether the army could be extricated from its position, with the victorious rebels on the hills above and a river in spate at its back. He managed to reach a telegraph office and send off this analysis in spite of the censors, but his story was so disheartening that the paper (rather fortunately) did not print it for days.

As the bad news filtered in, bit by bit, Lincoln came gangling over to the War Department and outwatched the bear, waiting for hope. Stanton kept the vigil with him, but on his feet, trotting in and out, working like a maniac at the mountain of details, contracts, matters of enlistment, anything to keep busy.

The next morning, Monday, December 15, brought Haupt, the railroader. He had been at the front and, indeed, in the battle, and felt better than the dispatches sounded. The army had dug itself in after its repulse, he said; there were adequate bridges for it to retreat on, and the northern heights were lined, hub to hub, with that wonderful Union artillery which from Gaines' Mill to Antietam had never failed to beat a Confederate attack into the ground.

His picture of Burnside was less reassuring. "Oh! Oh, those men! Those men over there!" the General had cried, and was with some difficulty dissuaded from placing himself at the head of his old IX Corps for a desperate charge up the hills, win or die on the field. Lincoln wanted Halleck to order a withdrawal north of the river, but Halleck said, no, it would be interfering with a commander in his own province. He agreed with the President and Secretary, however, that it would be wise to go down to the front for a look; and that night, in a storm of rain and wind, the Army of the Potomac slipped back across the Rappahannock without the Confederates even knowing it had gone.

Burnside gave out a manly public statement, saying that he alone was responsible for the failure, though he delayed it until Stanton asked him why he had not done something of the kind. It was certainly more than half true, since analysis showed that his efforts to deceive Lee as to the precise point of his crossing before the battle had been childish, and the crossing itself was so clumsily conducted that a whole precious day was wasted in the process.

All the same, the disappointment and anger over the defeat reflected up into the political field, and gave Lincoln one of his worst weeks. On that same night of December 15, when Burnside's men were filing glumly through the wet across the bridges, the Republican senators were in caucus. They decided they knew why the war was going badly; it was the namby-pamby line the government was taking, softness toward the slaveholders and England, the appointment of Democratic generals. The man clearly responsible for this was William H. Seward. They sent a committee to ask that Lincoln get rid of the man. Of course, one of the caucusers was a friend of Seward's, and took him the news even before it reached the White House; the Secretary of State wrote his resignation and began to pack.

Welles agreed with Montgomery Blair that the move was a "secret, underhand combination," engineered by Stanton to protect himself—from what, the Navy Secretary was not quite sure, though he was certain that people all through the North were bitter over the mismanagement of the War Department. The senatorial committee called on the President, discussed matters, and called again. Lincoln desired the full Cabinet to meet the committee; Chase demurred, was pulled into the meeting by the President's gentle insistence, and there publicly told the senators that the members of the Cabinet got along fairly well together.

This was not what he had said and written to several of them privately. Somebody must have reminded him of the fact, because after several days of whisper, whisper, and conferences in every corner, Chase and Stanton also wrote out their resignations. The President laughed triumphantly, told Stanton to go back to his department and forget about it, but held onto Chase's paper, and killed the palace revolution on the ground that neither Chase nor Seward could be spared.

This strain was hardly relieved before another came down in the form of news that all communication with Grant's army in central Mississippi had suddenly been lost; and while it was still lost, yet another tension was added to those of that unhappy Christmas season. Two days after the holiday, Stanton and Halleck were summoned to the President's office. They found Burnside already present, and both men grave. In a few words Lincoln brought the newcomers abreast of the situation. The Army of the Potomac had cooked three days' rations in preparation for another operation, and its cavalry had already begun to move, when Lincoln sent a telegram, asking that nothing be undertaken until there had been a conference of powers. The reason was that two generals from the army had lately called at the White House and described the troops as utterly dispirited and dejected. When a cheer for the General was called for, they hooted instead; the figure of desertions among the men and resignations among the officers was utterly alarming; it would be "dangerous folly" to attempt another campaign while the troops were in such a mood, and the reason they were in it was because they had no confidence in the General who had thrown them at the heights above Fredericksburg.

Burnside wanted to know the names of the officers who had been bearing tales about him, but Lincoln said he believed he had the right to withhold them. Halleck then remarked that such officers should be dismissed, and the four men turned to the material point. Burnside said frankly that he had had differences with the corps and Grand Division commanders—they did not wish to attempt another crossing of the Rappahannock —and he agreed they did not have much confidence in him. (After leaving, he wrote a letter in which he took some of the edge off this by saying they had no confidence in Halleck or Stanton, either.) The question, however, was how true were the charges about the morale of the body of the army.

Burnside, who made the only record of the conference, does not mention Stanton's part in it, but one can hardly imagine the Secretary's not coming in at this point, for he had the figures at his fingertips. Ever since the Army of the Potomac came back from Harrison's Landing, there had been trouble about desertions, straggling, and overlong absences on leave; most of this was due to McClellan's carelessness and his indulgence of the soldiers. In fact, on the day the first commander of the Army of the Potomac was relieved, his returns showed over 88,000 men absent—some of them in hospitals, to be sure, but most of them without any reason. Since then, the background situation had grown measurably worse, not only because of the defeat at Fredericksburg but also because practically all the states were offering bounties for enlistments. This produced a new class of military criminals—bounty-jumpers, who stayed long enough to be recorded at the recruiting bureaus, then slipped away to collect another bounty by enlisting again. Yet, in spite of these factors, the number of absentees in the army under Burnside had declined both absolutely and percentagewise.

This did not look like mass desertions or a morale of despair. Nevertheless, after the conference broke up, Lincoln asked Halleck to go down to the army, talk with the various subordinate commanders, form his own judgment, and tell Burnside what he thought of the plan for a renewed attack. Halleck would not; it was interference with a commander in the field again, he said, and against all military precedent. When Lincoln tried to insist with: "Your military skill is useless to me if you will not do this," the general wrote a resignation. It took all Stanton's persuasiveness to induce him to withdraw it, and withdrawn it had to be, for whatever his faults, there was no one quite like "Old Brains" for chasing details and correctly answering requests from the field.

In the meanwhile, Burnside was back with his command, the British press was highly unfavorable to the Emancipation Proclamation; there were the first flash reports of Rosecrans, fighting a hard battle in middle Tennessee, which looked ominously like the frightful disaster Stanton had predicted; word came at last from Grant, and it was not good.

These were the notes on which 1862 miserably expired.

IV

MOST of Grant's trouble was made in Washington, and Lincoln himself was largely responsible. Back in August, while Pope was feeling southward in the preliminaries to Second Bull Run, there waited on the President one of Grant's division commanders on leave, a certain John A. McClernand.

This McClernand was no ordinary soldier, but a politician from southern Illinois, who had given up his seat in Congress to fight for the Union. Lincoln knew him well, a Douglas Democrat and a powerful orator with a straight black beard and no sense of humor whatever ("Glorious! Glorious!" he used to be heard muttering on the battlefield, "My star is ever in the ascendant!") plus enormous drive—in part, the sort of man Stanton might have been if he had followed politics instead of stepping aside into the law. McClernand had done much to hold to the Union that blackland district of southern Illinois which had so many ties with the South, and as an officer had fought well at Donelson and Shiloh. Now he had an idea.

The business community of the wheat-growing states was extremely anxious, he said, to have the Mississippi reopened for the normal transit of grain to the sea and Europe. This was true, as both Lincoln and Stanton (who was present at the conferences) knew. In addition, the capture of Vicksburg, the most important barrier on the stream, would automatically sever the Confederate lateral supply lines from the producing states in the west to the consuming states in the east. Grant was operating down the line of the Mobile and Ohio Railroad, well inland from the river, in a region so thoroughly fought over that there were no local supplies, and he had to get all his bread and bullets by the cars, down from Columbus, Kentucky. (The influence of Halleck and his map board is traceable at several points in this transaction, not so much from what was reported said as from the considerations that ruled the decisions.) On the upper Mississippi was the navy's fine fleet of ironclad gunboats, which had shown they could work effectively with troops. Here was the proposition: McClernand should go west, raise a quite new army in Illinois, Indiana, and Iowa, and, with the gunboats supporting, take Vicksburg from the front, while the forces defending it were facing Grant in the back country.

McClernand talked so convincingly that he won Lincoln and the Secretary to his plan, and they gave him a secret order to raise the troops and take Vicksburg. It seems that Halleck protested the order and then did not even tell Grant it had been issued; the General-in-Chief was soundly grounded in military protocol, and knew that no commander of a department could tolerate the presence in it of an entirely independent command. But Admiral Porter, who was to head the fleet and who had an intense dislike of West Pointers, was enthusiastic; glad to co-operate.

About mid-November, 1862, letters and telegrams began to come from McClernand, saying that so many men had already gone to war in the Northwest that even his personal magnetism was finding recruiting difficult; and as for cavalry horses, they were simply not to be had. He wanted command of a few thousand troops belonging to General Curtis' southwestern command, now at Helena, Arkansas; more particularly, he wanted orders to start the expedition at once, because as fast as he sent troops to Memphis, Grant took them over.

It developed later that Grant had worked out a strategic plan of his own, not very different from McClernand's, under which his trusted subordinate, Sherman, should go to Memphis with one division of the army, pick up the new levies gathered there (which Grant assumed were solely to reinforce his command), and attack Vicksburg from the river, while Grant himself worked down into the rear of the fortress. This plan Grant submitted to Washington by wire on December 8, at the same time mentioning a certain uneasiness over newspaper reports that McClernand was to have a separate command. Halleck gave Grant's plan his blessing, but with the somewhat cryptic addendum that "the President may insist upon a separate commander."

It took until December 18, when Sherman was at Memphis ready to sail downstream, McClernand still in Springfield, Illinois, for the three men in Washington to realize that they had set up a tangle. They tried to straighten things out by wiring Grant that McClernand was to command the river expedition, and Grant passed this word along to Sherman, telling him to wait at Memphis for McClernand's arrival.

But Sherman never got the word, for early on the morning when Grant sent his wire, a big Confederate cavalry force under Nathan Bedford Forrest struck Grant's railroad lifeline in middle Tennessee and began the job of destroying sixty miles of it, while next morning more Confederate cavalry under Van Dorn ate up the depot of supplies at Holly Springs and about thirty more miles of railroad. Thus the news that came to Washington with the New Year was that Grant's hungry army was in full retreat toward base, that Sherman had got away before anyone stopped him and was irretrievably launched in a frontal assault against the fortress on the tall bluffs of Vicksburg, and that McClernand was steaming down the river with only a few regiments of the troops assigned to him.

The melancholy of this situation was somewhat palliated as the news began to come in from Rosecrans that after two days of terrific battle at Stone River, it was still not a disaster; the Union lines had been driven in, but were standing firm. President and Secretary clung to the wires, eating where they sat, sleeping anyhow, and now Lincoln began to make jokes, for the news was of a brightening picture; after two days of battering the Army of the Cumberland had passed from defense to counterattack, hurrah! and before dawn of January 3, 1863, it was clear that Rosecrans was driving the enemy from the field, after a battle as bloody as Shiloh and more decisive than Antietam.

Even Welles was moved to momentary graciousness, but some of the weight came back on January 6; the Capitol learned that Sherman had attacked and been repulsed at the bluffs of the Mississippi, with the loss of 3,000 men. The question now was what McClernand would do when he arrived on the scene. Washington found out by means of an angry dispatch from Grant on the eleventh, saying the amateur general had kidnapped the fleet and all Sherman's troops, and gone "on a wild goose chase" up the Arkansas River to a Confederate fort known as Arkansas Post. Halleck's comments on this as military procedure must have been a little more pungent than usual. He was allowed to wire Grant the next day that he had complete authority to order McClernand where he wished, and to relieve him if Grant saw fit. After the two officers met, this produced—as might have been expected—

a letter of almost tearful anger from McClernand: "How can you expect success when men controlling the military destinies of the country are more concerned at the success of your volunteer officers than the very enemy beaten by the latter in battle? Something must be done to take the hand of oppression off our citizen soldiers."

But the immediate net result was not too bad, for the guns of the warships had beaten in the embrasures at Arkansas Post, and the place was taken with 5,000 men, while Grant had recovered control of an augmented army, and marched off with it, to have another try at reaching the high ground where Vicksburg stood.

Marched off out of mind; while the tangled affairs of the Army of the Potomac once more emerged from the wings, with blue fire burning on both sides of the stage. On January 20 the troops were in motion up the Rappahannock—apparently in pursuance of some plan to surprise a crossing there and swing round Lee's left flank, though Burnside never told his plans to anyone. But that day it came on to rain in torrents, and so held for a week more. The tortured columns pressed on through ankle- and hub-deep mud for one and a half days more, then struggled miserably back to their cantonments across the river from Fredericksburg.

"The Mud March," it was called almost at once. Washington filled up with ugly rumors that the army was demoralized to the point of mutiny and some of them got into the papers. That Hooker might lead such a mutiny was suggested to Burnside by Raymond of the *Times*, who was informed that if Hooker tried it, he would swing before sundown. The words "military dictatorship" began to appear in the press, calling up the old, vague, dark threats McClellan had made in days not less dispiriting; and, on January 23, there was a wire from Burnside to Lincoln—could he see the President alone with regard to some important orders?

The General brought the orders with him: generals of division Newton, Cochrane (now identified by Burnside as the two talebearers), and Brooks, with Hooker, were to be summarily dismissed from the service of the United States; Franklin, W. F. Smith of the VI Corps, "One pinch of owl dung" Sturgis, general of brigade Ferrero, and a staff colonel were to be dismissed from the Army of the Potomac. Otherwise, this was Burnside's resignation.

Stanton's concurrence was required for either of the alternatives, but there is no record that Lincoln even consulted him before accepting the resignation.

BACKDROP

Governor Curtin (Pennsylvania) to Stanton

Please give me the reliable news from the army at Fredericksburg. Please indicate what the Government desires. If the disaster is serious I will move with the utmost dispatch, and the loyal people of this State will again rally to the support of the Government.

Washington Intelligencer

THIRTEEN MONTHS IN THE REBEL ARMY being a Narrative of Personal Adventure, by an impressed New Yorker, price 30 cents. For Sale by Blanchard and Mahan, Corner of Penn. and 12th street.

IRON FOR THE CAPITOL DOME. A very large cargo of cast iron embracing about a half a million pounds, has arrived for the new dome of the Capitol and is being discharged at the foot of Jersey avenue. We understand that this shipment embraces the entire interior finish over the rotunda, and all the exterior ornaments to the height of the base of the lantern. It is anticipated that the entire work will be completed during the ensuing year.

Near Murfreesboro, Dec. 31. Our entire line suffered terribly this morning. Four regiments of regulars lost half of their men and all of their commanding officers. The Anderson troop suffered severely. Majors Rosengarten and Ward were killed and Generals Stanley, Rousseau and Palmer were wounded.

New York Times

The Administration looks with distrust upon the Army of the Potomac. It might be added that the Army of the Potomac looks with distrust on the Administration.

Anson Stager to Stanton

The following is just received from Cincinnati, dated Murfreesboro, Jan. 1. "A terrible battle was fought yesterday. The latest from the field is up to noon. The rebel centre had been broken and things looked favorable. The losses reported are enormous."

Washington Intelligencer

The Printers employed in the Government Printing offices, to the number of one hundred and eighteen, have petitioned Congress for an increase in wages proportioned to the advance prices in living.

New York Tribune

Battle field in front of Murfreesboro, Jan. 2, P.M. The battle on Stone River is not yet decided, although it has continued for three days, with intermissions yesterday and today. Tomorrow morning the battle will be resumed. We now feel confident of ultimate victory.

Washington Intelligencer

SENT TO THE OLD CAPITOL. Two men named James C. King and Emanuel Weller were arrested last night near the Chain

Bridge, and sent to the Old Capitol, on the charge of having attempted to convey contraband goods and letters into Virginia.

New York Tribune

GREAT AND GLORIOUS VICTORY. The Rebels Run Away in the Night. Their Army Utterly Demoralized. Our Forces in Pursuit.

New York Evening Express

It is useless to deny that, during the inactivity of the past month, a universal murmur has gone forth from the soldiers who have been, many for six months, most of them four months, without a penny of their hard-earned wages. Thousands of letters have been sent to the men from their half-starved and destitute families, which have made the inactivity of the camp almost intolerable. Had not the Potomac been in their rear, we should have heard of thousands of desertions.

An unusually serious feeling pervades the officers of the army. It is felt to be a very critical period. The tone of the troops has been despondent for the last two weeks, and another decided repulse would bring results unpleasant to contemplate.

16

A STUDY IN CONTRASTS

THE manuscript reports that followed the first telegraphic dispatches from Stone River must have given
Stanton a certain amount of satisfaction: they demonstrated that the resolution which had held firm the shaking lines
was the resolution of his man, Thomas; and this was confirmed
when the tale arrived of how the old man woke from sleep in
his chair at mention of the word "retreat" during the midnight
council of war after the first day, said: "This army doesn't retreat," and made it stick. Young Sheridan had led a division;
was the soul of the battle; let us mark him down for attention.

For the moment, however, the important problem was that
of finding a replacement for Burnside. On the straight military
ground that they were the best leaders, who had shown both
ability in tactics and a stomach for hard fighting, Stanton
wanted Reynolds or George Gordon Meade of the Pennsylvania Reserve. But the matter was as complicated as the inside
of a clock; Meade was only a division commander, and the
army had now been on foot long enough for the development
of rights of seniority and an order of precedence. All the leaders of corps and divisions senior to Meade would feel aggrieved
if he were promoted, and would find support for their griefs in
Congress. No chance for him now.

Of the Grand Division commanders, the most senior by the
strength of their commands, Sumner promptly eliminated himself by asking for retirement, an old man and tired. Franklin

was infected with McClellanism, his behavior at Antietam had been less than spectacular, and, already before Christmas, the snooping Committee on the Conduct of the War was after him, trying to find out why one of the two corps he commanded at Fredericksburg stood idle while the other took the heaviest casualties of any corps in the battle. They could not turn up any precise misconduct, or any especially good conduct either, and, feeling that the leader of a two-corps unit should be something more than a device for transmitting the orders of the general in command, gave him a vote of censure which made his relief necessary.

Reynolds quietly let it be known that he would refuse. That left only Hooker; he drank so much that the soldiers altered their march song to take cognizance of it, he was insubordinate, talked loudly about the shortcomings of Burnside, Halleck, Lincoln, and the Secretary of War; and there was a good deal of doubt about whether he could handle so many men. Stanton did not want him. But some of Hooker's friends pointed out to Chase that the man who beat the main enemy army would have the next Presidency at his disposal, and Chase, who never let anything slip that might bring him the coveted nomination, put on the screws, both personally and through his Congressional connections.

So Hooker it must be. Stanton somewhat surprised the new General by cordially supporting every move he made. Hooker fiddled around with Burnside's Grand Division idea for a couple of weeks, found it made too many staffs and sets of orders, and on February 1, went back to the corps organization, with a new alignment of commanders. Reynolds kept the I, Couch the II. The cavalry were concentrated in a single corps, like the Confederate, and George Stoneman came over from III Corps to head it. Dan Sickles, whom Stanton defended in the murder case, moved up from a division to this corps, one of the first purely political officers to lead so many men in a fighting army. Butterfield became Chief of Staff and Meade took his place at the head of the V Corps. The VI went to Division Commander Sedgwick—John Sedgwick, a Connecticut nutmeg with a square open face and a square white beard; a strict disciplinarian, but so affable in contact that the troops called him "Good Uncle John." A soldier once mistook him for a commissary; he gave the man an order for a canteen of whisky. He played solitaire a lot, and was right in the middle of every battle, where he had already been twice wounded.

Old "Fight Mit Franz" Sigel was senior to Hooker on the army list, and refused to serve under him; his XI Corps went to O. O. Howard, a man who had lost an arm at Fair Oaks and was known as "the Christian soldier" from his psalm-singing habits. At West Point he had several rows with southerners and knocked a couple of them down; he was a good tactician and never drank. Slocum remained at the head of the XII Corps, and the IX, peculiarly identified with Burnside, was sent down to be the garrison at Fortress Monroe under a subordinate officer.

Morale? Hooker introduced insignia for each corps, and set up a program of regular drills, which no one had thought of before. Furloughs he granted so freely that both Lincoln and Stanton were disturbed, but he accompanied them with carefully prepared lists of absentees, which was more than McClellan had ever done. Stanton turned heat on the process of finding willful absentees so effectively that McClellan's 88,000 absent were reduced to nearly half that figure by the end of March. General Hooker also thought that the substitution of pack mules for wagons would reduce his train; they were provided with immense effort on the part of the Department, but the experiment failed to work, and was soon abandoned.

The Army of the Potomac began to feel better in its winter quarters, even if Charles Francis Adams, Jr., thought headquarters was a combination of a barroom and a brothel, but Stanton had more trouble with the hospital service when a report from the medical inspector-general came in. The inspector had been down to Fredericksburg; said the regimental hospitals were in bad shape: the stores were worthless, the provisions nothing more than government rations for well men —which meant mainly hardtack and salt pork—the hospital clothing so deficient that typhoid patients often suffered from frostbite in addition. This hit Stanton, whose particular pride it was that Union soldiers should want for nothing. Already at odds with the forceful Surgeon-General Hammond, a wonderful organizer, but as arbitrary as the Secretary himself, and less careful, he suspended the man. Hammond went to Lincoln with a request either to be cleared or court-martialed, and had influence enough to force the issue. The court-martial acquitted; but while it was sitting, Stanton turned up the fact that one of the reasons behind the shortage of hospital supplies was that some of Hammond's contracts had been distinctly queer. The court-martial was ordered to reconvene; it took testimony for months, while the Secretary traced involved pages of accountancy with the same patience as in the California land fraud and pork cases. The end of it was Hammond found guilty and dismissed the service, with Lincoln refusing to intervene. This Surgeon-General's later history was interesting; in the postwar world of Crédit Mobilier and the railroad grabs, his curious contracts seemed almost virtuous in retrospect, he became very respectable, a pioneer in neurology in New York, who also wrote successful novels. In 1878 he got the court-martial verdict reversed.

There were appeals from Rosecrans for more cavalry—the Confederates were raiding around his wings—and letters from government agents in the west, saying that cavalry horses were not to be had, which failed to satisfy Rosecrans. There was a report to be compiled on the surrender of a small force at Spencer Court House in Virginia, and a recommendation that the President summarily dismiss for cowardice the two officers concerned—which was done. General Curtis in Missouri broke loose again, with an order to arrest "notoriously bad and dangerous men and disloyal preachers"; he had to be spanked with an order that his own order be suspended as an unwarrantable interference of the military with the civil power.

Volunteering and state drafts were not producing the necessary reinforcements. It took debate, conferences, maneuvers, to persuade Congress to pass a general draft law, and when it was passed, there was the necessity of setting up the machinery; all to be done in a hurry, because it was a Lame Duck

Congress, and the new, unfavorable one must be faced with a *fait accompli.*

One other measure Stanton and Lincoln pushed through on the last day they had their solid Republican majority; an act authorizing the suspension of *habeas corpus* writs, which had been suspended without any authorization in the turbulent first weeks of the war. At the same time, the act called on the President and Stanton to furnish the courts with the names of all persons held as prisoners, and prescribed that no one should be held for more than twenty days without action by a grand jury. The hand of Congress is visible in the completed law, insisting that the control of *habeas corpus* lies with the legislative; but Stanton had a finger in it, too. He had made arbitrary arrests in no small number, but it seemed to bother the legal part of his mind, and he resorted to the procedure far less frequently than Seward had in the early days when jurisdiction in such matters lay with State, before Stanton came into office. The War Secretary kept insisting that only his office could make arrests, and not infrequently later laid a restraining hand on military commanders in the home departments who did their arresting for themselves.

A naval attack on Charleston failed, and Governor O. P. Morton of Indiana came unhappily to town. The opposition party in the legislature of his state had only narrowly been prevented from recognizing the Confederacy, then tried to seize all authority over the troops raised in the state, and ended by adjourning without appropriating any money at all for the state government. When Stanton gave him $250,000 from a fund earmarked for "munitions of war where rebellion exists," Morton remarked that it would be a lifelong mess if the Union cause failed. Stanton gave him a look and said: "If the cause fails, I do not wish to live."

And always and ever, as the snow changed to forsythia in that elongated tail of winter, the question of Vicksburg came back. The correspondents sent stories from Grant's front about discouragement, fever, smallpox, swamps, rain, and hard fighting, and there was no progress. One of the Ellet rams was

captured on the river by the rebels; and the commander of
the ram fleet, Ellet's son, refused to turn his ships over to the
navy as ordered. He had to be placed in arrest, which Stanton
did unwillingly, protesting that Admiral Porter of the river
command was a fussy gas bag and Ellet rather close to a hero—
which Welles admitted to be true, though he did not in the
least withhold the arrest because of it.

Grant sent hardly any dispatches, not even an answer to an
addlepated offer by Halleck to him and Rosecrans jointly that
whichever first won a victory would be made a major-general
of regulars. Delegations opposed to the commander of the
Army of the Mississippi began to appear as they had against
Buell, only this time most of them were churchmen, who railed
at Grant as an un-Christian sot. Stanton sneered at them; they
went to Lincoln, who inquired where Grant got his liquor, as
he wished to send a barrel of it to the other generals.

Yet there seemed so much substance in the complaints, they
were so general, and there was so little evidence of real progress
from Grant, that Stanton thought it would be a good idea to
send a pair of eyes and ears out west and learn the truth, as
nearly as it could be hit.

Stanton chose his old connection and correspondent, Charles
A. Dana, who had already proved his quality by a mission to
the west in May of the previous year, during the cleanup of
Simon Cameron's tangled business dealings. At that time one
of the worst tangles developed in the quartermaster's office at
Cairo, Illinois; it was the logistic support of two armies, and
the young men who had been hastily thrust into it understood
nothing either of accountancy or the proper forms for military requisitions and returns. The result was a pile of claims
that would have filled a trunk and cries of "Fraud!" from the
press. Stanton gave Dana full authority to pay or reject under
the famous order of January 29, 1862, most of the claims not
having been filed within the specified time. In five weeks Dana
cleared up the whole mess in a highly satisfactory manner.

After this, the ex-newspaperman formed a combination with
George W. Chadwick and Roscoe Conkling, the rising New
York politician, to buy cotton. Dana was the operator, and

from his friend Stanton, he secured a letter of permission to the commanders of the western armies, who held the only territory where there was cotton to buy. Dana was a man in whom people confided, and also an honest one; after a month in Memphis, he came back to tell the Secretary that the private trade in cotton was a rotten bad business. He thought the evils could only be cured by ending it entirely, making the government sole cotton broker, and selling all the captured staple at auction for the national account.

This fell in happily with Stanton's own ideas on the subject. He ordered it done, and having put Dana out of business on Dana's own recommendation, now sent him back west, technically to regulate the service of the paymaster's office, actually to find out what made the major officers of the western commands tick. Dana promised to write every day, and more than made good on his promise; from the end of March, when he reached Grant's headquarters, the mysterious movements through the swamps across the river from Vicksburg were no longer a mystery in Washington, nor were the men who made them. Lincoln learned with distress that McClernand's operations were disorderly and badly staffed; Stanton with surprise (for he had never chimed with the man) that Sherman was the best soldier in the army, precise and a powerful hitter; while James Birdseye McPherson, the other corps commander, was nearly as good. Grant's staff was not perfect (said Dana), but the man himself sound as an oak. Leave him to his own devices.

II

It was April, 1863; Halleck wrote Hooker a letter, gently intimating that it was time for the great army to be put to use. In a week of clearing weather Lincoln went down to Falmouth with Stanton and Attorney-General Bates to see for himself how matters stood. It was a several days' trip, with visits to the hospitals and company streets, where the President was cheered; then reviews, with the pennons of the Pennsylvania lancers fluttering gaily in the washed spring sunshine, and the long lines of muskets in an order notably good. An atmosphere of hope, cheer, and strength pervaded all, and though Hooker was even more niggardly than McClellan about specifying a plan of campaign (he even kept his corps commanders in the dark), President and Secretary came back well satisfied that the General had a plan and that it was for action.

One of the typical spring rains of Virginia began to come down and kept on for days, while those in Washington waited for news. But the only news was an irritated complaint from General Hooker that the *New York Times* and the *Philadelphia Inquirer* were saying things about army movements that gave information to the enemy. Stanton launched an investigation, meanwhile wiring the General that nothing had been allowed to go to the papers by the telegraph through Washington. The city filled up with "thick rumors" that the Army of the Potomac was already across the Rappahannock and a battle was either imminent or already in progress. May's first day, a Friday, came in with a tension that built up through the Saturday, on which date Stanton, having completed his investigation of the news leak, wired Hooker that it was useless trying to control information from Washington while staff officers of the Army of the Potomac wrote letters which betrayed everything. "A letter from General Van Allen to a person not connected with the War Department describes your position as entrenched near Chancellorsville. Can't you give his sword something to do, so that he will have less time for the pen?"

"Entrenched near Chancellorsville" was as much as anyone knew of the army that day, or on the Sunday, except that there was heavy fighting going on. By Monday the pressure had grown so intense that Lincoln was nearly all day at the War Department, constantly up and down, talking a little, but not making the customary jokes. It became known that General Stoneman had led the cavalry on a raid deep in the enemy's rear, Stuart model. That night Lincoln could stand it no longer and wired questions to Hooker, from whom he received a brief and unsatisfactory answer, which he read to a listless

Cabinet meeting the next morning. It merely said that the rebel works behind Fredericksburg had been taken.

It was three in the afternoon of Wednesday before the President came into a room in the White House, "his complexion that of the wall," and handed a visitor a telegram—the army had been withdrawn north of the river and was "safely encamped."

"My God! My God! What will the country say?" demanded Lincoln, pacing the floor, as near despair as he had ever been. There is a circumstantially detailed account that a little earlier he had been so close to suicide that it took Stanton's intervention, with his favorite palliative of action, to draw the President back from the pit.

There was still fighting going on that night (said the wires) but it was all over by the seventh, when Lincoln took Stanton's advice to go down to the army with Halleck. As they went, they crossed many boatloads of wounded coming back from what soon became evident as a defeat as bad as Fredericksburg; worse, maybe, since the Union had lost 17,000 men to a Confederate army only half its own size, while inflicting but 12,000 casualties on the enemy. Hardest of all to bear was the discovery that it had been agonizingly near a victory; mischance sent the torrential rains that held up Stoneman's cavalry raid for four days, mischance brought a Confederate cannon ball crashing against a porch pillar on which Hooker was leaning during the second day of the battle, leaving him conscious, but so little possessed of his faculties that some of his orders were gibberish.

But, no—no; the more one studied the maps and reports under Halleck's calm, if somewhat pedantic, guidance, the clearer it became that there was mismanagement, too. Instead of making his raid a hard blow at the enemy's rear, as ordered, Stoneman spread his men out across the country, destroying some supplies, bridges, and railroads indeed, but doing nothing to impede Lee's army. The day after having won a surprise crossing of the upper fords of the Rappahannock, Hooker had abandoned an apparent intention to attack Lee's rear on the high ground behind Fredericksburg, taken position and waited to be attacked; then accepted a visible Confederate movement across his front as evidence of a retreat, and did nothing about it, allowing it to get around his flank for a terrible surprise attack that demoralized and decimated the whole of Howard's XI Corps. "Be sure to put in all your men," Lincoln advised Hooker earnestly during the April visit, but the splendid corps of Reynolds had not fired a gun, and Meade's V Corps hardly any.

Stoneman's failure could be, and was dealt with by Hooker himself; he was relieved and the cavalry command given to Alfred Pleasanton, who had been leading a division. He was a Washington, D.C., man with powerful friends at court and a good head for organization; cold and sarcastic in manner, and a notable marcher at the head of horse, of which he had brought a regiment from Utah all the way to Washington at the outbreak of war. Hooker believed he had saved the army on the second day at Chancellorsville by throwing the Eighth Pennsylvania Cavalry into a suicidal charge on the rebel head of column after Howard's corps broke.

The problem of Hooker himself was more complex. His behavior seemed to add up to indecision in moments of crisis, he needed reassuring, and to this object Stanton addressed himself in the days following the President's visit to the army. He sent the General long dispatches telling how the Richmond newspapers were dismayed over Stoneman's destructions; that the Confederates had lost their great general, Jackson, killed in the battle; with a cheering word indicating progress from Rosecrans, and the news that Chancellorsville had produced no panic in 'change or in the country, the New York newspapers were more concerned with the Coburn-McCool prizefight than with the battle. The Secretary could afford to be a little cheerful in the face of defeat at that moment, for he had word that Grant was at last broken loose from the toils of the bayous, and his steady lines were pouring in on the defenders of Vicksburg like a dusty blue avalanche.

The first news of Vicksburg came on Saturday, May 2, along with the tidings of the Army of the Potomac entrenched near Chancellorsville, and it was a correspondent's dispatch saying

"The whole army is in motion, leaving tents and baggage behind." On the tense Monday another dispatch, that sent men scurrying to their maps, to find out where Bruinsburg might be—on the east bank, but still below the bluffs, and there was tension over this, too. Two days more, Grant had fought a battle, had taken Grand Gulf, on the high ground below Vicksburg at last; he expected to fight another and (Dana added) McClernand was behaving badly.

Stanton to Dana, May 5

General Grant has full and absolute authority to enforce his own commands, to remove any person who by ignorance, inaction or any other cause, interferes with or delays his operations. He has the full confidence of the government.

Two days wheeled by again; Grant was behind Vicksburg, marching on Jackson; nobody knew where Pemberton and the defending Confederate army were. Then a sudden silence, a dreadful silence of lost communications, as during the previous winter, in which the only news was that which filtered through from Richmond about heavy fighting in the west. Halleck twirled dividers across the map, worried desperately about what happens to armies when their communications are lost, and finally telegraphed Memphis to send an officer downstream by fast steamer; recall Grant to base at once, before his army was lost.

But on May 21, with Intelligence reporting Lee making movements south of the Rappahannock, the lines of wire sprang open, and the news blazed out like a star; Grant's communications had not been cut, but abandoned; he was carrying everything right away before him. With forces very little more than equal to Pemberton's he had marched 200 miles in 18 days, halting on the way to fight battles at Port Gibson, Jackson, Champion's Hill (a hard fight, that), and the Big Black River, always victorious; had taken 79 guns, inflicted 8,000 casualties on the enemy, and suffered only 3,500 himself. Jackson, with its railroad center and workshops, was destroyed; Halleck's messenger of recall had arrived ironically at the moment when the rebel line broke across the Big Black under a whirl-wind charge of the Army of the Mississippi; and now Pember-ton and his army—what was left of his army—were penned in Vicksburg, and Grant had his iron grip on the place and was building forts along the bluffs that frowned down on Sherman in December.

The only complaint was from an accompanying congress-man that Grant lacked military manners. "On this whole march for five days he has had neither a horse nor an orderly nor a servant, a blanket or overcoat or clean shirt. His entire bag-gage consists of a toothbrush."

All the papers shouted for joy; even the *New York Herald* and the *Evening Express* were slightly ecstatic. But it meant dizzy days in the War Department, for it was clear that the Confederates would not let their great fortress and communi-cations center go without trying everything, and Joe Johnston had been appointed commander for the Confederacy in the west to make a relief. Recruiting bureaus and troop reception cen-ters throughout the northwest were gingered up to reinforce Grant; heavy guns swung down the river from Pittsburgh to arm the siege lines; ammunition, food, uniforms, shoes, poured forth in a flood. Nor was all this easy:

Dana to Stanton, June 16

Most of the ammunition supplied to this army is very bad. A board of survey just held here reports that the Parrott shells are uniformly defective from sand-holes. Some of them are filled with putty; some are left undisguised. The small arms ammunition from Indianapolis is rascally; the powder worthless and deficient in quan-tity.

From out on the borders of Kansas and Missouri came a new trouble; a group of wildmen, more bandits than soldiers of North or South, sacked Lawrence and killed many people. The enraged Kansans planned a retaliatory massacre in Mis-souri. The local commander was General John M. Schofield, who had spent most of his life as a teacher and philosopher and kept a long beard down which he drizzled tobacco juice. His force was the grandiloquently named Army of the Frontier, an adjunct of Curtis' Missouri command. He refused to permit the retaliation, and Curtis backed him up, whereupon the matter instantly became entwined with politics, the Missouri and Kansas Radicals sending delegations to Lincoln to protest against softness to rebels. Curtis resigned under their pressure. Stanton put the interferers in their place by giving the command to Schofield—whereupon Brigadier-General F. J. Herron, a thorough Radical, who had six regiments on the frontier, said that if Schofield remained, he would have to go. Stanton told Herron that "insubordination will be met as insubordination," but ordered Herron and his regiments to join Grant as part of the reinforcements for the siege of Vicksburg.

A major's commission was made out for Dana, to protect him in case of capture, and now he began to send more detailed reports on Grant's officers—Rawlins of the staff, not a particularly brilliant man, but one who kept Grant from drinking; Sherman's staff, small and efficient; and a note on a young officer:

Lieutenant-Colonel Wilson, Inspector-General, has rendered valuable service. The fortifications of Haynes' Bluff were designed by him and executed under his direction. His leading idea is the idea of duty and he applies it vigorously and often impatiently to others. In consequence, he is unpopular with all who like to live with little work.

This was one which the Secretary of War noted for future reference. But now everything else paled out before the news that Lee was marching again, and marching north.

17

DOUBLE CONCERTO WITH
A FINALE DIMINUENDO

AS May turned the corner into June, counsel darkened and the air filled up with rumors. General Hooker complained to Stanton that he could get no information, the spies he sent across the river had not returned; General Rosecrans wired peevishly for more cavalry, he could undertake nothing until he had it; the Independent Telegraph Company transmitted a strength and position report on Hooker's army over its wires and had to be slapped with the temporary seizure of its lines; the *New York Tribune* thought Lee was making north to shake Grant's grip on Vicksburg, or to take Philadelphia in retaliation; Chase, Blair, and Bates "expressed their mortification" that Stanton was not more coming-forward with information about what the rebels were doing; Governor Curtin of Pennsylvania came down to see what could be done for the defense of his state; and there was an explosion in Chicago.

The blow-up began with Burnside, who had been sent to rusticate in command of the Department of Ohio after being replaced by Hooker. Illness had made him bad-tempered, and he was being driven to absolute fury by the remarks of the antiadministration papers, which were, in fact, something more than constructively critical of a government engaged in a desperate war. The *Chicago Times*, for instance, accused the President's son of making $500,000 on government contracts (without specifying how), and said that Jefferson Davis deserved the sympathy of all humanity. To deal with this sort of thing, Burnside issued a General Order, No. 38, whose operative sentence was: "The habit of declaring sympathy with the enemy will not be allowed in this department."

This touched off one Clement L. Vallandigham, a tainted character. He was a tall, self-righteous pacifist from Dayton, who had distinguished himself in Congress just before the expiration of his term there by urging the soldiers of both armies to fraternize and force their governments to negotiate a treaty of peace. Stanton had known him in the long ago; even loaned Vallandigham the $500 with which he set up his law business. He was an effective public speaker, in the demagogic tradition of enormous simplifications and sweeping invective; General Order No. 38 gave him a talking point which he considered he might use to get back into office, and he began a speaking campaign of steadily increasing violence, which reached its climax at Mount Vernon on May 1. An enraptured audience heard him say that the government had no intention of restoring the Union, had rejected peace offers from the South, with many similar matters, and the advice that soldiers should desert and a united people should "hurl King Lincoln from his throne." Three officers in plain clothes were taking notes; when Burnside saw the transcriptions, he had Vallandigham arrested.

A military commission ordered the prisoner to a fortress for the duration, and the courts refused a writ of *habeas corpus*. The *Chicago Times* handled the story with a violence even beyond its best previous efforts; Burnside sent a file of soldiers to the office of the *Chicago Times*, closed the plant, and pronounced the paper suspended.

Now two quite different things had become badly confounded, for a government at war could hardly allow anyone to persuade its troops that desertion was a sweet and decorous thing, but editorial comment on an arrest comes within the domain of free speech, no matter how intemperately made, and the Chicagoans quickly showed they were aware of it. The news that reached Washington on June 2, along with accounts of the mysterious maneuvers of Lee, was that a mob of 20,000 had only barely been prevented from burning the building of the proadministration *Chicago Tribune* in reprisal. It was a thorny question for the Cabinet; somewhat to his own surprise, Welles found Stanton agreeing with him heartily that although both Burnside's acts wanted doing, he had done them in the wrong way and on the wrong ground. ("Must I shoot a simple-minded soldier boy who deserts, while I must not touch a hair of the wily agitator who induces him to desert?" wrote Lincoln.) The *Chicago Times* case was the easier to solve; Stanton merely issued an order revoking that of Burnside, with a circular saying that no more papers were to be suppressed by local authorities.

But Vallandigham's case being now mixed with that of the newspaper, the confinement sentence obviously could not be allowed to stand. Lincoln himself found a solution that turned him from a martyr to a figure of fun; he was furnished with a flag of truce and a cavalry escort and sent through the lines into the Confederacy he had been praising so warmly. Vallandigham himself aided the discrediting process by escaping in a blockade-runner as soon as he possibly could and going to live in Canada. Stanton had nothing to do with this deal; it was about at the same time he became much involved in the question of prisoner-of-war exchange, which had become as hard to handle as a freshly baked potato.

The difficulties dated back to, and were entwined with, the second and definitive Emancipation Proclamation of January 1, 1863. Long before this date there had been discussion of the advisability of enlisting Negro soldiers. Anyone could see how dangerous such a step might be in the slave states still faithful to the Union, and though there is every evidence that Stanton favored the step, he had gone no further in his annual report for 1862 than to advise that such troops should be enrolled to garrison fortified places and to raise cavalry forage, of which there was a perennial shortage. But with all the slaves—except those in Kentucky, Maryland, Delaware, and Missouri—free either by law or proclamation, the weight became irresistible. The January proclamation itself declared that Negro enlistments would be received, and as of May,

1863, so many of them had joined the colors that five companies were drilling outside Washington, and Stanton had set up a special bureau of the War Department to handle the affairs of Negro troops.

The reaction of the Confederacy to Negro enlistments in the North was immediate and, as might be expected, violent. Jefferson Davis issued a proclamation that Negro soldiers taken in arms should be turned over to the state authorities under the laws against insurrection, and their white officers should be tried for "inciting servile insurrection," which was a hanging matter throughout the South. Stanton promptly suspended the paroles of all Confederate officers, and there the matter hung until April, when the Confederacy began to feel the pinch, both because it had lost so many more men by capture than it had taken and because the growing shortage of food in the South made it hard to care for Union prisoners.

At this date Robert Ould, who had once prosecuted the case against Dan Sickles, and who was now Confederate agent of exchange, tried to get things going again. Stanton told him that the Davis proclamation would have to be withdrawn; the Union could not consent to a partial exchange while some of its fighting men, taken in uniform, faced capital charges. Ould replied that the proclamation would not be withdrawn, even if the prisoners on both sides had to "rot, starve, and die," and the Confederate Congress backed him up by passing a law which reaffirmed the Davis proclamation in still more ferocious terms.

This doubtless confirmed for Stanton the opinion of Ould he had expressed at the trial, but something more practical than an opinion was needed inasmuch as there were plentiful and well documented reports about the living conditions in Confederate prisons. At the end of May, the Secretary issued orders that no more Confederate officers should be paroled or exchanged, that all should be placed in confinement under guard, and that a selection should be made from them for retaliation if any Union officers were hanged for leading Negro troops. With this the matter hung once more; no negotiations, and conditions would grow worse before they were better.

II

ALL this time the tide of war was moving west and north, and the War Department worried because Hooker would lose 16,000 men at the end of June through expiration of their enlistments. The aeronaut of the Army of the Potomac reported some of the rebel camps along the Rappahannock deserted, Hooker continued to complain that Washington sent him no news, and the army's trains were too cumbersome.

Stanton to Hooker, June 6

I have been trying to keep the women out of your camp, but finding that they were going in troops, under passes, as they said, from your provost-marshal and commanders, I have given up the job. I think no officer or soldier should have his wife in camp or with the army. If you will order them away, and keep your provost-marshal and other officers from issuing passes, not one shall be issued here, and all that profess to come from the Department will be forgeries.

Next it was Darius Couch, commander of the II Corps, second in rank to Hooker himself, visiting Washington grave and disturbed. He had from the beginning been profoundly distrustful of Hooker's Chancellorsville plan—what he knew of it—and everything that had happened since only hardened his opinion. He wished to be relieved from serving under such a general. Accorded; let Winfield Scott Hancock have the corps, a tall, strong handsome man and dandy dresser, famous for his purple language even in an army that treated profanity as a fine art; taught his men to work hard, forage hard, and, by God, to fight hard. They loved him; his division had saved the day at Chancellorsville, when everything was going to pieces.

On June 9 there was a cavalry fight at Brandy Station in the shadow of the Blue Ridge, and for a wonder the Union riders won it—very heartening after the remark that had been going round since Stoneman's raid: "Who ever saw a dead cavalryman?" Hooker wanted to strike through Fredericksburg again toward Richmond, and had to be discouraged from the idea; there was the mark of Halleck's thinking in Lincoln's telegram of disapproval: "I think that Lee's army, and not Richmond, is your sure objective point."

Sunday, June 14, was one of the bad days. It started with word from Pleasanton that Negroes had seen Ewell with one of the outsize corps of Confederate infantry, bound for the Shenandoah, two days before. As the day wore on, the rumors became so thick that Mr. Secretary Welles went over to the War Department to find out what was going on. He found the President there, and Halleck, smoking a cigar. Stanton fussed in and out, his jaw set like a snapping turtle's; and there was a telegram from General R. H. Milroy, who had a garrison at Winchester in the valley, relayed through from Baltimore, the direct wires being out. A "mighty raid" was in progress, Milroy thought, into Pennsylvania; he could hold out where he was for five days, a remark which caused Lincoln to say sadly that probably Milroy would soon be captured. "It is Harpers Ferry over again."

Already the possibility of a drive into Pennsylvania had engaged the Department. As early as the tenth, Stanton began to cover the likeliest points of impact. He sent General W. T. H. Brooks to Pittsburgh, as commander of a new Department of the Monongahela, with authority to call out the local militia in case Lee turned in that direction; Couch was dispatched to Harrisburg to take command of a new reserve corps, Pennsylvania men to be raised at once. On the fourteenth, while Welles was hanging around the Department came a telegram from Governor Curtin:

After full consultation this morning, it has been deemed advisable to postpone for a short period the issuing of general orders, now ready, for recruiting troops for three years or during the war, in order to fill up speedily the army corps for General Couch.

That is, Curtin wanted to return to the old short-term enlistments under state control, which had produced so much trouble already without any visible number of fighting troops.

Stanton to Couch

I hope that you have had nothing to do with such agreement. The recruiting for three years or during the war should not be postponed an hour. You will spare no effort to carry this recruiting into effect. If Governor Curtin neglects to act under the authority given him to recruit for three years, that is his own affair. But you are to give his neglect no countenance or assistance, but on the contrary, do everything in your power to promote the three years' recruiting.

Lincoln went home to dinner, then came back to sit waiting late for news; but when it came, it was such that sent him staggering; Grant heavily defeated before Vicksburg, and his army dispersed.

The next morning, June 15, 1863, things were better; the news about Grant was false; the iron grip on Vicksburg was unrelaxed. On the contrary, Union cryptographers had just cracked a cipher dispatch from Joe Johnston, saying he considered it hopeless to save the fortress. But not too much better: Milroy had too long delayed his retirement from Winchester, losing all his stores and 3,000 men. Stanton was very busy that day; a long exchange of wires made it evident that time and Lee would not wait for the formation of Couch's new corps of three-year men; the defense of Pennsylvania must be cared for by troops immediately available. Telegrams went out asking governors for six-months men from the militia: Maryland, 10,000; Pennsylvania, 50,000; Ohio, 30,000; West Virginia, 10,000; even New York being asked for 20,000 in spite of the fact that her governor was a Peace Democrat who had promised not to send men to war. Authority went to Couch to seize railroads to move his troops and supplies.

By the following day, Tuesday, there began to grow in Washington an uneasy consciousness that the near presence of the enemy exercised a corrosive effect on Hooker's mental processes, so clear and sharp when he was in fighting contact. He opened the day by telegraphing Lincoln: "You have been aware, Mr. President, that I have not enjoyed the confidence of the major-general commanding the army, and I can assure you so long as this continues we may look in vain for success, especially as future operations will require our relations to be more dependent upon each other than heretofore." Later in the day he was after Stanton, too: "I wish it might be the duty of some person in the telegraph office in Washington to keep me informed of the enemy's movements in Maryland"; and "I should very much like to have reliable and correct information concerning the enemy on the north side of the Potomac. So far, we have had only the wild rumors of panic-stricken people."

The first dispatch triggered the President into a telegram that there should be no question of the relationship of the generals; Halleck's command was the higher echelon, and Hooker's duty was to obey orders when he received them—with a following letter which told the General that Halleck had given and was giving him the fullest support. (It did not mention that Halleck was not giving and never would give orders.)

As for reliable and correct information concerning the enemy, that was exactly what Washington wanted from the commander whose cavalry were in contact with it, but Stanton replied reasonably: "You shall be posted on information received here as to the enemy's movements, but must exercise your own judgment as to its credibility. The very demon of lying seems to be about these times, and generals will have to be broken for ignorance before they will take the trouble to find out the truth of reports."

But Hooker was not in a reasonable mood. Sometime during the day, between these wires and the replies to them, Halleck sent him word that Harpers Ferry was being invested and no relief was to be expected except from the Army of the Potomac. It was perhaps not the clearest statement in military history, but after he received Lincoln's telegram, at three o'clock in the morning, Hooker issued march orders to four of his corps, then wired to Halleck: "In compliance with your directions, I shall march to the relief of Harpers Ferry."

This crossed another wire from Halleck, saying the report of Harpers Ferry invested had turned out false, and the

General-in-Chief immediately followed it with still another saying that he had given no such orders. This straightened things out tactically, but it did not efface the impression that Hooker was doing everything he could to place responsibility on Washington. Couch reported from Harrisburg that 13,000 New Yorkers had arrived and looked well; his artillerymen were untrained.

The president of the Philadelphia and Baltimore Railroad asked Secretary Welles for a gunboat to protect his bridge across the Susquehanna at Havre de Grace, and the naval man went round to inquire whether Stanton thought it necessary. Stanton laughed; Lincoln, who was present, quoted from Orpheus C. Kerr, and said that anyone who did not read him must be a heathen.

Hooker's conduct was all the more straining because the powerful New York papers—*Tribune, Times,* and *Herald*—had begun to cry for the General's head, demanding that some-one—anyone else—lead the army. Hooker did nothing to ease matters by another peevish wire to Halleck, and Senator Sum-ner told various Cabinet members that the General was a blasphemous wretch; the army would be better off if he had been killed at Chancellorsville. This combination of forces so disturbed Chase that he rushed off to visit Hooker at his headquarters, and brought back word that everything was as well as it possibly could be with his favorite officer. He made it clear that any attempt at relieving Hooker would encounter the whole Chase interest—in Congress and country. By the next day, June 17th, there were enough reports from Mary-land country people and the scouting cavalry to establish beyond doubt that Lee's bulk was in the valley, with some units forward into Maryland, while Hooker, well concen-trated, lay between the enemy and Washington.

Now the pace slowed, and the date-lines showed that the two armies were swinging around a vast circle, with Wash-ington as its pivot and the Cumberland Mountains between. Dana from Vicksburg reported that Grant's patience with McClernand had snapped at last; he had summarily removed that officer, the proximate cause being a vainglorious order in which McClernand praised his own corps and ran down the other two as well as Grant himself. The order had not even been submitted through channels, but published in the Memphis papers. The news affected Lincoln painfully; McClernand had been one of his high hopes. Stanton only snorted over it and turned to the reports—hourly growing more precise—about Lee's advance and the size of his army. Hooker flashed briefly into the city, demanded to be placed in command of the troops in Washington and the Department of Maryland, then flashed out again.

Through the next week the papers filled up with rumors—Jeff Davis had positively been seen in Pennsylvania, and Hooker, half-drunk, in Willard's Hotel. But some Union men in Maryland banded together and took a count of the marching rebels that would have done credit to a staff officer. They were 79,000 with 275 guns, said the report. It was forwarded to Hooker at once, but failed to satisfy him; he had been to Harpers Ferry, found 10,000 men in the garrison there and at Maryland Heights, wanted to abandon the place and add them to his mobile forces. Halleck replied that Harpers Ferry was important and heavily fortified; he could not approve the abandonment "except in case of absolute necessity."

Sunday morning, June 28, the Cabinet members were summoned to an extraordinary session, at which Lincoln pulled a telegram from his pocket. It was from Hooker:

My original instructions required me to cover Harpers Ferry and Washington. I have now imposed upon me, in addition, an enemy in front of more than my number. I beg to be understood, respectfully, but firmly, that I am unable to comply with this condition with the means at my disposal, and I earnestly request that I may be relieved from the position I occupy.

In spite of the imminence of a big battle, there was no doubt about giving the General the relief he asked; it was hardly necessary for Lincoln to remind his advisers that the "greedy call for more troops" and false statement of the enemy's superiority were a perfect reproduction of McClellan. The question was the replacement. Reynolds?—he had refused the command once, and would do so again. Couch?—he had left his corps and could hardly be rewarded for it with the command of an army. Sedgwick? Hancock?—good men, but very junior. Therefore, Meade, by pure elimination.

That same day word ran in that there were Confederate cavalry between the Army of the Potomac and Washington; the Governor of New Jersey wired to ask Stanton whether he should accede to a request from the Governor of Pennsylvania for militia to reinforce Couch; and there was a wholly mysterious telegram to the War Department from the postmaster of Philadelphia, saying that four notorious rebel sympathizers of the city were sending a man to "request General McClellan to come to Philadelphia and take military charge of things generally." Stanton authorized General Dana at Philadelphia to impress tugs and steamboats to carry away the machinery of the arms factory if the enemy approached, and sent special appeals to the heads of affected railroads to keep their lines running at any expense; he was sending Haupt, who was to do whatever he pleased.

III

THE papers of June 30, 1863, had the news of Hooker's removal, and greeted it with relief as that of a man brave and useful in lesser positions, but unfit for high command. Of Meade they said nothing: "At least he is unembarrassed by the hostility of the McClellan interests in the army and elsewhere," remarked the *New York Tribune*, the only journal even to come near an estimate.

The evening of the same day Haupt wired from Harrisburg, to which Couch's outposts had been driven from Carlisle, that the Confederates had evacuated their forward line and were falling back on Chambersburg or Gettysburg. Stanton passed this word to Meade at midnight, with the remark that the rebels were apparently concentrating for a blow at his army. A little earlier Meade had notified Washington of the positions of his separate corps, and said he was not fully satisfied that the enemy had withdrawn from the Susquehanna. Halleck and Stanton went over the map, discovered that Meade had broken up Hooker's tight concentration, and wired him back with a note of anxiety to ask whether his weight were not too far to the east.

The fact was that Meade, suddenly given the world to carry, had not only grown slightly confused over whether he was to attack or to be attacked (his orders showed this later), but was not quite certain about his instruments; had slid three of his corps to the east, to get nearer the Baltimore-Harrisburg main line and his sources of supply. He was quite unaware that the indefatigable Haupt was driving railroad forward almost as fast as the army moved, and would have a spur in operation from Hanover Junction to Gettysburg in four days.

Meanwhile Stanton had personally arranged with President Garrett of the B & O to have a locomotive running every three hours between Baltimore and the current railhead at Westminster for the transmission of messages, the first one hauling a horsecar with twelve good horses for a courier service between Westminster and Meade's headquarters. But by the hour when Halleck's inquiry about the eastward shift reached Meade, all inquiries were already too late; out along the Cashtown road John Buford's blue troopers were shooting, low and straight, at masses in gray; from his seminary tower Reynolds was watching the Wisconsin Iron Brigade swing into line behind the cavalry; and the greatest battle of the war had begun.

July 1, 1863, was a quiet day in Washington; it was only along toward midnight that whispers began to run around about heavy fighting in Pennsylvania. Mr. Secretary Welles rose early the following morning, met Mr. Senator Sumner, and with him went to the War Department for news. They found that Lincoln had been there since before dawn, and Stanton, buzzing in and out as he handled a thousand details. Both men were pretty cheerful, but not too much so, and with the memory upon them of the early hours of other battles when the news had been good. The tall General Reynolds was killed; Meade had five of his corps in hand

and was fighting a general battle; the tone of his dispatches sounded firm and ready. The telegraphic service was very poor —messages arriving late and often garbled.

Mr. Welles toddled over to call on Postmaster-General Blair and the latter's father. He learned that after the Seven Days' fighting, McClellan had accused Stanton of sacrificing the army, and Stanton "replied cringingly"; also that at the beginning of the conflict the present Secretary of War had acted with the secessionists. Mr. Welles found no difficulty in believing this, although he knew that the Postmaster-General had entertained a low opinion of Stanton ever since the previous winter, when Blair's pretty niece, Louisa Buckner, had been caught trying to sneak across the lines with 600 ounces of quinine and a pass approved by the Postmaster-General. Stanton had put her in prison, and although he let her out after a short while, Blair never forgave the act nor the remarks he had to hear.

Mr. Lincoln remained at the War Department telegraph with the man they were talking about, waiting for news. The pair were up most of the night at it, taking catnaps, but the first solid tidings came in a dispatch that arrived at ten in the morning, written by Meade at three on the previous afternoon. It was good in tone, and the army was concentrated, but Meade was "awaiting the attack of the enemy"; he spoke of "falling back on" his supplies at the Westminster railhead, and would "act with caution." This was so ominous a recollection of McClellan that it did little to inspire encouragement in President or Secretary, and it was very little helped by the press dispatches that presently began to filter in, describing the position as held, but also hard fighting and heavy losses. All night the town filled up with rumors, on which there presently floated a scum of unpalatable fact—the Confederate cavalry between Meade and Washington had been Stuart, once more riding right around the Union army, and he had captured a wagon train. (No one knew it, or would for many days, but it made him late for the battle.) All night there was nothing, nothing positive from the front, and most of the next

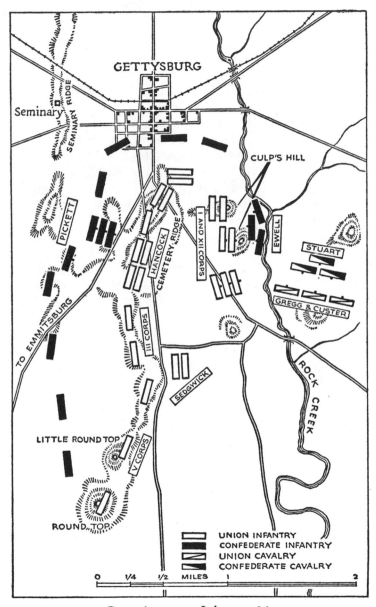

GETTYSBURG

Seminary

SEMINARY RIDGE

CULP'S HILL

PICKETT

HANCOCK

CEMETERY RIDGE

I AND XII CORPS

EWELL

STUART

TO EMMITSBURG

III CORPS

GREGG & CUSTER

ROCK CREEK

SEDGWICK

LITTLE ROUND TOP

V CORPS

ROUND TOP

	UNION INFANTRY
	CONFEDERATE INFANTRY
	UNION CAVALRY
	CONFEDERATE CAVALRY

0   1/4   1/2   MILES   1   2

Gettysburg on July 3, 1863

301

day was equally blank, a Friday, the day before Independence Day.

It was five in the afternoon before word came from Meade; but when it came, it was good, saying as of eight that morning that the action had commenced at early dawn, and "the enemy have thus far made no impression upon my position." Things looked better still when five minutes later there came in a dispatch that Meade had sent off the night before, but which had been held up for nearly twenty-four hours by the inexplicable vagaries of the telegraph: "The enemy attacked me about 4 P.M. this day, and after one of the severest contests of the war, was repulsed at all points. I shall remain in my present position tomorrow."

In the evening, as Stanton walked back to the Department from supper at home, things began to take on an even more hopeful air. Firecrackers and rockets bought for the Fourth were going off around the streets, and without anyone's knowing where the news had come from, people began to say that Lee was whipped. At ten in the evening a wave of excitement went through the town; the *Star* office had hung out an immense bulletin saying it was a victory, and, on the rising hope that it was true, President and Secretary got what rest they could that night.

But it was not until six in the morning of July 4, 1863, that definitive news came in—Meade's lines standing where they had stood, the battered Confederates beaten back under shattering losses, and as one excited officer put it: "Nine acres of prisoners!" All day crowds gathered in the White House grounds and there were parades of militia regiments and the veterans of 1812 behind bands; all day more dispatches dribbled in, climaxed toward evening by one from Haupt's reliable railroad telegraphic service that told of the Confederates in full retreat. They had lost 28,000 men in the battle, and Lee was crippled; the Union loss was 23,000.

IV

THERE are few battles without a tomorrow; Gettysburg had
several. In those delirious hours while bands were playing on
the White House lawn and strangers shaking hands in the
streets, the field of battle lay under a drenching rain, and
Meade issued a congratulatory order to his troops: "An enemy
superior in numbers, and flushed with the pride of successful
invasion, attempted to overcome and destroy this Army. Utterly baffled and defeated, he has now withdrawn from the
contest. The Commanding General looks to the Army for
greater efforts to drive from our soil every vestige of the presence of the invader." This came in just after Haupt's wire
describing the Confederates in retreat, which had led Stanton
to telegraph General Dix at Fortress Monroe to see whether
some advance could not be made up the James against Lee's
communications. It drew an outburst from Lincoln:

" 'Drive the *invaders* from our soil!' My God! This is a
dreadful reminiscence of McClellan. Will our generals never
get that idea out of their heads? The whole country is our
soil."

On July 6 came Haupt in person, direct from the front,
and officers with eyewitness accounts of the battle, including General Sickles, who had had a leg shot off on the second
day. Haupt was no more comforting than Meade's order; he
had seen the General the day before to tell him that the new
railhead and telegraph had been carried through Hanover
Junction to Gettysburg (which surprised Meade very much),
and to plead with him to follow the enemy hard. Meade replied that his men needed rest; Haupt told him they could not
be as tired as the Confederates. "You must pursue Lee and
crush him. His ammunition and stores must be exhausted,
and his supply trains can be easily cut off. He is in desperate
straits, like a rat in a trap, and you can whip and capture him."

No result; Haupt hopped on a locomotive to tell his story
in Washington. It dumbfounded Stanton, who sent Halleck
and Haupt around to the White House, while he himself got

off a message to Meade which was deliberately, but rather unfortunately, kept out of the records. When the Secretary joined the others, it was decided to send Haupt back to put on more pressure, with a remark from Stanton that Meade could be removed as easily as he had been appointed. Halleck puffed a cigar and rubbed his elbows; he contributed little to the conference.

No result again; through a week Meade only made excuses, crawled on at five miles a day, called a council of his corps commanders, and reported that only two of them were in favor of closing with and attacking Lee, though the Confederates had been penned in a bridgehead, with the rain-swollen Potomac unfordable at their backs. The fact was that Uncle John Sedgwick opposed the attack, or rather, could think of no way to make it a certain success, and since Reynolds' death, he was Meade's brain, as far as offensive maneuver went. On July 14, Stanton entered a Cabinet meeting looking dour, and whispered the bad news to Lincoln; Lee had escaped. Mr. Welles thought he had never seen the President look so dejected.

The next day there was bad news from New York.

BACKDROP

Washington Intelligencer, June 5

The different correspondents with the Army of the Potomac continue to differ very widely on their guesses about the rebel movements and intentions in Virginia.

New York Tribune, June 11

Beyond a doubt some interesting and important movements are in progress in Hooker's Army—something more than merely finding out Lee's position. One thing seems certain, the Army of the Potomac is not going to rust in inactivity.

New York Tribune, June 16

The enemy are advancing in three columns, one toward Waynesboro and Gettysburg, one direct to Chambersburg, and one toward Mercersburg and Coal Mountains.

Washington Intelligencer, June 17

Harrisburg, June 14. The whole of Gen. Lee's army, we are informed, is now moving on the offensive. The Cumberland Valley is therefore no doubt intended as his route to the vowed plunder and renown.

ARTIFICIAL LIMBS. By E. D. Hudson, M.D. Clinton Hall (up stairs.) Astor Place, N.Y. Soldiers provided without Cost, by commission of the Surgeon General of the U.S. Army. Descriptive Pamphlets, with reference, sent free.

New York Tribune, June 19

General Lee is believed to be still in Virginia with the main body of his army.

The Invasion excitement is rapidly subsiding, and the great questions are: where is Lee? What is he going to do? and what is Hooker about?

Washington Intelligencer, June 20

The Quartermaster's department of the army suffered quite a serious loss yesterday on the Rockville Road, seven or eight miles beyond Georgetown. A train of some 120 wagons was suddenly attacked by a band of mounted rebels. We had no idea that any rebel troops were so near us.

New York Tribune, June 26

The weight of evidence seems to show that the rebels are moving in force across the Potomac, and have already a large body of troops on this side, in Maryland and Pennsylvania.

New York Tribune, June 27

There is no longer any doubt that another great battle will be fought in Maryland probably, in Pennsylvania possibly. That one corps of the rebel army is already north of the Potomac and that the others have followed is almost certain.

New York Herald, July 8

Washington, July 7. About dark this evening a call was published for a gathering of the Union people of Washington to call upon the President to congratulate him upon the glorious news of the fall of Vicksburg. The band of the Thirty-fourth Massachusetts headed the procession, which had begun to be formed at the National Hotel. By the time it reached the White House an immense crowd was there assembled, filling all the available space in front of the mansion. After a few patriotic airs from the band, the President responded to the call and spoke. After the close of the President's speech, the band marched out into the avenue, and proceeded to the War Department.

Stanton came out and returned thanks to the assemblage for the honor done him. He said that the first thing that brought General Grant into prominence was his answer at Fort Donelson that the enemy should surrender, affording him six hours in which to reply, and that he proposed to move immediately upon the enemy's works. From that time he has been moving upon the enemy's works, and has taken them one after the other, until the crowning triumph of all had been achieved on the anniversary of the national independence, by taking possession of the greatest of the rebel strongholds, Vicksburg.

As soon as the fall of Vicksburg was bulletined here today the whole populace seemed wild with excitement. On the street corners and in all the public resorts crowds of men and boys assembled, giving cheers for Generals Grant and Meade. Even the women participated in the excitement, and manifested their appreciation of the recent great victories by waving Union flags and handkerchiefs.

Baltimore, July 7. Bands of music are now parading the streets playing national patriotic airs, the crowds upon the street corners and at the newspaper offices are cheering, and even the secesh are catching the contagion, and would get drunk if the barrooms were not all closed by the Provost Marshal. "Lee whipped and Vicksburg is ours," is the cry of ten thousand throats.

Hornellsville, N.Y., July 7. The news of Vicksburg was hailed by a general rejoicing. Thirty locomotives have blown their whistles for half an hour, all the bells are ringing, cannon firing, bonfires blazing. Speeches were made by Elijah Grey and others.

Bridgeport, Conn., July 7. An enthusiastic mass meeting was held here today on the reception of the news of the fall of Vicksburg. Bells were rung, the light battery fired a salute of one hundred guns, and in the evening an immense meeting was spontaneously called together at Franklin Hall. P. T. Barnum presided. Major General Anderson, who was in town, came on the stand, and was received with immense cheering.

New York Express, July 8

The news of the victory was signed PORTER, and we will not be absolutely satisfied until news comes along signed ULYSSES S. GRANT. However if the news IS true the war is very far from being over. Oceans of blood and mountains of treasure are yet to be consumed, if the white man, North, is to fight only to free Negroes, South.

18

ASSEMBLY OF THE DECISIVE PIECES

THE enrollment of men for the federal draft should have been everywhere completed by the end of June, 1863. In New York it was delayed, and the first names drawn from the wheels of chance did not come out until Saturday, July 11. Horatio Seymour, the Peace Democrat elected governor in the 1862 sweep, had been denouncing the act ever since its passage. He said his state had already furnished more than her share of men, he wanted the act suspended, he wanted it postponed, he refused to see Stanton when the Secretary asked him to confer about the execution of the law, he said it was unconstitutional. ("Ah!" said Stanton, when this was reported; "So it is the Constitution and not the country he worries about!")

The Democratic papers, led by the *World, Journal of Commerce,* and *Express,* picked up where the Governor ended, and told their readers that they would be dragged off to be the cannon fodder of an evil-minded tyranny, with various other remarks of similar odor. These remarks, delivered in a high tone of voice and with repeated daily emphasis, fell with peculiar force upon the ears of New York City's 200,000 Irish recent immigrants; this group furnished the command and most of the commanded in the brickbat army which appeared on July 13 at a dozen points at once, with a simultaneity that more than suggested careful organization. So did the time factor; the militia of the State Guard were still with Couch's command at Harrisburg, and the forces of the law were represented by 1,500 police, neither well armed nor well organized.

The first objective of the mobs was the draft offices; but it was so much fun to smash and burn them that the rioters turned on everything else an ingenious vandalism could suggest, looting, then burning the home of a former mayor who was a Republican, the postmaster's house, a Negro orphan asylum, a Methodist church, and, of course, all the liquor stores. By the evening of the first day, the police were practically out of business, all dead or disabled; the mob was lynching individual Negroes and beating to death any member of the State Guard caught in the street. On the second day, the mobs were in undisputed possession of the city; Stanton ordered the temporary suspension of the draft, but in the meanwhile withdrew eleven regiments of New York troops from the Army of the Potomac and sent them to the turbulent town with John A. Dix to take command of the area, in place of old General Wool, who was pretty ancient for such rough work.

The first companies came on Wednesday, July 15; were greeted by the rioters with showers of stones and did not hesitate to reply with those orderly sheets of flame that had stopped the Confederate army along Cemetery Ridge. One battle drove the canaille back to their holes, but it failed to drive Governor Seymour back to his. He was determined that there should be no draft if he could prevent it, and he tried everything he could to accomplish this laudable object, including sending James A. Brady, a lawyer Stanton had known in the court days, with a proposal that Brady and Seymour together should have the New York Court of Appeals rule on the law's constitutionality. The plan produced one of Stanton's best state papers:

If the National executive must negotiate with State executives in relation to the execution of an act of Congress, then the problem which the Rebellion aims to solve has already been determined.

The Rebellion started upon the theory that there is no National Government, but only an agency determinable at the will of the respective States. The governor of New York stands today on the platform of Slidell, Davis and Benjamin; and if he is to be the judge of whether the conscription act is constitutional and may be enforced or resisted as he and other State authorities may decide, then the Rebellion is consummated and the National Government abolished.

It also produced—after August had made it clear that Seymour would do nothing whatever to help the draft and everything to hinder it—a request from Dix for more troops. They were sent; the New York draft began again on August 19, with 10,000 armed men in the city and artillery protecting the draft offices. Seymour and his Tammany associates switched to legal and quasi-legal evasions, and so effectively that out of 291,000 names drawn in New York only 35,882 recruits actually reached the army.

But there was no retreat on principle, and there could not be, since this was no affair of a petty Pennsylvania township. The moment the news began to come from New York, the War Department wire was inundated with requests for postponement and even the abandonment of the draft. Kingston, Buffalo, Elmira, Oswego—in Seymour's New York bailiwick—all predicted trouble and said that the draft could not be carried through at present; Ironton, Missouri, and Chicago asked for troops to enforce; Philadelphia feared riots; the provost marshal at Peoria said the city government was "in the hands of the Irish" and would do nothing to help him if a riot broke out; Iowa City telegraphed urgently that unless the New York riot were put down, not a man could be drafted in the west.

Throughout that late summer of 1863, while the Army of the Potomac and the Army of Northern Virginia did nothing but make faces at each other across the Rapidan, while General Grant was tidying up the debris of Vicksburg and distributing troops on police duty, while Rosecrans and Bragg were maneuvering obscurely through the pine barrens northwest of Chattanooga, Stanton was feverishly busy at putting on a national basis a matter which had always been handled by the states and in which not only local pride but also local patronage were intimately twined.

The letters and telegrams—mostly the latter—ran to dozens a day. Every governor in the North wanted some special privilege or special arrangement with regard to the draft in his state. H. A. Swift of Minnesota would have frontiersmen exempted because of Indian troubles on the borders of his state; and James Y. Smith of Rhode Island wanted drafted Block Islanders assigned to a "special corps" to defend their island against Confederate privateers. Strongly German Missouri wished to recruit regiments to be led only by one of the German generals, preferably Sigel, but Schimmelpfennig or "Sowbelly" Osterhaus would be acceptable. Gilmore of New Hampshire wanted the draft to be conducted, not according to districts laid out by the provost marshals, but according to towns, as prescribed by the legislature; also his men would never accept smoothbore muskets—they must have the best modern Springfields. Andrew of Massachusetts thought drafted men should be allowed to enlist and collect a bounty, a procedure which Stanton denounced as a steal. Salomon of Wisconsin asked that old regiments from his state should be brought back to fill up with recruits, which might make a draft unnecessary; Yates of Illinois and Tod of Ohio both asked for postponement—till after the crops were in, till after elections, till the Greek kalends.

Above all, state control died hard; Wisconsin, Illinois, Pennsylvania were all hotly insistent that any filling up of depleted regiments must be done by means of the conscripts; volunteers should go into new regiments, with new colonels appointed by the governor. New Jersey felt so aggrieved over the lack of higher command among her citizens that the governor wanted to raise troops for service under New Jersey generals only; and practically every governor, in the face of repeated refusals from Washington, kept raising or trying to raise regiments of six-months men, especially cavalry, for whom the federal government would have to find horses and arms but who could not be sent to the front because of the time limit.

Stanton to Governor Salomon of Wisconsin

You are utterly mistaken in supposing that you are the exclusive judge as to whether arms and ammunition of the general Government are to be sent to your State. The President must be the judge. You have not until now stated any fact for the judgment of the President, but have contented yourself with imperious orders. The Department has borne, and will continue to bear with them patiently, and will act upon any facts you may communicate. Orders have been given to send ammunition.

The requests were not always refused, however:

O. P. Morton of Indiana to Stanton

The rebel cavalry have made a raid into Indiana and as making raids seems to be their stable policy, I beg that you will send 1,000 pistols, 1,000 sabres, and 1,000 carbines to Indiana, that I may organize a company of cavalry in each border county for State defense. The cavalry heretofore raised for State defense have left the State and gone to the front long ago.

Stanton to Morton, same day

Your request shall be attended to forthwith.

Cutting across all state lines, cutting across everything, was a snowstorm, a whirlwind of requests for blanket exemptions from the draft. Railroad managers wanted their employees set free (Stanton gave them locomotive engineers actually at work, the others no); steamboat companies wanted exemption for their pilots and engineers, engravers for their artists, towns for their fire companies—one village of a thousand population listed one hundred men as belonging to the fire company. Welles of the Navy and Chase of the Treasury kept up a constant row about drafting clerks from their departments; Stanton had to keep telling them that he would grant relief in individual cases on application, but that there would be no blanket exemptions. Then there was trouble with the foreign ministries, especially those of the German states, who wanted exemptions for their nationals—but who was a national? The rules differed, and Salomon of Wisconsin wanted to set up boards to determine whether a given man was a German or an American. Stanton merely wired back that if a man had voted, he was enough of an American to go to war, and the voting records would give the provost marshal an adequate basis for conscription in all cases.

A feature of the draft act which gave constant trouble was the provision that a man could buy himself out for $300, or could provide a substitute. Seymour and his tail made it their main point of attack: "A rich man's war and a poor man's fight." The provision was not very defensible; when Lincoln tried to write a letter to the New York governor justifying it, he found his logic taking him into places where he did not care to go, and never put the missive in the mails. The only trouble was that the commutation feature was so practical politically that without it no draft law at all would have been possible. In the application of the law, Stanton did a good deal to mitigate the substitute feature by a ruling that a recruit should be credited to the district where he lived, regardless of how or where he had been brought into the service—which knocked on the head the practice of rich men hiring substitutes from poverty-stricken districts.

At the same time, another War Department order struck a blow at bounty jumping, which assumed painful proportions as soon as the draft act came into force, and every district, rather than every state, had to furnish its quota of men. The system was for local authorities to offer big bounties, report their quotas filled by enlistment, then let the provost marshal try to find the actual men. Stanton's order required the physical presence of the men in camp before any credit was given.

All told, his operation was a success; by the end of 1863 he was raising troops at a cost of $9.84 a man, where under the straight volunteering system they had cost the government $34.01 apiece. But the problem was never really solved; it came up in a thousand daily details to grind the Secretary down.

II

DANA was the first man from Vicksburg to reach Washington. He found that everybody wanted to pump him, especially Lincoln, Stanton, and Halleck, who kept him for nearly an entire day going over the details of the great campaign, drawing sketch maps, describing the parts played by the various generals, and giving his opinions of them. Sherman, he thought, was the best man the Union had yet found, a complete soldier; the intellectual McPherson was not far behind. Not that there was anything wrong with Grant; the newspaperman had the highest praise for his sweeping concepts, his grasp of large issues, his ability to co-ordinate the widespread movements of many men.

The President badgered Dana a good deal about McClernand, leaving the impression that he was not altogether satisfied with the dismissal, which presently brought it about that Grant's staff man, Rawlins, also came east, ostensibly with dispatches, actually for a long session with the Cabinet. The McClernand matter was gone into thoroughly, and a final decision against the politician-general was somewhat reluctantly taken.

Dana himself went on to New York and his family, even, for about a week, considering a business partnership. But before he closed the agreement, there arrived an appeal from Stanton to do another inspector's job, this time with Rosecrans and the Army of the Cumberland. The reports from that front were producing an uneasy feeling in Washington, in spite of the fact that the map showed geographical progress ever since June 24, when the campaign began. Rosecrans kept asking for more cavalry and complaining that the mounted men he had were badly found and badly armed. The Confederates outlined the point for him by shooting a raiding force under John H. Morgan all the way up into Indiana and Ohio. Morgan and his whole command were killed or captured at the end of July (some of the pursuers were using the thousand carbines Stanton had sent); but the basic problem remained, and it was one of straightening out the supply of cavalry remounts and weapons. On July 28, accordingly, Stanton set up a Cavalry Bureau in the

War Department, along the lines of the Quartermaster service, to have charge not only of remounts and weapons but also of cavalry training centers.

It was also true that everyone who had ever been in central Tennessee agreed that Rosecrans faced considerable geographical difficulties. Before him stood range on range of high-rising terraced hills covered with sparse pine, a country nude of supplies, a country whose rare roads became quagmires at the slightest rain, and where he would have to fight his way across numerous military rivers easily defended. Beyond this region the immense barrier of the Cumberland Mountains covered Chattanooga—Confederate base and railroad center, gateway to Georgia, the main geographical objective of the campaign.

Now although the lines of pins were moving toward Chattanooga in a satisfactory manner, there was nothing in the dispatches about fighting, prisoners taken, or casualties inflicted on the enemy—the items in which Grant's telegrams from behind Vicksburg had been so rich. Bragg was trapped, and trapped again; but he kept slipping out of the traps without losing any hide. He even slipped out of Chattanooga on September 9, and Rosecrans marched in—a piece of news that brought rejoicing to the northern press, but a somewhat more qualified reaction in the War Department, where Halleck pointed out that Rosecrans had worked himself into a position with an unfordable river at his back and several defensible mountain ranges across his front.

Nor were matters much helped by the news from General Ambrose Burnside, who, at Lincoln's urgent insistence, had pushed down the valleys to bring some relief to the distressed Unionists of eastern Tennessee. Instead of falling in on Bragg's flank, Burnside sat down in Knoxville and sent distressful telegrams about the bogeymen in them thar hills.

Dana reported from Rosecrans' headquarters on September 11, saying he had found the army much spread out, and feeling for the enemy across the lofty summit of Missionary Ridge and into the woods and ravines beyond. The Union general was convinced that the Confederates were in force behind the next ridge, Pigeon Mountain, and he was concentrating. Rosecrans (said Dana) was a friendly man, but with flashes of temper; when he saw the letter of introduction, he burst into an angry tirade against Washington—he had not been sustained, his plans were thwarted, Stanton and Halleck were doing all they could to prevent his success. Dana added that everything General Sheridan did was well done.

So many unfriendly judges were releasing drafted men under *habeas corpus* writs that on September 15, after much Cabinet discussion, the President suspended it; and there was the usual snowstorm of dispatches from Dana, almost hourly detailing something else Rosecrans thought he needed. The general reaction to the suspension of the writ was not unfavorable; and on the eighteenth Dana reported Rosecrans' concentration as complete, with sharp skirmishes that held a presage of battle going on along the line of a creek named Chickamauga.

The next day was Saturday. Already by late afternoon dispatches had begun to come from Dana, beginning with a terse, "There is fighting." Lincoln came over to the telegraph office in the Department, but not to keep one of his late vigils, for Dana's almost hourly wires brought such tidings as: "Everything is prosperous" and "Thomas is driving the rebels." Sunday morning for breakfast Stanton and the President had a late night dispatch from Rosecrans himself that he had taken ten cannon and could promise a complete victory the next day. Lincoln talked the matter over with the Secretary, and then told young Hay that he was uneasy about this promise, particularly as Dana's latest word was that Longstreet's Corps from the Army of Northern Virginia had joined Bragg, while from Burnside there came nothing at all.

Dana was a good reporter; his second-day telegrams from the field began arriving about noon, but now there were longer intervals, and toward night they broke off. Lincoln went out to the Soldiers' Home, as he often did when in need of rest; Stanton stayed on at the Department. It must have been some time after midnight, and the President had just succeeded in getting to sleep, when he was wakened and handed the appalling dispatch which had just come in, and which the Secretary thought too important to hold until morning:

My report today is of deplorable importance. Chickamauga is as fatal a name in our history as Bull Run. Van Cleve on Thomas' right was seen to give way, but in tolerable order, borne down by immense columns of the enemy. Before them our soldiers turned and fled. It was a wholesale panic. We have lost heavily in killed today. The total of our killed, wounded and prisoners can hardly be less than 20,000 and may be much more.

It was dated Chattanooga, September 19, 1863. Lincoln got up and went over to the War Office. It must have been a frightful night, with few words spoken, but toward daybreak the sky lightened a little on another message from Dana, saying that the earlier one had "given too dark a view of our disaster." Halleck came; so did a first report from Rosecrans himself, saying he was back in Chattanooga, but not in too desperate straits, and could hold on.

Through that day and the next the story began to come clear in more long dispatches from Dana, whose prose turned a little purple at the edges; how an accident (which turned out to be a badly written order) caused a gap in the Union right wing, through which the Confederates rushed, tearing the whole wing to pieces, driving it into an utter rout that bore away two corps commanders and Rosecrans himself; how Thomas on the Union left drew back his flanks and all afternoon long, supporting in turn every part of the line with his presence and detailed orders, beat off the assaults of more than double his numbers of victorious rebels, until moonlight saw bayonets and clubbed muskets drive back the last waves from the feet of the "Rock of Chickamauga." A defeat, yes; but a defeat not without glory, and the Confederates had taken 18,000 casualties to 16,000 for the Union.

Yet it left a situation. That same evening, September 22, there came a telegram from Brigadier-General Charles K. Graham, who had been taken prisoner after being badly wounded at Gettysburg. He was in Fortress Monroe, having just been exchanged out of Richmond, and he confirmed to the hilt that Longstreet's whole corps, with eighty-six pieces of artillery, had gone to join Bragg. It did not need Rosecrans' latest dispatch from Chattanooga—"We will hold this point and I can-

not be dislodged except by very superior numbers"—to make
things ominous, for Bragg's numbers obviously met the condition. On the first news of the defeat, Grant had been ordered to
send Sherman and his corps to Chattanooga, but they had to
go by steamer to Memphis, then make a long march. Burnside
had nearly 20,000 at Knoxville, but neither command, prayer,

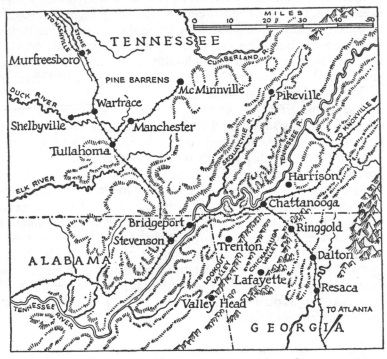

The Campaign in the Tennessee Mountains—Summer 1863

nor entreaty would budge him out of there; and even if he did
move, there was now a good chance he would be destroyed
while isolated. What to do?

Stanton called in Meade and put the question. The General
did not know. Well, then, Stanton asked Halleck, how long
will it take to send 15,000 men from the Army of the Potomac
to Chattanooga? "Three months," said Halleck. Eckert the
telegrapher, now a colonel, was summoned; Stanton explained

that Rosecrans needed reinforcements at once to meet an enemy attack. For that matter, if Rosecrans were not reinforced in far less time than Halleck said it would take, he would be starved to death; Dana had made it clear that the Confederates held all routes of ingress to Chattanooga except one poor mountain track that would by no means support an army, even if there were transport enough to carry the necessary supplies over it. A reinforced Rosecrans could bruise a path through the circle. Eckert believed that by using the railroads, Halleck's three months could be cut to forty days; was told that this was nowhere near good enough, and went out to study maps and timetables with McCallum, now a general and Director of Military Transportation.

That night, after Lincoln had gone out to the Soldiers' Home, young Hay was summoned to Stanton's office. He found the Secretary with two or three others, deciphering a partly garbled and intricate dispatch in which Rosecrans explained the reasons for the failure at Chickamauga. Stanton was snorting: "I know the reasons well enough. Rosecrans ran away from his fighting men and did not stop for thirteen miles. No, they need not shuffle it off on McCook. He is not much of a soldier. I was never in favor of him for a major-general. But he is not accountable for this business. He and Crittenden made pretty good time away from the fight to Chattanooga, but Rosecrans beat them both." Finally noticing Hay, the Secretary told him that he wanted the President summoned from bed at once; messengers had already been sent for Chase and Seward.

The various goings and comings took time. It was already one in the morning (with Lincoln's face showing the worry that beset him, since Stanton had never so sent for him before) of a hot moonlit night when the party assembled at the White House, with Halleck and (of all people!) Joe Hooker. Stanton opened matters by reading Rosecrans' urgent call for reinforcements, and saying that if he did not get them, the Army of the Cumberland would be destroyed, and probably Burnside, too. "I propose to send 30,000 men from the Army of the Potomac. There is no reason to expect that General Meade will attack Lee, although greatly superior in force, and his great numbers are, where they are, useless. In five days 30,000 men could be put with Rosecrans."

Lincoln: "I will bet that if the order is given tonight the troops could not be got to Washington in five days."

Stanton had evidently been primed by Eckert and McCallum as to their progress with the schedules. He said: "On such a subject I don't care to bet, but the matter has been carefully investigated, and it is certain that 30,000 bales of cotton could be sent in that time; and by taking possession of the railroads and excluding all other business, I do not see why 30,000 men cannot be sent as well. But if 30,000 can't be sent, let 20,000 go."

Hooker and Halleck were against the idea, and the President inclined in their direction, but when Stanton read a telegram from James A. Garfield of Rosecrans' staff about the imminent starvation of the army, Seward and Chase swung to the idea that saving the Army of the Cumberland was more important than weakening the Army of the Potomac, and their arguments had a visible effect on Lincoln. Stanton turned to McCallum: "If you have supreme authority and abundant transportation how quickly can you make the transfer?"

"I can complete it in seven days."

"Good! I told you so! I knew it could be done!" Stanton swung to Halleck: "Forty days, indeed, when the life of the nation is at stake!" Then again to McCallum: "Go ahead, begin now."

"Mr. Secretary," said Lincoln mildly, "I have not yet given my consent." This launched Stanton into an outburst of oratory about the danger to Rosecrans and Burnside and the superiority Meade would still have over Lee. It was 2:30 in the morning when Lincoln finally agreed and the conference turned to details. Hooker was placed in charge of the movement (after all, he had few superiors as a fighting corps commander), and the XI and XII corps were to be his command. Lincoln went back to the Soldiers' Home with an orderly, and the other Cabinet members left; Stanton sent one messenger to wire Meade that the two corps should be in Washington not later than the morning of the twenty-fifth, and another to wire

Dana that 20,000 troops were on the way. A long message went to Louisville inquiring about the gauges and condition of the railroads between there and Nashville, and the availability of rolling stock; an order was prepared giving Hooker authority to seize railroads and cars. Urgent telegrams summoned Garrett of the B & O, Thomas Scott of the Pennsy, and other railroad men—W. P. Smith from Baltimore, S. M. Fenton from Philadelphia. A reply from Meade said the XII Corps was on picket; he had to be told to get it off picket and into Washington.

It was after daybreak by the time all this was done; Stanton went over to the War Office, and was greeted by Eckert with his detailed schedules. How about crossing the Ohio at Louisville with artillery and horses? It had been thought of; the river was full of coal barges and a temporary pontoon bridge could be laid across them in twenty-four hours. How about feeding the men? The Quartermaster Department could establish a force of cooks and waiters every fifty miles along the route to have hot food ready to take aboard the trains, distributing the food during the run, and themselves returning by regular trains moving in the other direction. Stanton approved the plan at once and sent it over to the Quartermaster Department for execution. The railroad men arrived while the Secretary was having breakfast, and there was a good deal to take up with them, particularly the report on the gauges beyond Louisville, where, it appeared, there were several changes. It was agreed that Scott should go west at once and impress rolling stock from other roads for the Louisville-Nashville run; the gauge on a stretch between Louisville and Lexington would simply have to be changed, because it was a peculiar one and the amount of rolling stock for it was very limited. Scott was given an authority to gather a work gang of 8,000 Negroes for the job.

Details kept coming up, such as the necessary wires to military officers along the route to having the drinking saloons in the stations closed during the movement; and how many cars per train would the grades through the mountains allow. It was after nine on the evening of the twenty-fifth before telegrams came saying the XI Corps was on the way, and Stanton could lie down for the first time, with a handkerchief soaked in cologne around his head. He was not allowed to rest long; General Schurz of the Third Division of the XI Corps tried to hold his command at Grafton until he could join it, and had to be told that Hooker had authority to relieve and arrest anyone, anyone who delayed the movement; men went to sleep on the tops of the cars and fell off. A storm of messages kept coming in with more details for decision, and it was October 6 before Hooker telegraphed that he was at the front, and the Secretary could send telegrams of warm praise to his subordinates and go home for the first time in nearly two weeks. Stanton had accomplished the first mass railroad movement of troops in history, and it has been the model for every one since.

III

AMID all this, the dispatches from Dana took on a gloomy tone. There was a bad command situation in the Army of the Cumberland. Crittenden and McCook, the refugee corps commanders of Chickamauga, had never been too popular with their subordinates, and their conduct in the battle finished them; several of the brigade and division commanders, including Sheridan and Palmer, the two best, said they did not wish to serve under the pair any more. This put Rosecrans in a cruel position; not only did he dislike dismissing officers at any time, but he could hardly do it in this case without underlining the fact that he, too, had fled from the field. Dana wired that the removal of Crittenden and McCook by Washington had become a necessity (it was done at once), then slipped back to Nashville for a confidential wire chat with Stanton:

Dana to Stanton, September 30, 1863

The soldiers have lost attachment to Rosecrans. On the other hand, General Thomas has risen to the highest point in their esteem, as he has in that of everyone who witnessed his conduct on that unfortunate and glorious day; and should there be a change in the chief command, there is no other man whose appointment would be more welcome to this army.

Stanton to Dana, same day

The merit of General Thomas and the debt of gratitude the nation owes his valor and skill are fully appreciated here, and I wish you to tell him so. It was not my fault that he was not in the chief command months ago.

As a matter of fact, Stanton and Lincoln had already made up their minds as to what the situation called for, and the Secretary was only waiting for the completion of his railroad movement before acting. As soon as he absorbed a couple of days of what he called rest—in which he only worked ten hours a day instead of the usual twelve—he climbed on a train for Indianapolis. Grant had been ordered to the same point by telegraph, expecting to be sent on to Nashville as a co-ordinator of troops and supplies for the beleaguered Rosecrans. At the station there, a short, quick-moving, powerful man with abundant whiskers climbed aboard his car—Stanton, whom the General was seeing for the first time in his life. The newcomer rushed up to Dr. Kittoe of the staff with outthrust hand and: "How do you do, General? I recognize you from your pictures."

There was a moment or two of embarrassment, but both men were too busy to waste time; the Secretary pulled from his pocket a pair of orders and wordlessly handed them to Grant. The opening paragraphs were identical; they made the conqueror of Vicksburg commander of a new military Division of the Mississippi, including everything from the Alleghanies to the great river; but the second order relieved Rosecrans in favor of Thomas. Grant said he would take that one, and the two men sat down to exchange views on military matters and personalities, east and west. The train pulled into Louisville in a chill, drizzling rain, which gave Stanton a horrible cold, there to find a telegram from Dana which said it was growing difficult to believe that Rosecrans was of sound mind; unless prevented, he was going to abandon Chattanooga and retreat.

Grant, who had been out when the message reached Stanton, returned to find the Secretary pacing the floor in his dressing gown, sniffling, and much disturbed. The General promptly telegraphed Thomas to take over the command and to keep the army where it was. Before dawn, before Stanton could leave to take his cold back east, the answer was at hand: "We will hold the town till we starve." The record said that if Thomas decided to hold anything, he would probably do it, but Stanton wrote him a letter anyway:

General Grant, who bears this brief note, will thank you in behalf of the people, the War Department, and myself, for the magnificent behavior of yourself and your gallant men at Chickamauga.

You stood like a rock and that stand gives you fame which will grow brighter and brighter as the ages go by. God be praised for such men at such a time. You will be rewarded by the country and by the Department.

Election news came aboard the train on the way back; Pennsylvania was safe to the Union, and Ohio had returned to the Republican column with a highly satisfactory majority. Stanton stopped off at Steubenville to visit a few old friends. One of them, Moses Dillon, had fallen on evil days. "Come to Washington, Mose," said the Secretary, "and I will give you employment. I suppose, of course, that you are a steadfast Union man?"

"Well, I voted for Vallandigham for governor."

"Voted for Vallandigham! Then you shall never have a position under this government if I can prevent it."

BACKDROP

Washington Intelligencer

For Sale at a Bargain—One of Ericsson's patent CALORIC ENGINES at four-horse power, can be seen at Gray and Noye's Iron Works, Seventh Ward.

SUBSTITUTES! SUBSTITUTES! Drafted men can be supplied *at once,* by calling at the office of Wm. M. Robertson, corner Fifteenth street and Pennsylvania avenue.—T. A. Mitchell

STAMPEDE OF HORSES. In the course of Tuesday night several hundred horses in the corral, near the Observatory, got out and stampeded, running over the city in droves. A number of men were sent out to recapture them, and we believe, during the night, succeeded in taking the most of them.

CHANGE OF BASE. In consequence of the high price of board and rents in this city, about one thousand clerks in the various Departments have been contemplating the advantage of moving over to Baltimore, where everything appertaining to living is so much cheaper. House rent and board can be had in that city fifty per cent less than in this. The prominent individuals in this movement state that if they can effect an arrangement with the Baltimore & Ohio Railroad so as to fix the time of going and returning to suit them they will most assuredly make the desired movement.

New York Herald

We have the positive information from an intelligent source, that the late defeat of Gen. Rosecrans was not the result of any

326

deficiency in generalship on his part, but the consequence of a blundering peremptory order from Washington, which compelled him, against his better judgment, to advance into the plains of Georgia against a vastly superior army, while he was in the very act of falling back to the strong defensive heights around Chattanooga. It is only the old story of Bull Run, the Richmond peninsula, the disastrous defeat of Pope and the heights of Fredericksburg over again. In the case of Rosecrans, however, it appears that a special commissioner from the War Office did the business.

New York Evening Express

The Pennsylvania and Ohio elections continue to be fruitful topics of discussion. The Republican Journals are saucy, and in ecstatics. There is no knowing now what such a half-mad man as Stanton may do.

19

THE WAITING WINTER

Stanton to His Wife, August 24, 1863

I was very glad to learn that you safely arrived at Bedford and I hope you are enjoying the comfort of the mountain air. The weather is still extremely hot here, but not so severe as some of the days before you left home.

On the morning that you started a fine basket of peaches was sent by Dr. Barnes, but they were too soft and ripe to be forwarded so I distributed them between Mrs. Harrison and the President. Mr. Newton also sent a couple bunches of grapes and a fine bouquet.

On Sunday to escape the heat I spent the day on the Potomac and by night the weather had become much cooler. The day after you left here a woman came whose name I forgot, but she said she was a milliner on 8th between L and M, called and said you owed her $14 and was to leave it with the servant. I declined paying her until you could be heard from. Shall I pay her and what is her name?

I think if you could get a good doctor to vaccinate the baby, it had better be done at the spring than here and before you return. With much love to yourself, Eddie and the children and your mother, I am ever Yours.

There is an infinite distance between this letter and those written from S.S. *Star of the West* to the same address. To begin with, the burning intensity of emotion, which would almost be called passion in another man, has settled down into something more bland; they are sure of each other. It is also a different kind of letter. Of course, Stanton had no unfamiliar surroundings to describe for Ellen, but he says nothing whatever about any presence but those affecting their mutual home-life, and compared to the California letters, he is very brief.

Most important of all, this letter practically stands by itself. There is no other private correspondence from the period, all the documents signed "E. M. Stanton" are in the official records. No one sees the man at the great trotting races at the New Course, or at the theatre, which Lincoln enjoys so much; he is unaware of the courtesans who flood the streets and provide such juicy items for the *Star;* he is unmentioned in connection with social gatherings, except the rare formal Presidential dinners for the Cabinet. Doubtless this social abstinence was to some extent prepense, for the Secretary of War could hardly avoid being buttonholed for favors over the coffee cups; but the ruling factor was that a change had taken place, so gradually that it was only visible when complete, and he was now absorbed in the struggle to such a degree that it filled his whole horizon. The man had disappeared into the official.

It was not that Stanton engaged in "empire building" in the modern and pejorative sense of that term; rather that empires thrust themselves upon him. Even before the western journey (from which the Secretary returned with his chronic asthma no little augmented by the Louisville cold), there were long, difficult conferences about the Army of the Potomac and its command. To a letter from Halleck suggesting that a rested army and the fine September weather made an attack on Lee possible, Meade replied only: "I can get a battle out of Lee in very disadvantageous circumstances, which may render his inferior force my superior and which is not likely to result in any very decided advantage, even in case I should be victorious. In this view I am reluctant to run the risks without the positive sanction of the Government."

Stanton sent this along to Lincoln "for reflection overnight." He himself had already reflected, and decided that the significance of the protest was that Meade had become a Mc-Clellan, who could never be persuaded to fight except by the enemy—an uncomplaining, straightforward, soldierly McClellan, but not an attack commander. Lincoln did reflect, and then put his thoughts on paper for Halleck: "For a battle, then, General Meade has three men to General Lee's two. Yet, it having been determined that choosing the ground and standing on the defensive gives so great an advantage that the three cannot safely attack the two, the three are left simply standing on the defensive also. If the enemy's 60,000 are sufficient to keep our 90,000 away from Richmond, why, by the same rule, may not 40,000 of ours keep their 60,000 away from Washington, leaving us 50,000 to put to some other use?"

The logic was unanswerable, but it produced no result except more conferences and the decision that nothing could be done for the time being. The President summed up the result of these consultations for Secretary Welles: Halleck and Stanton knew the generals better than he, and "Who among them is any better than Meade?" Sedgwick was so close to the commander that their brains might almost have been inside the same skull; Hancock was at home with his Gettysburg wound and Sickles with his; Sykes had acquired the name of "Tardy George," not because his military movements were slow, but because his brain worked as though its bearings were rusted; would not do even as a corps commander, and would be removed from it soon. To appoint a new chief from the Army of the Potomac, one would have to clear away all the old heads and go down to some divisional officer like Warren or A. A. Humphreys, who used to go into battle giggling, one of the very few men who really enjoyed being shot at. Lincoln: "To sweep away the whole of them from chief command and substitute a new man would cause a shock and be likely to lead to combinations and troubles greater than we now have." Not to mention that for the public, Meade was still the victor of Gettysburg, who had done nothing to forfeit confidence.

During Stanton's western trip it began to look as though Lee himself would solve the difficulty; he slid forward by his left, near the sources of the Rappahannock, crossed the stream and made a gesture toward Meade's rear. The Union army retreated to Centerville, near the old Manassas battleground, and Warren with the II Corps rapped a Confederate advance sharply over the knuckles, taking five guns and 4,500 prisoners. But there was no counterattack, and Lee trotted back to the river.

How much of the earlier comment on Meade's strategy came out of Stanton's mind and how much from Lincoln's own is uncertain; but while the two armies were in face at Centerville, the President wrote another letter to Meade, one that owed nothing to anyone else: "If General Meade can now attack [Lee] in a field no more than equal for us, and will do so with all the skill and courage which he, his officers, and men possess, the honor will be his if he succeeds, and the blame mine if he fails."

The President took the unusual step of making this assumption of responsibility public, in the hope that it would urge Meade to action, and after some epistolary argle-gargle between the General and Halleck (the letters of the latter take on a sharper tone after Stanton's return, but it is impossible to allocate authorship precisely among the three men who were running the war), Meade did move forward toward the Rappahannock—cautiously, inchingly. Early in November Lee slipped across; on the seventh, late in the afternoon, Sedgwick closed up on the stream with the V and VI corps, and found the Confederates had left a bridgehead behind at Rappahannock Station, consisting of two pretty strong redouts. Sedgwick instantly attacked under cover of smoke and falling night; carried both redouts, with 1,600 prisoners, all the rebel guns, and eight stand of colors.

It was a clean small victory, but tempers in Washington were not improved by the fact that the first field dispatches described it as one of the great triumphs of the war, and that, instead of following it up, Meade only sent the captured colors to the Capitol with a guard of honor consisting of a company from each regiment that had participated in the attack, with General David A. Russell, who had headed it. Stanton, one of whose main worries all along had been that of keeping fighting men at the front, refused to receive the delegation; his act caused Russell some heartburning, but had no effect on Meade, the real objective.

Meanwhile, Grant had arrived at Chattanooga, "wet, dirty and well," according to the ebullient Dana, and as usual when he appeared on the scene, things began to heat up. He found Thomas' men on half rations, the army administration in a confusion which even Dana declared he had no words to describe, and Sherman with the corps from Vicksburg approaching at only about an inch a day, rebuilding the lateral railroad from Corinth. This last was Halleck's order; the General-in-Chief had cherished an inexplicable affection for that railroad ever since the early months of 1862. Grant promptly countermanded the railroad work and ordered Sherman by road to the right of the Chattanooga position, on the northeastward flank, in which direction heavy Confederate movements were reported.

Two days after the new commander's arrival, Dana reported that a plan had been worked out for seizing the nose of the peak called Raccoon Mountain and supplying the Army of the Cumberland by a route along the southern bank of the Tennessee and pontoon bridges across the river loops; two days more, at midnight on October 28, Stanton stood by the wire as the machine tapped out: "Everything perfectly successful. The river is now open." By morning there was the detail that Hooker, still "Fighting Joe" when it came to a battle, had carried the rebel lines with the bayonet, and beaten off a furious counterattack; but he grumbled, complained, and made so much trouble that Grant wanted to remove him.

Not yet, General Grant; it is politically impossible, with Chase and the Treasury interest still so strong for the man. But Stanton did accede to another request in the same wire that asked for Hooker's relief, and sent out a pair of general's stars for Staff Officer Wilson, which the young man donned just after his twenty-sixth birthday. Grant wanted him to go into the cavalry, which had not been doing too well in the western commands; in the meanwhile, the new general accompanied Dana on a mission to find out how matters progressed at Knoxville, it now having become certain that the movement toward Grant's left was Longstreet's Corps, swinging out of the Chattanooga lines for a thrust against the Burnside command.

On November 13, Dana reported from Knoxville in terms that caused both Lincoln and Stanton to send Grant anxious telegrams. Longstreet was coming with 20,000 to 40,000 men, Burnside did not have the strength to resist them, and in addition was talking of abandoning Knoxville for a desperate plunge southeastward. "I found him possessed of the idea that he must expose his whole force to capture rather than withdraw from the country. General Wilson overcame it by representing that Grant did not wish him to include the capture of his entire army among the elements of his plan of operations."

On pure military grounds the right thing to do was doubtless to remove Burnside from his command; but he was prompt, loyal, and politically important, and it was another case of Meade, or no one better in sight. "The command is in great want of first rate officers," wired Dana, so the only resource was pressing Grant to make so much trouble for Bragg that he would have to recall Longstreet. Grant was willing enough, but found it hard to make Washington understand that in the face of towering, fortified ridges, he did not wish to hazard battle without Sherman and his corps. That General reported in person from Chattanooga on November 15, but his head of column did not approach until five days later, and then it began to rain in torrents that still further delayed the movement of the troops who, lacking the support of a railroad, had to move their impedimenta by wagon train.

This was one of the times which Stanton called "distressing periods," when he slept at the War Department with one of the cipher men nearby and only went home for a meal now and then; he was also busy with the report for the year, which had to be considered with care, since it could not fail to play a part in next year's Presidential campaign. On the twentieth, the same day Sherman's first troops were reported nearing Chattanooga, the wires to Burnside went dead; he was besieged in Knoxville, a fact of which Grant was made aware the same day by telegram from Washington.

Not that he needed urging; no man could be more urgent. On the twenty-third Washington learned that the battle had begun with the seizure of a low hill out before the Union position—Orchard Knob. The next day was Monday; no news till late at night:

Grant to War Department, November 24, 1863

The fight today progressed favorably. Sherman carried the end of Missionary Ridge, and his right is now on the tunnel and his left on Chickamauga Creek. Troops from Lookout Valley carried the

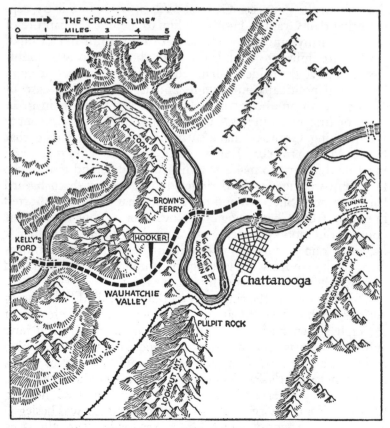

Chattanooga—November 1863

point of that mountain, and now hold the eastern slope and a point high up. Hooker reports 2,000 prisoners taken.

The maps showed how Grant was now menacing both flanks of the enemy line along huge, dominating Missionary Ridge, and the morning papers told of a spectacular "battle above the clouds," in which Hooker stormed Lookout, with the guns flashing like meteors through a morning mist, and the sun burst through to show the stars and stripes on the highest crest, while all the men in Chattanooga cheered.

Lincoln to Grant, late November 24, 1863

Well done. Many thanks to all. Remember Burnside.

President and Secretary knew that Grant would fight again the next day, one of electric tension in Chattanooga, Knoxville, Washington. Probably Lincoln and Stanton were not the only men who waited late for news from the field, but the news was worth waiting for, for when it came it told of the most incredible and glorious feat of arms in the whole war —Sherman stopped on one flank, Hooker on the other, but the soldiers of the Army of the Cumberland running quite away from their orders to charge straight up the face of a mountain studded with cannon and rifle pits full of men determined to kill them, madly shouting "Chickamauga!" till they burst across the summit, tearing the Confederate center to pieces, and drove Bragg's army across the border of Georgia in prone rout, leaving 6,142 prisoners and 40 cannon behind. Sheridan was in the heart of that insane assault; had been seen to throw his whisky flask up the slope and climb after it at the head of his men.

The news, with a copy of Grant's dispatch, was sent down to Meade; it might encourage him to do something. As a matter of fact, it did stir him on a little; on the twenty-sixth the report from the Virginia front was that in spite of rain and bitter cold, the Army of the Potomac was across the Rapidan, feeling for Lee's right flank, with Warren and the II Corps leading the advance. But then things went confusing, and, by December 1, Stanton was forced to write the other generals that "Meade is on the back track again without a fight."

When the details came in they showed that Warren had not made his turning maneuver as widely as expected, and ran into entrenched lines that he did not think he could carry; whereupon Meade called off the whole show in spite of the fact that Sedgwick, on the other wing, had already opened a cannonade preliminary to attacking across good ground and unfortified. Toward evening, after looking over Warren's position, Meade told Sedgwick he might go in, but by this time it was too late; the rebels had dug in on this part of the front also, Sedgwick no longer thought an attack would succeed, and "the heart was taken out of everything."

This about completed the picture of Meade's mind. He was an able tactician, as witness the fact that every time he clashed with Lee, he had the better of it. But he lacked offensive spirit and, above all, any power of improvisation; demanded engineering certainties, which are usually unobtainable in war; kept saying he had not wished for the command and would be content to quit it. The plain fact was that the Army of the Potomac had produced a number of fine corps leaders, of whom Meade might even be considered the best; but no one with the will to command an army on the offensive against Robert Lee. There would have to be a new man found for that, and there was very little doubt who it would be.

II

THE Chattanooga fighting had a not inconsiderable effect on the unhappy business of prisoner-of-war exchanges, about which the Confederates grew progressively more unreasonable. There was no doubt about it; Union prisoners were being treated abominably, left without clothing or medical care, ill-fed, and practically not housed at all. Here is how a Southern woman saw Andersonville, with the warning that this was the worst of the prisons, so bad that its superintendent, Henry Wirz, was tried and hanged for civil murder after the conflict:

Father Hamilton said that at one time the prisoners died at the rate of 150 a day, and he saw some of them die on the ground without a rag to lie on or a garment to cover them. Dysentery was the most fatal disease, and as they lay on the ground in their own excrements, the smell was so horrible that the good Father says he was often obliged to rush from their presence to get a breath of pure air.

On the very day he took office, Stanton had issued an order that Union soldiers' pay and rations should continue during captivity, and he sent Hamilton Fish with Bishop E. R. Ames to Richmond under a flag of truce, carrying $50,000 to buy supplies for Union prisoners. This worked reasonably well for those held in Libby Prison in Richmond, and partially for prisoners held in the smaller camps at Belle Isle and Salisbury, but the two commissioners never succeeded in getting anything past the brutal Wirz at Andersonville. The tales which came out of that place were appalling, and Stanton was the recipient of a good deal of steady pressure from Northern press and governors—notably Curtin of Pennsylvania—to make exchanges regardless of Confederate Commissioner Ould's continued refusal to include Negro troops or their white officers.

It did not seem to the Secretary that a government which was fighting a war, one of whose objectives was to make the black man free, should recognize the right of its opponent to make him a perpetual prisoner, and he refused to budge. But as provisions and clothing in the Confederacy grew scarcer, conditions grew worse, and on November 9, just after his western trip to meet Grant, Stanton approved a recommendation of General Sullivan A. Meredith, who had charge of prisoner exchanges at Fortress Monroe, and who knew pretty thoroughly what was going on. It said that Confederate prisoners should be "reduced to conditions similar to those of Union captives in rebel prisons." Nothing came of this; old General Ethan Allen Hitchcock, who had come far enough from his metaphysical retirement to take general charge of prisoner exchange, protested on the ground of common humanity.

Stanton now tried to improve things by ordering 24,000 army rations to Libby for distribution. In reply the truculent

Ould excluded all Northern commissioners for prisoner relief from Southern prisons, said he himself would distribute any rations sent for the prisoners, and if this arrangement did not satisfy Stanton, he could simply stop sending rations. Ould made it quite clear that he would be satisfied with one thing, and one thing only—a full general agreement for the exchange of whites, no exchange for Negroes or the officers who led them. At the same time, Hitchcock reported that even if Ould were willing to exchange Negroes (which he was not), it would be impossible for him to do so: "Not a single colored soldier or officer of colored troops was ever permitted to reach his hands." Those not shot or hung under the barbarous servile rebellion acts were put to work as slaves for government account or sold as slaves to private buyers.

There was a certain Colonel W. P. Wood in Washington, a great hand in under-the-table affairs, smooth and plausible, who had worked for Stanton in the McCormick reaper case as what would now be called a private detective. Now the Secretary called him in. The War Department had several million dollars in Confederate bills, confiscated from various rebel spies. This money was not worth much, about twenty-two cents on the dollar gold, since the Richmond government had never succeeded in setting up a true circulating medium, and most business in the Confederacy was done on a barter basis. But if the prison-camp guards were like human beings elsewhere, the sight of even mildly valuable portable wealth might entice them into doing something for the prisoners. Would Wood try to get the money through? Wood said, yes, and ultimately succeeded, dressed as a Confederate officer on a tour of inspection, and after some hair-raising adventures.

But this was only a cupful in the bucket of misery, and at the end of November the matter was still further complicated by the Battle of Chattanooga. Among the 6,000 prisoners captured by Grant, a very considerable number turned out to be men who had earlier surrendered at Vicksburg and who had been paroled "not to fight again until properly exchanged." Being questioned, they said they had been forced back into service under their state conscription laws. Of course, there was only one thing to do about such a situation; Stanton issued an order that all paroled prisoners should be "reduced to actual physical possession" as soon as possible and no more paroles should be granted. This produced another explosion from the newspapers and governors, Tod of Ohio arguing that Union prisoners would not be paroled either. It also produced the most indefensible of Ould's efforts to apply pressure in the North; on December 12, he notified Stanton that the Confederates would no longer receive provisions or supplies for Union prisoners.

Stanton made one more try by sending off several batches of sick and wounded Confederate prisoners to be exchanged for Union men in similar condition. Ould made the exchange, but only once; on December 28 he notified Stanton that he would exchange sick no more except as part of a general prisoner cartel—from which Negroes were to be excluded. There for the time the matter rested, except as Northern governors and papers kept hammering at Stanton to get their men out of the Southern hellholes.

III

THAT same December the pot of trouble in Missouri began to boil again. It was primarily local politics; the Conservative and Radical factions had carried their struggle to a point where no reconciliation was possible, and the Radicals, though stout Union men all, were trying to hang the Copperhead label on Conservative Governor Gamble—something that Lincoln denounced as monstrous. Stanton came into the picture because the Radicals were trying to hold a convention to write a new state constitution, so rigid in its test-oaths that no Conservative could hold office under it. Now Missouri and Kansas were a military department because of rebel raiders at their southern edges; the long-bearded General Schofield, head of the department, refused to allow the convention, whereupon the Radicals turned up in Washington with fire in their eyes and whisky on their breaths.

They wanted Schofield dismissed for having exceeded his instructions and prevented the much-desired merger of all Unionist elements. Lincoln sent for the General, heard him tell how no real merger was possible and was convinced: "I believe you, Schofield, those fellows have been lying to me again." But the situation remained, and was doubly complicated by the fact that the Missouri Radicals refused to work in concert with those in Kansas, from whom their views differed with the vehemence of early Christian sects.

Fortunately, a way out opened up. After the Chattanooga battles, Grant sent Sherman toward Knoxville at the head of a corps. Longstreet had no stomach for an encounter with this force in addition to Burnside; raised his siege and fell back toward the Great Smoky Mountains. There was some telegraphic conversation among Grant, Stanton, Halleck, and Sherman over whether Sherman should follow the Confederate corps hard enough to drive it from the state. The decision was against; Longstreet's men were less damaging where they stood than they would be if reinforcing Lee or the Confederate army in the west.

In the meanwhile, Dana had gone back to Washington with a report that Burnside would have to go, in spite of a telegram from Governor Andrew Johnson: "He is the man of the hour; the people want him and he will inspire more confidence than anyone else." The relief was General John G. Foster, next-ranking officer in the little army; for a few weeks he and Longstreet circled each other like a pair of quarreling cats through alternate periods of drenching rain and sub-zero cold. Then the weather caught up with Foster and he asked to be relieved for illness, about the time Schofield reached Washington.

Technically, the command was that of an army and a department—that of the Ohio—which called for a high-ranking major-general, while the actual problem was one of civil administration and a buildup with new recruits, one for a proved administrator. Stanton wired Grant to ask whom he wished in the job; Grant replied that either McPherson or Schofield would do, but neither had enough seniority to rank the generals now commanding in the Army of the Ohio. This made possible a solution to both problems at once; Schofield was promoted, thereby demonstrating that there was no dissatisfaction with his performance in Missouri, and assigned to the Army of the Ohio, while Rosecrans was resurrected from the shadows to take over Missouri, and Kansas was made into a separate department.

It was a quiet winter for the most part, in which Washington expressed a sense of resolution perfumed with the hope of coming victory. There was little social life. The President returned from making his Gettysburg address with an illness at first diagnosed as a bilious attack, but which presently developed as a mild case of smallpox, while an epidemic of the disease ran through the city. One of Jefferson Davis' slaves appeared in town with a tale of how Madame President had taken him by the hair and banged his head against a wall. Southern faces were seen in the streets that had not been there since 1860; the *Star* called attention to them under the headline: "Rats Leaving the Sinking Ship." So many people came to watch Belle Boyd, the famous rebel spy, take her walks in the park that Stanton had to put a stop to her excursions; and the Secretary had a run-in with General Grant.

The origins of it dated back to his first weeks in the War Office. Eckert, the telegrapher, was a dabbler in cryptography, and had read the famous works of Edgar Poe on the subject. He thought that the Confederates might be getting some of their obvious preinformation about Union moves by cracking the army cipher, which had been devised by another telegraphic expert brought in by McClellan, Anson Stager. Stanton called Stager in, had him and Eckert devise a better cipher, and set up a cryptographic unit in the Department, with a dozen operators. They were a good group; none of them ever betrayed a secret, and one of them refused a bribe of $20,000, with a guarantee of immunity.

Four of these cipher men, Eckert himself, A. B. Chandler, C. A. Tinker and D. Homer Bates, remained in the Department, and at least one was always on duty or asleep in the building. The rest went out to the armies, and they alone had the keys of the cipher in use; not even Lincoln or Stanton could read the messages without their aid.

The ciphers were almost childishly simple by subsequent standards, but the system worked wonderfully well; cryptography was at a low ebb in the Southern Confederacy, and not a message was ever broken down. Even the capture of a couple of operators with their keys in their pockets failed to bother Stager; he changed ciphers so quickly that the rebels got no juice from their prizes. The operators did more than keep communications secret; they cracked Confederate messages right and left, including some very important ones during Grant's Vicksburg campaign, and another that led government agents to a New York engraving shop where plates for Confederate money and bonds were being made. (It became very easy to spot counterfeit Confederate bills; after the loss of the New York plates, new ones had to be made in the South, and the job was so badly done that fake Confederate money always looked better than the genuine article.)

But the informal and forthright Grant found it a trial to have someone else handling his messages. During the Vicksburg garrison period, he appointed one of his staff, a Colonel John Riggin, as head of telegraphs for his department. Like all new brooms, Riggin began by installing a new system and shifting the operators around. One of them reported to Stanton; Grant placed him in arrest. Stanton sharply informed the General that Stager was the head of telegraphs and must not be interfered with, countermanded Riggin's orders, refused to honor his requisitions, and ordered the release of the arrested operator.

Grant took this defeat in silence, but in January of 1864, when he wished to make a trip from his headquarters at Nashville up to Knoxville to see whether the Army of the Ohio could be supplied through Cumberland Gap, he wished neither to take along his cipher operator, A. C. Beckwith, nor to wait for his dispatches until his return. He accordingly ordered Beckwith to give the key to one of his staff. Beckwith did so without informing anybody, but Stanton immediately noticed that he was getting ciphered dispatches from two sources in an army where only one man was supposed to be in the secret. He promptly dismissed Beckwith from the service, had Stager prepare a new cipher, and advised Grant that a new operator was bringing it out, and that no one, whatever his rank, was entitled to have the key. The incident doubtless contributed to Grant's later remark that Stanton did things for the pleasure of being disobliging.

BACKDROP

New York Herald

A fresh and formidable movement is on foot to procure the removal of the present Secretary of War whose imperious mode of administering that department and overruling the President himself has aggravated his unpopularity to such a degree that many of the most influential supporters of Mr. Lincoln are about to demand a change in the War Department as a *sine qua non* of their cooperation in his re-election.

Washington Intelligencer

THE RUSSIAN FLEET. It is stated that three of the vessels of the Russian fleet, Admiral Lisovski, were at Piney Point on Tuesday waiting for others of the fleet, and that it is possible they will reach the city today. On their arrival, it is said, they will proceed up the Eastern Branch, where salutes will be exchanged.

COME OUT OF "THE DRAFT." *Those who desire to escape the draft* may find a capital plan to enable them to do so in the "Constitutional Union" today. Peruse it carefully. Office Number 330 E street, near Grover's Theater.

RAID ON THE WHISKEY SHOPS. On Tuesday the invalid patrol by orders from the Provost Marshal went to a number of little shanties on New Jersey avenue in the vicinity of the depot, and tore them down. This seemed to be the only means by which the furnishing of whiskey to soldiers could be put an end to, as the parties occupying them had been repeatedly fined.

LIFE OF GENERAL GRANT, published and for sale at Shillington's Bookstore, Odeon Building, corner 4½ st and Pennsylvania avenue.

ANOTHER DEATH FROM CHLOROFORM. Mrs. Jane E. Ward on Tuesday night last was suffering severely from pain caused by a carbuncle on one of her fingers and sent to a druggist for an ounce of chloroform to relieve the pain by bathing her finger. While thus engaged, sitting on an ottoman, she left the bottle near her uncorked and unconsciously inhaled sufficient of the powerful fumes of the chloroform to induce insensibility. When found a short time afterward she was discovered in a kneeling posture before the ottoman with her head resting on a pillow and breathing heavily. Although a physician was immediately summoned, before he arrived Mrs. Ward was dead.

20

THE ATTACK, AT LAST

OWEN Lovejoy of Illinois went to Lincoln with the idea that, since Hooker's Corps had done so well in the west, a mutual exchange of troops between the armies would benefit the war effort, and persuaded the President to suggest this transfer in a note to Stanton. The Secretary asked whether Lincoln had given the order for it, and said if he had, he was a damned fool—which word Lovejoy, of course, immediately carried to the White House.

"Did Stanton really say I was a damned fool?" asked Lincoln.

"He did, sir, and repeated it."

"If Stanton said I was a damned fool, I must be one. For he is nearly always right, and generally says what he means."

The project died, and Stanton turned to the question of his recently established Cavalry Bureau. Under General Stoneman, whose raid in the Chancellorsville campaign failed so badly, it was by no means yielding the desired results, the main trouble being that the supply of remounts was always inadequate and of poor quality. Stoneman was removed as a failure before the Chattanooga battles, and Kenner Garrard, another respectable old body who had seen cavalry service on the western plains, was no improvement. When Dana came east in January to make a personal report on the winter strategic conferences at Grant's headquarters, the question of whether one of the western officers could not clear things up came to the fore.

Dana said Grant and Sherman had a drive on Atlanta in

mind; believed that an expedition should be launched from New Orleans against Mobile; and that as the Confederates had demonstrated that their two main armies could co-operate by the dispatch of Longstreet to Bragg for Chickamauga, Grant thought a new commander of the Army of the Potomac ought to take over, one who could work out a similar integration of east and west for the Union side. He proposed W. F. "Baldy" Smith, who had opened the "cracker line" that relieved the starvation at Chattanooga. As for the Cavalry Bureau, Dana could suggest no one better than his young friend, Wilson.

On the questions of integrating the armies and appointing Baldy Smith, Stanton only grunted; he already had his own plan in that direction. Wilson he accepted at once, having Dana wire for him that very day. Within a week a tall youth appeared in Washington, wearing a mustache and imperial to achieve a factitious appearance of age, which apparently did not help much, for as Wilson himself recorded it:

He received me with a scowling countenance. He was evidently disappointed by my youthful appearance, but proceeded at once to lay down the law; "I have sent for you," said he, "because I understand you do not fear responsibility. My life is worried out of me by the constant calls of the generals in the field for more cavalry horses, and the dishonesty of the contractors who supply us with inferior horses, or who transfer their contracts to sub-contractors who do not fill them at all. They are a set of unmitigated scoundrels and I want you to reorganize the business, drive the rascals out and put the cavalry service on an effective footing. I don't want you to fail as Stoneman did, nor to say, as Garrard did: "I cannot hope to surpass the efforts of Stoneman." "Don't tell me you can't swing the job. I give you *carte blanche* and will support you with all the resources of the department. While I have called you here for this particular purpose, please remember that if you see anything else in the War Department which requires attention or ought to be changed, you are to come and tell me about it. That will do, sir." He afterward told a friend of mine that my body was too short for my legs.

The principal horse contractors immediately invited Wilson to a little dinner for the cementing of cordial relations, a procedure that had worked very well with Stoneman and Garrard. He refused the invitation, assembled the contractors and told them that in the new contracts for 11,000 horses, they would be held to the letter of the document, and that no subletting would be permitted.

Apparently, they did not quite believe him; a St. Louis man furnished the 2,500 horses according to bid, but all the others failed to furnish or tried to sublet. Wilson waited only until he had a clear case, then went round to Dana, who had been named as one of the Assistant Secretaries. Dana went to Stanton; Stanton had the defaulting contractors arrested and tried by courts-martial, which found them guilty, one and all. They paid fines and went to jail, whereupon a tempest burst over the Cavalry Bureau, with congressmen trotting wrathily in and out, threatening the brash young man that if he didn't back down, they would prevent his confirmation as a general. Wilson took the tale to Stanton. "Who said that?" growled the Secretary, and when he had received a couple of names: "Oh, I know them. They are both damned cowards; neither one of them will ever come within five hundred yards of the War Department. I'll take care of them; you leave that to me and go fearlessly about your business."

The new head of the Cavalry Bureau found his chief "rough, overbearing, and outrageous to his inferiors; negligent and contemptuous to his equals," exciting "neither affection nor sympathy," but of "tremendous energy and comprehensive judgment." Dana alone could handle him, says Wilson—a valuable *portrait parlé*, whose impact is somewhat diminished by the fact that the occasion of the row over the contractors and their pocket congressmen was the only time when Wilson saw the Secretary between his arrival in Washington and the date when he left the Department to take the field with the Army of the Potomac. When things were well done, Stanton rarely bothered people; he approved by messenger and without further inquiry, Wilson's recommendation that a radical new weapon should be made standard throughout the cavalry service—Mr. Spencer's ingenious carbine, which could fire seven shots without reloading.

Wilson would live to bless his foresight about that carbine on the field of battle; but in the meanwhile even what happened in the Cavalry Bureau was a small matter compared to what should be done about the command of the Army of the Potomac. The reasons both for and against the replacement of Meade were as operative as ever, the more so since the coming military campaign would be accompanied by one before the electorate. The only real solution, a semipolitical one, that suggested itself (it is impossible to say precisely where the suggestion started) was to leave Meade in command, but to place over him someone who would give him the positive attack orders that Halleck steadily refused to issue. Perhaps Grant's views on strategic integration, as reported by Dana, played their part; in any case, it was clearly not an autochthonous inspiration on the part of Congress which led that body to pass, on February 26, a bill reviving the grade of lieutenant-general, which had been held by only two men in American history. On the twenty-ninth, Lincoln signed the bill, appointed Grant the next day, and wired for him to come east.

He arrived on March 8, a plain, scrubby man whom Washington found looking not in the least like a general by comparison with such beautiful figures as McClellan and Burnside. There was nothing in the least "brilliant" about him; but he was cheered in the dining room at Willard's and went around to the White House, where he stood uncomfortably on a red sofa to be looked at. After the crowd left, there was a short conference with Lincoln and Stanton; subject, mostly the protocol of the next day, when the Lieutenant-General's commission would be formally delivered and received. Lincoln did manage to get in that he had never professed to be a military man; all he wanted was someone to take the responsibility and act, and call on him for assistance.

Stanton accompanied the General back to his hotel, cautioning him on the way not to tell Lincoln his plan of campaign, as the President sometimes leaked. Grant felt that he knew the Secretary better than the President, after their many conversations by wire, in which the same type of expressions had been used. After the little ceremony on the ninth, the new

General went down to see Meade at his frontline headquarters at Brandy Station.

The interview was a brief one, Grant merely announcing his intention of making his headquarters with the Army of the Potomac, since he wanted to be in touch with the complex Washington situation, yet not subject to the city's influences. He refused Meade's offer to stand aside for another commander. The Lieutenant-General's subsequent stop in Washington was only to record a favorable impression of Meade; then Grant took off for the west to co-ordinate things with Sherman, who was to lead the armies assembled at Chattanooga. When Grant came back, on the twenty-sixth, he set up headquarters at Culpeper Court House, and the conferences began—with Lincoln, Stanton, and Halleck, the last now formally assigned to the Chief-of-Staff position he had always really occupied.

The first item was strategic planning. Grant took hold of this with a grasp that delighted the others; he proposed to send flags forward on every possible front on a single given day. He himself, with the Army of the Potomac, would make his primary objective Lee's army, his secondary, Richmond; Sherman's primary would be the Confederate western army, his secondary, Atlanta. ("I see," remarked Lincoln, "you propose to hold the leg while Sherman takes off the skin.") At the same time, Benjamin F. Butler would move up the James with an army of two corps toward the backdoor of Richmond. Franz Sigel, now in command of the Shenandoah, would attack up that valley toward Lee's left flank. Banks, with the Gulf command, was off on an expedition toward Shreveport and eastern Texas, partly political, partly one of Halleck's pieces of map strategy, designed to break up rebel concentrations in that area and bring the line of the Union forward from the Arkansas River to the Red. As soon as he returned, he was to move overland against Mobile, while the navy secured the place from the outside. Crook would operate in West Virginia, possibly into eastern Tennessee.

Next, officers. The little Aulic Council seems to have agreed that Sigel and Butler, at least, were dubious as commanders. But their efforts were diversionary, and both had an importance well beyond the downright military. Butler claimed to be the senior major-general of the army and said he could prove it by the almanac; was so potent a political personality that to remove him would be courting opposition in country and Congress just when such opposition could least be afforded, at the outset of a Presidential campaign. Lincoln called him "the damndest scoundrel that ever lived, but in the infinite mercy of Providence, also the damndest fool." He could be propped up with good corps commanders and might even accomplish something. Banks, not much better in the confidence of Washington, was at least doing a good job on the political side of his mission.

Grant put in a strong bid for his old friend Baldy Smith, whom the Senate had refused to confirm as a major-general sometime before; Lincoln and Stanton would work out the confirmation, and he would have a corps under Butler—just the right man. How about employing some of the other high-ranking officers now "awaiting assignment"—as a matter of general military morale? No, was the answer on McCook, Crittenden, McClellan, and Frémont; their military records were altogether too bad. Buell could be useful; let us offer him a corps under Sherman. Burnside is also politically important, a good organizer who draws the best out of his command, and a competent soldier under someone else's orders. Let him be returned to his old IX Corps, which had been withdrawn from Tennessee to recruit its thinned ranks at Annapolis earlier in the month, after Schofield's organization of the Army of the Ohio had progressed so far that it was evident Longstreet could accomplish nothing against him.

The question of Burnside brought up another plan, proposed by General James R. Gilmore, who had the command in the North Carolina sounds. Governor Vance of that state, said Gilmore, was shaky in his allegiance to the Confederacy. If a force of 20,000 men under Burnside—who was known and well liked in that region for his kind treatment of the people when he had commanded there—were to take Wilmington, it was rather more than likely that Vance could be persuaded to rebel against the rebels and bring his state back into the Union. No, said Grant, he could not spare that many men from the concentration against Lee; this was a war of guns, not intrigue. He wanted Burnside and his corps at the Manassas position, ready to reinforce Meade or Butler as the case might call for.

Now Grant expressed dissatisfaction with the work of the cavalry; thought that if Meade's mounted arm were brought together under a first-class leader, the best man available, it might deal with the Confederate horse. But who? Stanton proposed several names without drawing anything more than a grunt from the impassive Grant; it was Halleck who broke the log-jam with: "How would Sheridan do?"

Grant stirred: "The very man I want!" Forthwith a telegram to Sheridan. He came early in April, a little man with preternaturally long arms, young-looking and rather comic, who made a poor impression on the Secretary by doubting his own ability. Grant told him he would have a free hand as long as he took care of Stuart; Sheridan accepted glumly, and disappeared down into the Virginia scrub, followed by a cloud of secretarial doubt.

There were no questions or objections from anyone about Grant's reorganization of the Army of the Potomac, in which the old worn I and III Corps were dissolved into the II and V. Hancock was back; he would take over the II Corps with which he had done so valorously at Gettysburg, while Warren moved over to the V, replacing "Tardy George" Sykes, who was moved out to an area command in Texas, where slow thinking would not matter.

II

THESE were the main lines of military policy, the major factors of movement which have received the highlight of history. Stanton had no part in the decisions, except as they touched on the field of choosing personalities in which he particularly operated; and even there, he gave way to Grant on Sheridan and Baldy Smith, and to Lincoln on Sigel and Butler. He was in the conferences on the point of information; to learn how much in men, money, and material of war would be required for the machine he superintended, and what was to be done with those resources.

That he did not mingle more was partly due to Grant, who quite early in the game put Stanton in his place about troop movements, and as effectively as the Secretary had doused him on the cipher question. Grant had been rapidly drafting off the troops in the Washington forts to fill up his cadres. Stanton worried about cover for the Capital in case of one of those rapid and destructive Confederate raids; and when Grant said he had ordered the men out and no one could order them back, as he "ranked the Secretary in this matter," Stanton took him to Lincoln.

"Now, General, state your case," said the Secretary, a lawyer's trick if there ever was one. But Grant ducked it with: "I have no case to state. I am satisfied as it is."

Stanton was not satisfied, and told why. It made no impression. Lincoln merely said: "Now, Mr. Secretary, you know we have been trying to manage this army for nearly three years, and you know we haven't done much with it. We sent over the mountains and brought Mr. Grant, as Mrs. Grant calls him, to manage it for us; and now I guess we'd better let Mr. Grant have his way."

It hardly mattered that Stanton would turn out to be right on the military point; the important thing was to establish the lines of relationship with the new commander, and it was precisely the type of point which Lincoln could see better than Stanton.

One of the men ordered down to the army was young Wilson, to take over a division of cavalry, which he promptly equipped with the new Spencer repeaters; all three brigade commanders had to be transferred because they were senior to him. He called on the Secretary to say good-by, and remarked that it was a mistake to assign Colonel James A. Ekin of the Quartermaster Corps as his replacement in the Cavalry Bureau.

"What the hell is the matter with Ekin?" demanded Stanton, for the Colonel had been recommended by Quartermaster-General Meigs, one of the best men in the service, and the problem was one that could be presumably handled by a man with quartermaster experience.

"Nothing," said Wilson, "except that he is a volunteer without rank or experience for the position."

"Why can't he give his orders in my name?"

"He can," said Wilson, "but you will not have the time to explain what you want, nor he the knowledge to decide what he should do."

Stanton: "Well, I wish the whole damn thing were in hell. What do you recommend?"

Wilson thought the point of the whole anecdote was that Stanton shouted and swore, thereby justifying the adjectives earlier applied. He missed completely the fact that underneath the pyrotechnics there was a hairspring analysis of the problem, resulting in the instant acceptance of Wilson's suggestion that the Cavalry Bureau be placed under Halleck's command echelon, in charge of an experienced officer of the service, A. V. Kautz. There are not many men in whom emotion fails to interfere with judgment.

Certainly during those weeks when everyone was trying to guess the date of Grant's grand attack, there were plentiful causes for irritation in the problems surrounding the support of the armies; every time they were settled, they seemed to reappear in a new form. It took a long hearing before a committee and finally an act of Congress to settle the ambulance question, for instance; the law placed them under the medical officers of corps. More hearings, more urgings, and another law were necessary to set up a project for printing all the records of the war. (Stanton himself, well aware of the way Congress could regurgitate old issues, had from the beginning kept every important paper, and in duplicate.) A long correspondence over the damage done in Ohio by Morgan's cavalry raid of the previous summer—whether the federal government ought to pay for it, and how much. Some of the teamsters in the Quartermaster Department went on strike and the matter was passed to Stanton for settlement. Minnesota protests

that the British in Canada are selling arms to the Indians raiding her frontier; Stanton must handle it. General Dix of the
New York command has an elaborate controversy with Governor Buckingham of Connecticut because the Governor
wishes to pay enlistment bounties to the order of recruits instead of to the men themselves, a procedure which (Dix says,
Stanton agreeing when it is referred to him) leads to fraud.
Has a slaveholder the right to hire a substitute for a drafted
slave? Stanton to rule.

Word from beyond the Mississippi: Banks's lack of military
capacity has been estimated at less than its importance; he has
been badly defeated, his men running worse than at Bull Run;
he has almost lost the river fleet, must go back to New Orleans,
and will be unable—he or anyone else—to move against Mobile as desired. Remove Banks, regardless of politics. And
what about New York, where Governor Seymour's opposition
to the war and to furnishing men for it is stout as ever, with
many cogent objections? Stanton finally appointed a special
commission, which found that in this case the quotas of New
York City and Brooklyn had indeed been set a trifle too high,
so much of the census population consisting of aliens not liable
for military service.

But there must be another general draft; we shall need 200,-
000 men on February 1 to fill the thinned ranks, another
200,000 on March 14, and the Secretary recommends (for the
dozenth time) that Congress repeal the privilege of letting a
man buy himself out of service for $300 or a substitute. All
spring and early summer this issue was fought out; in spite of
all the pressure Lincoln could bring to bear; in spite of all the
help given by the three Blairs, honorably on Stanton's side in
this issue, honorable members still wanted loopholes. The best
obtainable, and this not till the desperate July battles, was a
new draft act that still allowed substitutes, though it abolished
commutation payments.

Buell refused a corps command on the ground that he was
once Sherman's senior and would not now serve under him
(he was Sherman's junior before that); he must have a soothing
letter of regret. The states compete with each other to fill up

their quotas, sending agents to recruit Negroes behind Sherman's lines, which irritates Sherman. Maine tries to gain credit for militia assigned to a series of absurd forts built in 1812 against the British—and a young man comes to Stanton's back door at night, offering to be a spy for the Union. He turned out to have connections South; when he showed up later at the headquarters of the cavalry command with compromising possessions, Sheridan hanged him.

In the midst of this flow of business some wounded arrived at Memphis, and the whole question of Negro troops and prisoners of war leaped from the domain of quiet negotiation into that of white-hot public debate. Early in April, N. B. Forrest rocketed up into eastern Tennessee on a raid, with 4,000 cavalry. Sherman had foreseen something like this, and moved General Sooy Smith with 7,000 horsemen to intercept; but Smith's men were neither well trained, well mounted, nor well led; Forrest repulsed them sharply and pushed on to Paducah, Kentucky, where there was a depot. The fort covering it and the gunboats in the river were more than the raider could deal with; he swerved back and on April 12 struck the Mississippi at a small fort—Fort Pillow—garrisoned by 295 men of the 13th Tennessee Cavalry and 262 of the 6th United States Heavy Artillery (Negro). The Confederates assaulted, broke in, and when what was left of the garrison tried to surrender, shot down nearly every Negro and most of the whites in cold blood, including one officer who was taken a day's march away before being executed.

The sense of shock with which the North learned of Forrest's troopers shooting down men who had their hands up, and knocking Negro children on the head with rifle butts amid cries of "Kill the God-damned niggers!" was undiminished by the remark of an officer under a flag of truce that he believed the men had got out of hand. For while Ben Wade and D. W. Gooch, of the Committee on the Conduct of the War, were in the west to investigate the affair on the ground, Forrest's report came out in the Richmond papers. "The river was dyed with the blood of the slaughtered for 200 yards," it said, and then in a tone of unmistakable exultation: "The approximate loss was 500 killed, but few of the officers escaped. It is hoped that these facts will demonstrate to the northern people that the negro soldier cannot cope with Southerners." "I regard captured negroes as I do other captured property," he said in a communication through the lines, "and not as captured soldiers."

After the Wade-Gooch committee made its report, Lincoln called a Cabinet meeting and asked his advisors to give written opinions on how the matter should be dealt with. The opinions came three days later; Seward's for caution, as might be expected, but at least for confining an equal number of rebel prisoners until the Richmond government should disavow. Chase said the same, with the modification that the prisoners confined should be of the highest rank. Stanton came next with a long document, adopting both the earlier suggestions and adding that Forrest and Chalmers, his second, with all other officers involved, should be exempted from any future exchange and held for civil trial if captured; that Richmond should be notified that hostages were being held for the delivery of Forrest and Chalmers for such trial; and that from this time forth, rebel officers should be given "precisely the same rations and treatment as Union prisoners in the South."

Welles was generally favorable to Stanton's program, particularly the part about no exchange, and civil trial for Forrest and Chalmers. Blair, Bates, and Usher of the Interior wanted to limit action to a proclamation that the guilty parties would be hunted down, the last saying that great battles were imminent and it would be inexpedient to start any retaliatory action at such time.

This was May 6; the meeting broke up with a sense of unhappiness and no sound line determined. Just at this juncture there arrived an emissary from an association of kind-hearted pro-southern Britishers, who had collected a $75,000 fund and wanted permission to spend it in providing comforts for Confederate prisoners in northern hands.

"Almighty God! No!" shouted Stanton.

III

Grant to Halleck, May 4, 1864

The crossing of the Rapidan effected. Forty-eight hours will determine whether the enemy intends giving battle this side of Richmond. Telegraph Butler that we have crossed the Rapidan.

Stanton to Governor Brough, Columbus, Ohio; Governor Morton, Indianapolis, Indiana; Governor Yates, Chicago, Illinois; Governor Stone, Davenport, Iowa; Governor Lewis, Madison, Wisconsin, May 4

General Grant crossed the Rapidan this morning and is moving on Lee. Sherman today moved on Johnston from Chattanooga. Your forces cannot be ready for the field too soon. Let me know whatever is wanted and it will be supplied.

No news but this. Once more the old tensions began to build up in the War Department, once more Lincoln strode gaunt through the corridors, once more the city filled up with rumors. May 6, in the evening, Dana was at a reception, when a messenger came in to say he was wanted at the Department. He found Stanton and Lincoln talking, both very sober. "Dana," said the President, "you know we have been in the dark for two days since Grant moved. We are very much troubled, and have concluded to send you down there. How soon can you start?"

Dana said he could start in half an hour, but he evidently did not get away quite that soon, for he was still in the Department when a dispatch came for him from an acquaintance of newspaper days, a cub correspondent for the *Tribune* named Henry A. Wing. Wing had been at Bull Run; had just left Grant and was trying to get a dispatch through to his paper over the military wire. The operator would not let him send it. Dana went out to borrow a pistol and have a locomotive readied at Alexandria to take him to the front, while Stanton took over the telegraphic conversation. Where was Grant when Wing left him?

The cagey reporter instantly realized that he had a scoop, and wired back that if he were allowed to send a one hundred-word dispatch to his paper he would tell everything he knew. Stanton replied that if he didn't tell, he would be arrested as a spy. Wing was just refusing to tell anything when the receiving key began to click at his end—would he tell the President where Grant was? He was smart enough to realize that this must mean Lincoln had come into the War Department, and he could get a better deal than from the Secretary, so he repeated the first offer.

Back came an acceptance with the addition that he was not limited to a one hundred-word dispatch and that a locomotive was being sent. At two in the morning he was in the White House, dirty and tired, being crossexamined by President and Secretary on details of fighting so furious that no man in North America or the world had seen anything like it, not even at Stone River or Chickamauga, for the battles there flared up and down and in local areas, while this was all along the line with thousands of men, and did not cease for weariness or night. A desperate blind struggle through dense scrub forests, which caught fire and burned the wounded to death, already being named "the Wilderness." One wing of the VI Corps had been driven in; the casualties were certainly over 15,000 of Grant's 120,000 and would go higher. General Wadsworth was killed, General Hay killed, Generals Getty and Bartlett wounded; Burnside and the IX Corps were in, rebel casualties unknown, battle continuing. There was some light; Sheridan had stopped Stuart cold; a good many rebel prisoners had been taken; nothing seemed to upset Grant except the fact that the soldiers threw away so many of their blankets and new overcoats to lighten their march loads.

(Unknown to the three men talking in the White House until dawn stole their lamps, there was more light than they had heard; for this was the electric night when the troops of the Army of the Potomac, drawn from their lines to march, with no expectation but retreat, found instead a stumpy man with a cigar, silently gesturing each formation deeper into the Wilderness, forward to another battle; this was the night when the tired men marched cheering on, having found their leader.)

The wounded began to come in on May 9, more of them than Washington had seen before, and the same afternoon, so did the first dispatches from Dana, not much more informative than those from Grant himself, that the army had moved from the Wilderness toward Spottsylvania Court House, slanting toward Richmond, and the battle was continuous. Positions, precise course of events, obscure. The next day, word that Good Uncle John Sedgwick was killed in action; Horatio Wright, known as a sound but rather formal soldier, took over the VI Corps; he was sometimes taken for an Englishman.

Sherman to War Department, May 10

Johnston acts purely on the defensive. I am attacking him on his strongest fronts till McPherson breaks his line at Resaca, when I will swing round through Snake Creek Gap and interpose between him and Georgia. Yesterday I pressed hard to prevent Johnston detaching against McPherson, but today I will be more easy, as I believe McPherson has destroyed Resaca.

Welles noted that "A craving, uneasy feeling pervaded the community through the day."

Sherman to War Department, late May 10

General McPherson reached Resaca, but found the place strongly fortified and guarded, and did not break the road. I must feign on Buzzard Roost Gap and pass through Snake Creek Gap and place myself between Johnston and Resaca, when we will have to fight it out. I am making the preliminary move.

It was not until the twelfth, Thursday, that Grant's old friend, Congressman Washburne, who had visited him at headquarters, brought back the note that Stanton gave to the country:

We have now ended the sixth day of very hard fighting. The result at this time is much in our favor. But our losses have been heavy as well as those of the enemy. I propose to fight it out on this line if it takes all summer.

The losses were indeed heavy enough to have stunned a nation not by now inured to losses; they would run 18,000 for the Spottsylvania battle. In addition, Sigel got himself defeated

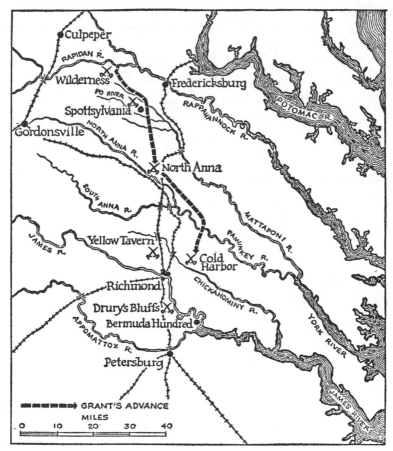

Attrition—Spring 1864

in the Valley of the Shenandoah and Butler proceeded to demonstrate a military capacity equal to Banks's by moving up the James to a place called Drury's Bluffs and sitting still. Grant sent his chief engineer, General J. G. Barnard, to find out why, then reported to the Department that Butler had taken up a fortified position on a narrow neck of land between the James and Appomattox rivers, very strong, but attended by a certain inconvenience—that the Confederates had fortified lines as strong as his own across the same neck, and he was corked up like a genie in a bottle.

But on the same twelfth that brought the note via Congressman Washburne, the Army of the Potomac delivered a furious assault at Spottsylvania that broke Lee's trench line, captured a whole division and two generals. With this came a piece of news that set all Washington jubilant over the thought that it was now the Union cavalry that imposed restrictions on the enemy, for Sheridan was loose around Lee's flank, had torn up ten miles of his supporting railroad, and won a battle at the gates of Richmond.

Sherman to War Department, May 14

We have been fighting all day, pressing the enemy and gaining substantial advantage at all points. The troops fight well and everything goes smoothly. We intend to fight Johnston until he is satisfied, and I hope he will not attempt to escape.

That day a letter from Grant; he had promoted Colonel Emory Upton of the 121st New York on the field of battle for gallantry; he wanted formal promotions for Wright, Hancock, divisional General Gibbon, and two other colonels. "General Meade has more than met my most sanguine expectations. He and Sherman are the fittest officers for large commands I have come in contact with."

It began to rain; a dispatch from Dana said the Army of the Potomac was on the move again, though nobody in Washington could divine in what direction, and Grant sent his siege train back to the capital, evidently meaning more war of maneuver.

Sherman to War Department, May 16

We are in possession of Resaca. We saved the road bridge, but the railroad bridge is burned. Our columns are now crossing the Oostenaula. We will pursue smartly to the Etowah. Our difficulties will increase beyond the Etowah, but if Johnston will not fight us behind such works as we find here, I will fight him on any open ground he may stand at.

Sherman to War Department, May 17

Tonight I propose my three heads of columns to be abreast of Adairsville. Johnston will be compelled to fight on this side of the Etowah, or be forced to divide his army or give up either Rome or Allatoona. It will take five days to repair the railroad bridge here.

The Richmond papers brought the news that their great cavalryman, Stuart, had been killed trying to hold off Sheridan at Yellow Tavern; and on the eighteenth, with little trickles of news about more fighting coming from Virginia, a thoroughly aroused Seward strode into Stanton's office. He was in receipt of wires from New York; the *World* and *Journal of Commerce*, antiadministration sheets, which had been using terms like "butchery" and "brutality" about Grant's campaign, had that morning reached a climax by printing under a Washington dateline a purported proclamation from Lincoln. It set aside May 26 as a day of fasting and prayer because of Grant's failure and called for an extraordinary new draft of 300,000 men. This was tantamount to printing enemy propaganda. He had ordered (said Seward) the sailing of the English mail steamer to be delayed until the matter was cleared up, and had started spreading denials at once. What he wanted to know was whether the fake proclamation had gone over the regular wires.

It had not, said the War Secretary; he himself had only heard of the forgery a short time before, immediately investigated, and since the Independent Telegraph Company must have forwarded it, had ordered the seizure of that line and the closing of its offices. Seward remarked that those two scurrilous sheets had been published one minute too long; Stanton said he would be delighted to close them up if the President would permit it. There was a little more conversation, then Stanton sent off an order to arrest the editors and publishers, without waiting for Presidential permission.

On the twentieth, when it developed that the new fighting in Virginia was only a minor affair that cost the lives of barely a thousand men on either side, there was a reply from General Dix in New York. The arrests had been carried out and the forgery traced down. It was the work of an ill-omened newspaperman named Joseph Howard, who had been in trouble about faked news before, and it was fundamentally a stock-jobbing operation to send up the price of gold. In spite of the fact that the forgery had been so blatant that the other papers, also recipients of the faked wire, refused to have anything to do with it, this put a slightly different face on the matter, and after two days of silence, the *World* and *Journal of Commerce* were allowed to resume. Howard went to jail but stayed there only a few weeks, then was released on the intercession of Henry Ward Beecher, the great pulpit orator, whose secretary he had once been.

Sherman to War Department, Adairsville, May 18

Johnston passed last night here. We overtook him at sundown yesterday and skirmished heavily with his 'rear till dark. In the morning he was gone, and we are after him.

Sherman to War Department, May 19

We entered Kingston this morning without opposition. The enemy has retreated south of the Etowah. Tomorrow, cars will move to this place and I will replenish stores and get ready for the Chattahoochee. I apprehend more trouble from our long trains of wagons than from the fighting.

Sherman to War Department, May 20

Our cars are now arriving with stores. I give two days' rest to replenish and fit up. On the 23rd I will cross the Etowah and move on Dallas. This will turn the Allatoona Pass. General Davis' division occupies Rome and finds a good deal of provisions and plunder.

Grant was moving by his left again, taking his right-most corps and swinging it around the rear into the advance, an operation whose difficulty and skill of execution were no more to be understood by nonprofessionals than the turn from defense to attack at Stone River.

Sherman to War Department, May 21

Weather very hot and roads dusty. Nevertheless, by morning we will have all our wagons loaded and be ready for twenty days expedition. Returned veterans and regiments have more than replaced all losses, and we move tomorrow with full 80,000 fighting men. I allow three days to have the army grouped about Dallas, whence I can strike Marietta or the Chattahoochee. You may not hear from us in some days.

On the twenty-third the rebels were found in position behind the North Anna River, covering the Virginia Central Railroad, a strategic line; there was a fight and Hancock's men forced a crossing, breaking the enemy line. On the twenty-fourth, twenty-fifth, and twenty-sixth, there were more obscure combats against what returning officers and correspondents described as a new Confederate entrenched position, and the medical officer reported 2,100 wounded during the three days.

Dana to Stanton, May 26

One of the most important results of the campaign thus far is the entire change which has taken place in the feeling of the army. The rebels have lost all confidence and are already morally defeated. This army has learned to believe that it is sure of victory. Even our officers have ceased to regard Lee as an invincible military genius.

The dispatches of the twenty-seventh, twenty-eighth, and twenty-ninth had Grant on the move again, always by the left flank. There was a cavalry fight, which Wilson won with his repeaters.

Sherman to War Department, May 28

The enemy discovered our move to turn Allatoona, and moved to meet us here. Our columns met about one mile east of Pumpkin

Vine Creek and we pushed them back about three miles, to where the roads fork to Allatoona and Marietta. Here Johnston has chosen a strong line and made hasty but strong parapets of timber and earth, and has thus far stopped us. I am gradually working by the left to approach the railroad in front of Acworth.

Sherman to War Department, May 29

Yesterday we passed our lines up in close contact with the enemy. The enemy massed against McPherson and attacked him at 4:30 P.M., but was repulsed with great slaughter and at little cost to us. Loss, 2,500 and about 300 prisoners. McPherson's loss not over 300 in all.

News of the next two days was obscure; at nearly midnight on the thirty-first, another dispatch from Dana: "General Grant means to fight here if there is a fair chance—" the dateline on the wire demonstrating that Lee must have been pushed back to a position near the old Seven Days' battlegrounds, with his right resting on the Chickahominy. Baldy Smith's XVIII Corps had been pulled from the bottle on the James and added to the main army.

It was not until the night of June 4 that news began to come in of another battle, a heavy one.

21

DARK AUGUST

Sherman to War Department, June 5, 1864

The enemy discovered us creeping round his right flank, abandoned his position and marched off last night. General McPherson is moving today for Acworth, General Thomas on the Marietta road, and General Schofield on his right. It has been raining hard for three days, and the roads are very heavy. I expect the enemy to fight us at Kenesaw Mountain, but I will not run head on his fortifications.

It was not until June 7 that the dispatches from Cold Harbor, where Grant had fought his battle, reached the press. The *New York Times* headed its dispatch, "The Loss of our Key Position," and, without saying as much in so many words, called it a defeat. The other papers had a different story (the *Herald* even called the *Times* a liar), but their explanatory manner gave the show away. Nor were matters helped when Burnside, with his usual genius for doing quite reasonable things at the wrong time and place, had *Times* correspondent William Swinton arrested and sentenced to be shot for being altogether too nosy around headquarters, even though Grant commuted the sentence to one of banishment from the area of the army.

The Cabinet, of course, knew early that Grant had assaulted a fortified line and taken a bloody repulse. The General's own dispatch of June 5 made that much clear: "Without a greater sacrifice of human life than I am willing to make, all cannot be accomplished that I designed outside the city. I have therefore resolved upon the following plan. I will continue to hold the ground now occupied by the Army of the Potomac until the cavalry can be sent west to destroy the Virginia Central Railroad from above Beaver Dam for some 25 or 30 miles west. When this is effected, I will move the army to the south side of the James River." Welles confided to his diary that "the immense slaughter of our brave men chills and sickens us" and "the bodies of our brave men, slain or mutilated, are brought daily to Washington by hundreds. Some repulse we have had beyond what is spoken of, I have no doubt." But it was only gradually and by grapevine that there reached the public the tale that Grant had lost 10,000 men at Cold Harbor, twice as many as the Confederates, and that men in the attack had little pieces of paper bearing their names pinned to their blouses, so certain were they of death.

In that public domain the wave of discouraging, almost despairing, reports encountered two other tides that had been running beneath the whole campaign, reinforced them and brought them to the surface in a tangle that Stanton had to deal with. One, of course, was the political question, the question of whether Lincoln could or should be renominated and reelected. It must be remembered that the field was more than theoretically open; in the thirty-two years since Andrew Jackson had left office, a tradition of one term per President had grown up, the sort of tradition not lightly discarded, like making a successful campaign manager Postmaster-General.

Chase wanted the post so badly that he had been trying all sorts of manifestoes, devices, efforts to get state legislatures to pronounce in his favor (none of them did), and trial balloons in the newspapers, as favorite son of the Radicals. The Radicals were dissatisfied with Lincoln all right, but some did not wish to break the party, and the rest could not see taking a man out of Lincoln's Cabinet; they held a quiet little convention in Cleveland at the end of May, while the troops were moving into position around Cold Harbor and nominated John C. Frémont.

A week later the administration convention met in Baltimore. It was called the National Union Convention, not the Republican, and great efforts were made to draw in as many Democrats as possible. Lincoln was easily nominated by acclamation; but Henry Raymond, publisher of the *New York Times*, was his manager, and there were those upon whom it was not lost that only the day before the delegates cheered the President, it was precisely Raymond's paper that burst out about the failure at Cold Harbor.

Sherman to War Department, June 11

Johnston is intrenched on the hills embracing Lost Mountain, Pine Hill and Kenesaw. Our lines are down to him, but the ground is so boggy that we have not developed any weak point.

The *World* declared that Stanton was the friend of thieves, protecting them from court-martial, and on June 14 Grant began to move down to and across the James. The intent was to swing wide behind Butler's bottle at Drury's Bluffs, and quickly gain possession of Petersburg, where two railroads from the south and one from the west met to form the main supply sources of Richmond. Hold Lee from the Chickahominy to the James, take those main supply lines, and he would have to move out into open country where he could be attacked.

To achieve this, Baldy Smith's XVIII Corps, technically returned to Butler's command, but actually acting under Grant's orders, was to cross the James on the fifteenth, come up against Petersburg from the south, and slide into the place; Hancock with the II Corps, Warren with the V, following in support.

But Meade failed to tell Hancock he was wanted for battle; only said pass to the south bank of the James and pick up rations there. By another blunder the rations were not sent. Smith did get into position (and as the records showed later, Lee was completely deceived, thinking the march of the Union army portended attack across the old battleground of the Seven

Days); but once in position, everything in the XVIII Corps went to pieces. The cavalry did not clear the roads, the reconnaissance discovered nothing, the artillerymen went off to water their horses. The attack on the Petersburg lines, which looked very grim, but had few defenders that day, was so disjointed and half-hearted that it gained only a few of the outer redans.

Hancock came up the next day without his rations and there was a real Hancock assault, driven home with a hurrah into the outer lines; but now the rebels were reinforced; they could not be broken then, nor on the next day, when Warren joined the attackers.

The country could hardly know how near a thing it had been, nor of the blunders and mischances (which cost Baldy Smith his command); nor that Lee heard the first stroke of the death knell for the great Army of Northern Virginia when Grant safely crossed the James; nor that the Confederate losses were so insupportable that they were kept secret; nor that Lee's sword was broken—he was no longer capable of delivering such counterstrokes as at Chancellorsville and Second Bull Run, could only cling to his defenses and hope for a miracle. The people saw the dead; they heard the wounded.

Sherman to War Department, June 21

This is the nineteenth day of rain, and the prospect of clear weather is as far off as ever. The enemy holds Kenesaw, with Marietta behind it, and has retired his flank to cover that town and his railroad. I am ready to attack the moment weather and roads will permit.

Grant said he knew what Lee's condition was: "The rebels can protect themselves only by strong entrenchments, while our army is not only confident of protecting itself without entrenchments, but that it can beat and drive the enemy whenever and wherever he can be found without this protection." Dana thought he knew the same, but it is doubtful whether Stanton really believed either of them, for Dana had been down to the front with Lincoln, and reported in writing that

Meade was approaching crash point. He had violent fits of temper, the corps commanders were losing confidence in him, and Grant, beneath his reticences, made it clear that he held the commander of the Army of the Potomac much to blame for the Petersburg failure. Meade's orders left the corps commanders too much to their own devices, implied that they were incapable of playing their parts in a wide general plan.

The people saw the dead; they heard the wounded; they knew there had been another battle in Virginia with 10,000 casualties, and for what? That Grant might attain approximately the same ground as McClellan reached on his spring picnic two years before, while Sherman's dispatches from the pine mountains of Georgia kept telling how the enemy had slipped away from places with meaningless names.

Sherman to War Department, June 23

The whole country is one vast fort, and Johnston must have full fifty miles of connected trenches, with abbatis and finished batteries. As fast as we gain one position, the enemy has another ready, but I think he will soon have to let go Kenesaw, which is the key to the whole country.

Gold climbed to 250, higher than it had been during the war, the *New York World* reported that the Treasury Department was little better than a bagnio, full of loose women who attended lewd performances at night, and had affidavits to back the story; and on June 29, Chase resigned. With elections coming on, the department must be headed by someone at least as eye-catching as that powerful figure. Lincoln sent the nomination of Governor Tod of Ohio to the Senate, but before that body could confirm it, Tod refused by telegraph. Senator William Pitt Fessenden of Maine, head of the Senate finance committee—about the only man left who combined public prominence with a real knowledge of money—was nominated and refused verbally. The ship was leaking.

Enter Stanton, with what Welles called an "intrigue," waiting on Fessenden. "You can no more refuse than your son could have refused to attack Monet's Bluff (the Senator had four sons in the service, one killed in action), and you cannot look him in the face if you do."

"It will kill me."

"Very well, you cannot die better."

At the first Cabinet meeting attended by the new Treasury Secretary, Lincoln brought up the question of cotton-trading permits, which had always been a sore point during Chase's tenure. Fessenden said he was not posted; Stanton said he was wholly opposed to fighting the rebels and trading with them at the same time, and said it in a manner that even Welles thought "sensible and correct." Blair, Bates, and Seward agreed. There would be changes made.

II

THE sign manual of the second, more difficult underrunning current of this period of stalemate and despair was that on the day of Fessenden's first Cabinet meeting, Governor Seymour of New York had General Dix arrested and placed on trial for the suppression of the *World* and *Journal of Commerce* for publishing the fake proclamation. (The case never got past a grand jury.) Jacob Thompson, the glum man who had felt Stanton's lash in the Buchanan Cabinet, was in Canada ostensibly to persuade someone on the Union side to meet him and discuss peace, actually to see whether the antigovernment and pacifist feeling in the northwest would not be developed into some kind of rising that would paralyze the forces in the field. These "copperheads" had organizations—the Knights of the Golden Circle, the Sons of Liberty—of which Vallandigham was the Grand Commander; they had a badge, a head cut from a copper cent; a program—striking hands with the Democrats in a movement half political, half conspiratorial, to get rid of Lincoln and the war.

How much conspiratorial, how much political, was the movement? It is known now—but was not then—that they were looking for an occasion, preferably the Democratic National Convention. But that gathering was postponed from

July 4 to wait for the military campaigns to fail, and as it touched Stanton and the War Department the whole thing was a nebulous menace, cockroaches crawling out of corners as though they had been spontaneously generated. Even the political part had a curious impalpability. Twice Stanton sat with a warrant in his hand while the wires ticked off a speech by the egregious Fernando Wood which was expected to furnish ground for arrest, but the politician never quite stepped over the line.

The only man behind the Secretary who really knew what was going on in those muddy waters was Colonel Lafayette C. Baker, the head of his secret service, whose taste for telling a good story was uninhibited by any squeamish tenderness about facts. Baker was a character: handsome and quick of movement, strictly temperance, and a great hand at disguising himself—he tracked down everything from organized gambling to a syndicate dealing in bawdy photographs. All that summer he was supposed to be with a cavalry regiment, but there is no record of its being in action or drawing supplies. Postmaster-General Blair kept trying to get Baker dismissed —Baker was the detective who tracked down the pretty niece smuggling quinine—but when Lincoln took the matter up with Stanton, the Secretary only answered that Blair's dismissal would be more beneficial to the country than that of Baker.

June deepened; from deep in the South correspondents reported that Sherman had tried Grant's game of assault against the Kenesaw position and had been repulsed. Partial payment for the Fort Pillow slaughter was extracted from Forrest when he attacked a depot at Tupelo in Mississippi and got himself well rapped over the knuckles by a peppery little character named "Whisky" Smith. June swung to July; returning from a visit to Fortress Monroe for the national holiday, Mr. Welles found Stanton grumbling over the "cursed mistakes of our generals," and learned that David Hunter had been driven from the Shenandoah right off the map into the mountains of West Virginia. A new rebel force was across the Potomac into Maryland. That day Stanton thought "it seemed to be a raiding expedition by some of the partisan robbers that infest that region." He said as much in a telegram to Governor Curtin of Pennsylvania, who was suffering from one of the fits of shakes usual to him when Confederates approached his state.

But Grant got to worrying whether this movement might not be more serious; offered a corps for the defense of Washington, and actually embarked a division for Baltimore the next day. It was not until the night of July 9 that news ran in of the rebels in Maryland with really important forces. They beat a little command of militia on the banks of the Monocacy and were sweeping on Washington. The tenth was a day of wild alarm; telegrams to Northern governors for hundred-day militia, panic in the city, and clerks saying that rebel pickets were on the outskirts of Georgetown, within the District lines. Cabinet members and congressmen crowded the War Department, asking for news that no one could give them, and that night, when Lincoln went out to the Soldiers' Home to sleep quietly, a squadron of cavalry sent by Stanton routed him from rest to escort him back to the White House.

Sherman to War Department, July 9

General Schofield effected a lodgment across the Chattahoochee last night and has two good pontoon bridges. General Garrard crossed at Roswell Factory and has a secure lodgment at the ford. These crossings will be strongly covered with forts.

The reason for the Secretary's anxiety became clear the next day—a day on which gold reached the panic figure of 285 in New York, the highest of record—when rifles began to snap at forts only two miles from the Soldiers' Home, all the wires to the capital went dead, and mails stopped. Mr. Welles went around to see Stanton, but found him exhibiting "none of the alarm and fright I have seen in him on other occasions." In fact, while Confederate General Early was sitting his horse within sight of the Capitol dome, Horatio Wright and the steady VI Corps were marching through the streets behind their bands and the first regiments of the XIX Corps from Louisiana were landing at the city docks. On July 12, the rebels were still there; the President, with Seward and Mr. Welles, went out to see war at first hand, heard bullets whistle and watched wounded being carried past. Stanton stayed in his office, working.

Dana to Grant, July 12

The Secretary of War directs me to tell you, in his judgment Hunter ought instantly to be relieved, having proven himself far more incapable than Sigel. He also directs me to say that advice or suggestions from you will not be sufficient.

July 13 woke to show the rebels gone from Washington, but they left marks. Blair's fine home with its library was burned, and he let loose bitterly about the "poltroons and cowards" in the War Department. Even the mild-mannered Halleck wrote a letter to Lincoln about this, demanding that if he approved the remarks of his Cabinet member, he dismiss the officers in the Washington and neighboring commands. The letter came through Stanton, who passed it on without comment, though he knew that a good deal of this, and of even sharper criticism—from Mrs. Lincoln, for example—was directed at him as being responsible for Early's raid. He had no time to bother with criticism, being intensely busy in trying to assemble a force from Washington city, Baltimore, and the surrounding districts, to pursue and fight the raiders.

The main question about such a force was the over-all commander; Dana wired Grant about it as early as July 12, and Grant designated Wright. But Wright was too dainty, too precise; by the end of another week it was evident that Early had slipped away from him and was posted comfortably at Strasburg in the valley.

That week the Richmond papers brought news that down in Georgia, retreating Joe Johnston had been replaced by

Hood, the most renowned battle leader in an army famous for its leaders in battle. That meant fighting; nor was fighting long delayed.

Sherman to War Department, July 21

Yesterday at 4 P.M. the enemy sallied from his intrenchments and fell heavily on our line in the direction of Buck Head. For two hours the fighting was close and severe, resulting in the complete repulse of the enemy with heavy loss. He left his dead and many wounded in our possession. We have gained important positions, so that Generals McPherson and Schofield have batteries in position that will easily reach the heart of the city, and General Howard, on the north, also has advanced his lines within easy cannon range of Atlanta. The city seems to have a line all round it, at about a mile and a half from the center of the town.

Two days later there arrived a long letter from Grant; he wanted the diverse departments of the Susquehanna, the Middle, West Virginia, and Washington consolidated into one under a single commander, and he wanted Franklin to be that commander. Why Grant wanted him is inexplicable; perhaps because he talked so good a war. But this was one request that clearly could not be granted, not only because of doubts about Franklin's ability—he had done no better in Banks's misbegotten Red River expedition than in the east—but also because all the straws pointed to the nomination of McClellan by the Democrats. The presence of one of his intimates in command of an important army, perhaps the most important army for its effect on the public, in the midst of a political campaign would create intolerable tensions.

But who else was there to command? Grant suggested Sheridan, Stanton said he was too young for independent command and Lincoln agreed. Grant offered Meade, with Halleck taking over the Army of the Potomac, but that would be a demotion for Meade, and anyway could he handle cavalry in that cavalry country? So President and Secretary worked out the compromise of giving the command of the consolidated departments to Halleck himself, hoping he would go into the field and use it.

Sherman to War Department, July 24

I find the result of Hood's attack on our left more disastrous to the enemy than I supposed. Our loss will not foot up 2,000 killed and wounded, whereas we have found over 1,000 rebels dead, which will make, with the usual proportion of wounded, a loss to the enemy of full 7,000.

This was the hard battle of Atlanta, a rebel defeat and a bad one; you could follow on the maps how the Union lines were closing in; but McPherson was killed—Grant's friend and Sherman's—and Grant got drunk.

He recovered in time for a new attack on the Petersburg lines, an ingenious scheme in which a section of the Confederate works in front of Burnside's IX Corps was mined. The mine explosion was to be followed by an assault by Warren and the V Corps on one flank, and on the other the XVIII Corps, now led by E. O. C. Ord, a quiet, able man from Maryland, very popular with the soldiers, who was always getting wounded. For several days the papers carried dispatches about obscure minor engagements north of the James—Grant had shifted Hancock thither to draw men from the Petersburg lines—but the first Washington knew of the mine plan was on the night of July 30; and then the news was that it had exploded and been a ghastly failure, 4,000 men lost for no gain at all. Worse than a failure; the court of inquiry which presently examined the matter found that the two division commanders who should have led the attack were cowards, and that Burnside had played the part of an utter incompetent, not even clearing the abbatis from in front of his own lines so the troops could advance.

That same day there was more discouraging news from the Shenandoah, where Halleck had not taken the field, nor even given any very clear orders. Early had defeated the West Virginia force of General George Crook and flung an arm of cavalry up into Pennsylvania. Not getting the $100,000 in gold they demanded from the inhabitants of Chambersburg, the Confederates drove them out into the fields and burned the town to the ground.

Sherman to War Department, July 28

The enemy again assaulted today, this time on our extreme right. The blow fell upon the XV Corps, which handsomely repulsed it, capturing four regimental flags. Our loss is comparatively small, while that of the enemy is represented as heavy.

III

THE mine and Shenandoah incidents triggered Grant into drastic action. Burnside was relieved at once, replaced by John G. Parke, a quiet, long-headed man, whose modesty had much to do with his having thus far been held down to a division command. As for the valley, a telegram went to Washington on August 1: "I want Sheridan put in command of all the troops in the field, with instructions to put himself south of the enemy and follow him to the death." Hunter could go home or to the devil, in spite of the fact that Grant had defended him when Stanton had asked his removal in the spring and again later.

Sheridan left for Washington at once; so did two of his cavalry divisions from the Army of the Potomac. In the capital, the strange little man—"a Punch of a soldier, a Rip Van Winkle in regimentals," one of the correspondents called him —went with Stanton to call on the President, and was told that both of them had objected to the appointment. Sheridan did not tell them that he had objected, too, doubtful of his own capacity and his ability to get along with senior generals, and had had to be talked into the acceptance by Grant. He left the White House with the Secretary and was much impressed by the fact that Stanton treated the objection as an utter bygone, only talked about the necessity for success, battles, victories, from a political point of view; things were going badly out in the constituencies.

Sherman to War Department, August 3

We have had pretty lively times today generally. Under the pressure I got two divisions across the head of Utoy Creek, well toward the railroad, and tomorrow will push still more on the flank. My lines are very strong and cover well all the bridges across the Chattahoochee. I will use my cavalry hereafter to cover the railroad, and use infantry and artillery against Atlanta.

Mr. Welles felt a "blight of sadness like a dark shadow," and doubted the competence of Grant; August 4 was appointed a day of fasting, humiliation, and prayer, and time slid down into the dark month of the war. There had to be another draft, and it was going badly, too, prices for substitutes up to $900 or more, corruption and bribery rampant among the surgeons who conducted the physicals, men slow in coming forward. Stanton had to tell Grant that not a regiment or even a company of volunteers would reinforce him from Illinois or Indiana. From Ohio, Governor Brough wired the Secretary to ask whether anything could be done to prevent the sale of Henry rifles; one agent had peddled fifty in Columbus in two days, and was taking orders for more throughout the countryside. Guerrilla gangs were terrorizing southern Illinois; General Pope from Milwaukee reported that further drafting there would provoke more resistance than he could deal with; Morton of Indiana said his state was boiling with plots and commotions.

Sherman to War Department, August 17

I have a tight grip on Atlanta, and was on the point of swinging round to the southeast when Wheeler went to my rear with 6,000 cavalry; he has passed into East Tennessee, having damaged me little.

Horace Greeley to Mayor George Opdyke, New York

Mr. Lincoln is already beaten. We must have another ticket to save us from utter overthrow. If we had such a ticket as could be had by naming Grant, Butler or Sherman for President, and Farragut for Vice, we might make a fight yet.

The two correspondents met with other influential New York Republicans on the fourteenth to consider what might be done. Raymond thought a peace offer to the Confederacy might be helpful. Grant wrote a letter intended to influence voting by killing the peace party, but Stanton consulted with Lincoln, and they agreed to withhold it, since now only results could speak, and from before Petersburg there were no results, only casualty lists. On August 23 Lincoln gravely handed each Cabinet member a little folded sheet of paper, asking them to sign their names across it:

This morning, as for some days past, it seems exceedingly probable that this Administration will not be reëlected. Then it will be my duty to so coöperate with the President-elect as to save the Union between the election and the inauguration, as he will have secured his election on such ground that he cannot possibly save it afterward.

A. Lincoln

There it was and the reasons for it everyone knew; all the campaigns deadlocked. Sheridan doing nothing back at Harpers Ferry, which had become "Harper's Weekly" on the soldiers' tongues; Grant held. The only possible chance lay with Sherman: "All now depends upon that army before Atlanta." It was almost terrifying to follow it on the War Department maps, to realize that he hung there at the end of a single line of rail reaching back to Chattanooga and Nashville, that it might be cut at any moment. Stanton was moving the roots of the mountains for cars and locomotives in the west, sending forward all the new men from the instruction camps, shoes, bullets, guns, tents, ammunition—but to what end? The people saw the dead and heard the wounded.

There was soon no doubt about who Lincoln's "President-elect" would be. Less than a week after his melancholy note, the Democrats met in the same hall where he had first been nominated, in an atmosphere of music, waving handkerchiefs, and delight. What conferences, what private deals with the underground were made no one has ever told; but the sense of those present was clear—there was no use trying armed rebellion when everything needed could be had through the ballot box. They nominated McClellan, of course, and gave him a platform which could be summed up succinctly as: "The war is a failure." All that was now necessary was going through the motions.

That was August 31; but on September 3, late in the evening, Stanton and Lincoln together at the War Department, took from the wires a dispatch with a phrase in it that would send men shouting into the streets:

Atlanta is ours and fairly won.

W. T. Sherman

22

THE LIGHTNING AND THE SWORD

A DECENT elderly lady to whom Lincoln had given a pass through the lines with baggage was caught by one of Baker's detectives in Syracuse, her trunks stuffed with contraband for delivery southward; and Stanton received a curious letter from his old friend and gossip, Judge Black. Some weeks before, being in Washington, Black mentioned to the Secretary that he thought he might go to Canada and see Jacob Thompson, not in the latter's capacity as spy master, but as a commissioner for peace, which was the Confederate's ostensible errand. Now he was reporting the result of the contact; said he had told Thompson that his visit was approved by "a Cabinet officer," and had drawn the reply that the Confederates were only afraid that the war would be carried to the point of subjugation, spoliation, and execution. They would return to the Union under a guarantee of self-government "on all subjects as they had that right under the federal Constitution." Slavery had apparently not been mentioned.

"I do not presume to advise you," wrote Black, "but if I were in your place I would advise the President to suspend hostilities for three or six months, and commence negotiations in good earnest, unless he had irrevocably made up his mind to fight it out on the Emancipation issue."

At the same time, Thompson was writing to a friend in the

Confederate government that Black represented himself as Stanton's personal emissary, sent because Lincoln could not be reelected—which was something the War Secretary could not know at the time, and which Black would later deny. But even without that, here was a pretty business, which Stanton knew would have to be scotched before it bloomed, particularly in view of the fact that Black's letter had not been marked "private," and bore internal evidence of having been set down with a view to publication.

Stanton to Black

I do not suppose anybody cares when or how often you visit Thompson, nor what you talk about with him, but when you called in the morning to pay me, as you professed, a private, friendly visit, I did not suspect that you would afterwards talk about it as a visit to a "cabinet officer," and while we were talking of public persons and things, past and present, and you expressed a desire to see Thompson, and your belief that he would tell you the truth about southern feeling, I did not imagine you were making out credentials as an agent of my "wishes" or a seeker of my "approbation." But this is a matter of trifling importance. You have seen Thompson and no harm has been done to anybody, but as in what you report of him your desire may have "helped you to the conclusion," so the wish to see him may have helped you to the belief that I wished what was to me a matter of perfect indifference, and approved what I did not care about one way or the other. The upshot of it all is that you go for an armistice, which is nothing more and nothing less than what South Carolina wanted when the Rebellion began. You and I then opposed it as fatal to our Government and our National existence; I still oppose it on the same grounds.

This killed the matter except for an anguished protest from Black, but it was hardly dead before a petition came from Curtin of Pennsylvania; the Confederates had thrown twenty-six people of his state into the Salisbury war prison, not soldiers at all. This was more or less a political opportunity; a delegation of peacemakers had just been begging the Secretary to patch up the differences between himself and the Pennsylvania Governor for collaboration in the electoral campaign, and had received the reply: "Tell Governor Curtin that if it will help carry Pennsylvania for Lincoln, I will lie down and let him walk on me." Now Stanton translated his promise of good will into sharp action by ordering twenty-six Confederate Virginians imprisoned as hostages—and then fell unconscious across his desk.

He had been overworking. His health was far from good in many respects that fall, and he used to say to Joseph K. Barnes, the new Surgeon-General: "Keep me alive till the Rebellion is over, and I will take a rest—a long one, perhaps." But until it was over, there could be no relaxation; he had to take a potion and keep going. The details piled in as the political campaign heated up, and Baker's detectives and the cipher operators here and there got their fingers on some thread of the underground movement. Hooker had lost his temper and resigned when Sherman would not give him command of the Army of the Tennessee after McPherson was killed; Stanton sent Hooker to take general charge of guarding the Middle West against rebellious movements, and arranged for Butler, with troops from the Army of the James, to be in New York on election day—one-eyed Ben might be a fool as a field soldier, but civil-military administration and restraints on a turbulent city he thoroughly understood.

More directly political were orders for Sherman to send home six ranking Indiana officers, with corps commanders John A. Logan and Frank Blair; now that the war of movement in Georgia was over with Atlanta's fall, they could be more useful before the electorate than in the field. It took a good deal on Stanton's part to use Blair in this way; he exchanged feelings of mutual dislike with the whole family, and in the spring had relieved Frank of his command after the latter denounced Chase in unmeasured terms; but Lincoln overruled the dismissal. Putting the officers into the campaign, however, turned out to be a thoroughly good idea. Telegrams from political managers presently began to say that prospects were improving in Indiana, while "Black Jack" Logan was carrying everything before him in southern Illinois.

But nothing they said, nothing they did, was half as good as the campaign documents that unexpectedly began to come off the wire on September 19:

Stevenson (Liaison Officer) to Stanton, September 19

Sheridan moved on enemy this morning at daylight. Soon after movement heavy and continuous fighting for two hours, then ceased, apparently receding; resumed about 9 o'clock and has continued up to this hour.

Stanton to Garrett, B & O, September 19

Be ready to move troops from Washington to Harpers Ferry rapidly on short notice.

Stevenson to Stanton, September 19; 4:30

Fighting in the direction of Winchester much heavier.

Stevenson to Stanton, September 19; 5:50

Just heard from the front. Our cavalry, Averell and Merritt, engaged Breckinridge's corps at Darkesville at daylight and up to 1 o'clock had driven him beyond Stephenson's Depot. Every indication is most favorable to us.

Stevenson to Stanton, September 20; 7:40 A.M.

Sheridan has defeated enemy heavily, killing and wounding 5,000 of them, capturing 2,500 prisoners, five pieces of artillery and five battle flags. Our loss about 2,000. Sheridan in Winchester.

Stanton to Sheridan, September 20

Please accept for yourself and your gallant army the thanks of the President and this Department for your great battle and brilliant victory of yesterday. The President has appointed you a brigadier-general in the Regular Army, and you have been assigned to the permanent command of the Middle Division. 100 guns were fired here at noon today in honor of your victory.

This correspondence went to the papers straight, carrying its own annotations, but on the same day came a nastier note. In Cabinet, Stanton unfolded a telegram saying some armed rebels had taken possession of the packet boat coming from Canada across Lake Erie and were presumably bent on raiding the prison camp at Johnston's Island. Mr. Welles asked for army transportation to send a hundred picked sailors and some guns to Buffalo, but before the meeting broke up, there was another wire saying the rebels had run their capture aground and deserted her after sinking one small ship.

Two days later, Frémont unexpectedly withdrew his candidacy, and Montgomery Blair left the Cabinet in a movement that both aroused quite justified outcries about a deal, and united the National Union party. The very next day left little doubt that the black hours of August were brightening toward a golden autumn, for Phil Sheridan hit the enemy again, hard, at Fisher's Hill, and "only darkness saved the whole of Early's army from total destruction"; the rebels were flying up the valley with Union sabers in their backsides. Stanton ordered hundred-gun salutes fired from every major command; all the papers hung out banners, and Chase left his retirement to make speeches in favor of reelecting Lincoln. McClellan accepted his nomination in a speech that left his backers with their jaws hanging down, for he said the war was not a failure at all, the only difference between him and Lincoln was that he could more quickly bring it to a tighter conclusion.

Amid these clearing airs the old, tortured question of prisoner exchange came up again in two forms, neither of them pleasant. Welles privately made an agreement for the exchange of naval prisoners; his service had no Negroes. Stanton objected; there was something like a Cabinet meeting about it at the Navy Department on October 5, to which the Secretary put his case, adding that he also thought it dangerous to address the Confederate Secretary of the Navy by that title, as it would be an act of substantive recognition, something the rebels had been trying by every device to obtain, since it would count ten points in the diplomatic game.

Mr. Welles said he had not fallen for the recognition dodge;

also that "to absolutely stop exchanges because owners held onto their slaves when they got them was an atrocious wrong" —which gives an interesting picture of Mr. Welles' system of ethics. But he carried his point on naval exchanges as a *fait accompli.*

That agreement seemed to soften the Confederates a little. Two days later their Commissioner Ould proposed a new plan for prisoner care. Stanton accepted it at once and worked out the details; the Confederates would be allowed to buy food and medicines for Union prisoners in the North, paying for it in cotton, to be delivered at Mobile or New Orleans and carried in federal ships, all expenses borne by the Union. Supplies began moving at once under the agreement, but the plan lasted less than three months; agents for the Union soon reported that the death rate in Southern prisons was as high as ever, the prisoners were getting nothing, because the supplies were intercepted and used up. That is, the arrangement had merely worked out into one by which the Confederates were making the Union break its blockade to take cotton in exchange for the goods its armies and people needed.

Washington began to fill up with soldiers on furlough, going home to vote; October 11 was the day of state elections in Pennsylvania, Ohio, and Indiana, and late at night Lincoln went over to the War Department to get the news. The place was closed, under bright moonlight, and Stanton was upstairs, sick and asleep with the key in his pocket, but a sentry recognized the President and let him in a back door. The news looked good; Pennsylvania close, but inclining to the right side; Ohio a smashing victory for the Union party, and all but two Democratic congressmen turned out of their seats; Indiana solidly Union. Maryland had abolished slavery by constitutional amendment in a special election. Two days later, as this was being confirmed, Lincoln came to the telegraph office and drew up for Stanton and Eckert an estimate of the electoral vote very different from the unhappy memo of August 23. McClellan (he now thought) would carry the border states, with New York, New Jersey, Pennsylvania, and Illinois, just failing of election by three votes; he forgot to count on either side the electoral vote of the new state of Nevada, as Eckert pointed out.

But one week later Little Phil Sheridan delivered his third campaign document, with its news that the Union had a Jackson and more than a Jackson, and there was no longer any reason for worry:

My army at Cedar Creek was attacked this morning before daylight, and my left was turned and driven in confusion, in fact, most of the line was driven in confusion, with the loss of 20 pieces of artillery. I hastened from Winchester, where I was on my return from Washington, and found the armies between Middletown and Newton, having been driven back about four miles. I here took the affair in hand, and quickly united the corps, forming a compact line of battle, just in time to repulse an attack of the enemy, which was handsomely done at about 1 P.M. At 3 P.M., after some changes of the cavalry from the left to the right flank, I attacked with great vigor, driving and routing the enemy, capturing according to the last report, 43 pieces of artillery and very many prisoners. Affairs at times looked badly, but by the gallantry of our brave officers and men disaster has been converted into a splendid victory.

Lincoln was at a hospital when the telegram was brought. He pushed up his spectacles and beamed. "This is good news indeed," he said. "This Sheridan is a little Irishman, but he is a big fighter."

Even he underestimated the effect; no other battle ever so epitomized a whole campaign, a whole war. The country went wild over the account of Little Phil's dashing up from Winchester on his big black horse, gathering the wreckage of a defeat already established, and turning it into a victory, while two hundred bugles sounded rally. Campaign speeches were speeches no longer, but elecutionists declaiming the poem Thomas Buchanan Read promptly wrote for the occasion, and the price of gold told the story. From a steady 254 on the day McClellan was nominated and a brief 281 when Early stood before Washington, it dropped to 191 after the Confederate commander was hurled from the valley, with his organization permanently broken.

II

THAT same day, October 19, 1864, Confederate raiders crossed the border from Canada, and fell on St. Albans, Vermont, killing two people, looting the banks of $200,000, and making an unsuccessful effort to burn the town.* About the same time, either the cryptographers or Baker's men—probably the latter—really got their noses into the plans of the western underground, and Stanton dispatched identical letters to Generals Hooker and Dix:

This Department has received information that the rebel agents in Canada design to send into the United States, about this time, a large number of refugees, deserters, and enemies of the government, and to colonize them at different points for the purpose of voting at the approaching Presidential election and also, perhaps with a view to organizing a system of robbery and incendiarism in such cities, towns, villages and districts as they may find unprotected. Persons who have come into the United States from Canada upon this business belong to one or the other of the following classes:

First. Citizens of insurgent states who have been engaged in the rebel service.

Second. Deserters from the military service of the United States.

Third. Persons who have been drafted or subject·to draft, and have fled to escape this obligation to their country.

All these persons are liable to punishment under military law.

This was not all; there were plots turned up to kidnap Lincoln and Stanton both. The latter was a near miss. As for the President, Stanton threw a cavalry guard around the Soldiers' Home, to be kept constantly under arms, and refused to let

---

* The by-products of this raid have some interest. Baker's smart detectives had no difficulty in identifying the perpetrators, had them arrested in Canada, and brought to trial for civil crime. The court dismissed them as belligerents conducting an act of war, but that cost the Canadian government money, an international tribunal not unreasonably holding that it is the business of a neutral to restrain belligerents from using his territory as a base for warlike operations.

Lincoln leave the War Department, day or night, without being accompanied by an infantry patrol.

It was difficult to draw the line between legitimate political activity and the plots, a point which the dynamic Secretary seems to have simplified by not drawing any, presumably on the ground that a defeat at the polls would be as bad as any other kind. Governor Seymour of New York vetoed a bill permitting soldiers from his state to vote in the field, but the Unionists in the legislature outflanked him by amending the state constitution. Seymour promptly sent a commission to Washington to gather up Democratic votes and to see that all the Democratic soldiers voted; Stanton threw the commissioners into prison, and would not let them out until after the election. He also imprisoned a Democratic vote-getter from Pennsylvania named Jere F. McKibben, but that led to a row and McKibben's release.

November 8 was a strangely quiet day in Washington, the departments almost crippled into inactivity by the absence of those who had been allowed to go home and vote for the Union. In the evening a storm of wind and rain came on, and at about seven Lincoln took Secretary Hay through it to the War Department to watch the wires. The first was from New York: "the quietest city ever seen" under Butler's good management, who had kept his troops aboard ferryboats, out of sight of the electors, but very ready to reach any spot where there was trouble.

Forney from Philadelphia claimed 10,000 majority, which provoked remarks about overenthusiasm, but then Baltimore reported Maryland unexpectedly for Lincoln, and two Massachusetts Union congressmen were elected by unprecedented majorities.

There began to be a few jokes and amusing anecdotes, into which dropped the news that New York was Union, too, and even Henry Raymond, who had taken on the impossible task of running for Congress in a solidly Democratic district, had won his seat. The President asked Dana if he had ever read any of Petroleum V. Nasby's works, and then proceeded to read some of them aloud himself, pausing now and again to glance over telegrams, while Stanton looked on, speechlessly indignant at the profanation of this high moment with levity. The Secretary was just out of a sickbed, and would go back to it as soon as the excitement was over. At midnight, with enough returns from the west to make everything certain, there was jollity and a fried oyster supper; by two o'clock in the morning, when the President and his guard left, the storm was over, serenaders with music were already beginning to assemble, and groups of men were moving along Pennsylvania Avenue, singing "The Battle Cry of Freedom" at the tops of their voices.

That night Thompson's underground tried to burn New York, members of the organization repeatedly renting hotel rooms and setting chemical fires in them. It was a failure; the chemicals did not work in some cases and the fire department was too alert in others. The bigger attempt scheduled for Chicago had been squashed earlier and harder, due principally to the fact that the conspirators seemed unable to conduct their business on any other basis than that of talking about it in saloon bars. Early in November, Colonel B. J. Sweet of Camp Douglas, where there were 8,000 Confederate prisoners, learned that the "colonization" was coming from Canada, with four Confederate officers and a British colonel to lead the movement, and it would be joined by the Sons of Liberty on no small scale. On Sunday the sixth, suspicious characters began to be noticed in various bars and houses already identified as suspicious; on the morning of the seventh, militia patrols were sent into the streets, the camp guards were doubled, and raiding began. By afternoon the city police had 106 prisoners and the military authorities were in possession of all the officers and a couple of arsenals, one containing two hundred muskets. The British colonel got the heaviest sentence—life on the Dry Tortugas.

III

ALL through those middle weeks of October, 1864, while Sheridan was making the valley ring, there had been an exchange of telegrams among Sherman, Grant, and the Department, beginning with one on October 11 from the general at Atlanta:

I am loath to remain on the defensive, and want to break up this line back to Chattanooga, leave Thomas to defend Tennessee, and collect my forces to go to the seashore, taking Macon, Milledgeville, and Savannah en route. I can do it.

This wire, forwarded to Grant the same day, brought from him an immediate reply with reasons for disapproval: Hood might get away on a new invasion of the north, like Bragg's in 1862—he was edging westward as though for such a purpose; a divided Union army of the west might not be strong enough to hold him and strike for the seacoast, too; Sherman himself would be driving into the unknown, would have supply difficulties, and might encounter a terrible flame of guerrilla warfare. Halleck reinforced all this in conversations with Stanton and Lincoln; Napoleon's campaign to Moscow was mentioned, and the Secretary wired Grant about the President's solicitude, but with something more than an implication that the decision on releasing the western army rested with the Lieutenant-General alone.

In the meanwhile Colonel Horace Porter of Grant's staff returned to headquarters from a visit to Sherman at Atlanta, full of the project in all its details. Defense against Hood was a holding mission, the kind Thomas did best; Sherman would let him have the veteran IV Corps, with John Schofield to lead it, and the dashing young Wilson to head up the cavalry. Whisky Smith had been ordered to Nashville with his three divisions from Missouri, and all the garrisons now defending the rail line from Atlanta to Chattanooga could be added. Thomas himself was confident; thought he would have "men enough to ruin Hood unless he gets out of the way very rapidly."

As for the march to the sea, Sherman proposed to take none but the best men, wreck the whole country and its railroads across a wide belt, so that Lee could no longer draw supplies or recruits across the area of devastation, then turn north against Lee's rear. All the shops and railroad yards at Atlanta would be burned. As for the comparison to Moscow, Sherman wanted to know where the Confederates would get the weather. Supplies? Sherman wired Stanton: "Convey to Jeff Davis my personal and official thanks for abolishing cotton and substituting corn and sweet potatoes. These facilitate our military plans much, for food and forage are abundant."

John Rawlins, also a staff man, was violently opposed. He and Porter had an argument that lasted until one in the morning, when Grant sent them both to bed, Rawlins so much unconvinced that he went up to Washington and laid his case before Lincoln and Stanton, as a result of which they wired Grant, asking him not to let Sherman go. But Porter had done too good a job of explanation; Grant replied next day that "Sherman's proposition is the best that can be adopted."

Stanton to Sherman, October 13

You will see by General Grant's dispatch that your plans are approved by him. You may count on the cooperation of this Department to the full extent of the power of the Government. Supplies will be furnished with the utmost dispatch to the points indicated. Whatever results you have the confidence and support of the Government.

Now the election intervened; Sherman dropped out of the papers and only came back to them when he dropped out of sight completely, with headlines crying "The Mystery of the Day. Where is General Sherman and his Army?" There was nothing that Washington could do further but wait, as it had waited while Grant was lost behind Vicksburg, or Meade and Lee circling each other in Pennsylvania, the long-scale strain replacing the flash strain of knowing that battle was already engaged.

Into this nervous quiet, at 3:40 in the morning of December 1, there burst the news that battle had already been engaged the previous evening at Franklin in central Tennessee— a sudden, savage battle, far into the night. The result could not have been better for the North; Hood repulsed with frightful loss, while in the wings, Wilson's cavalry had beaten Forrest soundly. But the repulse had been inflicted by Schofield's corps alone, against Hood's whole army, and was followed by the retreat of the victors. Where the hell was Thomas, and what was he doing? He was not the first good corps leader who failed to show up well in independent command. Not only that; the field reports showed that Schofield had dug George Stoneman out of the boneyard and made him his second in command. Stanton wired Grant:

"The President feels solicitous about the disposition of General Thomas to lie in fortifications for an indefinite period, 'until Wilson, the commander of the cavalry, gets equipment.' This looks like the McClellan and Rosecrans strategy of doing nothing and let the rebels raid the country. The President wishes you to consider the matter." Another wire contained an enclosure of an order relieving Stoneman: "I think him one of the most worthless officers in the service, who has failed in everything entrusted to him."

Grant did not see eye to eye with the Secretary on the Stoneman matter; put the relief order in his pocket, and rapped back at Stanton that a commander should have what subordinates he chose. But he was inclined to agree about Thomas, toward whom he had always maintained a certain reserve. He wired that officer, urging him to attack Hood at once. At the same time, looking over the record, Grant thought that if Wilson was complaining about not having enough horses for his cavalry, he was probably right; Wilson was a young man who usually knew what was needed. The General sent Stanton a supplementary wire, suggesting that Wilson be given authority to seize horses anywhere in the Department of the Ohio.

The Secretary put Wilson's authorization on the wire that night, and the young cavalryman went to work with vigor. He got 7,000 horses in a week, including those from the Nashville streetcars and a circus; but he also got into a row with Andrew Johnson, military governor of Tennessee and Vice-President-elect of the United States. Johnson's carriage horses were taken, which he liked very little, and still less did he like the fact that Wilson had broken up twelve regiments of one-year cavalry raised by the Governor, and court-martialed a goodly number of the officers Johnson had appointed. The Governor made trouble; secure in the knowledge that Stanton would back him up, Wilson exhibited his authority, and told Johnson he was "a politician of the commonest sort." That egg laid into the future would hatch a curious chick.

Meanwhile, Grant was growing more and more impatient over the lack of news from Thomas, and on December 8 he wired Halleck that if Thomas had not attacked, he should be relieved by Schofield. Halleck replied that if Grant wanted Thomas relieved, he should give the order. Stanton (it is clear from side evidence) did not want him relieved, merely fired to action. Now Grant began dashing off telegrams to Thomas which made that dignified commander say: "They treat me like a schoolboy"; and when, on the eleventh, the wires from the West said that a storm of sleet had delayed the attack for one day further, Grant's patience snapped. He ordered Logan to Louisville, on the way down to relieve Thomas, and himself started for Washington. There he had a conference with Halleck, Stanton, and Lincoln on the fifteenth; wrote out and put in the War Department hopper a telegram notifying Thomas he had been removed.

He might have spared the trouble; that night at eleven a telegram came in that sent Eckert bounding down the stairs of the Department and out to Stanton's home. When he rang the bell, the Secretary appeared at a second-story window. "Is that you, Major? What news?"

"Good news," Eckert called back.

Stanton shouted "Hurrah!" and as he disappeared from the window, Mrs. Stanton and the children could be heard echoing him. In a moment the Secretary was at the door and the two men were on their way to the White House, where Lincoln, also roused from rest, received them in a nightshirt with a candle in his hand, and learned that Thomas had struck with all his strength, taken 17 guns and 1,500 prisoners, was still in contact, and would fight again next day. On the way back,

Stanton asked if the telegram of relief had gone out. No, said the telegrapher, he had detained it on his own authority, not having heard from the cipher operator with Thomas that day; feared he had violated a military rule, and would be court-martialed.

"If they court-martial you, they will have to court-martial me," said Stanton, putting his arm around the telegrapher. "You are my confidential assistant and in my absence were empowered to act on all telegraph matters as if you were Secretary of War. The result shows you did right."

On the next evening there was another vigil, this time of hopeful expectation, and the news was worth the wait, for on that second day at Nashville, Thomas hit so hard that he achieved something not previously seen in this war and seldom in any. Even the papers could hardly believe that Hood's army was wiped out, scattered, captured and destroyed, driven right off the map.

Yet even this news took second place in the headlines of December 17; Sherman was at the coast, had taken some of the forts covering Savannah. The general and his troops were in the best of health, and the Confederacy cut in half. Even Mr. Welles thought that "present indications are an early close of the Rebellion."

BACKDROP

Washington Intelligencer

Lieut. Gen. Scott once more begs to be spared by correspondents—principally applications for autographs—as he cannot answer one in thirty of the letters he receives.

A HARROWING SIGHT. On Wednesday evening, just before dark, one of the most pitiful scenes ever presented to our notice passed up Pennsylvania avenue, in this city. It was a procession of some seventy of the most fearful looking men we ever saw, guarded by a number of cavalrymen, armed with carbines and revolvers. These men were chained to each other by the ankles, in threes and fours. They were all dressed, in a measure, like the poorest of Confederate prisoners brought here. Some of them were hatless and coatless and all of them filthy in the extreme. As they passed up the avenue at a slow gait, their chains clanked on the pavement, giving us an idea of the chain gang in France going to the galleys in the days of Vidocq. These men were sent here from Kentucky, under a guard of forty-five Kentucky Mounted Infantry. Many of our citizens mistook these men for Confederate prisoners, as they were mostly dressed in gray. They are Federal deserters and bounty jumpers, who deserted to the Confederates in western Virginia and east Kentucky, and again deserted from the Confederates, and banded themselves together for plunder and murder. They were exposed by six escaped Federals when near Lexington, Kentucky.

SALE OF MONTICELLO. Monticello, the former residence of Thomas Jefferson, in Albemarle county, Virginia, was sold at auction on Thursday under the sequestration act, for $80,500. Benjamin F. Ficklin, purchaser.

FEMALE PRINTERS. The Boston papers state that the printers' "strike" in that city is practically at an end. The withdrawal of printers belonging to the combination has led to the engagement of women, and experience has thus far proved that they are equal to the workers who have hitherto debarred them from the best situations.

CHRISTMAS, CHRISTMAS, CHRISTMAS. George T. Smith and Co. beg to call the attention of the ladies and gentlemen to their large and varied stock of Fine Family *Groceries, Wines* and *Liquors* generally consisting in part of—
Imperial Prunes, in glass and tin; Plums, Figs, in large and small boxes; French Loyer Raisins; New Citrons; Jellies of every kind, and of the best quality; Preserves of all kinds; Canned Peaches, the best on the market. Also Tomatoes, Green Corn, Salmon (Spiced and Fresh), Lobster, Crabs, Clams, Smoked Salmon; the best Mess Mackerel in the market; Sardines, Petit Pois; Champignons, Pate de foi Gras; Olives Farcies; French and Spanish Olives; French and English Mustard, and a large variety of all kinds of goods for family use and for presents on the holy days.
P.S. Don't forget the old M.D. and Nectar Whiskey.

23

IT CAME OUT THE WRONG WAY

AFTER the election Attorney-General Bates resigned as tired and unwell. Chase and Blair had already gone; and by one of the illogical but firmly established customs of American politics, this brought up the question of remaking the Cabinet completely, with Stanton also resigning. There was a place he could be sent without demotion, for the ancient Chief Justice Taney of the Dred Scott decision had died in October, and it seems that several persons, including Governors Morton and Andrew and Methodist Bishop Matthew Simpson, urged Lincoln to give Stanton the appointment. Bishop Simpson was a personal friend of both President and Secretary; Lincoln often used him as a persuading influence toward leniency in cases involving Confederate sympathizers. But when the question of the Supreme Court appointment came up, the President merely told the Bishop: "If Mr. Stanton can find a man he himself will trust as Secretary of War, I'll do it."

That was just the rub, as it appeared in conversations with Grant early in December, when, after Chase had already been given the Supreme Court job, the question of Stanton's retirement came up between President and General on the heels of newspaper stories. Lincoln said that if he did make a change, the new man would be subject to Grant's approval.

Grant: "I doubt very much whether you could select as efficient a Secretary of War as the present incumbent. He is not only a man of untiring energy and devotion to duty, but even his worst enemies never for a moment doubt his personal integrity and the purity of his motives, and it tends largely to reconcile the people to the heavy taxes they are paying, when they feel an absolute certainty that the chief of the Department which is giving out contracts for countless millions of dollars is a person of scrupulous integrity."

The General was working rather closely with Stanton just then, planning an expedition against Fort Fisher, at the mouth of the Cape Fear River, a project Welles had been urging in the Cabinet since spring, when it could not be undertaken because all the troops were needed for the Virginia campaign. The fort was clearly of strategic importance; it covered Wilmington, the last port through which the Confederacy could receive blockade-running supplies, and with weather locking the siege lines around Petersburg, the men could be spared. Welles detailed his best man, Admiral Porter, with a big fleet of ironclads to conduct the naval bombardment, and, for the landing forces, Grant chose General Godfrey Weitzel of the XXV Corps, which had just been formed from the Negro troops of the Army of the James. This produced an inconvenience; namely, that the orders to Weitzel had to pass through Ben Butler as army commander, and Butler decided to take charge of the expedition himself.

It arrived off Fort Fisher on December 15, the day Thomas attacked Hood, and delays promptly began. First, a ship loaded with powder, which was to be run in under the fort and exploded to stun the garrison (Butler's idea) was not ready; then Butler's transports ran out of food and water and had to go back to the advanced base at Beaufort; then there were storms, and the clock ticked to December 23 before the powder vessel could be run in and touched off.

Next morning the fleet moved into range, while the army landed on the peninsula behind the fort, Butler staying aboard a transport. The advance troops gained a footing, and reported everyone inside down behind the traverses, but the fort in-

considerably damaged either by explosion or gunfire, so Butler decided to call the whole thing off without fighting.

This was the news that came for Christmas, together with
tidings that Sherman presented the nation with the city of
Savannah, but that the defenders had escaped, a combination
that Stanton regarded with some disappointment. Grant did
not mince words about the Fort Fisher fiasco: "A gross and
culpable failure," he called it, in obvious preparation for the
wire he sent to the Secretary on January 4, demanding that in
spite of his political importance Butler be relieved and sent
home.

Stanton must have known this was coming, but he was not
in Washington to receive the wire. After seeing the Fort
Fisher expedition reorganized under General A. H. Terry, he
had taken ship for Savannah. Quite aside from the fact that the
sea voyage might be some help with the asthma which was
crippling him badly that winter, he wanted to make contact
on the ground with the two problems that had already caused
a good deal of Cabinet discussion—what to do about the 35,000
bales of cotton taken with the city, the largest single haul yet
made, and what to do about the liberated Negroes?

In Savannah Stanton found that much of the cotton was
being claimed as British property—"had the British mark on
it," which Sherman had already annotated to the effect that
the British mark was on every battlefield of the war. The
Secretary quickly sent the British claimants packing and turned
to his other problem. He interviewed about twenty of the leading Negroes about what they wanted and what they thought,
taking down their depositions in his own hand, and speaking
with as many of their former masters as he could locate. When
he returned to Washington, he reported in Cabinet that the
situation among the captured rebels was not too hopeful;
little evidence of loyalty to the Union, and the women especially "frenzied, senseless partisans" of the tottering Richmond
regime. The trip took two weeks and it did help his health;
he arrived off Fort Fisher on the way back in time to learn
that the place had just been taken after a whirlwind assault
lasting far into the night. The Secretary promptly promoted

Terry and several others for gallantry, one of them being Colonel Galusha Pennypacker to brigadier, the youngest general in American history, not quite twenty-one when Stanton gave him his stars.

The Secretary had hardly sat down at his desk before the singular business of the Blair mission began to add its complexities to the total picture. This started back in mid-December, when old Frank Blair, the last surviving relic of the great days of Andrew Jackson, was visited with the inspiration that a real peace could be made by negotiation. He asked Lincoln for a pass to go to Richmond and talk it out with Jefferson Davis, whom he had known of old. "Come to me after Savannah falls," said the President, and after the capture of the city was announced, duly gave Blair his let-pass, though without allowing him to explain what message he intended to carry to Davis. This was just as well; when Blair got to Richmond he told his old friend that it would be easy to bring the two parties together on the basis of united action to throw the French out of Mexico, with the combined armies commanded by Jefferson Davis.

Of course this story-book scheme got no further than the ears of the two presidents, but Davis thought the contact might be developed into an occasion for sending commissioners to a conference "to secure peace to the two countries," and Lincoln thought the idea not a bad one. He consulted Seward, who said the matter was a political one and he wanted nothing to do with it; then consulted Stanton, who said: "There are not two countries, Mr. President, and there never will be two countries. Tell Davis that if you treat for peace, it will be for this one country; negotiations on any other basis are impossible."

Lincoln took this advice, but Davis overlooked the dialectic point, and appointed three commissioners to meet the President of the United States. Stanton sent Eckert of the telegraph office down to Grant's lines to greet the trio, which was done on February 1. Eckert reported back that the Confederates were by no means prepared to negotiate on the Lincoln formula of peace for "our one common country," or to accept the preconditions Lincoln had laid down that the national authority must be restored, the executive must not recede on the slavery question, and there would be no armistice until the Confederate armies were disbanded.

This seemed to settle matters, and it would have but for Grant, who had talked with the commissioners, and telegraphed to Stanton that same night; he thought the men were sincere, and wished the President could meet them. Finding the wire at the War Office next morning, Lincoln decided he ought to go.

Said Stanton: "You observe, Mr. President, that Davis himself does not propose to meet you; he sends underlings who have no discretion beyond their instructions and whose acts can be repudiated if necessary. But go, if you think the proposition is not a trap, and I will remain here and push our plans for crushing the enemy, which is the only thing that will save the Union."

He was worried, telling Eckert: "I fear that Lincoln's kindness of heart and his desire to end the war might lead him to make some admission which the astute Southerners would wilfully misconstrue and twist to serve their purposes." But Lincoln went, and on February 3 there was a meeting aboard a steamer at Fortress Monroe, the President with Seward for the Union, Alexander Stephens, Senator R. M. T. Hunter and former Supreme Court Justice John A. Campbell for the Confederacy. They talked pleasantly enough for about four hours. Result: absolutely nothing; there was no reconciliation possible between the formulae of one country and two.

That same month the dynamic Lafayette Baker succeeded in working his way into a New York ring dealing in bounty jumping and forged enlistment papers, and arrested them all in a series of sensational raids. Things were quiet with the Army of the Potomac, but young Lieutenant Carpenter, coming into the War Department one day, was asked to help hold a big map, while the President, with a copy of a telegram in one hand, searched for a place named Salkehatchie. The wire told only that the terrible Sherman was on the march through the South again under pillars of fire by night and smoke by day;

it was only long later that there began to be details of that incredible progress through a country sodden with bogs and swimming with rain, where no roads or bridges were. One of the greatest achievements of history was being worked out among the swamps, where men waded shoulder-deep with cartridge boxes over their heads to drive off rebel pickets, while behind them the axmen toiled to build the corduroys and bridges on which wagons and artillery never ceased rolling forward. But Washington would soon know that Columbia had been taken, and one day later came the news that sent streamers of joy across the tops of all the papers—the fall of naughty Charleston, cradle of the rebellion.

It was in the glare of this fire running through the Carolinas that on March 3 there arrived a telegram from Grant; Lee wanted an interview to arrange a peace. It came to the White House, where Lincoln was going over the last of the legislative business left by the expiring Congress; in his delight he proposed that General Grant give the rebels almost any terms they desired if they would stop fighting.

"Mr. President," said Stanton, "tomorrow is Inauguration Day. If you are not to be President; if any authority is for one moment to be recognized or any terms made that do not signify you are the supreme head of the nation; if generals in the field are to negotiate peace, or any other chief magistrate to be acknowledged on this continent, you are not needed and you had better not take the oath of office."

Lincoln's face fell a trifle, then he looked thoughtful. "I think the Secretary is right," he said, and that night Stanton sent a dispatch which, like all those expressed in its formula, was the product of a collaboration between them:

The President directs me to say to you that he wishes you to have no conference with General Lee unless it is for the capitulation of General Lee's army, or on some minor or purely military matter. He further directs me to say to you that you are not to decide, discuss, or confer upon any political question. Such questions the President holds in his own hands and will submit them to no military conference or convention. Meantime you are to press to the utmost your military advantage.

It turned out to be unfortunate that no copy of this dispatch went to Sherman.

II

NEXT morning the new Vice-President pronounced a harangue that caused Mr. Welles to whisper to Stanton that the man must be either drunk or crazy, and Stanton to reply that there was certainly something wrong. Mr. Lincoln pronounced for malice to none and charity to all; there was a really brilliant inaugural reception, into which came the news that Columbia had burned and Sherman was over the border into North Carolina. By this time there was pretty good information about what the Confederates had in front of him, and it was not very much, even though Joe Johnston had been recalled to command.

To make things certain, Stanton had brought Schofield's IV Corps of Thomas' army around by rail to Annapolis, and it was now already on the way up through Wilmington to join Sherman, carrying a vast convoy of new uniforms for the men of the Army of the West, who had worn out their pants legs in the Carolinas. The jig must be nearly up; Confederate deserters were pouring in every day, 3,000 of them moving through Washington alone that month. Grant described Lee as "robbing the cradle and the grave for men," and was only worried lest the Confederate force slip from its lines and, moving light, escape westward. "Lee can keep his army just where it is, but he cannot attack nor can he fight a battle. Victory or defeat would be alike ruinous."

Stanton went down to see the General during the month, and was given this viewpoint with its supporting evidence in person, but the major purpose of his trip seems to have been something quite else; namely, the singular affair of General James W. Singleton, one of the most curious in which Lincoln was ever involved. This Singleton was from Illinois, a strictly noncombatant general, who in January appeared to have secured from the President a permit to pass through the lines and another one to return with anything he wanted to bring back. The first time Stanton heard of the transaction was early in March—a long, angry telegram from Grant, saying that Singleton had appeared at the lines from the Confederate side with 200,000 pounds of cotton and tobacco as personal baggage. Grant had seized and burned the stuff, since the transaction was obviously part of a stupendous scheme to make millions of dollars by trading with the enemy.

That evening Orestes Browning, Lincoln's friend, dropped in on the Secretary and found him boiling over the incident. "Every man who goes through the lines to buy cotton ought to be shot. It is trading in the blood of our soldiers, and sacrificing the interests of the country to enable mercenary scoundrels to amass fortunes." Browning intimated that there was more to the story than met the eye; produced a letter from Grant to Singleton, which seemed on its face a permit to trade, and said the latter general had acted in perfect good faith for the benefit of the government, and Browning personally would hate to see the trader ruined.

"We'll not ruin him bad," said Stanton, no doubt a trifle grimly, and went down to headquarters, where the affair began to sprout subplots as a sheep dog does hair. He discovered that Grant had written the letter as charged; it was the result of a note borne to him by Singleton's hand from Lincoln, saying that the trader had arranged to bring some produce from Richmond and, while Grant was to be the judge of the arrangement's propriety, "I would be glad for this to be done." Grant let Singleton go in, but recoiled sharply on discovering that "some produce" consisted of 200,000 pounds, and that the trader held options on $7,000,000 worth more, which he now expected to bring out.

On the face of it, this did not look too good for the General, and still less so for the President; and it became important to find out just what was behind the affair and put a damper on it before it became a public scandal. This took more pressure on Browning before Stanton could gather in all the threads, but then the story was not so bad. Lincoln's wife had a half-sister living in the South, Mrs. B. H. Helm; she owned 600

bales of cotton and was worried about losing them to the
Union army. Singleton (probably through Browning since
he was mixed up in it, too) offered to take care of the matter,
but said he would have to have a trading permit to do so. This
was the background of the January blank check permit. But
when the trader came back from a first visit to Richmond on
January 30, he already had the $7,000,000 option, and was in-
tending to get financial backing to make use of it. How Lincoln found this out is uncertain; but he did find it out and was
so startled that he wrote the letter making any arrangement
subject to Grant's approval. Grant also was apparently deceived as to the extent of the operation and did give a qualified approval, the one Browning brought to Stanton.

What to do now? Singleton's tobacco was burned, and
his scheme brought up short, but Mrs. Helm remained. It is
not certain who made the final arrangement, and Stanton may
have had no more part in it than hushing the whole business
up, but the way it was worked out was for Mrs. Helm herself to
come through the lines, while Grant gave orders that her property was not to be harmed.

III

On March 25, the day of Stanton's final interview with Browning on the Singleton matter, Lee suddenly assaulted the IX
Corps lines before Petersburg and, under cover of a rolling
fog, broke into them. There his attack lost steam, the gap was
closed ahead, Union artillery put a cross fire down behind the
assaulters, and they were all killed or captured to the tune
of 4,000 men. When the news reached Grant, he immediately
deduced that Lee was trying to dislocate his positions as a
preliminary to abandoning the Confederate capital and slipping away southward. In Washington, Stanton, Halleck, and
Lincoln reached the same conclusion, and overriding the worries of the Secretary, the President determined to go down
close to the front for what might be the final act.

It rained hard for the next three days and there was business to be cleared up in Washington, so it was March 29 before Lincoln arrived at City Point, to find that Sheridan had already been to headquarters, pounding one fist in the opposite palm and begging to be let go. "I am ready to strike out now and smash them up." Go, then, said Grant; the troops were already moving for a smash at Lee's left flank and communications.

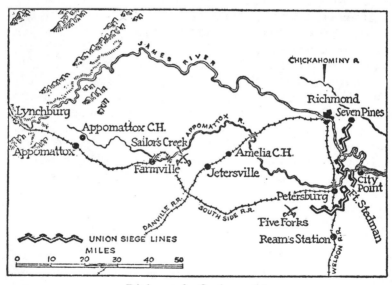

Richmond—Spring 1865

Lincoln to Stanton, March 31, 1865

There has been much hard fighting this morning. Our troops, after having been driven back on the Boydton plank road, turned and drove the enemy in turn and took the White Oak road. There have been four flags captured today.

Sheridan was in the vanguard now, aiming at a place called The Five Forks, key point on Lee's left rear, and the fight at White Oak Road made it clear that the Confederate lines at Petersburg were so denuded of troops that they might be attacked.

Lincoln to Stanton, April 1

Dispatch just received, showing that Sheridan, aided by Warren, had, at 2 P.M., pushed the enemy back so as to retake the Five Forks. The Five Forks were barricaded by the enemy and carried by Devin's division of cavalry. This part of the enemy seem to now be trying to join the main force in front of Grant, while Sheridan and Warren are pushing them as closely as possible.

The newspapers made more of it; 4,500 prisoners taken, in a battle where Sheridan blazed across the field like a star, on the big black horse that had carried him from Winchester, his battle flag in one hand with bullets going through it; the rebels badly broken, three batteries of artillery and a wagon train taken.

The next day was Sunday. Mr. Welles attended divine service and went over to the War Department, where he found a wire just in.

Lincoln to Stanton, April 2

All going finely. Parke, Wright and Ord, extending from Appomattox to Hatcher's Run, have all broken through the enemy's intrenched lines, taking some forts, guns and prisoners. Sheridan with his cavalry, Fifth Corps, and part of the Second, is coming in from the west on the enemy's flank.

There was another wire from Selma, Alabama; Wilson had stormed the town and destroyed the last remnants of Forrest's command, which had escaped the rout at Nashville by not being present. There was an air of excitement in the city, and Monday morning early it was justified.

Lincoln to Stanton, April 3, 8:30 A.M.

This morning General Grant reports Petersburg evacuated, and he is confident Richmond also is. He is pushing forward to cut off, if possible, the retreating enemy. I start to him in a few minutes.

Stanton to Lincoln, April 3

I congratulate you and the nation on the glorious news in your telegram just received. Allow me respectfully to ask you to consider whether you ought to expose the nation to the consequence of any disaster to yourself in the pursuit of a treacherous and dangerous enemy like the rebel army. Commanding generals are in the line of their duty in running such risks, but is the political head of a nation in the same condition?

This dispatch had hardly been put on the wire when one of the cipher operators began decoding a dispatch, stopped to stare at the dateline, then ran to the window and shouted into the street: "Richmond has fallen!" At once the crowds began to collect and extras to pour from all the newspaper offices. Clerks left their desks, stores closed, bars opened, and all the houses sprouted flags. There were thousands in front of the War Department, yelling "Speech! Speech!" so Stanton gave them one, then hurried back to get off messages and to receive them:

Stanton to Dix, for Distribution to State Governors and Press

It appears from a dispatch of General Weitzel, just received in this department, that our forces under his command are in Richmond, having taken it at 8:15 this morning.

Governor J. A. Andrew to Stanton, Boston, April 3

I give you joy on those triumphant victories. Our people by a common impulse abandon business today for Thanksgiving and rejoicing.

Governor James Y. Smith to Stanton, Providence, April 3 . .

Accept the congratulations of Rhode Island upon the glorious consummation of General Grant's campaign in the capture of Richmond. I have ordered a salute of 100 guns throughout the state.

Governor R. J. Oglesby to Stanton, Springfield, Illinois, April 3

Your dispatch announcing the fall of Richmond has electrified our people. We are firing salutes over the restoration of the Union, and the hearts of our people are throbbing in unison with the reverberation of Grant's artillery. God bless Abraham Lincoln, E. M. Stanton, U. S. Grant, W. T. Sherman, Phil. Sheridan and the soldiers of the Union.

In the evening Mr. Welles and Attorney-General Speed walked to the Department through the shouting streets to see if there was anything more precise about the movement of the armies. There was not much, but Stanton entertained the other two in this hour of victory by an account of the weird late meeting of Buchanan's Cabinet when the question of Sumter was being debated, and for Mr. Welles' benefit, added an anecdote about his predecessor in the Navy Department, also from Connecticut, and one of the evacuationists. Did he ever expect to go back to Connecticut? asked Stanton, when Toucey announced his position. Toucey said, yes, he did, but why? "Oh, honestly to know the character of the people of Connecticut," replied Stanton, "for if I were to take such a position and then go back to Pittsburgh, I would be stoned through the streets and then thrown in the river."

The other two Cabinet members left cheerful and leaving their colleague cheerful. It must have been that night, after writing a letter to Chase, in which he described himself as "feeble and in broken health," that Stanton prepared the carefully worded resignation he presented to Lincoln, as soon as the President returned to Washington the next morning. Lincoln read it through, then tore it up with firm hands, and put both of them on the Secretary's shoulders:

"Stanton," he said, "you cannot go. Reconstruction is more difficult and dangerous than construction or destruction. You have been our main reliance; you must help us through the final act. The bag is filled. It must be tied and tied securely. Some knots slip; yours do not. You understand the situation better than anybody else, and it is my wish and the country's that you remain."

Without a word the Secretary went back to his desk, and two days later there was the news that the rebels were really crumbling; the devil Sheridan was after them again—he had taken several thousand prisoners from them in a battle at Sailor's Creek, including a long list of Lee's top generals. But it was not until nine on the night of Sunday the ninth that Stanton, who had been home for supper and was lying down, was roused to be handed the message so long awaited, so ardently desired:

Grant to Stanton, April 9

General Lee surrendered the Army of Northern Virginia this afternoon upon terms proposed by myself.

Stanton was not ungrateful:

Stanton to Grant, April 9

Thanks be to Almighty God for the great victory with which he has this day crowned you and the gallant army under your command. The thanks of the Department and of the Government and of the people of all the United States, their reverence and honor, have been deserved and will be rendered to you and the brave and gallant officers and soldiers of your army for all time.

But there was still work to be done:

Stanton to Grant, 11 P.M., April 9

Some thousands of our prisoners in the hands of the rebels are still undelivered. Can any arrangements be made to hasten their release?

IV

DURING March a beefy but pallid War Department clerk named Lewis Weichmann, who often talked about studying for the Catholic priesthood and resembled a timid slug, told a fellow clerk in the Department a tale—one of those things a man can either no longer keep to himself or else has imagined to gain a little attention. He lived in a boardinghouse run by a Mrs. Surratt on H Street. A gang of men who habitually met at the house—he did not give their names—were planning to redress the balance of the war by kidnaping President Lincoln and delivering him to the Confederate authorities. How was this extraordinary feat to be accomplished? During one of Lincoln's not infrequent visits to the theatre, said Weichmann. Two men would enter his box from the rear, gag him, truss him up, lower him to the stage on a rope during some bit of dramatic action that would permit the performance, and take him out the stage door at the rear. When was this to be accomplished? Originally set for Inauguration Day, said Weichmann, but probably only postponed.

Weichmann begged his fellow-clerk, whose name was Captain Gleason, to keep the thing secret, but, of course, Gleason passed the information up the line. It is not at all difficult to see why it should have been received with skepticism amounting to contempt. In the first place, Abraham Lincoln, the rail-splitter, was a powerful figure of a man; the idea that any one, or any two persons could subdue him, truss him like a fowl, and lower him to the stage in full view of the audience, without arousing the whole theatre, was simply absurd. In the second place, whenever he went out he was accompanied by members of the Washington city police force, one of whom had the assignment of placing a chair just outside the single door giving on the Presidential box and sitting in it until Lincoln was ready to go home.

In fact, the whole thing looked like one of those "plots" that would-be informers dream up to get a little credit or a little money for themselves. This was most especially true after April 9, when there were no more Confederate authorities to whom a kidnapped President could be delivered. Still, there had been so many alarms of plot through Lafayette Baker and others, and so many of them had some substance, that Stanton became acutely uneasy. When he held a reception on the evening of Thursday, the thirteenth, for the victorious Grant, and serenaders came around, the Secretary told the General that he was opposed to either Grant's or Lincoln's appearing in public while the popular excitement endured, and himself went to the window to make whatever reply was necessary to the popular ovation.

The next day the papers announced that General and Mrs. Grant would accompany the Lincolns to Ford's Theatre for a farewell performance of "Our American Cousin." Stanton immediately and violently opposed the whole project. There was, he said, a genuine danger of an assassination attempt on both General and President. He urged Grant not to go, and Grant, to whom a party in the company of Mary Todd Lincoln was no treat and who had given only a conditional acceptance, withdrew his adhesion during the afternoon and took the train to Philadelphia to see his children.

The invitation was transferred to the Stantons, who promptly turned it down—Stanton having been to the theatre only once during the war, and then to carry a message to Lincoln as the President sat in his box. But when Lincoln dropped in at the War Department about six, after an early supper, to see if there was any news from Sherman, the Secretary expostulated once more. If the President would not give up this dangerous project, let him at least take a special guard with him. Lincoln countered teasingly that he would take Eckert, on the ground that the superintendent of telegraph could bend a poker over his arm. This was a joke, and Stanton treated it as such; the President went off to see the play, accompanied by a Miss Harris and her fiancé, Major Rathbone of New York.

None of them knew that the Washington police guard outside the Presidential box that night would be a man named John F. Parker, who had been in trouble before about his inexhaustible thirst for high liquors and low women, and while the play was in progress, he would take occasion to slip out to gratify one taste or the other.

That evening Stanton went to call on Seward, whose carriage horse had run away with him on the sixth, and who had suffered a painful multiple fracture of the arm and a broken jaw. The War Secretary was just undressing at home when a man came banging at the door (the bell-pull was broken), shouting that the President was shot and Seward was murdered. Humbug, Stanton told Ellen, he had left Seward only an hour before. But he had hardly finished saying it when another messenger arrived with a still wilder tale. The undressing was postponed; Stanton took a hack to Seward's house, where he arrived almost as soon as Mr. Welles, to discover that practically everybody in the building had been slashed almost to death by an insane giant with a bowie knife, who dashed through the building, shouting; "I'm mad! I'm mad!" Before they had been there long a frightened hackdriver arrived with an insistent summons to Tenth Street, the building across from Ford's Theatre. The President had really been shot, and was thought to be dying.

By 1:30 in the morning, it was obvious that there was no hope. Stanton retired to another room and began to send orders. Grant was notified of the assassination and told he had better return to Washington at once; Police Chief Kennedy of New York was to send on his best detectives; Colonel Baker was to come; President Garrett of the B & O to provide a special train for Grant. There was a note to Chase to be ready to administer the oath of office to Vice-President Johnson; a note to Johnson to be ready to take the oath; bulletins to the newspapers and the country.

People gathered silently in the street under a cold rain. It was not until half-past seven of the morning of April 15, 1865, that the breathing ceased and Secretary Stanton walked across the room to pronounce the famous valedictory: "Now he belongs to the ages."

BOOK III

The Third Career

24

EXPLANATIONS ARE
IN ORDER

ALMOST at once the controversies began, in an atmosphere as superheated as that of the secession winter.
The first row was of Sherman's making, and it left a
broad moraine of bitterness. On April 17, 1865, while the
hunt for the assassins was in vigorous progress—it had not
taken long to identify John Wilkes Booth as the man who
staggered across the stage at Ford's, brandishing his weapon
and crying: "Sic semper tyrannis!"—there arrived a telegram
from the general of the western army to Grant and Stanton:

I send copies of a correspondence begun with General Johnston,
which, I think, will be followed by terms of capitulation. I will accept the same terms as General Grant gave General Lee, and will
be careful not to complicate any points of civil policy. I have met
ex-Governor Vance and others, all of whom agree the war is over,
and that the states of the south must resume their allegiance, subject
to the Constitution and the laws of Congress.

This was straight enough, and read almost as though Sherman had had a look at the March 3 telegram to Grant. But on
the twenty-first, after the train draped in black had left Washington to move across a sorrowing nation, there came another
wire, accompanied by an order of the day, which promptly
got into the newspapers. The latter said that Sherman and
Johnston had reached an agreement "which, when formally

ratified, will make peace from the Potomac to the Rio Grande." Grant took one look at the contents of the agreement, then asked President Johnson to summon an emergency Cabinet meeting at once, at eight o'clock in the evening, and when the agreement had been read, there were long faces around the board.

For "complicate points of civil policy" was precisely what Sherman had done. His terms provided that all the Confederate state governments should be recognized as legal, that the people of the seceded states be guaranteed in the franchise and rights of property, that the government of the United States was not to "disturb any of the people by reason of the late war," that this document was a general amnesty.

What in the world led Sherman to sign such a paper? The desire for a quick peace was behind it undoubtedly, and very comprehensible. But also he had allowed himself to talk across the conference table with that very slick article, John C. Breckinridge, and had been roundly diddled. There was no question in the mind of anyone at the Cabinet meeting that these terms must be repudiated, emphatically and without the slightest delay. An amnesty, though it might have been a good thing under normal circumstances, could hardly be conceded with Lincoln lying dead and no one yet certain how deeply the officers of the Confederate government were involved in suborning the assassination. In view of the operations of the Thompson organization in Canada and certain other evidence that presently came to hand, there was strong suspicion that the Confederate government was mixed up in it.

More than this, guaranteeing the property of Confederate citizens involved guaranteeing them their slaves—at least the legal claim could be made—since slaves were property by the laws of all the states that had left the Union. Far more than this; the Confederate government was not merely the act of "We the people," like the old one; the secessionists had been careful to justify their act by making their new constitution the work of "each state acting in its sovereign and independent character." Recognizing those state governments as legal therefore recognized the Confederacy itself as legal, along with the debts it had contracted to fight a war against the United States, and implied that the struggle for the Union was nothing but a naked war of conquest against a perfectly valid entity. It was an invitation to another secession as soon as the seceders were strong enough to make it stick.

Indeed, Lincoln himself had seen the pitfall of such an admission and put his foot down hard on it two days before his assassination, less than a week before Sherman fell into the pit and made the admission. To General Weitzel, in occupation of Richmond, came former Judge Campbell, the same who took part in the Hampton Roads conference, with a brilliant idea, while Lee was still retreating from Richmond. He would convoke the members of the Virginia (rebel) legislature to withdraw the state's troops from the war. Lincoln, at City Point, thought some use might be made of this movement, and said so; whereupon Campbell carried on the correspondence in terms that caused Lincoln to send Weitzel a wire:

I have just seen Judge Campbell's letter to you of the 7th. He assumes, it appears to me, that I have called the insurgent legislature of Virginia together, as the rightful legislature of the State, to settle all differences with the United States. I have done no such thing. I spoke of them not as a legislature, but as "the gentlemen who have acted as the legislature of Virginia in the support of the Rebellion." I did this on purpose to exclude the assumption that I was recognizing them as a rightful body. I dealt with them as men having power *de facto* to do a specific thing, to wit: "to withdraw the Virginia troops and other support from resistance to the general government," for which, in the paper handed to Judge Campbell, I promised a special equivalent, to wit: a remission to the people of the State, except in certain cases, of the confiscation of their property. Inasmuch, however, as Judge Campbell misconstrues this, and is still pressing for an armistice, contrary to the explicit statement of the paper I gave him, let my letter to you and the paper to Judge Campbell both be withdrawn or countermanded. Do not allow them to assemble.

The matter of canceling Sherman's armistice could be— and was—handled by sending Grant down to Raleigh to take command in person. But there was also the question of public

reaction, since Sherman's terms had followed his order of the
day into the press. Stanton telegraphed a bulletin to General
Dix at New York for distribution. It cited nine reasons for the
rejection, including that Sherman had no authority to grant
any such terms, and that Lincoln had specifically refused to
grant like ones; and to complete the record, it included a copy
of the March 3 telegram to Grant, and a dispatch coming
through Richmond, which said that Johnson would try to
make terms that would let Jeff Davis escape to Europe or Mexico with the Confederate gold reserve in his pocket.

Sherman took this pretty hard. He had never been with the
Secretary in that relation of mutual easy confidence which
Stanton maintained with, for instance, Grant and Wilson;
both men were too prickly. (The incident of Sherman being
thought insane because he wanted 200,000 men for the Army
of the Cumberland took place before Stanton came into office,
and the official contacts of the pair were perfectly correct, if a
trifle cold.) But the General chose to accept Stanton's bulletin
as an imputation that he had seen a copy of the March 3
message, and that he could be bribed to let Jeff Davis escape.
Therefore, when he came to the grand review of troops in
Washington, he walked to the reviewing stand, shook hands
with everyone in it but Stanton, and then turned his back.
No other results are part of the story except as it forms part of
the background.

II

FROM the first there was not very much doubt that the assassination was a plot involving not only Booth, but a dimwitted
bravo named Lewis Payne, who had slashed Seward. Nor was
it difficult to establish that the plot had been hatched at the
boardinghouse of a Mrs. Mary Surratt, and that it included the
elimination not only of the President, but of Vice-President
Johnson, General Grant, and the whole Cabinet, and that the
men assigned to the other killings either got drunk or failed
through cowardice. Weichmann was probably of a good deal

of help in identifying the other members of the group—Arnold, O'Laughlin, Atzerodt, Payne, Herold—and so were the inmates of the Surratt boardinghouse, who were promptly lodged in prison, along with the actors and employees of Ford's Theatre, and those of a sporting house where Booth had installed his mistress.

This dragnet brought in one fish, a stagehand named Spangler, who had aided Booth's escape. On the seventeenth Payne was taken when he came out of hiding in the Maryland woods and went to the Surratt house to find it a police trap. O'Laughlin turned up on the same day in Baltimore, Atzerodt was found at his cousin's home in Maryland, and Arnold was taken trying to make his getaway at Fortress Monroe, all by elementary detective work. But Herold and the big number, Booth himself, remained invisible for a week after the killing, the former having simply dropped out of sight, the latter after having the ankle he broke in his leap set by a Dr. Mudd, who was also promptly arrested.

On his own authority (it was afterward ratified by Congress) Stanton got out a poster offering $50,000 for Booth and another $25,000 for Herold. The prisoners already captured he had placed in the hold of a monitor off the Washington Navy Yard, with chains on their feet and sacks over their heads, closely tied around neck and body, leaving only a hole for eating and breathing. This was later to produce a flow of words like "torture" and "barbarian," directed at the Secretary, but it does not seem to have disturbed anyone at the time, and a lot of people knew about it. It was already evident that the murder was the outcome of a fairly well-ramified conspiracy, and nobody yet knew how far the ramifications extended. Moreover, Lee's surrender had touched off something like a mass movement to Washington of the characters who had rushed south in 1861 in such numbers as to give the capital the character of a deserted city. Nor did they come at night or stay in corners; they arrived heads up and cheerful, going around to government departments to shake hands with old friends and ask for jobs, as though they had only been on a little trip somewhere. There were so many of them that the

Common Council considered a resolution to keep them out of town, and a mass meeting of protest against their presence was held in front of the City Hall.

How many of them were involved in the assassination and how deeply? In that fevered last week of April no one knew; but to Judge-Advocate-General Joseph Holt there came a newspaperman named Sanford Conover. He had been the *New York Tribune's* correspondent in Canada, and there had placed his finger on lines leading to the real backers of the plot. They were, of course, the Confederate mission in Canada—Jacob Thompson, Clement Clay, George Saunders, Beverley Tucker, and W. C. Cleary; and their project had the approval of Jefferson Davis. John Surratt, son of the boardinghouse keeper, had been their messenger between Richmond and the North, and doubtless between Thompson and Booth. Davis in person had told young Surratt that he needed no more authority to kill Lincoln than to kill any other Union soldier. Conover offered Holt his services as a volunteer to track down details and line up witnesses; he had one or two of the latter already available.

Holt gave the newspaperman some money for traveling expenses and put him on the trail. In the meanwhile, quick action was needed, since all the persons named were at liberty. On May 3 Stanton announced that the murder was "approved in Richmond and paid for in Canada," and a Presidential proclamation offered $100,000 each for the capture of Davis, Clay, and Thompson, with lesser amounts for the others.

By this date Booth was gone and Herold a prisoner. To Lafayette Baker came someone—an old Negro, he said, in a burst of wild improbability—with a tale that the murderous actor and his companion had crossed the Potomac at an indicated point. Studying the road net, the detective fixed Port Royal on the Rappahannock as the likeliest hideout of the pair and ordered a detachment of the Sixteenth New York Cavalry to scour the country round. They found their game in an old tobacco barn on April 26; Booth tried to shoot it out, and was extinguished by a soldier named Boston Corbett.

Stanton had the body sewn in a sack and placed aboard the

monitor *Montauk*, then secretly removed and secretly buried under the floor of a room in the old penitentiary building, the room being locked, the key delivered to the Secretary, and the burial party sworn to secrecy. This proceeding has received due comment as melodramatic, and even a little more than due. Stanton's own story was that he did not wish to see the corpse made "a subject of glorification by disloyal persons." There was certainly something in that, for while the body still lay aboard the *Montauk*, a group of people succeeded in paying it a visit, including one lady who had cut open the sacking and was possessing herself of a lock of the actor's hair when stopped.

The trial of the living conspirators, to whom were added Dr. Mudd and Spangler as accessories after the fact, opened on May 1, and was before a military commission, or court-martial, of three major-generals, two brigadiers, and two colonels, headed by General David Hunter; the legal ground for the procedure being Lincoln's position as Commander-in-Chief.

When people began taking pot shots at Stanton later, the avoidance of the civil courts and the whole manner of the trial was held up as an act of doleful tyranny on his part. Although he may have advised and wished it, however, the military trial was not an act of Stanton's at all. Attorney-General James Speed was the leading legal officer of the government, and it was up to him to decide what the charge should be and in what court the trial should be held. He decided on a general charge of conspiracy against the eight defendants, including Mrs. Surratt, about the only charge under which all could be tried and all the evidence presented at once. Conspiracy is extremely hard to bring home in a civil court unless one of the group turns state's evidence, but a military court is perfectly competent to handle it and its rules of evidence are more liberal.

The general atmosphere of tension must always be borne in mind—the fact that no one yet knew whether this group were the puppets of a larger conspiracy. While the trial was in progress, in fact, Beverley Tucker, one of the group named in the May 3 proclamation, issued from Montreal an "Address to the American People," in which he used the doctrine of *cui bono* to charge that the assassination had been procured by President

Johnson; and there were stories that since Grant and the Cabinet had been included in the murder plan, the whole thing had been set up with the idea of producing a military government under Sherman. Finally, the town was still full of rebel sympathizers; a military court could be given a military guard, a civil court, not.

The defendants were represented by good counsel, and the trial was orderly. It ended on June 30, with a general verdict of guilty. Payne, Herold, and Atzerodt, about whose implication in the violent features of the plot there was no doubt, were sentenced to hang, and so was Mrs. Surratt. Arnold and O'Laughlin, who had been in the kidnap plot but not that for murder, received life sentences on the Dry Tortugas; so did the accessories, Dr. Mudd and Spangler. Another of the criticisms against Stanton has been that he failed to introduce Booth's pocket diary in evidence, on the ground that it would have shown that the original conspiracy comprehended kidnaping only. It is hard to see what difference the diary could have made; certainly Payne, Herold, and Atzerodt were armed to kill.

There was a great deal of to-do about Mrs. Surratt, quite aside from the normal American sentimentalism about hanging a woman for anything. Her defense was that she knew nothing of the purpose of the meetings at her house—even though her son was a member of the gang—and Father Walter, her parish priest, believed her. During the day just before that fixed for the execution, July 7, he bestirred himself so much that Mrs. Surratt's attorney secured a writ of *habeas corpus* from a District of Columbia judge. The papers were at once sent to Attorney-General Speed, who drafted a proclamation suspending *habeas corpus* in the District; Johnson signed it, and Mrs. Surratt died with the rest.

In 1867 there was an epidemic of yellow fever on the Dry Tortugas, which carried off O'Laughlin. The surgeons all came down with the disease, and Dr. Mudd, with great gallantry, cared for both surgeons and prisoners. When the epidemic was over, the officers of the post sent President Johnson a petition for Mudd's pardon. It was granted in 1869, and

Arnold and Spangler were pardoned at the same time. All three went to Maryland to live.

Sanford Conover, the reporter turned detective, was just getting into his stride at the time of the trial. In August he found a highly important witness to the implication of Davis and Thompson in the kidnap plot, with a tale so detailed that Conover was sent to look for more. He pursued the hunt to Richmond, New Orleans, and Wilmington, from where he returned in November with an admirably detailed report and three witnesses, then reached out to New York for another one and to Canada for two more. They made a good impression on Holt, who reported that they were contrite former conspirators and that he believed them.

But a Congressional committee wanted to cross examine, and dispatched a Colonel Turner to New York to bring back Conover's witnesses for the purpose. At this point the structure began to crack. The witnesses said calmly that they had no intention of taking oaths or being cross examined, because everything they had told Holt, including their very names, was false, and had been dreamed up by Conover. What the latter's interest was it is hard to say; perhaps a desire for travel at the public expense, perhaps the thrill of mixing in great affairs and seeing important people dance to his tune, perhaps he genuinely believed in the involvement of the Confederate leaders, and was using the false stories to stall for time until he could strike the true trail. He got away to Canada, but later ventured across the border and was sent to jail as a swindler; Conover was not his real name.

III

In December, 1863, when it was already evident that only a military disaster of the first order could prevent at least part of the seceded territories being left in the hands of the Union at the close of the war, President Lincoln addressed himself to the problem of Reconstruction in a proclamation. It laid down the form of an oath of allegiance, on taking which former

Confederate citizens would receive full pardons. When in any seceded state the number of oath-takings reached 10 per cent of those who had voted in the Presidential election of 1860, they would be allowed to form a government which would be recognized by the Executive.

In view of how frequently this oversimplified outline has been cited as representing Lincoln's whole Reconstruction policy, it is rather important to note that it was hedged round by doubts and restrictions. Lincoln regarded it as a basis for experiment, not a final program. "While the mode presented is the best the Executive can suggest, with his present impressions, it must not be understood that no other possible mode would be acceptable."

As for the restrictions, Virginia was specifically exempted; it already had a loyalist state government sitting at Alexandria, which everyone knew to be a rump, but which had been made necessary to secure a legal state consent for the splitting off of the new state of West Virginia. The return of seized property offered in the amnesty section of the proclamation did not include slaves. The 10 per cent must have been voters by the election laws of the state at the time of secession. Finally, there were excluded from the benefits of the proclamation "all those who are, or shall have been, civil or diplomatic officers or agents of the so-called Confederate government; all who have left judicial stations under the United States to aid the Rebellion; all who are, or shall have been, military or naval officers of said so-called Confederate government above the rank of colonel in the army, or of lieutenant in the navy; all who left seats in the United States Congress to aid the Rebellion; all who resigned commands in the army or navy of the United States and afterward aided the Rebellion; and all who have engaged in any way in treating colored persons, or white persons in charge of such, otherwise than lawfully as prisoners of war, and which persons may have been in the United States service." The proclamation ended by stating that it was an executive act only; members of Congress elected under the 10 per cent governments would have to be passed on by the Senate and the House.

Tentative though this scaffolding was, it by no means satisfied the Radicals who, under the leadership of Charles Sumner in the Senate, had already developed a theory that the seceding states had committed governmental suicide, and were to be treated as conquered, unorganized territories. They grumbled, and Sumner pitched his books on the floor of the Senate chamber when the document was read as an appendix to the Presidential message. But the Radicals had no program of their own to offer, and there was nothing in the proclamation on which they could lay a finger, and so for the time being they sat still.

Well aware of how useful it would be to have a sample state government operating smoothly under his plan, the President transmitted certain intimations to General Banks at New Orleans, where the Union forces had been longest in occupation and were not facing any strong Confederate army. In February of 1864, Banks allowed the election of a governor and members of a convention to write a new Louisiana constitution and to provide for the election of congressmen. The governor chosen was Michael Hahn, of impeccable Unionism; he had already been in Washington to take a seat in Congress as the result of an election permitted by General Butler in December, 1862. But he only stayed three weeks, and returned to advise that it would be well to send no more congressmen to Washington until Reconstruction had been carried further along.

Lincoln gave Hahn authority as military governor also, and wrote him a private letter: "Now you are about to have a convention, which, among other things, will probably define the elective franchise. I barely suggest for your private consideration whether some of the colored people might not be let in—as, for instance, the very intelligent, and especially those who have fought gallantly in our ranks."

Undoubtedly the acceptance of this suggestion would have torpedoed the Radical opposition in Congress and the state suicide theory. But unfortunately the Presidential showpiece failed to work out well. The number of voters was above the required 10 per cent of 1860, but below 20 per cent, and anyone could see by the map that three-quarters of the area of the state was still in the hands of the Confederates, who had a governor of their own. They also had the capital at Shreveport, with the state archives; and Banks's Red River expedition, which was undertaken partly to drive them from there, was so dismal a failure that it hung an aura of incompetence around the whole Hahn administration. Moreover, the convention behaved badly. The free-soil men in it were split, and one group of them charged that the whole election was a fraud. As for the freedmen, the convention only authorized the coming legislature to establish free schools for Negro children and to give the ballot to what Negroes it chose; and when the legislature assembled, it promptly refused to do either.

In the meanwhile the Union command in Arkansas made the army posts centers for an election to a convention in January, and in March the convention met. It drew a document that was satisfactory in abolishing slavery and repudiating the Confederate war debt; but on what should have been the talking points it was no better than Louisiana—the number of voters barely scraped over the 10 per cent mark, and the new constitution absolutely restricted the suffrage to whites.

While this was going on, the Radical leaders in Congress recovered sufficiently from the surprise of Lincoln's proclamation to work out a Reconstruction program of their own. After long debate, they passed it on July 2, 1864. It called for provisional governors in the seceded states, conventions to set up new state governments, members of which would be chosen from those who could take an oath of allegiance like Lincoln's, and who had not served the Confederacy in any capacity, nor voluntarily borne arms against the United States. It declared that the assent of Congress was necessary for the President to declare a state reestablished, and until the Congressional consent had been won, senators, representatives, and Presidential electors from the states would not be recognized. Finally, it emancipated all slaves and disfranchised the top Confederate leaders.

The provision for the approval of the new state governments by Congress was clearly a reflection of the restiveness of that body under the impact of the Presidential war powers

—some granted, some assumed. Even the Democrats who spoke against the bill objected to it, not on the ground that it gave the President too little power, but that it left him with too much. Yet there seems to have been no objection to the bill—called the Wade-Davis Act—on the score of Congressional assertion. The real key section, in the President's eyes, was that abolishing slavery. Lincoln did not think it was constitutional, and every member of the Cabinet agreed with him.

The bill was laid on his desk for signature less than an hour before Congress adjourned. He gave it a pocket veto by not signing it within the required time, and since the adjournment deprived him of the opportunity of explaining why he was vetoing, he put his reasons into a proclamation. It mentioned his doubts about the constitutionality of freeing the slaves by law instead of Constitutional amendment, stood on the ground that it was not yet time to fix inflexibly and by law upon any general plan of Reconstruction, and that throwing out the Louisiana and Arkansas 10 per cent governments would be severely discouraging to the loyalists who had set them up.

This incensed hefty Ben Wade and his colleague on the House side, Henry Winter Davis; they turned out the paper called "The Wade-Davis Manifesto." It pointed out the slender numerical support of the 10 per cent governments, charged that Lincoln merely wanted the electoral votes of those states in the coming contest for the Presidency, asked what would happen if several different sets of 10 per cent governments were organized in a single state, and issued a warning that Congress meant to keep political Reconstruction in its own hands.

There might have been some question as to whether Wade and Davis spoke for the majority of Congress, but that point was at least partly settled in the following February, when the electoral vote was counted. Those of Arkansas and Louisiana were rejected, and this made the rejection of their members of Congress only a formality. That is, Congress had decided that Reconstruction had not yet reached the operative point; that no wholly satisfactory basis for it had yet been found. The reasons, as they stood at this time, came out pretty clearly in the debate about a Freedman's Bureau Bill, setting up an agency to care for the liberated slaves and to find them land. There was undoubtedly and understandably a certain desire, not confined to the Radicals alone, to punish the men who had plunged the country into four years of war, with all the blood and treasure it entailed. There was also a perfectly genuine apprehension that the reconstructed South would bring back slavery "under a new alias," as Charles Sumner put it, for although this very session had passed the Thirteenth Amendment, it might be held unratified without the votes of some of the Southern states. There was also the question of enforcing legislation to back up the amendment.

That is, the Radicals were both suspicious and somewhat vindictive. Lincoln was neither; to a crowd which gathered in jubilation before the White House on the night of April 11, he explained that his Louisiana plan had the full support of his Cabinet at its inception, and met with very little objection from any source. The question of whether the seceded states were technically in or out of the Union was a "pernicious abstraction"; the Louisiana government was by no means perfect—he wished it could have provided for at least limited Negro suffrage—but at the worst it offered a nucleus around which Reconstruction could coalesce. "Concede that the new government of Louisiana is to what it ought to be as the egg is to the fowl, we shall sooner have the fowl by hatching the egg than by smashing it." The crowd took it pretty well, but Senator Sumner thought it argued confusion in the future, and his mailbox filled up with letters saying Negroes had rights which must be respected.

This was the situation on April 14, 1865. On that day there was a Cabinet meeting, with Grant present. Lincoln remarked that "We must reanimate the states," that he was glad Congress was not in session, and then asked Stanton to read a long paper he had drawn up on Reconstruction at the President's request. Precisely what was in that paper no one can now tell. Welles, who seems to have taken a leading part in the brief debate that followed the reading, says he objected in the case of Virginia that the plan was in conflict with the principles of self-government; that Virginia already had a skeleton government and a governor who had been recognized all through the war. "The President said the point was well taken," and the meeting broke up, Stanton promising to furnish the other Cabinet members with copies of his plan for study.

Just what was Lincoln's own reconstruction policy, then? It is clear that he wanted to keep the 10 per cent governments in Louisiana and Arkansas and build them up; and the point about Virginia already having a government he considered well taken; but he would hardly have set Stanton to drawing a new plan if he intended to apply the 10 per cent scheme right down the line. That is, the indications are that Lincoln intended to treat each case as an individual entity, proceeding by trial and improvement, adopting no general rule until he had one that fully proved itself. It was a thing he often did in other areas, and it was the thing that made Sumner think he had a disorderly mind.

IV

THAT night Lincoln was shot and Andrew Johnson marched to the center of the stage. "Treason is a crime and must be made odious," he had said, and "The halter to rich, influential traitors. Traitors must be punished and impoverished, their social power broken." Remarks like these caused Ben Wade, the arch-Radical, to set the new President down as one of his group, and others to fear that Johnson would go too far in punishments and confiscations. They missed the point; the key phrases were "rich, influential" and "social power."

Johnson was a genuine hill-billy, whose passionate thirst for education had led him to supply his want of it by not unheroic efforts; brought up on the semifrontier, violently class conscious, using the rough-and-tumble methods of his Tennessee background, sometimes without being too nice. When Grant nominated young Wilson to command the Department of Georgia, Johnson paid the cavalryman out by refusing to appoint, and ordered Wilson to engineering duty on the rivers, with his permanent rank of a captain of engineers. Politically, Johnson was supposed to be a Jacksonian Democrat; actually, he was a proto-Marxian. It was not slavery, but slaveholders that he detested, and merchants in the cities. "The God-forsaken and hell-deserving, money-loving, hypocritical, backbiting, Sunday-praying scoundrels of the town," as he put it. This is not far from Jeffersonian of the unrevised model, heavily dosed with Rousseau—Jeffersonianism of the type that considered no purity existed outside agricultural life, and that commerce should be severely restrained. The new President was also utterly fearless and a hard worker. He was accused of being a drunk on the strength of the scene in the Senate room at the inauguration—but that was an accident. He was a wonderful family man—but that is unimportant.

He called a Cabinet meeting on the Sunday morning after the assassination, to which Stanton brought his Reconstruction plan, now a good deal altered into a part for Virginia and one for North Carolina, which he proposed making a test area. It seems to have been well received. That night the War Secretary held a conference at the Department with Sumner, Representatives Gooch and Dawes and a few others, and explained the plan to them. This conference has received a particularly bad press from those who use hindsight to accuse Stanton of working from the beginning with the Radicals and against Johnson's and Lincoln's policies. The viewpoint is not merely partisan; it is also myopic. The plan Stanton offered was the same as that he had put before the Cabinet in the morning without arousing the slightest objection; Welles says he saw the papers lying on the Secretary's desk as the conference began to assemble. It is a thoroughly well-established practice in American government for Cabinet members to consult with Congressional leaders on important steps, especially in such a case, where legislation would be required, and where Congress had unmistakably signified its intention of taking a hand. Since the South was under military government and Stanton had been asked to draw the plan, he was clearly the Cabinet member to handle the liaison. The meeting seems to have been harmonious; the only sign of future omen was when Sumner interrupted the reading of the Virginia program to ask what provision was made for the Negroes to vote. What Stanton replied is uncertain; Mr. Welles, who alone reported the conference, left between question and answer.

The next act was May 9, when Johnson recognized the rump government of Virginia by proclamation and declared the Confederate Virginia government to be without legal force. The same day the North Carolina question came up in Cabinet. Stanton, with Attorney-General Speed and Postmaster-General Dennison, thought the proclamation calling a state convention should announce some form of Negro suffrage; three other Cabinet members were opposed. Welles told his diary that this marked a change of attitude on Stanton's part.

The proclamation came out on May 29, appointing William W. Holden provisional governor for the purpose of calling a constitutional convention. It excluded from voting the same classes of individuals as Lincoln's 10 per cent proclamation, and added eight additional classes, compiled with the particular design of keeping wealthy slaveholders from voting. There was no provision for any Negro suffrage; in fact, the proclamation specifically stated that determining the qualifications of the electorate was a matter that rested with the states. The President did say—in the proclamation—that he thought no power but Congress could decide whether the new state government was legally organized, but this was hardly much of a concession in view of the fact that Congress had already claimed, and been conceded that power.

If he had been a less obstinate man and a less hard fighter, Johnson might well have taken warning from a letter, received just before issuing the proclamation from Thaddeus Stevens, the intellectual and moral leader of the House Radicals. Stevens held that the Virginia government was unsatisfactory, that Johnson had better postpone further Reconstruction until Congress could take a hand, or else call a special session. But Johnson had now chosen his line. He recognized a 10 per cent government in Tennessee and appointed provisional governors to call conventions in the remaining states.

The conventions met at once, and the step was hailed with transports of delight, but unfortunately for Johnson, the hosannahs came mainly from Peace Democrats, and still more unfortunately, the conventions failed to yield the kind of results that would have been helpful to the President. It rapidly became evident that both the Lincoln 10 per cent plan and that of the Wade-Davis Bill contained an error—the error that there were enough men of capacity for leadership and ability in administration to form viable governments without dipping into the disqualified classes. The Arkansas and Louisiana regimes were visibly wobbly; Johnson had been unable to get even a 10 per cent government together in his own Tennessee before the end of the war; and almost everywhere, the conventions which assembled during the summer contained a number of men on the disqualified list. For this, Johnson had a simple solution. In spite of another and still gloomier warning from Stevens, he issued pardons to nearly all those taking part in the conventions and the governments that grew out of them.

On top of this came the proceedings within the Southern states themselves. All the conventions, with the exception of Mississippi, ratified the antislavery amendment. But not one of them made provision for any class of Negro voters, although Johnson begged Provisional Governor Sharkey of Mississippi (and perhaps others) to "disarm the adversary" by providing that at least Negroes who could read the Constitution and sign their names might have the franchise. Georgia was only brought to repudiate the Confederate war debt with the utmost difficulty and under strong pressure from Washington. North Carolina ruled that unpardoned Confederate leaders could sit in the legislature. Mississippi organized a militia, and tried to take a prisoner from the military authorities under *habeas corpus*, which was legally suspended in the state.

In North Carolina, South Carolina, Mississippi, and Alabama, the new legislatures met before the December session of Congress and regulated the new relations between the races by a series of codes called the "Black Laws," which provided bright-burning fuel for Radical fires. Mississippi invented the Jim Crow car and wrote it into law; provided that all Negro orphans should be bound out as apprentices, preferably to a former master; provided that Negroes over eighteen without employment were automatically guilty of vagrancy, and their labor should be sold at auction by the sheriff until they had worked out a fine; and that Negroes could neither own nor rent land outside an incorporated town. South Carolina allowed the Negro to rent or own property only outside of town, and had a vagrancy law like Mississippi's. Florida provided for the whipping post and pillory as punishments for Negroes; Georgia enacted a curfew law for Negroes. Few of the states allowed Negroes to testify in any but cases involving their own race, and most of them fixed severe penalties for "enticing away" Negro laborers or apprentices.

Many of these laws were before Congress when it met on December 4, 1865. Honorable members could hardly know that most of the new legislatures were composed of old upland Whigs and Douglas Democrats, respectable, proud, and not very wise. They could hardly be aware that so far as the Black Laws were discriminatory, their operation would be suspended either by the Freedman's Bureau or the military commands. What they saw was that in spite of his own declaration of Congressional authority, Johnson had carried through his personal Reconstruction program singlehanded. His message called it complete, except in the case of Texas, and it left Congress with no other task than to pass on the personal eligibility of the new Southern senators and representatives. And the lines on which the Presidential Reconstruction were developing were not such as to commend themselves even to moderate Republicans.

The more one examined the eligibility of the proposed new members of Congress, the more dubious it became. It was not only that they were sent up by states which were conducting interesting experiments in Black Laws. The men themselves were often Confederate veterans; the new Governor of Mississippi had been a brigadier-general in the Confederate service, a member of a class specifically excluded by Lincoln's

10 per cent proclamation; the new governor of South Carolina had operated a blockade runner. The only test the Johnson-
reconstructed governments seemed willing to admit was
whether a man had voted against secession when it was moot
during the frantic winter of 1860. If he had done this, it appeared to be a clearance for everything he had done since.
And if those men were admitted to Congress, there loomed
before the Union party the spectre of a Congress constituted
as it had been before the rebellion, with the majorities in both
houses composed of Southerners who voted on the Negro issue
without party tags, and helped by Northern doughfaces. This
was in fact Sumner's "slavery under a new alias"; it was the
work of the war undone, the states-rights position admitted as
valid. The only possible answer to a sectional political group-
ing is an antisectional party.

This is not an attempt to justify the position or the measures
of the Thaddeus Stevens group of Radicals. It is merely an
effort to explain the atmosphere in which they moved, and
which they could no more escape than the air they breathed.
The bitter old man Stevens, whose factory in Pennsylvania
had been destroyed during one of Early's cavalry raids, made
his position perfectly clear in a speech at Lancaster in September, 1865. He had now worked out his program—and it
was one for vengeance. The South was conquered territory,
and he wanted the estates of the large secessionist landowners
confiscated—394,000,000 acres of them, which would dispos-
sess only 75,000 persons, according to his figures. This would
allow forty acres to be given to every adult Negro, and permit the rest to be sold for a sum that would go far toward ex-
tinguishing the Union war debt. The Negro must be given
the ballot at once, or nothing else done would be permanent.
Stevens left no doubt that by "ballot" he meant social equality.

It is not intended to contend here that this program, at that
time and in that way, was a wise one, or even a feasible one.
As a matter of fact, Stevens never succeeded in getting through
the half of his program. But it is intended to contend here that
as matters stood in December, 1865, a reasonably intelligent
Unionist had very little choice. He could go along with Stevens

—part way, at least—declare that the matter of Reconstruction was almost as completely unsolved as it had been on April 14, or he could accept the Johnson Reconstruction as complete, including Black Laws, Confederate officers in government, and (it certainly seemed at the time) the strong probability of slavery under a new alias, the paramount rights of the states and the struggle all over again. It would doubtless have contributed vastly to a more successful Reconstruction and the quicker achievement of a unified people if there had existed a "third force" with malice toward none and charity for all. But the only possible leader of such a force was dead; the only people who believed in such a solution were political dilettantes like Henry J. Raymond, and they were in the position of being an unrecognizable gray where all else was chalk and lampblack. It is curious how everyone around Lincoln seemed to shrink after his death.

Stanton's own position in the developing struggle deserves some analysis. The frequently stated thesis that he was on the vindictive side all along, even in Lincoln's Cabinet, will not bear the test of the record. It is true that throughout the war he stood for the root and branch destruction of the Confederacy, and was very stiff on Confederates and Confederate sympathizers; it is true that Lincoln not infrequently tried to moderate his ardor, principally through Bishop Simpson. But it is also true that Stanton never gave the slightest support to Stevens' confiscation idea, that with the rest of the Cabinet he approved the 10 per cent plan when Lincoln put it forward in 1863. There is not a trace of evidence that Stanton tried to sabotage this plan, or tried to get a harsher one accepted. There is no evidence that the dead President had any but criticisms of detail on the plan Stanton read to him on April 14. Moreover, it was specifically to handle the problems of Reconstruction that Lincoln begged Stanton to stay in the Cabinet after the fall of Richmond.

In fact, that Presidential request supplies a key. That, and any long-term examination of Stanton's record as an administrator, such as that made by James Ford Rhodes, whose summation it would be difficult to improve:

The Stanton of tradition is an austere man, standing at a high desk, busy and careworn, grumbling, fuming and swearing, approached by every subordinate with fear, by every officer except the highest with anxiety, by the delinquent with trepidation. The Stanton of the Official Records is a patient, tactful man who, bearing a burden of administration, disposes of business promptly, who takes into account many conditions and adapts himself to circumstances, keeping always in view the great result to be achieved. It is a man who does not obtrude himself. No one accustomed to affairs can go through the correspondence of the summer of 1864 without arriving at a high opinion of the executive ability of Stanton. He is patient and considerate with those to whom patience and consideration are due, but when he believes himself in the right, he is unyielding and resolute.

It was this patient administrator—able to take the long view and to wrench the possible from the jaws of the difficult—that Lincoln wanted in the control room of Reconstruction. Stanton was an executive, a mechanic, much less concerned with the abstract (which was settled for him by deep-abiding religious principles) than with getting things done. The date when he changed his position on Negro suffrage in the reconstructed states is very significant. So far as his personal opinion went, he was originally in favor of the kind of locally granted Negro suffrage on a limited basis suggested by Lincoln to the Hahn government of Louisiana. He gave up that idea because of the practical difficulties of administration. When he turned toward Negro suffrage again, it was after the April 16 conference with the Congressional leaders on the Virginia and North Carolina plan. At that conference Stanton learned that no Reconstruction program which did not provide for some form of Negro suffrage from the beginning would ever be approved by Congress. It became then a choice between including that feature and what Lincoln called smashing the egg. That is, a matter of straight realism.

Nor can Stanton have been very happy about the creeping secessionism that was manifesting itself in the Johnson-reconstructed states. The only opposition to it came from the group dominated by the Radicals. Stanton expressed his misgivings about what was going on to G. S. Boutwell of Massachusetts in a private interview just before Congress opened in December, 1865. He was concerned, he said, over the arbitrariness of Johnson's proceedings. In August the President had ordered a big expedition of three columns of troops into the Indian country, without even notifying either his Secretary of War or the Commander of the Army; and it was likely that Johnson would attempt to organize Congress arbitrarily on the prewar basis of a coalition between Northern and Southern Democrats.

V

ON December 4, 1865, Stevens introduced a resolution for the appointment of a joint Congressional committee of fifteen to inquire into the condition of the late Confederate states, and to report whether any of them were entitled to representation in the United States Congress. It passed the House by 136 to 36 and the Senate by 33 to 11, all the moderates voting for it, and only the Democrats against.

This made it clear that the members from the seceded states would not be seated, and they were not, although one of them was a Tennesseean who had been sitting almost since the beginning of the war. During the next two and a half months there was a good deal of torrid oratory on the subject of Negro suffrage, but the first real event was the passage in mid-February of a bill greatly enlarging and extending the Freedmen's Bureau. Johnson vetoed it in a message which repeated that the states were already fully restored, and the Radicals just barely missed passing it over his veto. The day after this was Washington's birthday; a meeting of the President's sympathizers was held at Grover's Theatre and marched to the White House, where Johnson gave them a little speech in which he attacked the joint committee of fifteen as "an irresponsible central directory," declared: "We are now almost inaugurated into another rebellion," and named Sumner and Stevens as the rebels—a speech not calculated to improve tempers.

There was pending a bill drawn up by Lyman Trumbull,

Lincoln's friend, in opposition to the Black Laws—the Civil Rights Bill, defining the Negro as a citizen and protecting his civil rights. Trumbull seems to have intended it as a conciliation measure, in view of the fact that in his December message Johnson had said that "good faith requires the security of the freedmen in their liberty and their property, their right to labor, and their right to claim the just return of their labor." That is, Trumbull thought that under the protection of the Civil Rights Bill the reconstructed governments might be accepted by Congress. The Radicals now took up the Civil Rights Bill and passed it. Johnson, who never conciliated anybody under any circumstances, and who would accept no conciliation from Radical hands, vetoed, saying it would put the federal government too deeply into the states. The Radicals unseated a New Jersey Democrat whose election had been irregular and passed it over his veto, along with a new Freedmen's Bureau Bill; then Congress hammered out the Fourteenth Amendment, which would place the Negro's civil rights beyond doubt when ratified.

With Congressional elections coming up in the fall, the campaign was now in the open, and the word "treachery" has been freely used of Stanton because he did not resign, like Harlan, Dennison, and Speed, the other three Cabinet members who could no longer stomach Johnson's policy. What the treachery consisted of it is somewhat hard to perceive. Stanton certainly made no secret of his position; at a Cabinet meeting on May 1 he made himself perfectly clear privately, and on May 23, when a Union-Johnson club serenaded the President and Cabinet officers, he was equally specific in public, declaring that he had advised the President to sign the Freedmen's Bureau Bill and the Civil Rights Bill. One section of the pending Fourteenth Amendment, a section which disfranchised "all persons who had voluntarily adhered to the late insurrection" until July 4, 1870, he disapproved; with its other objectives he was in sympathy.

Well, then, why did he stay on, completely disagreeing with Johnson's line on Reconstruction? Certainly not for the pleasure of clinging to an office he had already tried to give up under Lincoln, nor even for that of "spying" on Cabinet meetings, as has been alleged. If there were steps which Johnson did not wish to expose before his whole Cabinet, there was no reason he had to mention the subjects in question at a full meeting, and there were cases in which he did not, like Lincoln before him.

Stanton stayed on because, in spite of Johnson's repeated statements that the Southern states were fully restored, the military occupation continued. Without Stanton in the War Office to prevent it, or at least to raise a howl about it, the President could have reduced the occupying troops to skeleton staffs or withdrawn them altogether. In fact, he did try to disband the occupation force in Virginia in January, 1866, before the Reconstruction struggle really warmed up, and was only prevented by Stanton. Speculation on the ifs of history is a somewhat fruitless game, but it does not take much to prove that there would have been somewhat explosive possibilities in a condition of affairs in which the Southern states were turned over without let or hindrance to the governments elected under the Johnson Reconstruction, while Congress was refusing to recognize those governments. "Reconstruction is more difficult and dangerous than construction or destruction," Lincoln had told the Secretary. "You have been our main reliance. You must help us through the final act. It is my wish and the country's that you remain."

To the man who spent every odd moment he could set aside —and they were few—composing a work on "The Poetry of the Bible," these words were a trust and a duty. He had to stay on the job in the face of newspaper reports that he would resign and unconcealed suggestions that he should; and there were twice as many letters begging him to stay as there were urging him to leave.

There was also another factor, frequently overlooked. Although the President and his Secretary of War were diametrically opposed on the broad lines of reconstruction policy, their strictly official relations remained unimpaired. Johnson had discovered, as Lincoln had done, that Stanton possessed a keen legal mind and an immense capacity for business. Even the acidulous Mr. Welles set it down that "His [Stanton's] opinion and judgment, I think, the President values more than he does Seward's. Stanton studies to conform to the President's decisions and determinations when he cannot change them." Disagree he would; even put pressure on Johnson he would; but while the controversy was going on, he did not funk either his advisory or his executive duties, and he was the best executive in the Cabinet.

The Congressional campaign of 1866 was the place where the Reconstruction issue would obviously be decided. To get things rolling, the pro-Johnson forces issued through Henry J. Raymond, who as Lincoln's campaign manager in 1864 occupied the position that would today be that of the party chairman, a call for a convention of the National Union party in Philadelphia on August 14. It met amid intense enthusiasm, but unfortunately more than half the delegates were Democrats, some of them from the Johnson-Reconstruction governments, and still more unfortunately, two events supervened between the call and the convention to furnish spectacular evidence that Johnson's Reconstruction was not working well. There was a bloody riot in Memphis, with Negroes on the receiving end, and a still worse and more confused one in New Orleans.

The basis of the latter was complex. In the spring session of the Louisiana legislature a bill was passed through the House declaring that the constitution of 1864, the Lincoln government constitution, had been put through by "fraud and violence," and summoning a new convention, which by the nature of its backers would obviously produce a document less unfavorable to ex-secessionists. Johnson and Seward told Louisianans in Washington that this was an extremely poor time for taking such action; their remarks were reported back home, and the bill was tabled in the state Senate. But the predominantly free-soil elements who had made the constitution of 1864 took alarm and issued a call for the reassembly of their convention, having discovered a trick clause in the document they produced that gave them a basis for the summons. There was no doubt in anyone's mind what they intended to do; they meant to enfranchise the Negroes, and one of the Radical leaders told a Negro mass meeting as much amid thunders of applause.

Mayor J. S. Monroe informed General Absalom Baird, in temporary command of the military department, that he intended to break up the convention unless it were meeting with the sanction of the military authorities, to which Baird replied that the military authorities "held themselves strictly aloof from interference with the political movements of the citizens of Louisiana." The Mayor and the Lieutenant-Governor (the Governor was on the other team, and had sanctioned the convention) then informed Baird that they intended to have the sheriff arrest the convention members. Baird did not think the assembly should be prevented and, after obtaining Mayor Monroe's promise that writs of arrest would not be executed until he had countersigned them, wired Stanton that he would not allow the arrests without special instructions. No special instructions were sent. The Lieutenant-Governor then wired Johnson that members of the convention would be arrested "under process from the criminal court of this district," and asked whether the military were to prevent process of court. The President wired back that the military were to sustain, not obstruct the process of court, but he sent the wire to the Lieutenant-Governor only, and not a word to Baird. It does not seem that the Lieutenant-Governor bothered to communicate the wire to the General either.

The convention was to meet on July 30. On the night before the four or five hundred New Orleans police were ordered to assemble at their stations under arms. When the convention assembled, the hall was surrounded by a group of Negroes and the streets of the city were packed with whites. As a Negro procession approached the convention hall a shot was fired somewhere. The police came up at the run, surrounding the building, in which the Negroes outside had taken refuge, and another shot was fired, whereupon the police rushed to the windows and emptied their revolvers into the hall, being joined by a white mob. How many—both white members of the convention and Negro spectators—were killed and how many were injured in this frightful affair was never ascertained, but the bodies were carried away on drays like cords of wood.

General Sheridan, whose department it was, hurried back from a trip to Texas and four days later made a report which called down a pox on both houses, the leaders of the convention as low-minded political agitators, the mayor for having organized a police force out of the most unsavory elements he could find, the civil authorities for having done nothing to bring to book either police or rioters, but having arrested the members of the convention. He questioned whether the local authorities could protect Northern men in the South. This was perhaps merely a verbal point; but no one could miss the fact that, regardless of who was to blame, the civil authorities could not maintain order in a state which contained free Negroes. To complete matters, Johnson published the part of the report blaming the backers of the convention, but withheld that blaming the Louisiana authorities until Sheridan sent an indignant protest.

It was in the shadow of this event, which may be taken as the key point in the whole "bloody shirt" agitation, with its insistence that the slavery question would not be settled until Negroes had the vote, nor secession really put down until the men who made it were disfranchised, that Johnson's National Union convention assembled in Philadelphia. Even before it rose the Radicals had organized a convention called the Loyal Union, with many delegates from the South, to demonstrate that there could be found men of that section who favored another plan of Reconstruction than that insisted upon by Johnson. It was not a particularly brilliant gathering, but it did put before people in the north the idea that the riots in Memphis and New Orleans were by no means isolated events.

In the meanwhile, perhaps as a result of the communiqués he began to receive from the spirit world about this time, the President decided to carry his case to the people. Ostensibly his trip was to visit the tomb of Stephen A. Douglas, actually it was the famous "swing around the circle," the occasion for which the phrase was invented. Seward and Grant went with him; Stanton was invited but did not go. Johnson began badly by referring to Congress as "the Congress of only part of the states" and declaring that it was responsible for the New Orleans riot. He continued badly by losing his temper over being heckled and letting loose with some of the most dubious billingsgate that ever came from a President of the United States. The crowds became increasingly hostile; at the final stop in Indianapolis he was driven from the platform and it was evident that the Radicals were going to win. Actually they gained more than a two-thirds majority in both houses.

VI

THE winter war began early in January with the passage of an act giving the ballot to Negroes in the District of Columbia. In the Cabinet Stanton read a carefully prepared paper, advising that the bill be signed, but of course Johnson vetoed, and of course Congress passed it over his veto. But this was merely a statement of purpose; the real emphasis lay on three other pieces of legislation which were sent through in February. As a group the three bills were intended to break the deadlock brought about by the fact that while the bands were playing and orators spouting during the political campaign of the previous fall, Kentucky and ten of the eleven seceded states had rejected the Fourteenth Amendment—with Johnson's full approval and, in at least one case, on his recommendation. Tennessee ratified and Congress promptly accepted her senators and representatives, which made Johnson unhappy.

The failure to ratify was, of course, a demonstration to the Radicals that the South intended to enforce its Black Laws, keeping administrations in safely Democratic hands and sooner or later obtaining enough co-operation from Northern Democrats to get rid of the Civil Rights Bill. Well, that had to be prevented, and the only way anyone could think of preventing it was by setting up governments elected with the help of Negro voters.

Therefore the first of the new series of laws was the Military Reconstruction Bill. It declared that no legal governments existed in the South and split it into five military districts, each to be commanded by a general until "loyal and republican state governments can be legally established"; that is, until there were new state constitutions and new governments. It stated specifically that the conventions should consist of delegates elected by citizens "of whatever race, color or previous condition, who have been resident in the state for one year." Stanton spoke for this bill in the Cabinet.

The second bill was the Tenure of Office Act, providing that an officer appointed by the President with the consent of the Senate could not be removed without the approval of that body. It was openly intended to keep Stanton in office, in his key position for the administration of military Reconstruction, even over Johnson's objection. Stanton thought the bill unwise and unnecessary, opposed it in the Cabinet, asked J. A. Bingham to have it dropped, spoke publicly against it, and even wrote the veto message. This also has been described as treachery on the Secretary's part, but the acceptance of that definition requires the statement that he approved of everything Sumner and Stevens were doing, which was certainly not the case, even though he disapproved of much of what Johnson was doing.

The third bill required that the new Congress should begin its session on March 4 instead of in December, as watchdog to see that the program was not sabotaged. To it was added an act providing that military orders from the President or the Secretary of War should be issued only through the General of the Army—a throwback to Johnson's Indian expedition of the summer of 1865; he might try to order troops out of the South without consulting anybody. All the bills were vetoed and passed over the veto as fast as Congress could move.

As soon as the new session met, there began to be talk of impeaching Johnson; in fact, there had already been some in January, 1867, after the Radical election victory and the failure of the Fourteenth Amendment produced its deadlock. But the general opinion in the party leadership was that the new legislation would cover matters. This turned out to be not quite true. Sheridan, commanding the district covering Texas and Louisiana, removed Mayor Monroe of New Orleans, State Attorney-General Herron, who had refused to prosecute any of the perpetrators of the New Orleans riot, and Judge Abell of the New Orleans criminal court, who had promised there would be no prosecution of the rioters in his jurisdiction. Some of the other generals asked instructions, and this brought before the Cabinet the whole question of how military Reconstruction should be administered.

There was a long debate about how far the powers of the military commanders extended, and an interrogatory of seven questions submitted to the members by Attorney-General Henry Stanbery. With the exception of Stanton, the Cabinet was unanimous in supporting Johnson's view that the President had authority to supervise the generals, and they were bound to carry out their duties in accordance with his instructions; that if the commanders assumed powers they did not have, the President could rectify their acts; that the power to suspend or abolish state laws was not vested in the military commanders. Stanton held that under the Military Reconstruction Act, the military authority in the rebel states was paramount, that under the act the soldiers could remove state officers, that the powers conferred by Congress were vested in the commanders and could not be exercised by the President in person "any more than he could take on himself in his own person any other duty of military service vested in a specific officer by law; as for example the duties of the quartermaster-general, commissary-general," and the like.

Of course this opinion, whose legal validity was somewhat shaky, had no effect. Stanbery promptly issued an instruction that any prospective voter would be qualified on taking the oath, that none who had participated in the Rebellion could be disqualified from voting until they had been convicted in a court, and that boards of registration had no right to doubt anyone who did take the oath. "A broad and macadamized road for perjury and fraud," Sheridan called it. Stanton took the same view, and drafted a bill which Congress passed on July

19, over the Presidential veto as usual, wiping out Stanbery's interpretation and making the military commanders the direct instruments for the execution of the law.

Congress adjourned the next day, and Johnson promptly took up the counterattack. On August 5 he asked Stanton for his resignation; it was refused the same day, and there have been a lot of hard words said about the Secretary's "disloyalty." It is perhaps pertinent to point out that when Stanton took the oath of office it was not to Johnson, Lincoln, or any other man, but to the United States of America.

On August 12 Johnson suspended Stanton, appointed Grant as interim Secretary of War, and at the same time removed Sheridan in favor of Hancock. Instantly there was tumult, for Sheridan was one of the most popular of officers throughout the North (as Johnson had been warned, even by his supporters), and Stanton was by no means without friends, quite aside from the people who thought he was right. Among the latter belonged Grant, who told the President that he was a man under orders and would obey orders, but that the Tenure of Office Act made the removal illegal. "It is but a short time since the Senate was in session," wrote the General, "and why not then have asked for his removal, if it was desired?" But the fighter wanted to fight; "If Congress can bring themselves to impeach me," he told Mr. Welles, "because in my judgment a turbulent and unfit man should be removed, let them do it."

Stanton wrote a letter to Johnson denying the President's right to remove him, turned over the office to Grant, and went up to New England for his first vacation in five years, feeling ill and depressed. He was back in Washington in October and lived very quietly until December 12, when Johnson sent the Senate a message saying that he had suspended Stanton for the four several reasons that his refusal to resign was defiant, that he had advised the President to veto the Tenure of Office Bill and then taken advantage of it, that he had been the author of Johnson's Reconstruction policy, then disapproved it, that he had sent no instructions to General Baird at the time of the New Orleans riot, and had not "exculpated" the President from responsibility for the riot.

Stanton submitted a brief in reply to the Senate. He brushed aside the first point as silly; as a matter of fact, he had used exactly the same language in refusing to resign as Johnson had in asking for the resignation. He certainly had disapproved the Tenure of Office Act, but it was now law and should be obeyed. On the Reconstruction program, he pointed out that his own outline and Johnson's statements at the time described the Southern governments as provisional and "subject to the controlling powers of Congress" and—a point of great force— he had insisted that some provision must be made for some Negroes to vote. As for the New Orleans riot, Baird had not asked for special instructions; he had asked whether there were any changes in his existing instructions, and there were none. Exculpating the President from responsibility for the riot was hardly the duty of the Secretary of War; and Johnson had done his own exculpating by blaming the affair on certain members of Congress.

The Senate took the case up in executive session and, after a little sniping at Stanton for not having exchanged prisoners of war more rapidly, to which he made a crushing retort by sending to the Department for the carefully kept records, it was voted by 33 to 6 that the Senate did not concur in the suspension. This was January 13, 1868; the next day Stanton went round to the Department and took over from Grant again. In the Cabinet Johnson violently denounced the General for not having kept an agreement to remain physically in the War Office to bring the Tenure of Office Act before the courts; Grant denied there was any such agreement. Now Johnson tried to appoint Sherman, but he refused to have anything to do with the matter, so Johnson issued an order removing Stanton and appointing Lorenzo Thomas as Secretary of War.

He could hardly have made a worse choice. Lorenzo Thomas was the vain, pompous, incompetent, and probably dishonest man-with-influence who had been Adjutant-General when Stanton took office, and whom the Secretary had promised to pick up with a pair of tongs and drop in the Potomac. This was never achieved, but Stanton kept him on inspection trips in the West during most of the conflict so the work of the office could be done well, and everybody thought it was a good idea.

The removal order was February 21; on the same day Stanton transmitted a copy of it to the Senate and barricaded himself in the Department, sleeping on a sofa as in the old "distressing periods" while waiting for news from the front. On the same day the House followed Stevens in voting to impeach President Andrew Johnson of high crimes and misdemeanors.

VII

THE serio-comic trial of that impeachment belongs to another department of history, and no remarks on it are necessary except as to defense counsel's construction of the case that since Stanton was not appointed by Johnson, he was not Johnson's Secretary of War. As was, and is the custom, all the Cabinet officers offered their resignations when Johnson took over, and Johnson asked Stanton to stay. But this was merely the legal argument of the case. The real trial was conducted in a different field and on a different basis. Attorney-General Stanbery, who was one of Johnson's counsel, managed to persuade the President to keep his mouth shut during the proceedings, and that helped greatly; but what helped still more was the activities of William M. Evarts, one of the best and cleverest lawyers in American history. It occurred to him that even at this late date there was a possible basis of compromise. He held a little meeting with certain of the Republican senators, to whom he suggested that no compromise was a hell of a way to run a government based on checks and balances, and he made them a proposition. What if there were nominated in Stanton's place a man who could certainly be confirmed by the Senate as being in full accord with the idea of Reconstruction not exclusively controlled by the President?

They asked Mr. Evarts to develop his idea. He said he did not believe the President could be convicted on the law and the evidence, but he thought Republican apprehension about Johnson was rather from what he might do than what he had done. A reliable Secretary of War would keep him in bounds, whereas his removal by impeachment would be ruinous to the Republican party and perhaps to the republic, as having been made for political reasons.

Whom did Mr. Evarts have in mind? asked the senators. The scholar-general, John M. Schofield, said Mr. Evarts, and presented him. Schofield thought that many of the President's acts were irregular, and his procedures would have to be changed. The senators, while not precisely pronouncing themselves satisfied, made purring noises, and the conference adjourned. This was on April 21, one day after the taking of testimony in the high court of impeachment had begun; on April 24, Johnson sent Schofield's name to the Senate as Secretary of War. The nomination was held up until May 26, when the most important articles of impeachment were voted on and had failed by a single ballot, seven Republicans going against.

The next day Stanton wrote a note to Johnson:

Sir—The resolution of the Senate of the United States on the 21st of February last, declaring that the President 'has no power to remove the Secretary of War and designate any other officer to perform the duties of that office *ad interim*,' having failed to be supported by two-thirds of the senators present and voting on the articles of impeachment preferred against you by the House of Representatives, I have relinquished charge of the War Department, and have left the same and the books, archives, papers, and property heretofore in my custody as Secretary of War, in care of Brevet Major-General Townsend, subject to your direction.

On the day following, Schofield was confirmed and Congress sent Stanton away with a resolution:

That the thanks of Congress are due, and are hereby tendered, to the Hon. Edwin M. Stanton for the great ability, purity, and fidelity in the cause of the country with which he has discharged the duties of Secretary of War.

The ex-Secretary went back to Steubenville for a time, ill, very tired, and financially embarrassed, but the campaign for the Presidency was already on, and he was horrified at the sight of Horatio Seymour, one of the kings of the peace-with-the-Confederacy movement, running on the Democratic ticket. Stanton took the stump for Grant and spent himself unsparingly, was delighted with the result of the election, and then became very ill with something that seems to have been a combination of his old asthma with a worn-out heart. He conducted a few legal cases during 1869 to retrieve his financial status, including one in which the judge came to hear him make his argument from his bed. On December 16 there fell a vacancy in the Supreme Court; 38 senators and 118 members of the House petitioned Grant to give the place to Stanton. The nomination was sent in four days later and was confirmed by the Senate without even reference to a committee. Too late; on December 23, 1869, Stanton died.

APPENDIX

The Controversies

I

THE RIGGED REAPER, 1856

FRANK Abial Flower, who produced a biography of Stanton
that is a model of pains taken—for he personally interviewed
or wrote to practically every human being who ever had anything to do with his subject—tells a story about the McCormick Reaper case that has since been much repeated. There was
a certain Colonel William P. Wood in Washington, Flower
says, a mechanical expert who had made many of Manny's
models; a man of high ingenuity and low morals. When the
reaper case was due before the United States Supreme Court,
this foxy colonel went down into the valley of Virginia,
where McCormick had originally operated, and bought from
a farmer there an old McCormick reaper, made before the
1847 patents. It had a curved divider, like the later McCormick
and the Manny. Wood got a blacksmith to hammer the divider out straight, then treated it with salt and vinegar to give
it the rusty appearance of having been in that shape all the
time, then took it to Washington to be filed with the exhibits
in the case, as proof positive that there existed an early type
of divider, which McCormick and Manny had independently
modified. This exhibit, Flower says, won the case.

Wood apparently told the story on himself, as Flower
quotes him directly, at the same time quoting him as absolv-
ing Stanton from any part in the fraud, except to realize the
supreme importance of the exhibit when it was presented.

But was it important? Wood's doctored reaper (if there was

457

a doctored reaper—no one else mentions it) made no appearance in the Circuit Court at Cincinnati, where Stanton had already won his case without it. For that matter, Justice Grier, when he wrote the decision which was the unanimous opinion of the Supreme Court, never even mentioned the "old" straight divider. The decision of the lower court was sustained on grounds that had nothing to do with the shape of the divider.

The conclusion seems inescapable that Colonel Wood was telling the story of what he would like to have happened rather than what did happen.

II

STANTON THE TRAITOR,
1 8 6 0

In August, 1865, Montgomery Blair made a speech at Clarksville, Missouri. He was supporting President Johnson's Reconstruction program, and used the occasion for indulging in the American sport of blackguarding the opposition. So he told a story:

Mr. Stanton, then Attorney-General, was in full sympathy with the leaders in Congress who dragged the south into rebellion. He met Senator Brown of Mississippi, at the door of the Supreme Court, as he passed from the hall of the Senate after taking leave of it as a secessionist forever. He encouraged him, told him he was right; that it was the only course to save the south; firmness would give all he asked. This is proved by Mr. Brown, former Senator from Mississippi, who mentioned it at the time to the Hon. James E. Rollins of Missouri. Mr. Saulsbury, Senator from Delaware, by a resolution offered in the Senate last winter, proposed to substantiate it before a committee of that body, but the committee was not granted. I have been assured by one of his colleagues in Buchanan's cabinet that in his intercourse with his associates of that ilk he was most violent in denouncing any attempt at coercing the south to maintain the Union by force and continued his denunciations till he entered Mr. Lincoln's cabinet.

Now, aside from the grammar of this effusion, which leaves one in some perplexity as to which "he" is referred to at various points, it is a highly questionable story. It rests wholly upon the assertions of Brown of Mississippi, one of the fire-eating wing of the Southern party, the same Brown who at the Charleston Democratic Convention of 1860, offered the resolution guaranteeing slavery in the territories. Brown told his tale in the Confederate Senate on January 30, 1865, when Stanton was the enemy Secretary of War, a circumstance not exactly calculated to vouch for the disinterested accuracy of what he was saying.

The *New York Herald* picked up the tale from the Richmond papers, whereupon Senator Saulsbury of Delaware (an anti-Lincoln Democrat who did everything he could to embarrass the administration) moved to investigate the charge. The resolution never came to a vote; it could not even find a seconder, the whole matter being treated as too silly to be worth attention. The Honorable James E. Rollins never confirmed it. Stanton's colleague in Buchanan's Cabinet who, Blair said, described him as violent in denouncing the coercion of the South, was not mentioned by name and could never be found. There were found Stanton letters during the period between his seats in the two Cabinets, in which he let the Lincoln administration have it with both barrels—but it was not for coercing the South; it was for failing to apply the coercion quicker and harder. Moreover, the story is inherently unlikely in view of Stanton's statements about Southern aggression at the time he was in politics. Certainly nothing had happened to make him shift so violently to the other side.

There was also found Albert G. Riddle, Republican congressman from Ohio, who wanted Lincoln to take Stanton into his Cabinet before the inauguration. "I found him to be heart and soul against the conspirators," said Riddle to the incoming President, "that he fully understands their movements and was ready and anxious to defeat their plots." One night Stanton shook hands as he bade Riddle farewell, with: "Stand firm, you have committed no blunder yet."

III

THE BLACK MEMORANDUM
AND THE ECLIPSE
OF FLOYD, 1860

This is a controversy chiefly because Buchanan and Black made one of it.

On February 9, 1862, the *London Observer* printed a brief article:

In February, Major Anderson, commanding Fort Moultrie, Charleston harbor, finding his position endangered, passed his garrison, by a prompt and brilliant movement, over to the stronger fortress of Sumter, whereupon Mr. Floyd, Secretary of War, much excited, called upon the President to say that Major Anderson had violated express orders and thereby seriously compromised him (Floyd), and that unless the Major was immediately remanded to Fort Moultrie, he should resign the War Office.

The Cabinet was assembled directly.

Mr. Buchanan, explaining the embarrassment of the Secretary of War, remarked that the act of Major Anderson would occasion exasperation to the South. He had told Mr. Floyd that, as the government was strong, forbearance toward erring brethren might win them back to their allegiance, and that the officer might be ordered back.

After an ominous silence, the President asked how the suggestion struck the Cabinet.

Mr. Stanton, just now called to the War Office, but then Attorney-General, answered; "That course, Mr. President, ought certainly to be regarded as most liberal towards erring brethren, but while one member of your Cabinet has fraudulent acceptances for millions of dollars afloat, and while the confidential clerk of another—himself in South Carolina teaching rebellion—has just stolen $900,000 from the Indian Trust Fund, the experiment of ordering Major Anderson back to Moultrie would be dangerous. But if you intend to try it, before it is done, I beg you will accept my resignation."

"And mine, too," added the Secretary of State, Mr. Black.

"And mine also," said the Postmaster General, Mr. Holt.

"And mine, too," followed the Secretary of the Treasury, General Dix.

This of course opened the bleared eyes of the President, and the meeting resulted in the acceptance of Mr. Floyd's resignation.

The item was signed "T.W.," and there never was any doubt that it came from the hand of the oleaginous Thurlow Weed, who was then in London. Buchanan, who obviously could not be expected to take the references to his unheroic part and "bleared eyes" lying down, attacked it at once: first on the ground that some member of the Cabinet had violated the secrecy in which its meetings are supposed to be held, and then because it was not true. "Had such a scene transpired in my Cabinet, they should not have held office fifteen minutes." He seemed to feel that the members of his Cabinet should have contradicted the story as soon as it appeared. It apparently did not occur to him that if the story were untrue, no Cabinet secrets had been exposed.

Only Black offered a contradiction, in a personal letter to Buchanan, which pronounced Weed's story "sheer fabrication made out of whole cloth." About a year later, Augustus Schell of New York, who had been Collector of the Port in that city during the Buchanan administration, and who beat off a raiding party of the Covode committee, wrote to all the members of the Buchanan Cabinet, saying he did not believe the "slanderous" story, and asking for a true account of what went on at the historic meeting.

Thompson and Floyd were by this time citizens of the Confederacy and could not reply; Toucey, Thomas, Stanton, and Holt did not. Black replied that he could hardly oblige with an account of the Cabinet meeting "at present. The circumstances set out with precision would, I suppose, fill a moderate volume and anything short of a full account would probably do wrong to the subject. Besides, I am not convinced that the truth would be received now with public favor, or even with toleration." But "Major Anderson passed his garrison to Fort Sumter not in February 1861 but in December 1860. General Dix was not a member of the Cabinet—the real cause of Floyd's retirement from office had no connection with that affair. Mr. Stanton made no such speech as that put into his mouth by T. W., or any other speech inconsistent with the most perfect respect for all his colleagues and for the President. Neither Mr. Stanton nor Mr. Holt ever spoke to the President about resigning upon any contingency whatever, before the incoming of the New Administration."

Schell passed this missive along to Buchanan, who was extremely displeased with it, since, after hinting that there was a good deal of fire behind Weed's smoke, it merely picked out the obvious factual errors in date and in including Dix in the Cabinet at the time. Ten years later, when Stanton was safely dead, Black denounced the *Observer* story as a "pure and perfectly baseless fabrication."

Eight years later still, the old Judge gave the *Philadelphia Press* a copy of the "indissoluble Union" Memorandum of December 30, with the statement that he was its sole author, as well as of the early December memorandum, holding that "The Union is necessarily perpetual." At the same time, he said that Stanton had approved his November 20 opinion that force could not be used in a state where no federal marshals or judges existed "with extravagance and undeserved laudation." Stanton also praised the Presidential message of December 3.

This impressive series of denials and assertions is somewhat damaged by the fact that between December, 1860, and August, 1881, Black had become a peculiarly violent anti-Stanton man for reasons quite unconnected with what went on in Buchanan's Cabinet—and Black was a man who, when he hated anyone, hated him all over. More damaging to Black's assertion was the fact that the copy of the Memorandum of December 30 that went to the *Press* was in Stanton's handwriting. When this was called to Black's attention, he said it was because Stanton copied off the memo; he did not explain why Stanton should have made the copy and then given it to him.

It is also very hard to get over the fact that the two memoranda express opinions about the maintenance of the Union and the existing federal powers for suppressing insurrection within the states, which are fundamentally at variance with the Presidential message and Black's opinion of November 20. Indeed, when the December 30 memorandum asked Buchanan to take out the phrase about "coercing a state by force of arms to remain in the Union, a power which I do not believe the Constitution has conferred on Congress," it was a specific repudiation of both the opinion and the message.

There was no change in circumstance to bring about this change of heart except the emergence of Stanton. There is also the literary evidence that the two memoranda came from Stanton instead of Black. Plenty of the latter's writing has survived; it is solemn, balanced, repetitious, with very long sentences and occasional attacks of quainting, the style of a judicial decision. There is nothing in it like the short, hard-hitting sentences, the bold statements habitually used by Stanton, and which mark both the memoranda.

Finally, there is contemporary testimony of considerable weight. On the very day the December 30 memorandum was prepared, Stanton wrote to General William Robinson of Pittsburgh: "We are enveloped in a great deal of dust and fog, but the smudge is not so thick that I cannot distinctly discern treason all around us. Judge Black and myself have been dumbfounded by a meeting of the President, as President, with the so-called South Carolina commissioners. At first we agreed to resign at once, but after going carefully over the subject, thought it better to state our objections or views in writing before taking any step that might later be considered precipitate. Justice Black is closer to the President than myself and exercises a great deal of influence over him. He will present the written objections which I have just prepared, and stand by for the purpose of extricating the President from his present peril. If he shall refuse to recede, it seems to me there is no escape for Black, Holt and myself, except resignation. I tremble to think that the administration is already semi-officially committed to the theory that South Carolina is an independent nation or 'republic' capable of negotiating treaties."

Nor does the contemporary evidence stop here. The South Carolina commissioners saw Stanton in Washington, and were not in the least pleased with what they heard from him. Two of them—Orr and Trescott—laid the whole failure of their attempt to negotiate for Sumter at the Attorney-General's door. This, of course, does not mean that the failure came about in the way set forth in Thurlow Weed's story, and it is quite certain that Black, Stanton, and Holt did not fling resignation threats across the Cabinet table. But there is contemporary evidence on the essential features of the Weed story, too.

After Stanton's death, there was found among his papers a letter. It had been written in 1863, in reply to Augustus Schell's call for information. It noted the errors in date and with regard to the presence of Dix already mentioned, commented on the fact that the *Observer* article was an obvious condensation of events covering several days, and proceeded to take up *seriatim* the main statements. It was true, said Stanton, that Floyd opened the meeting by declaring that Anderson was in Sumter contrary to orders; that when the War Secretary was driven from this position, he took the position that the government had violated its pledge. It was true that Buchanan seemed determined to order the troops back, and that Floyd and Thompson repeatedly said a pledge had been given, without drawing any contradiction from the President. It was true that Stanton brought up the embezzlement of the Indian Trust Fund during the debate, and that he had said the evacuation of the fort would be treason. Floyd had certainly resigned as a result of the failure to evacuate. That Black, Holt, and Stanton would have resigned, if the evacuation had taken place, was substantially true, but he did not remember saying so in the Cabinet. "The principal error of the *Observer* article is, perhaps, in ascribing to me more credit than is due in awakening

Mr. Buchanan to the real character of Floyd's contemplated treason."

This letter made the main line of the story more or less a question of veracity between Stanton and Black; but the matter did not stay on that basis. Of the men who had been present at the hectic Cabinet meetings, Floyd and Toucey were dead when the letter came to light, Thomas and Thompson were living in melancholy retirement, and Black had already made public his reaction to the story. The letter was accordingly carried to Holt, who said, yes, he had seen it before. Stanton brought it to him in 1863, when it was written, but after talk, he and the then Secretary of War agreed that it would be better to send no answer at all to a man who evidently wished a quarrel.

As for the content of Stanton's letter, Holt declared that everything in it was perfectly true, and a great deal more besides. He supplied details and additional quotations that had been fixed in a retentive memory by the excitement of the crisis.

Later research (by Professor Corwin of Princeton) has established beyond much doubt that Weed got his account of the affair at third hand, from a private conversation between Stanton and Colonel George McCook of Steubenville, one of his law partners; and that the story had suffered the mutilation inevitable when a tale is passed verbally for such a distance.

IV

STANTON'S APPOINTMENT,
1 8 6 2

PRACTICALLY everyone in Washington at the time, and some people outside the city, thought themselves personally responsible for Stanton's nomination as Secretary of War. General Scott thought he was the moving spirit. He was back in Washington at the time having the attorney draw a will for him—an intricate business, since he was a Virginian by birth and much of his property lay in the seceded state. He was impressed by the flame of energy that burned in the fierce little man, by his quick grasp of problems, and by his devotion to the Union, and told Lincoln this was a person he ought to have in the Cabinet.

Simon Cameron thought the appointment was substantially his; in the vague conversations of half-finished phrases in which he specialized, he had suggested to the President that he would be willing to give up his Cabinet post if allowed to name his successor, and he named Stanton, who rated as a Pennsylvanian, though long a resident of Washington. Salmon P. Chase, who had worked with Stanton in rousing antislavery sentiment in Ohio during the old days of Van Buren's Free Soil campaign, recommended the appointment, in the conviction that he would gain a powerful and effective ally in the cause of antislavery radicalism. Seward also recommended it; on the basis of their intercourse during the secession winter, he seems to have believed that Stanton was a man who could be managed. McClellan was all for the idea and told Stanton he hoped he would accept.

The fact, however, seems to be that Lincoln himself chose his man and quietly let the others think they were behind it, since the impression did no harm and made them feel good when the appointment turned out a success. As soon as it was evident that Cameron would have to go, the President wanted to replace him with a prominent Union Democrat, preferably one who had been associated with the previous administration. It would place before the world, as it could be placed in no other way, the assurance that the war was not a party affair, but was being conducted by a united North.

In addition a reputation for incorruptibility was peculiarly necessary because of the doubts about Cameron in this respect; so was intimate acquaintance with the law of contract. In the McCormick Reaper case, Lincoln had become personally acquainted with Stanton's wonderful capacity for hard work and absorption of detail, and these were qualities also needed in the War Office.

On the showing of Carl Sandburg, who devoted much research to the point, Lincoln was rather inclined to give the appointment to Joseph Holt, Stanton's fellow Cabinet-member in the last days of the Buchanan administration. But Stanton met the requirements equally well, and when everyone around the President began speaking for him, Lincoln was quite amenable. It was a reputation appointment, not one based on personal contact. The two men had not met since the McCormick Reaper case, and though Lincoln apparently did not know about the remarks his new Secretary had been making to McClellan and Buchanan, it is not likely that would have been allowed to make any difference.

Joseph B. Doyle in "In Memoriam: Edwin McMasters Stanton" on this point quotes a lawyer who had been one of the attorneys in the McCormick Reaper case without naming him, but in a context which makes it clear that he is talking about George Harding. Harding called on Lincoln just before the appointment and quotes the President as saying to him: "I am about to do an act for which I owe no explanation to any man, woman or child in the United States except you. You know the War Department has demonstrated the great necessity for a Secretary of Mr. Stanton's great ability, and I have made up my mind to sit down on all my pride, it may be a portion of my self respect, and appoint him to the place."

One point deserves notice because it has been brought up repeatedly by a whole school of pseudo-historians who maintain McClellan was a great and grievously wronged man, and therefore find it necessary to tear down Stanton. This is the Plot Theory, first stated by McClellan himself in "McClellan's Own Story": "He climbed on my shoulders only for the purpose of throwing me down." In the biographical preface to that volume, W. C. Prime develops the theory to full flower and applies the colors. According to it, a quick and successful end to the war via McClellan's generalship—which was neither quick nor successful when the General actually took the field —would have been profoundly distasteful to the Radicals. (Bennett of the *Herald* seems to have been the originator of this part of the theory.) Therefore Chase and Stanton formed a "secret alliance" to get the latter into the War Office so he could hamper McClellan and prolong the conflict. The two men in concert succeeded in pulling the wool over Lincoln's eyes and even, for a time, over McClellan's own.

Now Stanton said very little to McClellan about Lincoln that he had not already said to Buchanan, and there is not the slightest evidence that he was trying to deceive anybody about his sentiments toward the President. Also, aside from the fact that Chase was not Stanton's only supporter for the appointment, one thing very clear is that the War Secretary had no hand whatever in obtaining it for himself. He had just made arrangements for a law partnership with S. L. M. Barlow, and was about to go to New York to look up living quarters and an office, when there came to him a verbal message asking him not to leave Washington, as the President wished to appoint him to an important office. "Tell the President that I will accept," said Stanton, "if no other pledge than that I will help to strangle treason shall be exacted." He told McClellan that "the only possible inducement was that he might have it in his power to aid me by devoting all his energy and ability to my assistance, and that together we could soon bring the war to a close" ("McClellan's Own Story"). The plot theory has to argue that both statements were just duplicity on Stanton's part.

The only person not very well satisfied with the appointment was James Buchanan. To his niece and White House hostess, Harriet Lane, he wrote:

Well, our friend Stanton has been appointed Secretary of War. What are Mr. Stanton's qualifications for that, the greatest and most responsible office in the world, I cannot judge. I appointed him Attorney-General when Judge Black was raised to the State Department, because his professional business and that of the Judge, especially in the California land cases, were so intimately connected that he could proceed in the Supreme Court without delay. He is a sound, clear-headed, persevering and practical lawyer and is quite eminent, especially in patent cases. He is not well versed in public, commercial or constitutional law because his professional duties as a country lawyer never led him to make those his study. I believe he is a perfectly honest man and in that respect differs from his immediate predecessor. He never took much part in Cabinet councils, because his office did not require it. He was always on my side and flattered me *ad nauseam*.

Stanton certainly did apply flattery to people he was working with—it was part of his technique of personal relations—but the closing lines of this communiqué would carry more weight if they were not preceded by the reference to Stanton as a "country lawyer," who did not understand commercial or constitutional cases. He had been a city lawyer for fifteen years, and commercial and constitutional law were precisely the fields in which he left permanent marks on American jurisprudence, as Buchanan had every reason to know.

V

BALL'S BLUFF, 1861

IT is hard for anyone at all familiar with the operation of armies to avoid the conclusion that the Committee on the Conduct of the War crucified the wrong man for the Ball's Bluff disaster. The officer who should have been placed in arrest was not Charles P. Stone but George B. McClellan.

He sent McCall's division up the Virginia side of the river as far as Dranesville to cover some mapping operations. On October 20, while McCall was at that point, McClellan telegraphed Stone, who was at Poolesville, Maryland, some distance north of the Potomac:

General McCall occupied Dranesville yesterday, and is still there. Will send out heavy reconnaissance to-day from that point. The General desires that you will keep a good look-out upon Leesburg, to see if this movement has the effect to drive them away. Perhaps a slight demonstration on your part would have the effect to move them.

Now if this means anything, it means that McCall, who had a big division, was going to behave aggressively toward the camp and entrenchments at Leesburg, and McClellan wanted Stone to co-operate, at least to the extent of finding out where the enemy was and what he was doing. The dispatch reached Stone at 11:00 in the morning; that afternoon he sent patrols to the south bank, then reported to McClellan:

Made a feint of crossing at this place this afternoon, and at the same time started a reconnoitering party toward Leesburg from Harrison's Island. The enemy's pickets retired to entrenchments. Reports of reconnoitering parties not yet received. I have means of crossing 125 men once in ten minutes at each of two points.

That is, Stone had made contact with the Confederate outposts, but had neither developed their strength nor their exact position, had not been able to "keep a good look-out on Leesburg," nor had he made "a slight demonstration." He had not yet carried out his orders, because the Confederates in front of him were a little too strong for the parties he had sent. The message carries a clear intimation that Stone intends to go ahead with the business. His means of crossing would enable him to get nearly his whole force over in a couple of hours, and he could expect to be helped by McCall from Dranesville, which was only 12 miles away on a good road—an easy march during the time it would take to pass Stone's troops to the south bank.

That evening McClellan summoned McCall back to the lines of the main army, without either informing Stone that he had done so, or countermanding the orders of the previous day for a thorough reconnaissance and "perhaps a demonstration." October 21 accordingly found Baker's brigade under attack by the Confederates, while McCall spent the day marching away from the battle. In "McClellan's Own Story," he says: "I did not direct him [Stone] to cross, nor did I intend that he should cross the river in force for the purpose of fighting."

McClellan never intended anybody to do anything for the purpose of fighting, which was foreign to his nature; but if he did not intend Stone to cross, he must have expected that officer to "keep a sharp look-out on Leesburg" by mental telepathy.

The Confederate commander at the spot, who was General N. G. Evans of the Seventh Brigade of the I Corps, reported locating McCall's force at Dranesville on the twentieth, and taking a "strong position" behind a creek, where he expected McCall to attack him on the twenty-first. Early that morning,

Baker's brigade of Stone crossed the river and got in behind Evans, but the Confederate merely swung round and attacked Baker from two directions. He was evidently under no apprehensions about McCall, for he devoted his whole attention to Baker, and his report does not mention the Dranesville group after the evening of the twentieth.

McClellan, however, managed to duck any responsibility when the investigating committee—either out of determination to get Stone or from lack of expertise—asked the unfortunate General the wrong questions. They inquired whether he had any orders from McClellan to make a reconnaissance in force toward Leesburg on the twenty-first, and he honestly replied that he had taken that step on his own responsibility. Of course, he had no such orders for the twenty-first; it would have been an outrageous interference with the commander at the front to have given them anew after the orders of the day before. Any other commander than McClellan would have thought Stone slothful or timorous if he had failed to follow through his orders of the twentieth.

The fact is that McClellan blundered, then shifted the onus to a subordinate already under fire for something else. He never made any effort to clear Stone or any protest against his arrest.

VI

THE 9TH OF MARCH, 1862

SOME remarkable transactions took place at the White House on the morning of March 9, 1862, when the news arrived that a Confederate ironclad (which everyone present wrote down as the *Merrimac*, though her original name had been spelled differently and the Confederates themselves called her *Virginia*) had destroyed the sloop-of-war *Cumberland* and the frigate *Congress* in Hampton Roads, with the loss of over 300 men. The account of what happened rests almost wholly on Gideon Welles's diary, and it has been quoted or otherwise used so frequently in producing pen portraits of Stanton and his character that it deserves rather close attention.

When he got the news, Welles says, he hurried to the White House. Stanton was already present, much excited, the President hardly less so. "He could not deliberate," reported the frosty Welles of Lincoln; had been to the Navy Yard, where he received only the coldest of comfort from Admiral Dahlgren. Seward soon came, very despondent. Dahlgren and Quartermaster-General Meigs, who presently joined the discussion were "by nature and training cautious, not to say timid"; were powerless to do anything, and had been infected by Stanton's fears.

As for the War Secretary, he paced the floor with whiskers bobbing, and shot out bursts of words. The *Merrimac*, he said, would destroy *seriatim* every naval vessel; could lay every city on the coast under contribution; could take Fortress Monroe. McClellan's purpose to advance by the peninsula must be abandoned, and Burnside's small army in the North Carolina sounds would be captured. Probably the *Merrimac* would come up the Potomac and disperse Congress. "Why, sir, it is not unlikely that we shall have from one of her guns a cannonball in this room before we leave it." What vessel or means do we have to prevent her from doing whatever she pleases?

Welles, says Welles, retained a glacial calm. The *Merrimac*, he said, could hardly visit Washington and New York at the same time; he had no apprehension of her doing either, as a matter of fact. Burnside and his forces in the sounds were safe, because the ship's draft of water was such that she could not approach them. The Ericsson battery, *Monitor*, had arrived at Hampton Roads, and Mr. Welles had confidence in her ability to resist, and he hoped, to overcome the *Merrimac*.

Seward, beginning to revive a little under these reassurances, remarked that Welles's statement about the *Merrimac*'s draft of water gave him the first relief he had experienced. But Stanton demanded how many guns the *Monitor* had, receiving the news that there were only two "with mingled incredulity and contempt. To me there was something inexpressibly ludicrous in the wild, frantic talk, action, and rage of Stanton as he ran from room to room, sat down and jumped up after writing a few words, swung his arms, scolded and raved."

The War Secretary dispatched telegrams to the governors of seacoast states that they should be ready to obstruct major harbor entrances with chains of rafts. Later in the day he ordered Admiral Dahlgren at the Navy Yard to make ready some sixty rock-laden canal boats to obstruct the Potomac. This produced a fine row when the Admiral, in the course of the evening, wired Welles that he had the boats and was now loading them, asking whether this were in conformity with the wishes of the Navy Department.

Of course not, said Welles, and on Monday morning took up the question with the President while Stanton was there. Stanton "with affected calmness, but his voice trembling with emotion" asked if Welles had prevented the boats being prepared and loaded. Welles said he had given no orders for the boats to be prepared. Well, said Stanton, I have—to Meigs and Dahlgren, and with the approval of the President. Lincoln confirmed this, remarking that on the previous day he had felt that something should be done for the security of the capital, and even if it did no good, no harm could come of the boat project.

Of course, by the time of this discussion, the *Monitor* had fought the *Virginia*, the Confederate ship was no longer a menace, and the stone-boats had become what Lincoln later called "Stanton's navy—as useless as the paps of a man to a suckling child. They may be of some show to amuse the child, but they are good for nothing for service."

Although the matter had become academic "the passages were sharp and pungent," and the total impression given by Welles is that on both days everyone except himself, but most especially Stanton, was frightened half to death. That was the word he used.

Now Welles bears a very high reputation as a witness of events; but it is also worth noticing that he is not quite so accurate at interpreting what he saw and heard, and that the diary account of the events of the ninth of March is obviously intensified by his approval of himself as the most collected man in the room.

For example, "cautious, not to say timid" is a rather strange description of John A. Dahlgren, the man who led the monitors into action against the forts of Charleston daily for a whole two months—personally flying his flag in ships that were hit four or five times a day by heavy shot. Nor was Seward accused of being a timorous man on any other occasion, in spite of his hesitancy of manner. And Lincoln's excitement, so great that he could not deliberate, did not prevent him from conducting some very serious and sensible deliberations with Stanton and McClellan later in the same day, when the news from Manassas arrived.

Nor did anyone report Stanton indulging in "wild, frantic talk" on other occasions, even in the dark days of the dispatches from Second Bull Run, Fredericksburg, and Chickamauga.

He undoubtedly did a good deal of buzzing around; when things were going wrong, he always did. He wanted immediate remedial action of some kind, and the inability of the others to think of anything that could be done, the bland calm with which Welles awaited events, must have been galling. So he did something himself, the telegrams to the governors and the futile canal boats.

He did more. He called for reports on the status of Fortress Monroe, and found that it had only sixty days' provisions and only two guns that stood any chance of damaging the *Virginia*—a 12-inch and a 15-inch, the latter not mounted. He ordered both guns mounted at once, and provisions and munitions put into the place.

These were perfectly reasonable precautions, and most of the other things he did that day were dictated by reason. To say that he was quivering with fright is a misreading of character (of which Welles was often guilty), and to accept the account in Welles's diary as thoroughly indicative is to say that account was all true. It was only all true except the adjectives.

VII

McCLELLAN'S FIGURES,
1862

THE actual figures in McClellan's return for the defense of Washington, while he was in the peninsula, were:

1. In Washington and forts	22,000	
To be sent to Manassas	—4,000	
Left in Washington		18,000
2. To be at Manassas:		
The 4,000 from Washington	4,000	
Troops now in Pennsylvania	3,500	
Troops guarding railways in Maryland	3,359	
		10,859
3. To be at Washington:		
Abercrombie's division and Geary's force	7,780	7,780
4. To be in the Shenandoah Valley:		
Blenker's division	10,028	
Banks's corps	19,687	
Cavalry	3,652	
Railroad guards	2,100	
		35,467
5. Forces on the Lower Potomac		1,350
		73,456

Actually, the forces in Washington and its forts were nowhere near what McClellan said. Nobody knows where he got the figures; certainly not from the commander of those forces, who reported much less. Moreover, if they were in Washington, they were not at Manassas; and they were all untrained, and partly unarmed recruits, as Wadsworth complained.

The facts that part of the troops listed were in Pennsylvania, that part were guarding railways in Maryland, and still another part on the lower Potomac, speak for themselves. How were they a part of the Washington defenses?

Abercrombie's division and Geary's force belonged to Banks's corps, and were thus counted twice. Blenker's division, as mentioned in the text, was in transit. The cavalry listed were all on outpost duty and not a fighting force. McClellan's own figures convict him.

VIII

DREYFUS? *1 8 6 2 – 1 8 8 6*

THE Fitz John Porter case caused a furious amount of pamphlet-
eering, which has not died down even today. It also became
heavily charged with politics, because McClellan was on the
fringes of it, and he had become a political rather than a military figure. Porter himself was in Europe on a holiday from
the Colorado mining business, in which he was quietly earning a living, when the war came to an end. As soon as the
Confederate documents were published, they demonstrated
that one of defense attorney Johnson's contentions at the trial
was perfectly correct. General Longstreet, with the major
portion of Lee's army, had in fact been in line on Jackson's
right during most of August 29, 1862, and if Porter had attempted to outflank Jackson as ordered, he would have run
head-on into a position held by Longstreet.

This information started Porter on a campaign for vindication. He appealed for a new trial, for the reversal of the former
verdict, but the man he appealed to was Andrew Johnson,
and the date he made the appeal was 1867, at which date Johnson was too busy trying to get some vindication for himself to
be bothered with obtaining any for the general. When Grant
became President, Porter tried again, but this time he made
his petition a fat pamphlet, issued to the general public. A large
part of it was devoted to ridiculing Pope and the officers of the
court-martial, and another part to a long statement from Mc-
Clellan, saying that Porter was a wronged man. This was not

exactly the way to influence Grant, an army man with an orderly mind, who believed in courts-martial as a device for ascertaining facts and did not particularly believe in McClellan. He simply ignored the matter.

Porter spent a good deal of time gathering opinions favorable to his case and, after a short interlude in New York City politics, made another assault under President Hayes. By this date all old soldiers were heroes and nothing they had done was wrong; Hayes appointed a board of inquiry, headed by General John M. Schofield, which heard 142 witnesses (why?), and on March 19, 1879, brought in a report, which not only exonerated Porter completely, but said he "had understood and appreciated the military situation," saved the Union Army from disaster on the twenty-ninth, and saved it from rout on the thirtieth. Even Grant now joined the let-bygones-be-bygones chorus, and in 1882 wrote an article, titled "An Undeserved Stigma," which was a good deal more creditable to his heart than his head, for its contents showed a close acquaintance with the report of the Schofield board and little, if any, with the proceedings of the court-martial. But Congressional action was necessary, and Congress split politically on the matter. It was not until 1886 that a bill was passed, reversing the verdict and restoring Porter to his rank in the army.

Out of this reversal there grew up a long series of countercharges, that the whole Porter trial was due to Stanton's hatred of McClellan, and that therefore he packed the court and railroaded the accused. Now the first point worth examining concerns the relative results obtained by the court-martial and the Schofield board. The board took the view that nobody should be condemned for not executing an order that could not be executed; and since it stood proved that Pope's 4:30 order was based on a misapprehension of Confederate strength and position, Porter was guiltless in not obeying it. In fact, the board thought it was meritorious of him not to obey it.

But if there is one thing perfectly clear from the trial record, it is that Porter by no means "understood and appreciated the military situation." He brought no evidence to indicate that he knew Longstreet's corps was in the path of a move toward

Jackson's flank; the only statement to that effect during the trial was made by Reverdy Johnson, and it was a rhetorical flourish. Porter never *knew* that Longstreet was there until the war was over and—a point completely neglected by the Schofield board—he made no effort to find out whether there was anyone in Longstreet's position. Nor did he mention the attack order to Division Commander Sykes, who was standing right beside him when the order came, and would have to do the attacking.

If Porter really did understand and appreciate the military situation, the case against him becomes rather graver than before. With part of an afternoon and a whole night to do it in, he made no effort to inform Pope that Longstreet was there; and on the morning of the thirtieth, it was precisely those troops of Longstreet who attacked and drove in the left flank of Pope's main body. To say that Porter knew they were there is to say that, having received from his commanding officer an order obviously based on a mistaken estimate of the enemy's strength and position, Porter left his commander in ignorance of the true facts. As for what he did to save the army from rout on the thirtieth, the Schofield board did not specify; it would be hard to.

As for the packed court and railroading charges, they are supported (in Porter's pamphlet) by charges against the members of the court. It is true that one of them was General Rufus King, whose own conduct during the battle had been distinctly peculiar; but there is only Porter's word for it that King was drunk during the whole two days, and there are the words of several other people that during part of one day, King decided to have an epileptic fit, a habit to which he was addicted. In any case, he was only one of the nine members of the court.

Of the court as a whole, Porter says that three members had become unfriendly to Stanton, three others were friendly to that Secretary or to Chase, and two were unfriendly to Porter himself; therefore (his argument apparently is) they formed a combination to convict. It is a rather bewildering line of logic, and it altogether fails to explain why Stanton, who certainly had it in his power to relieve Porter and send him home (as had been done with Frémont, Lew Wallace, Buell, and McClellan himself), should have taken the trouble to convict and cashier him. As a matter of fact, the indications are that Stanton wanted to smooth the whole thing over; repeated requests from Pope for a court of inquiry into the campaign had been refused.

Pope, Stanton, most of the members of the court, and the more vital witnesses, were dead when the Schofield board met. A good summation would be that Porter simply did not want to attack (he never did in any other battle), and found excuses for not doing so; and that he obtained his "vindication" less through justice than through longevity.

IX

A CALLING CARD FROM
MR. STEPHENS, 1863

On July 4, when every hour was bearing tidings that added to the certainty and magnitude of Meade's Gettysburg victory, there reached Washington a dispatch from the blockading squadron in the James: a small Confederate steamer had come downstream under a flag of truce from Richmond, carrying Alexander H. Stephens, Vice-President of the Confederacy, of all Southern leaders the one most likely to be *persona grata* in the North. He had a letter from Jefferson Davis, and wanted to see Lincoln personally—about the exchange of prisoners, he said. Stanton "growled and swore" when he heard of it, and joined Seward and Chase in saying that Lincoln ought to have nothing to do with the man, when the matter came up in Cabinet, and the conciliatory President wished at least to send someone down for conversations. Lincoln let the three Cabinet members talk him over when they produced the idea that Stephens' real mission had nothing to do with the ostensible one. But the incident left a little hangover of mystery, and was afterward used as supporting evidence for the charge that Stanton was unnecessarily callous about the fate of Union prisoners in Confederate hands.

Actually, the whole business did start with the prisoner-exchange question. When Stephens was in Richmond early in May, he saw a letter written by Union General David Hunter of the Department of the South, in which that officer said that unless Davis' order for the hanging of white officers commanding Negro troops were revoked, he, Hunter, was going to start executing captured slaveholders and Confederate officers. Of course, Hunter had no authority to do any such thing, and he was presently relieved of his command for having done it, but Stephens was much disturbed. When he got back to Georgia he wrote to Davis, saying something ought to be done about this. He himself would undertake a mission to do it; and while he was about it, he would discuss a negotiated peace, on the basis of recognition of "the sovereignty of the states" by the North. The moment for such a peace negotiation looked highly propitious, for Hooker had just been roundly beaten at Chancellorsville, Rosecrans and Bragg were making no impression on each other in Tennessee, and Vicksburg seemed immune to Grant's efforts. At the very least (it seemed to the Confederate leaders), the news of such a mission, allowed to leak out in the proper quarters, would strengthen the peace party in the North.

Davis took his time about making up his mind, and it was June 19 when he telegraphed Stephens to come to Richmond. He found the Vice-President had grown lukewarm about the mission plan. Hunter was clearly going to execute nobody. Lee's presence north of the Potomac, Stephens thought, would so stir up the Northern war party that nothing could be accomplished. There were the long discussions and persuasions that usually accompanied political decisions in the Confederacy before Stephens consented. The result was that he did not reach the blockade line until July 4, and then without any real intention of discussing prisoners; did not, in fact, carry authority to do so. He was there to discuss one thing only, a negotiated peace, and if Lincoln, Stanton, or anyone else had talked to him, he would have confined himself to that subject. But it would clearly have been a conversation in the back room, in view of the facts that Vicksburg was no longer immune to Grant, and Lee had just been crushingly defeated.

X

PRISONERS OF WAR, 1864

THE very idea that Northern prisoners were any worse treated in the South than Confederate prisoners in the North has caused so much hair tearing that it is pertinent to give the statistics:

	Union	Confederate
Died in prison	26,249	26,774
Released on oath		71,889
Exchanged and paroled	154,059	350,367
Illegally paroled	1,097	
Escaped	2,696	2,098
Joined Confederate army	3,170	
Joined Union army		5,452
Unaccounted for		3,084
Recaptured	17	
	187,288	459,664

There is no doubt some duplication here, as in the case of the prisoners Grant took and paroled at Vicksburg, who were later captured again while fighting in the Confederate ranks; not entirely by their own fault, it may be noted, since most of the Southern states passed severe draft acts, which took no account of paroles already given. But the really significant fact is that although the Confederacy held less than half as many prisoners as the Union, almost exactly the same number died in prison, or to put it otherwise, prison life in the South was twice as noxious as in the North.

This was not because the Union men were in prison longer, either; some of the biggest Union hauls came very early in the game, at Fort Donelson and in the operations at New Orleans and along the Carolina coast. The Union prisons were no rose gardens, as the figures demonstrate, but they were nothing like the places that killed off one man out of every seven confined.

XI

THE McKIBBEN CASE,
NOVEMBER, 1864

THE case of Jere F. McKibben is one of the most puzzling in
the whole Stanton saga because the evidence is tainted. It
comes from a single source, and goes like this: Governor Curtin of Pennsylvania, who certainly could not be accused of being anti-Union, wanted McKibben to represent the Democratic party in the counting of the soldier vote of his state, and
sent A. K. McClure to ask him to serve. McKibben said: "Why,
Stanton would put me in Old Capitol Prison before I was
there a day. He hates our family for no other reason I know of
than that my father was one of his best friends in Pittsburgh
when he needed a friend."

McClure said he did not believe Stanton would interfere
with a Pennsylvania state commissioner, and McKibben went
down, only to telegraph two days later that he was in fact
in Old Capitol Prison. McClure at once called on Lincoln,
found him very distressed, calling Stanton's act a "stupid
blunder," and being ready to discharge McKibben on parole.
McClure said he did not want parole for the man, but full
exoneration; Lincoln replied that it did not seem fair to go so
far without giving Stanton a chance to explain, made out a
parole for McKibben, and handed it over.

The next morning McClure was in the President's office
when Stanton came in, very angry and exploding: "Well, Mc-

Clure, what damned rebel are you here to get out of trouble this morning?"

McClure: "Your arrest of McKibben was a cowardly act; you know McKibben was guiltless of any offense and you did it to gratify a brutal hatred—" with much more of the same order, and another request for an unconditional discharge.

Stanton, pacing the floor: "I decline to discharge McKibben from his parole. You can make formal application for it if you choose, and I will consider and decide it."

McClure: "I don't know what McKibben will do, but if I were Jere McKibben, as sure as there is a God I would crop your ears before I left Washington."

Stanton thereupon walked out of the room without saying anything more and Lincoln spoke: "Well, McClure, you didn't get very far with Stanton, did you? But he'll come out all right; let the matter rest."

The application for full discharge was made, and Stanton dismissed it as not consistent with the public service.

This is the story. It has been used in building word portraits of Stanton almost as often as Welles's account of what happened on the day of the news of the fight in Hampton Roads (see Appendix VI), and it is subject to some of the same criticisms. In the first place, it is wholly McClure's story; nobody else mentions a word about it, and McClure did not publish it until well after the death of the only two men who could have contradicted any part of it. Even without anything else, it is subject to a certain amount of discount at source, for by the time he wrote it, McClure's opinion of Stanton had solidified into an active detestation over the Reconstruction issue, which found the two men in opposite camps. In the second place, the literary style arouses a certain amount of suspicion; did McClure really describe the arrest as a cowardly act dictated by brutal hatred, and say that McKibben ought to cut Stanton's ears off without drawing any more reply than that he gives? It all sounds rather like the remarks people wish they had made after the close of an altercation in which they have not come off quite as well as they wished.

Also the behavior of Lincoln is curious. "Stupid blunder"

is a most unusual phrase to hear from him, and when he did find anything was a blunder, he corrected it at once and very completely. There are too many cases of his releasing prisoners, granting pardons and discharges over Stanton's head, even when the Secretary was legally correct, for any comment to be necessary on this point. Yet here is a case in which Stanton is represented as palpably wrong in law and justice, as having acted out of pure personal spite, yet the President refuses to grant full exoneration, to clear a man's name. "Let the matter rest."

As to any reason why Stanton should have hated the McKibben family, there is simply nothing in the record. McKibben's own story, as repeated by McClure, clearly will not wash, even as sarcasm; when Stanton went to Pittsburgh, it was as a partner of Judge Shaler, and with abundant backing. He stood in no need of either money or the kind of patronage implied, and proceeded to do everything under his own steam. The contact with the McKibbens must have been very tenuous. There is no record of it among the historical and genealogical societies of Pennsylvania.

XII

THE CONTROVERSIES IN GENERAL

OF course, the Reconstruction program was a ghastly failure after the Radicals, with Johnson somewhat suppressed by the impeachment trial, pushed through the Fifteenth Amendment giving the Negro the vote everywhere, and made its ratification a condition of the reacceptance of the seceded states. It is not intended to defend or to palliate that manner of Reconstruction here. Even to Thad Stevens it was the alternative, the worser and more punitive program. After the old Jacobin of Lancaster failed to put through his confiscation plan, he opted for a Reconstruction under the sword of ten years' duration, during which the former slaves would be educated to the use of the vote. It is not improbable that even this would have worked better than the plan actually adopted. Reconstruction as it worked out, with its carpetbaggers, scalawags, and ignorant Negro legislators, was only what he told the South it would get if it did not co-operate in the acceptance of more reasonable terms.

But it is incorrect to blame Stanton for the failure, or to picture him as a member of a savage conspiracy to repress the Southern whites. He expressed himself with sufficient vigor about secession on various occasions, but as an advocate, accustomed by a lifetime of training to presenting his case in the most forceful terms possible. The words he used and the acts he performed were often in some contrast with each other. In the spring of 1864 Representative Grinnell of Iowa came to him with a request for the promotion to brigadier of a local colonel named E. W. Rice. Stanton said: "What we want is victories, not brigadiers," and when Grinnell declared he would take the matter to Lincoln, added that if the request were granted, he would resign. Grinnell did go to Lincoln, got a flat order that Rice should be promoted and took it to the War Department. Stanton pursed up his lips, tossed the paper into the waste-basket, said: "I resign," and went on writing. But as Grinnell shifted his feet in some embarrassment, he discovered that the Secretary was grinning at him and saying: "Wait, Mr. Grinnell, come over and take dinner with me"—and across the desk handed him Rice's commission. Now this was not the act of a grim conspirator.

In fact, it was the act of an executive, who did his best to influence decisions, but once the decisions were taken, one way or another, cheerfully took the steps to make them as effective as possible. He was not a great leader; he was a man who followed the best leadership he could find in the direction that came nearest his ideals. Nor, in spite of all the stories, was he an unkindly man. The orphans he kept around the house would attest that if there were nothing else. But there is much else. As soon as he learned that the captured Jefferson Davis had been placed in irons, he ordered the irons to be removed. And there is the Worthington case. The son of a D. B. Worthington was in a military hospital, dying of gangrene; the young man's mother engaged a physician who removed him to a private home, whereupon the military surgeon, much incensed at this violation of procedure, ordered him moved back. The father wired Stanton, who instantly issued a War Department order that young Worthington should be left where his mother had placed him. After he unexpectedly recovered the parents came to thank Stanton; the Secretary put them aside with: "Yes, I love to lay a heavy hand on those fellows when they need it."

The combination of fierceness of manner exercised on the side of the general humanities is so peculiar, and so unusual, that it is not altogether surprising that its essential nature es-

caped both contemporaries and later observers. But what has
this to do with the most criticized period and series of actions
—Reconstruction? This: Stanton, as an executive, had the
choice of only two policies to execute. From what is known
of the Reconstruction plan he submitted to the Cabinet on
April 14, 1865, and in a revised form to the Congressional leaders two days later, it is probable that his views were not too
different from those of Lincoln, or even those of Johnson in
the beginning, about setting up state governments in the hands
of men who could take a test oath without committing perjury.

Both Presidents fully expected that those new governments
would take Congress off their necks by adopting a form of
limited Negro suffrage. Louisiana and Arkansas disappointed
Lincoln in this respect earlier, but he apparently still had hopes
for them, and it is probably idle to speculate whether the
other states might not have done better, even pulling the first
two into line, if the business had been managed by the firm and
clever hands of Lincoln. It is hard to see Lincoln, for example,
permitting the passage of the Black Laws, which were so
effective in convincing the North that the intransigence of the
Southerners in the matter of prisoner-of-war exchanges was
still in determined existence, that the Confederacy had accepted
defeat on the right to secede, but was still refusing to make any
genuine change in its social and economic system.

In this conviction the North was perfectly correct; Dixie
is still making a fighting retreat on the issue today. In accepting the Southern attitude Johnson was behaving like an old-
fashioned strict constructionist, who did not believe that the
Constitution gave the federal government any right so to enter
the municipal affairs of a state as to determine the qualifications
of its voters or the guarantees that should be given its citizens.
This is probably an error in view of the Bill of Rights, but the
important thing in the Reconstruction period was not so much
the legal right as the practical effect. By clinging unshakeably
to this strict construction, by his refusal to compromise at any
point, Johnson set before Stanton, among others, an absolutely
clear-cut choice: (1) accept the Johnson governments, which
were indicated by the evidence as still Confederate on the Ne-

gro question, and which, if accepted, could almost certainly count on enough help from the northern Democrats to freeze the Negro in his status as a subcitizen; (2) follow the Stevens-Sumner line, and make the Negro a voter without any period of tutelage; (3) no Reconstruction at all, military rule for an indefinite period until things had died down.

A man of Stanton's general feeling for the humanities could hardly accept the first choice; a man of his religious feeling could not. A man of his temperament, an executive, desirous of some progress, some accomplishment, could hardly accept the third. But so far from being the rabid Radical that he is frequently pictured, the record shows that he did a not ineffective much to make the Radical program milder. His denunciation of the disfranchising section of the Fourteenth Amendment in the serenade speech was the key event in the defeat of that section. Through his control of the army and the Freedmen's Bureau he was in a position to make Stevens' confiscation program a practical fact, at least on an experimental basis; he did nothing of the kind. He was so definitely opposed to the Stevens program of occupying the South for ten years that the project never developed any steam—though it is fair to say that Stanton was not the only one who looked askance at that one.

Yet even before the fall of 1865, when the Black Laws made it clear that if the Negro were not protected from Washington he would not be protected at all, long before the rejection of the Fourteenth Amendment made it evident that the South did not wish to have the Negro protected from Washington, a highly practical consideration appeared. At the conference on the Sunday evening two days after Lincoln's death Stanton learned that Congress was not going to accept Reconstruction governments without some provision for Negro voters. To a man of his temperament there was only one thing to do—agree with Congress.

So much for Reconstruction, the area from which most of the shooting at the Secretary has been done. Is there anything more to be said about the rest? Very little; the record speaks for itself, and one can only summarize. When Grant wrote his memoirs, he set it down that Stanton was "timid," a judgment so odd that it can hardly be discussed without knowing what Grant had in mind. Traces of either physical or moral timidity are excessively hard to find in anything Stanton did; and, indeed, Grant contradicts his own adjective by also criticizing Stanton for being too ready to assume responsibility.

There should be noted Stanton's devotion to the Federal Union; manifesting itself as early as the date when he "went over to Jackson," and remaining so intense that if it be accepted as a fundamental part of his character and system of thought, it is unnecessary to explain his actions by resorting to such words as "intrigue" and "treachery." If the fact that the Union was meeting the most severe threat to its existence that it ever encountered, and that Stanton was in a position to do something to alleviate that threat be kept in mind, all his actions in the Buchanan Cabinet, including his converse with Seward while in that Cabinet, his course through the Lincoln administration, and even during Reconstruction, is perfectly logical, honorable, and even obvious. The fate of the men he dealt with, even his own, were insignificant beside that ideal of the Union. It was only the surface manifestations that looked eccentric; beneath them, he followed a singularly straight line.

Stanton had no humor whatever; but he was not lacking in a certain mordant wit. Which brings up another point; a perusal of the Rebellion Records, and of his briefs in cases, shows him a singularly able writer, one of the best in American public life, if the criterion be the quick and clear communication of ideas and their logical arrangement. His ability in analysis was enormous—see the court cases—and it was exercised on the vast masses of evidence he usually assembled.

That is, he was an advocate, a supreme advocate. But his historical place must be something more than that of an advocate merely, for he conceived of himself during the war and even after, as an advocate holding a brief for the Federal Union. Lincoln, himself no ineffective advocate for the same client, obtained his results through qualities of heart and human sympathy; in the area of advocacy, he made it clear that no man could be anti-Unionist without being something less than a man of good will. Stanton was the precise complement; however passionate his Unionism, it was intellectual at both the input and outflow ends; he made it clear that no man could oppose the Union without being something less than intelligent.

He often irritated people, but at least part of the irritation was caused by the maddening discovery that Stanton's snap judgments were more accurate than their careful considerations, that his mind neatly filed and ticketed the enormous quantities of facts he was always gathering. Mr. Welles had a series of contract and other scandals in his department, and dealt with them well; but Stanton did not have scandals, he caught the guilty parties before they stole anything.

This produced the singular incorruptibility of his administration of the War Office, one of the purest ever recorded of a nation in arms. It was also one of the most efficient. There is hardly an instance to be found of a Union battery or regiment running low on ammunition, and the war ended with the Union in possession of a reserve adequate to have equipped another army as large as the one already in the field. This is no little advance for a nation that began the conflict by sending to Europe for muskets dating from the French Revolution. The efficient Montgomery Meigs, Quartermaster-General, gets some of the credit here, but it was certainly Stanton who insisted upon American-made arms from his first day in office on, and it was Stanton who worked out the ingenious and effective supporting system. The basis of it was the purchase of small quantities of any promising arm—the Spencer carbine, for example—from a private maker, followed by the mass manufacture of the weapon in government arsenals if it proved out well in combat. There has been some criticism of Stanton for not going over to the breechloader earlier. It is unjustified. A board considered this question well before the war and found that although the breechloader might be the coming arm, no model then available could be relied on. The trouble was the lack of a good metal cartridge; paper cartridges allowed part of the explosion to come out the breech. Research was pushed on the problem throughout the war, and in October, 1865, Stanton issued an order for the conversion of 5,000 muzzleloaders to breechloaders.

In other respects, notably the handling of ciphers and in the use of the railroads which reached its climax in the great move to Chattanooga, Stanton was so far ahead of his time as to rank as one of the great innovators of military history. It took his special qualities of bold imagination, snap decision, and un-hesitating acceptance of responsibility to bring off things like this; and bringing them off, he contributed no little to what D. W. Brogan (among others) has recognized as the specifically American contribution to the art of war—the mobilization of the immense forces latent in a free and mechanically minded commonwealth, the provision of unlimited quantities of the very best matériel and the employment of this crushing "force without stint or limit."

Yet the achievements of those marching armies, growling guns, and smoking arsenals would hardly have been possible without one other event in which both Stanton and Lincoln curiously played key parts—the McCormick Reaper case. The Confederacy entered the war with the conviction that "Cotton is king," and made the aphorism the cornerstone of its policy. Too late it discovered that the monarch had been deposed, and that the scepter now rested in the wheat fields of the Middle West. It was the flow of wheat pouring from that area that paid for the munitions, it was the labor set free by the mechanical reaper that worked in the arsenals and manned the guns they produced. It is possible that some decision or some action would have made mechanical reapers universally available at a rea-sonable price in any case. But the thing that actually happened was that they were set free when Stanton won his decision.

INDEX

508 STANTON: LINCOLN'S SECRETARY OF WAR

Iowa City, 311

Iowa City, 311
Irish immigrants, 309–310
Ironton, Mo., 311
Isaac Newton, S.S., 46
Island No. 10, 183
Iuka, Miss., 246, 248

Jackson, Andrew, 16–21, 40, 41, 368
Jackson, Miss., battle, 285
Jackson, Gen. Thomas J. (Stonewall), 126, 179, 242, 284
  Manassas, 230–231, 233
  Porter case and, 480–482
  Richmond campaign, 208–212
  Shenandoah Valley campaign, 201–204
"Jacobin Club," 154
James, Army of the, 400
James gun incident, 207
James River, 211–212, 368–370, 377
Jefferson, Thomas, 398, 434
Jefferson County, Ohio, 24, 33
Jew Bill, 14
Jim Crow, 437
Johnson, Maj. A. E. H., 217
Johnson, Andrew, 154, 214, 415
  arbitrariness, 441, 442
  character, 434, 435
  elections of 1866 and, 446–447
  first presidential acts, 420
  impeachment of, 448, 452–453
  popular reaction to, 447
  Porter and, 480
  Reconstruction under, 434–438, 441, 491, 493–494
  Sheridan and, 450
  social concepts, 433–434
  Stanton and, ix, 405, 441, 443–444, 450–453
  Wilson and, 394–395, 433–434
Johnson, Reverdy, 61–63, 255
  Porter case, 480, 482
Johnston, Gen. A. S., 184
Johnston, Gen. Joseph, 159, 205–206, 286, 294, 405
  in the 1864 campaigns, 360, 362–366, 369, 371, 375
  surrender terms, 419–422
Johnston's Island prison camp, 386
Jouan, Auguste, 68–70, 72

Journal of Commerce, 309, 363–364, 372
Julian, George W., 154, 187

Kansas, 87–89, 286–287, 339–341
Kansas-Nebraska Act of 1854, 86, 87
Kautz, Gen. A. V., 354
Kearny, Gen. Philip, 188, 205, 211, 212, 233
Kenesaw Mountain, Ga., 369–373
Kennedy, Police Chief, N.Y., 415
Kentucky, 10
  Reconstruction in, 447
  secession and, 118, 123, 132, 133
  war in, 230, 238, 246
Kenyon College, 11–13, 19–21
Key, Philip Barton, 81–85
Keyes, Gen. E. D., 172, 173, 191, 192, 194, 205, 241
King, Gen. Rufus, 255, 482
Kingston, Ga., 364
Kingston, Jamaica, 71
Kittoe, Dr., 324
Knights of the Golden Circle, 372
Know Nothing Party, 68
Knoxville, Tenn., 319, 332–333, 335
Kohnstamm swindle, 256

Labor, 7, 52–54, 273
Lake Shore Railroad, 57
Lamon, Ward Hill, 118, 119
Lane, Harriet, 470
Lassie balloon, 114
Laughing gas, 196
Law, American vs. English tradition, 26–28
Lawrence, Kansas, 286
Lecompton constitution, 87–88
Lee, Gen. Robert E., 206, 252
  Antietam campaign, 241–246
  Burnside's campaign against, 259–263
  final war moves, 405, 407–412
  peace moves and, 404–405
  Richmond campaigns, 208–212, 369–370
  Sherman's march and, 392–393
  surrender, 412
  winter of 1863 fighting, 330–331, 335, 336
Leesburg, Va., 153, 471–473